FATHER JEREMY DRISCOLL, O.S.B., has been a Benedictine monk of Mount Angel Abbey in Oregon since 1973. He was ordained a priest in 1981. In 1983 he earned an S.T.L. in patristics from the Augustinianum Patristic Institute in Rome. He has been teaching theology in Mount Angel Seminary since then. In 1990 he was awarded an S.T.D., summa cum laude, from the Pontificio Ateneo Sant'Anselmo in Rome, where he distinguished himself with an original thesis on Evagrius Ponticus. He has published two books and fifteen scholarly articles on Evagrius and related topics in ancient Egyptian monasticism. Since 1994 he has also been teaching a semester each year at Sant'Anselmo in Rome.

EVAGRIUS PONTICUS
Ad Monachos

Ancient Christian Writers

THE WORKS OF THE FATHERS IN TRANSLATION

MANAGING EDITOR
Dennis D. McManus

EDITORIAL BOARD
Walter J. Burghardt
John Dillon

No. 59

EVAGRIUS PONTICUS: AD MONACHOS

TRANSLATION AND COMMENTARY
BY
JEREMY DRISCOLL, O.S.B.

THE NEWMAN PRESS
New York/Mahwah, N.J.

Jacket design by Cynthia Dunne

COPYRIGHT © 2003
BY
JEREMY DRISCOLL

Library of Congress Cataloging-in-Publication Data

Driscoll, Jeremy, 1951–
    Evagrius Ponticus : Ad monachos / translation and commentary
by Jeremy Driscoll.
        p. cm. — (Ancient Christian writers ; no. 59)
    Includes bibliographical references and index.
        ISBN 0-8091-0560-8 (alk. paper)
    1. Evagrius, Ponticus, 345?–399. Ad monachos. 2. Monastic and
religious life—Early works to 1800. 3. Spiritual
life—Christianity—Early works to 1800. I. Evagrius, Ponticus,
345?–399. Ad monachos. English & Greek. 2003. II. Title.
III. Series.
    BX 2435.D755 2003
    248.8'942—dc21

                                                                 2003009076

Published by The Newman Press
an imprint of Paulist Press
997 Macarthur Boulevard
Mahwah, New Jersey 07430

www.paulistpress.com

PRINTED AND BOUND IN THE UNITED STATES OF AMERICA

CONTENTS

PREFACE

Evagrius of Pontus (ca. 345–399) was educated philosophically and theologically under Basil and Gregory Nazianzus. He was deacon for Gregory in Constantinople and seems to have been helpful to him in carving out the solution to the trinitarian problems faced by the council in that city in 381. An amorous attachment to a lady highly placed in imperial circles caused him to flee to Jerusalem, where he was received by the monastic communities of Rufinus and Melania on the Mount of Olives. Under the influence of Melania, he retired to the deserts of Egypt to complete his monastic conversion; there he became the disciple of the two Macarii, living for two years at Nitria and thereafter at Cells until his death some fourteen years later. He was among the first of the desert fathers to articulate in writing the wisdom of the spiritual tradition of the monastic movement. His writings, much esteemed in his lifetime and after, eventually came to be the subject of controversy and misunderstanding, particularly because of their intentionally enigmatic style. Teachings associated with his name were condemned in the Council of Constantinople in 553.

My first serious encounter with the writings of Evagrius was by means of the text presented here, *Ad Monachos*. The text is a collection of 137 proverbs composed in a style that imitates the proverbs of biblical wisdom literature. My attraction to this text kept increasing, and the day came when I finally directly asked myself why. Why was this text so attractive to me and so compelling? What was it about it that could bring me to read again and again its seemingly simple lines? I kept discovering secrets tucked away in its structure. How many more might I find? What was the reason for these hidden surprises? I wanted to face these questions systematically. I had experienced a piece of spiritual literature of which I could not let go. Was there an explanation as to why? Could the text's attraction be accounted for theologically or literarily?

The following study is the result of these kinds of questions systematically posed. The principal method for pursuing my efforts to understand this text was clear from the start, and it remains the method for what is presented here. That method is reading Evagrius with Evagrius, commenting on Evagrius with Evagrius.[1] Characteristic of Evagrius is his ability to say things in short, condensed statements, often intentionally enigmatic. The only way to unfold all that has been condensed and to solve the enigma is to become thoroughly acquainted both by study and by meditation with his way of speaking, especially his use of biblical language. This way of speaking—fortunate indeed for the interpreter—is remarkably consistent. Thus, for example, by comparing the language of a given proverb in *Ad Monachos* with other instances where Evagrius uses that same language, all that is condensed and enigmatically expressed in that proverb can eventually come to light. This is why with Evagrius, more than with most other ancient authors, the author himself is his own commentator.[2] If Evagrius is in general a particularly condensed writer, *Ad*

---

[1] This is the method adopted by most serious scholars of Evagrius. It is fundamentally the method adopted by A. and C. Guillaumont in their commentaries on the *Praktikos* and the *Gnostikos* in *Sources Chrétiennes* (= SC) 170, 171, 356; by G. Bunge in his commentary on the letters in *Briefe,* on the *Chapters on Prayer* in *Geistgebet,* and on the *Praktikos* in *Praktikos oder Der Mönch;* by P. Géhin in his commentaries on the *Scholia on Proverbs* in SC 340, the *Scholia on Ecclesiastes* in SC 397, and *On Evil Thoughts* in SC 438. It is the method recommended by M. J. Rondeau, who is preparing the critical edition of the *Scholia on Psalms,* in her *Les Commentaires Patristiques du Psautier,* 1:125: "En fin de compte, pourtant, Evagre n'est vraiment semblable qu'à Evagre, et c'est la comparaison avec les autres oeuvres de cet auteur qui donne leur véritable sens à ces scolies hautaines, volontiers gnomiques, jouant avec prédilection du syllogisme." (The commentaries by the Guillaumonts and by Géhin will be cited so frequently in what follows that for convenience only the SC abbreviation with volume number will be used. When a work is by A. and C. Guillaumont together, it is cited as "Guillaumont." Otherwise, the title is specified A. or C. Guillaumont.)

[2] It is not always possible to clarify Evagrius only with Evagrius. When this is not possible, I turn for help to the theological influences that most strongly shaped him: Clement, Origen, Didymus, and Gregory of Nazianzus. There is much need for future investigation of the influence of each of these on Evagrius's thinking, but a first effort of the whole scholarly project in Evagrius's regard needs to be understanding as accurately as possible what Evagrius is saying in his enigmatic mode of expression. The present study hopes to be a contribution to this part of the scholarship on Evagrius.

Monachos can be considered in some senses a condensation of the condensation. This will become clear in due time.

The kinds of answers I began to be able to give to my systematically posed questions eventually dictated the organization of this study in its various parts. The Introduction is conceived as a preparation for a reading of the Evagrian text. It faces the standard questions of the condition of the text, its possible audience, and its relation to the other works of Evagrius. In addition, it attempts to summarize briefly the dimensions of Evagrius's thought that must be presumed for this study to advance. I will argue that in *Ad Monachos* Evagrius has created a text whose structure is an image of the whole spiritual journey of the monk as he conceives it. Obviously such a structure cannot be detected without a basic knowledge of how Evagrius does in fact conceive the journey.

Part One of the study presents the Greek text of *Ad Monachos* and my English translation. The translation is the result of my effort to express clearly, first for myself and now for my reader, how I understand Evagrius's text. It is the first translation of the text into English. I have tried in this translation, in addition to simply rendering the text accurately, to offer two additional advantages. First, I have translated technical terms with consistent English equivalents throughout. I extend this practice to the translation of all other Evagrian texts in this study.[3] Second, I have tried to create in the English a poetic rhythm that facilitates the recitation, even the memorization, of the individual proverbs. In this way I mean to acknowledge that Evagrius's text is poetic and designed, among other things, to create an auditory and imaginative impact.

Part Two of the study examines the structure of the whole text. This part is the result of what was for me one of the more exciting dimensions of my own progressive understanding of the

---

[3] In commenting on Evagrius with Evagrius, there will be many citations in this study from other Evagrian works. In each case the English translation is mine. In that way readers can know how I understand the text in question, and I am able to maintain Evagrius's consistent vocabulary in uniform English equivalents. Biblical translations are mine for a similar reason. I translate to indicate what Evagrius would have heard in the text. Old Testament translations are based on the Septuagint.

nature of *Ad Monachos*. A first impression of the text is that the proverbs are arranged in no particular order, apart from the fact that some proverbs on a same theme are found together in groups. Over time I discovered a very sophisticated arrangement of proverbs extending from start to finish. Every proverb has a precise reason for standing in the place where it is found. I think this section offers the most original contribution of the study. Other scholars have noticed that Evagrius organizes his short sayings into particular patterns, but to my knowledge this is the first study that analyzes such patterns in detail throughout the entire work. *Ad Monachos* has never been considered an especially important work of Evagrius. I believe that precisely because of this structure the text deserves more attention than it has heretofore received.

Part Three steps back from this close reading of the text and shares the results of asking a different kind of question. If the study to this point has revealed a text especially striking for its careful construction and for the amount of theological and spiritual content condensed into its brief lines, now the study asks where such a text came from. This part tries to situate *Ad Monachos* within the kind of human impulses and specific cultures that could have given rise to a text with its particular features. Using the close reading of the text as a basis, I look again from new angles provided by *Ad Monachos* at some of the basic issues that surround the monk Evagrius: why he wrote in a poetic style, what his relation was to the various monastic traditions of fourth-century Egypt, and how his classical background influenced his creation of a monastic literature.

Part Four returns to a close reading of the text, employing now a different approach. It contains commentaries on a wide variety of individual proverbs taken from various parts of the text. In Part Two I will have argued that detecting the significance of a proverb's placement in the overall structure is an important part of that proverb's interpretation. But each proverb is also worthy of meditation in its own right, and Part Four is an attempt to reveal how much has been condensed into the short lines of these various proverbs. The proverbs selected provide occasion, as they did when I first came to know the text, for entering into theological discussion of various dimensions of Evagrius's thought, for understanding more deeply Evagrius's way of conceiving the monk's spiritual journey.

Judging from the scholarly output since the Greek text of *Ad Monachos* was rediscovered and published in 1913, one would have to conclude that *Ad Monachos* is not especially appreciated among the works of Evagrius. This is the first major study of the text and, to my knowledge, the first study of any Evagrian work that examines that work's *structure* in detail from start to finish, attempting to gauge the intended effects of such a structure. More than anything I hope that the kind of study I am presenting here will let an Evagrian text that has not been much noticed speak for itself.

Before stepping into the work before us, it may be useful to recall that in previous centuries there was a greater appreciation of the text presented here. The fifth-century church historian Socrates, loud in his praise of Evagrius, mentions that "he wrote books of a most excellent kind" and then proceeds to mention six by name. Among these is *Ad Monachos.*[4] Evagrius had written many more than six works. If Socrates restricts his list to these six, or if his knowledge of Evagrius is restricted to these six, it could suggest that these are among the more appreciated of Evagrius's writings.[5] In any case, for Socrates *Ad Monachos* is "an excellent book." Evagrius's friend Rufinus very likely translated this work into Latin as part of his project of sharing Evagrius's writings in the West.[6] The work was very popular in the Latin monasteries of

---

[4] Socrates, *Church History* 4.23 (PG 67:516B). Socrates' Greek matches exactly the title of the Evagrian text. For this title, see the Introduction below, "The Addressees of the Text."

[5] *Ad Monachos* is also among six works of Evagrius mentioned by Gennadius in *De viris illust.* 11 (PL 58:1067A).

[6] See the testimony of Gennadius (*De viris illust.* 17 [PL 58:1070A]). Jerome, complaining in general of Rufinus's translations of Evagrius, may be referring specifically to *Ad Monachos* when he introduces his complaint with these words: "Evagrius Ponticus Hyperborita, qui scribit ad virgines, scribit ad monachos" (*Ep.* 133.3 [PG 22:1151A or CSEL 56:246]). It is not possible to say whether Jerome is referring to a title or simply to the fact that Evagrius wrote to both virgins and monks.

medieval Europe, as is witnessed by the many surviving manu-scripts.[7] Since that time one has not heard much about the text apart from mention of it among the extant works of Evagrius and the occasional citation of some of its proverbs.

At the beginning of this century the Greek text was redis-covered, critically edited, and published in 1913. It has been my good fortune to have read and studied this text slowly over some years, and now to share some of the answers I have been able to give to the questions I found myself posing. Can the text's attrac-tion be accounted for theologically or literarily? I think so. *Ad Monachos* is the poetic summary in biblical language of the whole spiritual life as Evagrius conceives it. It is a summary that rewards its reader for careful attention but at the same time requires of its reader a steep price: the price of practicing in actual living what is being read. It is an exercise, a spiritual exercise, which means to bring the reader into an experienced knowledge of the Holy Trinity. The following pages tell why I think so. The present study was first published in 1991 in the series *Studia Anselmiana* (no. 104) under the title *The "Ad Monachos" of Evagrius Ponticus: Its Structure and a Select Commentary*. It has been rearranged here for inclusion in *Ancient Christian Writers*.

---

[7] See Leclercq, "L'ancienne version latine des Sentences d'Evagre pour les moines"; idem, *The Love of Learning and the Desire for God*, 117–18. See also the testimony of Honorius Augustodunensis, *De luminaribus Ecclesiae* (PL 172:212C). The present study does not consider the text's history and influence in its Latin version except insofar as this brings some few improvements to the Greek text. However, this study could be the basis of an interesting inquiry; namely, did the Latin West read this text and understand it in the same spirit with which I will be suggesting it was designed by Evagrius to be read and understood?

INTRODUCTION

The Condition of the Text

The present study is based on H. Gressmann's critical edition of the Greek text of *Ad Monachos* published in 1913, accompanied by my English translation of this text.[1] Gressmann's edition is based on five Greek manuscripts, three taken from the Vatican library and two from Mount Athos, dating from the twelfth to the seventeenth centuries. The critical apparatus includes comparison with the Latin translation published in Migne and with one Syriac manuscript.[2] The following year, this apparatus was completed by reference to an Armenian version of the text.[3] The published text and its apparatus can be considered a generally reliable text.[4]

Nonetheless, scholarly gossip would suggest that Gressmann published his text hastily.[5] There are other Greek manuscripts that Gressmann did not consult. J. Muyldermans has examined two of these from the tenth and eleventh centuries, that is, manuscripts significantly older than those used by Gressmann for his critical edition. Muyldermans's observations are presented in the

---

[1] Gressmann, "Nonnenspiegel und Mönchsspiegel," 152–65.

[2] The critical edition of the Latin text, published by J. Leclercq in 1951, has shown that the translator of the Latin text published in Migne is less familiar with the language of Evagrius than the translator of the text of Leclercq's critical edition, which is discussed below.

[3] The results are published in *Zeitschrift für Kirchengeschichte* 35 (1914): 87ff.

[4] I rely here on the judgment of J. Muyldermans expressed in *A travers la tradition manuscrite*, 66: "Bref, rien n'a été négligé pour nous donner une édition dûment critique: les vieilles versions sont consultées et cinq manuscrits grecs sont examinés. Ce nombre cinq, bien que restreint, est déjà considérable, quand on songe combien il est malaisé de dépister de nouveaux textes grecs d'Evagre le Pontique."

[5] See Muyldermans, *Evagriana Syriaca*, 29.

1

form of a critical apparatus which can be added to that published by Gressmann.[6] This apparatus can function as a good test case of how dangerous Gressmann's haste may have been to the value of the critical text he published. The answer is, fortunately: not very dangerous. Leaving aside orthographic differences, the conclusion of the comparison with the two older manuscripts is that "les variantes de NP [the manuscripts examined] sont peu nombreuses."[7]

Some years later, Muyldermans and L. Th. Lefort suggested that Gressmann's edition could have benefited from a more careful comparison with the Syriac manuscript tradition. Gressmann compared his Greek with one Syriac manuscript, but there are in fact some ten.[8] Yet to date no one has undertaken such a task. It could be interesting for the Syriac tradition on Evagrius and could likely bring some improvements to the Greek text, but one is probably safe in assuming that such a study would not make for significant changes in the text of Gressmann.

In 1951 J. Leclercq published a critical edition of the Latin version of this Evagrian text, which has an interesting history of its own, based on a relatively large number of manuscripts.[9] Leclercq claims that his Latin version can in some cases improve Gressmann's text, though he only gives one example.[10] Though I follow him in this particular suggestion, the present study has not benefited (if benefit there would be) from an exhaustive comparison of the Latin and Greek texts and whatever conclusions for the Greek texts that such a study might offer. Again, it is safe to assume that such a study would not bring more than incidental improvements to the Gressmann text.

None of the manuscripts used by either Gressmann or Muyldermans have divided or numbered the individual proverbs as Gressmann does in his printed text.[11] He, however, did well to do

---

[6] Muyldermans, *A travers la tradition manuscrite*, 65–70.

[7] Ibid., 69.

[8] Muyldermans, *Evagriana Syriaca*, 29. L. Th. Lefort, "A propos d'un aphorisme d'Evagrius Ponticus," 70–79.

[9] Leclercq, "L'ancienne version latine des Sentences d'Évagre pour les moines," *Scriptorium* 5 (1951): 195–213.

[10] Ibid., 201 n. 43.

[11] So Muyldermans in *A travers la tradition manuscrite*, 68.

so. We can be virtually certain that Evagrius would have so written the text and wanted it so copied. He expressed himself explicitly on this concerning another of his works, the *Praktikos*, in which, as in *Ad Monachos*, individual chapters or proverbs in a particular order are critical to the nature of the text that Evagrius presents.[12]

In brief, then, apart from some few improvements permitted by the aforementioned studies, there seems to be no serious flaw with Gressmann's text.[13] It can form a secure base for the study that follows.

Presumed Understanding of Evagrius's Teachings

Evagrius's *Ad Monachos*, like a number of the works of Evagrius, presupposes much of his teaching. In many ways it takes for

---

[12] This interesting remark of Evagrius was published by Muyldermans in *A travers la tradition manuscrite*, 33–34, and conveniently reprinted by Guillaumont in SC 170, 147. Some of the manuscripts of the *Praktikos* introduce the text by the following request made to the copyist: "I beg the brothers who come upon this book and want to copy it not to join one chapter to another nor to place on the same line the end of one chapter which has been written and the beginning of the one about to be written. Instead give each chapter its own beginning according to the way we have divided them with numbers. Thus is safeguarded the order of the chapters and what is said will be clear." For the Evagrian authenticity of this text, see Guillaumont, SC 170, 384–85. (I follow Guillaumont in translating ὁ κεφαλαιώδης κανών as "the order of the chapters.") The present study will show how important the order and numbers of the text are in *Ad Monachos*.

[13] I note these improvements here. The most important concerns M 55. Combining the results of Muyldermans's work with a comparison of Leclercq's Latin text by M. Mühmelt in "Zu der neuen lateinischen Übersetzung des Mönchsspiegels des Euagrius," I accept the reading that Mühmelt offers for that proverb's second line: καὶ μὴ ἐκκλίνης ἐν καιρῷ πάλην ἐπωφελῆ. For M 112 I accept Leclercq's suggestion for reading in the third line ἐπὶ χρόνου αὐτοῦ. This is supported by Gressmann's Syriac text, by the Armenian version, and by one of the manuscripts examined by Muyldermans. More difficult to decide is M 115, where Muyldermans suggests reading μέλιτος instead of πνεύματος. This is supported by the majority of manuscripts, but an error could be explained with equal sense working in either direction. Either reading yields something of a mysterious proverb, both possible according to the manner of Evagrius's writing. Therefore, it seems best to remain with Gressmann's text here, opting for what should probably be considered the *lectio difficilior.*

granted the reader's understanding of many issues; or at any rate, it is a text composed with such understanding in mind. Some of the more important dimensions are summarized here, as they are necessary to a full understanding of the text: first, the notion of the relation between mind, soul, and body; second, the division of the spiritual life between *praktikē* and knowledge; third, Evagrius's analysis of the eight principal evil thoughts and their order; fourth, various levels of knowledge; finally, a position about biblical exegesis that is operative throughout the text, a method of commenting on the scriptures and using scriptural language. Some understanding of all these is necessary to read *Ad Monachos* with profit.

A number of previous studies have examined and exposed Evagrius's position on these issues. Because he hardly ever expressed himself in a systematic way, these studies have had painstakingly to gather various cryptic remarks from Evagrius's other writings and try to fit them together into some coherent picture. I do not repeat that work here; rather I rely on it. However, for the reader's convenience I briefly summarize here the teachings that must be presupposed for a proper reading of *Ad Monachos,* and I provide bibliographical indications for deeper investigations of the material.

Some studies are useful for tracing the main lines of all or most of the issues singled out here.[14] Concerning all of these studies, it should be noted that they are systematic presentations of Evagrius's material, though he himself nowhere offers such a

---

[14] The classical study in this regard is A. Guillaumont, ed., *Les 'Képhalaia Gnostica' d'Évagre le Pontique et l'histoire de l'origénisme chez les grecs et chez les syriens,* 15–123. Also useful is his introduction in SC 170, 38–112. More recent, and very comprehensive, particularly in its notes, is Bunge, *Briefe,* 112–64. In his introduction to Evagrius's *Scholia on Proverbs,* P. Géhin provides a useful summary of Evagrian themes, particularly as they bear on these scholia. See SC 340, 33–54. M. O'Laughlin examines these themes on the basis of many texts (*Origenism in the Desert*). His synthesis is useful even if I do not agree with all his interpretations. For a brief and reliable synthesis, see A. Louth, *The Origins of the Christian Mystical Tradition,* 100–113. Since all of these studies, except perhaps the last, are based on extensive collection and examination of texts, I may be forgiven if in summarizing them I do not myself cite Evagrius extensively. It would obscure the focus of the present study on the text of *Ad Monachos,* which, once begun, will rely heavily on citations of Evagrian texts.

presentation. As Guillaumont himself notes, this runs the risk of imposing a system where the author himself refused to give one.[15] The importance of that being granted, a systematic arrangement of the material does help modern readers to find their way around in the various concepts that unfold only in bits and pieces throughout Evagrius's work.

1. RATIONAL BEINGS: MINDS IN SOULS AND BODIES

To understand Evagrius's notion of the present condition of human beings and their relationship to God, it is necessary to understand how he uses all the terms listed in the title of this section. For this it is necessary to know something of his cosmology.[16] Before summarizing these I would like to draw attention to two hints that G. Bunge drops in his introduction to the letters of Evagrius, suggestions that can considerably reorient the attitude with which one reads Evagrius on these questions, particularly as regards his orthodoxy or lack thereof. In general it is presumed that the Origenist theory of preexistence of souls is shared by Evagrius and that this is to be understood as occurring within the temporal order.[17] Bunge points out that the application of temporal sequence to the relation of mind, soul, and body risks a serious misunderstanding of Evagrius, who, he claims, is attempting to speak of metahistorical realities with the language of space and

---

[15] Guillaumont, *Les Képhalaia Gnostica*, 37.

[16] A great deal of the material on these issues is found in *Kephalaia Gnostica* but scattered about. Since the time of Guillaumont (*Les Képhalaia Gnostica*, 37 n. 67), scholars have used the more orderly presentation of the *Letter to Melania* as an interpretive key for the *Kephalaia Gnostica* and for arriving at a general notion of how it all works. There is evidence for Evagrius's same understanding of these terms throughout his writings. One needs to be clear on the issue to read any given text in its fullest implications. For these as studied by Guillaumont, see his *Les Képhalaia Gnostica*, 37–39, 103–13. The anthropological focus of O'Laughlin's study is particularly useful in this regard; see *Origenism in the Desert*, 153–88. For an examination of the *Letter to Melania* on the basis of texts from the *Kephalaia Gnostica*, see M. Parmentier, "Evagrius of Pontus and the 'Letter to Melania,'" 33–36. For the themes as they occur in the *Scholia on Proverbs*, see Géhin, SC 340, 34–37, 45–48. For a fine summary study of the whole, see Bunge, "Der Zustand des Intellektes" in *Das Geistgebet*, 62–73. Also see his *Briefe*, 118ff.

[17] Thus A. Guillaumont, *Les Képhalaia Gnostica*, 103–4.

time, that is, with the only language available to speak of such elusive realities. Evagrius was aware of this difficulty and cautions that the mind in its relation to God admits in the strict sense the language of neither place nor names. Bunge would want a more sympathetic reading of Evagrius on these questions to which later generations (and many contemporaries) applied too literally the categories of space and time.[18] For the present, there are three issues to be discussed: (1) the original creation of the mind, (2) the mind's condition of being in a soul and a body, and (3) a threefold division of the soul.

Original Creation of the Mind

God's original creation was of reasonable beings (τὰ λογικά).[19] These beings were pure minds (νόες) created to know God, to know God as non-numeric Trinity and as essential unity. This knowledge is called essential knowledge. These minds were created equal among themselves in their knowledge of God and in their unity with him.

Mind in Soul and Body

By use of their free will these minds grew lax in their contemplation of essential knowledge, producing a rupture in the original unity and causing the minds to fall away from the essential knowledge and unity. This movement, this misuse of free will,

---

[18] Bunge, *Briefe*, 156 n. 19 and 396 n. 52. That such a reorientation of the evaluation of Evagrius would require considerable study is indicated by the fact that Bunge places these remarks in footnotes, only, as it were, trying to suggest a new line of thought to scholars. Thus, I do not take a position here but await further studies. However, following Bunge's suggestion, I do find it helpful to read Evagrius without such a strict application of chronological categories, which inevitably leads to the judgment that his opinions are heretical. New interpretations are suggested for much of what he says as a result. Such new interpretations seem to be the major project of Bunge's work. For much of what follows in this study, I am indebted to the new horizons his suggestions open. For the study that best summarizes the need for this reorientation, see Bunge, "Mysterium Unitatis."

[19] Here, in the perspective suggested by Bunge, "first" would be not so much a temporal term as a metaphysical and ontological term. For Evagrius, the mind being the icon of God, it must be immaterial like God himself.

introduces differences in once equal rational beings. It introduces a disintegration of creation's original oneness and a disintegration of what was originally created as a pure mind. The pure mind disintegrates into a soul that is joined to a body.[20] This situation is described succinctly in a passage from the *Letter to Melania:*

> There has been a time when, because of its free will, it [the mind] fell from this former rank and was called a soul. And having sunk down even further, it was called a body. But in time the body, the soul and the mind, because of changes of their wills, will become one entity. Because there will be a time that their wills and their various movements will have passed, the mind will stand again in its first creation. (Ep Mel 6, p. 12, lines 193–98)

As this text suggests, though the disintegration is lamentable, there is something provident in the arrangement, a providence that operates in such a way that body, soul, and mind will again become one entity. These fallen minds were not abandoned by God, who is merciful and provident. In his mercy and through his Logos, God undertakes to arrange what may be considered a secondary condition for the fallen mind.[21] He provides the rational *soul* as the direct extension of the fallen *mind*, and he arranges lower parts of the soul whereby he joins it (and the mind of which it is an extension) to a *body*.

A soul is joined to a body and established in a world in accordance with the degree of its fall from essential knowledge. This assignment of a body and a world to a fallen mind is called "the

---

[20] *Disintegration* is a word that Bunge prefers to use in an attempt to avoid words with strong temporal overtones. It has the advantage of showing the continuity of mind as the fundamental reality while at the same time showing that the present human condition does not represent a perfect manifestation of God's intentions in creation's regard. See *Briefe,* 118.

[21] Evagrius never uses the expression "second creation," as Origen does, because of the difficulty of the temporal conception noted above, which can make the term misleading. Even if Evagrius does speak of bodies as representing "second beings" or of the contemplation of the material world as a "second contemplation," the fact that he never says "second creation" should not go unnoticed. "Second beings" implies more a secondary condition at odds with God's original intentions, an ontological assessment, without necessarily implying an actual second creation.

judgment," while the whole arrangement, which is designed for the mind's reintegration, is called "providence." In this way there come about the bodies and the worlds of angels, humans, and demons, all of them fallen rational creatures, differing among themselves according to the degree of their fall and the degree of their level of return to their original unity. These bodies are formed of varying proportions of fire, earth, air, and water and by varying predominant proportions of the three parts of the soul.[22] Thus, angels are formed of a predominance of fire and reason, humans by a predominance of earth and concupiscence, and demons by a predominance of air and irascibility (see KH I, 68). In the proper use of the body and by establishing health in the soul, the disintegrated mind will recover its original unity. "[T]here will be a time when the human body, soul and mind cease to be separate, with their own names and their plurality, because the body and the soul will be raised to the rank of mind (this can be concluded from the text 'Let them be one in us, as you and I are one')" (Ep Mel 5, pp. 11–12, lines 158–61, citing John 17:22).[23]

The Three Parts of the Soul[24]

The Platonic threefold division of the soul is a major dimension of Evagrius's anthropology: the rational part (λογιστικόν), the irascible part (θυμικόν), and the concupiscible part (ἐπιθυμητικόν). The spiritual struggle of the monk is conceived as a battle for establishing virtue in these various parts. Different virtues are suitably established in a part of the soul to which they correspond, while various vices can also be identified as trouble in one or another part of the soul.[25]

---

[22] It was noted that the soul's highest part is its rational part. Its lower part is actually dividied into two parts, the concupiscible and the irascible, discussed below.

[23] From our present perspective this reintegration is in the future, that is, in time. Thus, "there will be a time . . ." Yet in itself, ontologically and metaphysically, it is beyond time (cf. KG VI, 9).

[24] See Guillaumont, SC 170, 104–7; Géhin, SC 340, 34–36; Bunge, *Briefe*, 120–25; O'Laughlin, *Origenism in the Desert*, 164–71.

[25] The classical expression of this in Evagrius is TP 89, where the various parts of the soul are clearly identified along with the corresponding virtues. This

The rational part is the most noble of the parts of the soul. It is, as I have mentioned, a direct extension of the fallen mind. The other two parts of the soul, together called the passionate part,[26] are the parts whereby the soul is joined to the body. The mind is extended to a soul in a body as a result of the fall from essential knowledge. By means of a purification of the body and of the passionate part of the soul, the intellectual part (which is a direct extension of the mind) will once again be united to the essential knowledge.

In the proverbs of *Ad Monachos* the terms *mind, soul,* and *body* are all used, and in each case their precise Evagrian sense is operative.[27] Each encounter with these terms will be occasion for developing a fuller understanding of how Evagrius uses them. The analysis of the literary structure of the whole as well as the commentaries on individual proverbs will need to be based on what Evagrius intends by his particular use of each particular term.

2. THE SPIRITUAL LIFE DIVIDED BETWEEN *PRAKTIKĒ* AND KNOWLEDGE

This understanding and description of the human condition (mind in soul joined to body) are the basis for the various divisions in Evagrius's conception of the spiritual life. There are two major divisions: *praktikē,* where the concern is purifying the passionate part of the soul;[28] and knowledge, where the rational part of the soul devotes itself to contemplation and knowledge.[29]

---

clear statement can function for all other occurrences of the terms in the writings of Evagrius.

[26] Cf. TP 38, 49, 78, 84, and Guillaumont's commentaries in SC 171.

[27] "Soul" is used in no less than twenty-five proverbs; "body" is used in four proverbs, though the related term "flesh" is found in five others. "Mind" occurs in only three proverbs, but, as we shall see, each of these uses is extremely significant.

[28] Thus, TP 78: "*Praktikē* is the spiritual method which purifies the passionate part of the soul."

[29] Cf. TP 89. There are divisions within the realm of knowledge also, which are discussed below. But the main lines of division are between *praktikē* and knowledge (in general).

Thus, the monastic life as conceived by Evagrius is the entire struggle to rid oneself of *evils* (related to the passionate part) and *ignorance* (related to the rational part) and to establish in the soul *virtue* (related to the passionate part) and *knowledge* (related to the rational part). For Evagrius there can be no knowledge in the higher part of the soul without virtue first being established in the passionate part of the soul. So it is that the beginning of the monastic life is concerned with *praktikē*, while knowledge can be hoped for later, after the monk has reached the goals of *praktikē*.

The teaching of Evagrius on *praktikē* has been carefully studied by Guillaumont in his introduction to the *Praktikos*.[30] The *Praktikos* is Evagrius's principal work devoted to this stage of the spiritual life. It can be seen there that *praktikē* basically consists in doing combat with evil thoughts. The *Praktikos* analyzes eight principal evil thoughts and offers sage advice for how to defeat them.[31] The immediate goal of this purification of the passionate part of the soul is passionlessness, ἀπάθεια.[32] Passionlessness makes true love possible, and only from love can the monk pass on to knowledge.[33]

Perfect passionlessness means that health is established in the two passionate parts of the soul, the concupiscible and the irascible. Then these two parts work together to maintain the soul in this state and to leave it free for its higher part, the rational, to function for knowledge. The concupiscible part *desires* virtue and knowledge. The irascible part *fights* the evil thoughts that attack all three parts of the soul. In the passionless soul, thoughts from

[30] Guillaumont, SC 170, 38–112. All other discussions of *praktikē* in Evagrius rely on this study. The only place where something significantly new is added is Bunge, *Praktikos oder Der Mönch.*

[31] See further the next section of this part of the study.

[32] The second half of the *Praktikos* is devoted to a description of the condition of passionlessness. Guillaumont says that passionlessness can be considered "le sujet essentiel" of the treatise. The first half (TP 1–53) explains how to reach it; the second half (TP 54–90) describes it and indicates what are the signs for recognizing its presence. See SC 170, 98ff.

[33] This concern for passing on to knowledge is expressed, among many other ways, by the fact that the *Praktikos* is the first of a three-part work, the second and third parts being devoted to knowledge, that is, the *Gnostikos* and the *Kephalaia Gnostica.*

the passionate part no longer mount up to darken the mind (cf. TP 74), and thereby is the rational part ready to pass into knowledge.

These two major divisions of the spiritual life everywhere obtain in the writings of Evagrius, particular treatises generally concerning themselves with one or the other. Thus, Evagrius's works tend to be classified as either ascetical or theoretical, that is, as concerned with *praktikē* or with knowledge.[34] Keeping these divisions in mind will explain much in *Ad Monachos,* and it is particularly necessary for an accurate analysis of the literary structure, as we shall see shortly. Furthermore, one of the major points Evagrius wishes to make in the text he has designed here concerns not only the difference between *praktikē* and knowledge but also their intimate connection. Among the works of Evagrius no work expresses with such insistence the intimate nature of the relation between *praktikē* and knowledge as does *Ad Monachos.*

3. THE EIGHT PRINCIPAL EVIL THOUGHTS AND THEIR ORDER

Praktikē has been said to consist in combating evil thoughts. *Thoughts* (λογισμοί) is a technical word in the Evagrian vocabulary, its use widespread throughout his writings. It almost always has a pejorative meaning, even when unaccompanied by an adjective that secures its pejorative sense. The simple mention of "thoughts" in Evagrius generally can be taken to mean "evil thoughts."[35]

Evagrius devotes much space in his writings to the analysis of evil thoughts and to methods for overcoming them. The *Praktikos* is a detailed analysis and set of remedies for each of eight principal thoughts identified by him. The *Treatise on Evil Thoughts* is an equally acute analysis of the way in which demons work through thoughts. So also is the *Eight Spirits of Evil, spirit* being a synonym for *demon* in Evagrian vocabulary. It is a key feature of his theory

---

[34] But see below, pp. 29–31 for my remarks of these classifications.

[35] The evidence is collected by Guillaumont in SC 170, 56–57. For a study of Evagrius's use of this term and for the roots of his usage, see pp. 55–63.

that to each λογισμός there corresponds a demon or spirit who specializes in it. Thus, to be troubled by a thought is to be troubled by a demon. The true battle of the monk is with the demons themselves. Thoughts are the means used by the demons to trouble the monk. On the other hand, it is by doing battle with evil thoughts and conquering them (that is to say, battling and conquering the demons) that the monk in fact discovers true virtue in the counterpart of the evil thoughts.[36]

Evagrius identifies eight such thoughts. "Eight is the number of principal thoughts in which every thought is contained. The first is that of gluttony and after it comes fornication. The third is that of love of money, the fourth that of sadness, the fifth that of anger, the sixth that of listlessness, the seventh that of vainglory, the eighth that of pride" (TP 6). Evagrius's analysis of these thoughts is keen and filled with practical wisdom, often showing how one thought will work in conjunction with another.[37] There is a certain logic to the order of the thoughts as Evagrius lists them and analyzes them, an order derived from experience. Thus, for example, fornication follows rather naturally from someone who gratifies his desires for food and comfort. Or if one loves money and is frustrated in his aims to amass it, he will become sad or angry. Vainglory and pride are dangers for the monk who has had some success in his fight against the other thoughts. Thus, in a general way the order of the eight thoughts follows the order of spiritual progress.

Certain evil thoughts are especially related to one or other part of the passionate part of the soul (i.e., to the concupiscible or the irascible), though Evagrius does not express himself with precision in this regard.[38] Thus, gluttony and fornication can be considered to be in the concupiscible part, as also probably love of money. Sadness and anger are clearly related to the irascible part. On the other hand, listlessness is said to embrace the entire soul, while vainglory and pride are not assigned to any particular part.

---

[36] See Evagrius's explanation of this in TP 82, 83.
[37] On the order of the thoughts, see Guillaumont, SC 170, 90–93.
[38] Ibid., 93 n. 3.

The demons have as their goal keeping the monk from reaching passionlessness, so they attack that part of the soul where the passions reside in such a way as to set them in motion. Evagrius describes this with a language typically precise. *Demons* inspire *thoughts,* and these, when they are allowed to linger, unleash the *passions* in us. The remedy against this system of demonic attacks is constant vigilance over thoughts, never allowing them to linger. *Praktikē* is learning this art.[39] "Whether all of these [thoughts] trouble the soul or do not trouble it does not depend on us. But whether they linger or do not linger or whether the passions move or are not moved, that depends on us" (TP 6).

Evagrius's teaching on the eight principal thoughts will bear on this study of *Ad Monachos* in several important ways. Each of the eight thoughts is dealt with in the text, and they must be recognized as such for a proper interpretation.[40] The order of the thoughts is followed in part in various portions of the text. Knowing this order will help us to uncover the structure of the text's entire arrangement, and it is precisely this structure to which, among other things, the present study wishes to draw attention. Finally, not only the individual thoughts and their order are mentioned, but the technical term λογισμοί is found in no fewer than nine proverbs. A number of these proverbs play key roles in the overall structure precisely because of the way in which this term is employed in them. The literary analysis of the text will make this clear.

4. VARIOUS LEVELS OF KNOWLEDGE

When the soul has reached passionlessness, the rational part may turn, unobscured by evil thoughts, to knowledge. Thus does the monk pass from one major division of the spiritual life to another, from *praktikē* to knowledge. Ultimately the knowledge to

---

[39] Ibid., 97–98.
[40] The technical terms φιλαργυρία (love of money) and ὀργή (anger) do not occur, but both issues are major ones in *Ad Monachos,* as our study will show. So also with the other evil thoughts, it is not simply a question of mentioning the technical names but of dealing with the issues that these technical names cover.

which the mind is given over is that of the Holy Trinity, that is, the knowledge for which it was originally created and from which, in its present condition, it has fallen. Yet as the mind returns to this knowledge, it must follow a particular path arranged by the providence of God. The mind in soul joined to body, once having reached passionlessness, must climb by stages through various levels of knowledge until at last it reaches the essential knowledge for which it was originally made.

Thus, there are in Evagrius's understanding two major divisions within the realm of knowledge, the first and highest being knowledge of the Trinity, the second being generally all the lesser forms of knowledge. Various terms cover both of these areas of knowledge, and within the lower forms Evagrius distinguishes different levels and different angles of the same level. It will be useful to fix with precision these various terms, for most of them are used in *Ad Monachos*. We take them here in their ascending order, that is, from the point of knowledge at which one enters after having reached passionlessness.

Several general terms cover the whole area of the knowledge that lies below that of the Trinity. It is called natural contemplation (φυσική)[41] or also contemplation of created things (θεωρία τῶν γεγονότων). The scope of such contemplation is not the observation or enjoyment of the wonders of nature—though it does not exclude that and even in some ways is based on it—but rather a discovery of the reasons (λόγοι) with which the Logos has made the world. What these reasons show, step by step, is that all things have been made toward the end of leading the mind to knowledge of the Trinity. This contemplation discovers reasons (λόγοι) in bodies and in the worlds and times that they have been assigned. These discovered reasons reveal to the gradually purified and sharpened vision of the contemplative a world beyond the material world perceived by the senses. This incorporeal world, discovered by discovering the λόγοι in the corporeal,

---

[41] In English the best translation of φυσική seems to be "natural contemplation" as opposed to something like "physics" or "nature." The latter two terms now carry too much a modern scientific overtone. A contemplation is always implied when Evagrius uses the term φυσική. Unfortunately, there is no single English word that can convey what it implies.

reaches far beyond the corporeal world and its wonders. And this incoporeal world has its own λόγοι waiting to be penetrated. In this knowledge the contemplative sees that in his reality as creature the most fundamental dimension is not his material body. Rather, he sees that in him there is something created; yes, created but immaterial. It is his immaterial mind, and this mind has a reason for being. It is an immaterial instrument made and perfectly adapted for knowledge of *the* Immaterial, God as nonnumerical Trinity and perfect unity. The mind is the immaterial icon of the immaterial God.

This movement of the mind upward to a discovery of its own condition as created knower of the Trinity is identified in its various stages by a technical vocabulary. The knowledge that discovers reasons in the material world is called knowledge, contemplation, or reasons of the corporeals. Understanding the reason for the worlds and times in which these bodies are found is called contemplation or reasons of worlds and aeons. The *that* and the *why* of God's assigning fallen minds to bodies of a certain type in a certain world are called the reasons and contemplations of the judgment. Closely joined to this is the contemplative vision that such a judgment is a great act of mercy on the part of God, for the body and its world have been filled, have been provided, with reasons which, once discovered, will lead the mind to the final blessedness for which it was made. Seeing God's mercy and the arrangement of the plan of restoration it entails is called contemplations or reasons of providence. Discovering the immaterial world and its purposes which lie behind this material world is called knowledge, contemplation, or reasons of the incoporeals, or sometimes also, but less frequently, knowledge of rational beings or seeing intelligible natures. Finally, any knowledge that covers some aspect of the material world is called the second natural contemplation because it treats of a secondary condition of the creation. Knowledge of the immaterial created world is called the first natural contemplation because it treats created reasonable natures in their original condition as knowers of the Trinity.

It is clear that there is a certain logical (λογικός) progress to the knowledges that end in the Trinity. The last two proverbs of *Ad Monachos* state it with a splendid succinctness: "Contemplations of worlds enlarge the heart; / reasons of providence and

judgment lift it up. Knowledge of incorporeals raises the mind /
and presents it before the Holy Trinity" (M 135–36). This final
knowledge is likewise given several different names. Most com-
monly, of course, it is called knowledge of the Holy Trinity. But
Evagrius also means Trinity when he speaks more simply of
knowledge of God. He also sometimes speaks of knowledge of
the Unity or the One. The sense of the word *theology* (θεολογία)
is reserved by Evagrius to refer to the Trinity. In addition, the
Trinity is called "the final blessedness."[42]

Clarity about these different levels of knowledge will help in
a number of ways to interpret with accuracy various dimensions
of *Ad Monachos*. Virtually all of this terminology is found in different proverbs of the text. In order for the meditating mind to
follow what the proverbs suggest it is necessary to understand
what is meant by each of the terms. Furthermore, the progress
from one type of knowledge to another is the subject both of individual proverbs and of some of the chains. These proverbs cannot be interpreted without reference to these levels, nor can the
chains be identified as chains without awareness of them. Finally
the way in which Evagrius conceives of the whole spiritual life as
a return of the mind to the essential knowledge of the Holy Trinity is a conception both magnificent and profound in its various
dimensions. This profundity is shared with the reader of this text.
It is an indication of the level of the audience for whom the text
is intended. It would be misleading to think of it as an elementary
treatise when so much about the various levels of knowledge is
included in its contents. In the structure of *Ad Monachos* Evagrius
has created an image of the whole movement of the mind's
return, beginning in *praktikē* and moving through many levels of
knowledge to culminate in knowledge of the Holy Trinity. The
present study seeks to analyze this structure, and a major feature
of the structure will be seen to be levels of knowledge culminating in the Trinity.

---

[42] All these levels of knowledge are presented in diagram form by O'Laughlin in *Origenism in the Desert*, 136.

5. Evagrius's Biblical Exegesis

The language and style of *Ad Monachos* are intentionally biblical. Many words and phrases echo different parts of the scripture, and the style and structure of the proverbs are an imitation of the proverbial style found in the wisdom literature of the Bible, particularly the book of Proverbs itself. Evagrius was steeped in the language of the scriptures, and so were the people to whom he wrote. He could justifiably expect his readers to recall whole passages or scenes from scripture by his merely mentioning a key word or phrase from that passage. This permits him a tremendous economy of language, and it is ideal for what this genre of writing would promote, namely, meditative reading. The more familiar the reader is with scripture, the more possibilities for meditation are uncovered in the text.[43] In this study we shall sample a number of examples of the directions into which these scriptural citations and allusions are meant to lead the meditative reader.

We can hope to secure with greater accuracy the meaning of the intentionally biblical language of *Ad Monachos* by attention to Evagrius's own explanation of this language, particularly in his scholia on Proverbs and Psalms. In both the literary analysis and the commentaries that follow, I shall have many occasions to turn to Evagrius's scholia in order to clarify the meaning of some of the proverbs in *Ad Monachos*. In the scholia, a specific method of exegesis is unabashedly operative and is extended to the biblical language of *Ad Monachos*. It will be useful to prepare the reader

---

[43] These remarks are valid for all of Evagrius's works. Bunge makes a similar observation regarding the letters, and it can apply here as well. "Evagrios lebt wie seine Zeitgenossen vollkommen in den Gedanken und Bildern der Heiligen Schrift, und zwar in einem solchen Maße, daß seine Sprache oft nur ein überaus feines Gewebe von Schriftzitaten und -anspielungen ist. Es wird offenbar vorausgesetzt, daß auch der Empfänger des Briefes die Schrift nahezu auswendig kennt, was damals, zumal unter Mönchen, auch durchaus keine Seltenheit war, und zudem mit einer geistlichen Schriftauslegung vertraut ist, die sich stark an Origenes orientiert" (*Briefe,* 113). Pp. 113–17 offer a number of useful remarks about Evagrius's way of reading the scripture and writing with scriptural language. For scripture as the central text of learning in all of desert monasticism, see Burton-Christie, *The Word in the Desert.*

for the encounter with this exegesis by tracing here its main lines and intentions.[44]

In his scholia on Proverbs and Psalms, as well as in his use of scriptural language in the rest of his works, Evagrius invites his reader to a spiritual reading of the scriptural text. This involves seeing through the sensible realities (δι' αἰσθητῶν πραγμάτων) and sensible words of the text to the intelligible realities (πράγματα νοητά) they signify (see In Prov 1:1 [G 1]). Evagrius does not deny the literal level of the text any more than he denies the goodness and providence of the material creation. But this level is not his principal interest.[45]

Evagrius wants to find in the scriptures God's own word, God's own teaching about *praktikē*, natural contemplation, and theology (cf. G 18).[46] One misunderstands his effort if this is evaluated as a forcing of scripture into his own categories. Evagrius

---

[44] A fine, even if brief, sketch of Evagrius's exegesis is found in Géhin, SC 340, 26–32. A thorough study of Evagrius's exegetical method and the contents it yields would be a very fruitful and interesting study. We cannot presume that the method is unique to him. The wide range of his correspondents suggests a number of people familiar with and congenial to his methods. He stands squarely within the Alexandrian exegetical tradition. For a study expressing little sympathy for Evagrius's exegesis, see Berthold, "History and Exegesis in Evagrius and Maximus."

[45] It could be said that it is a question of finding the λόγοι within the text in the same way that this is to be discovered in the creation. But the whole reality of the Incarnation and of the death and resurrection of Christ is assumed within Evagrian theology. On this, see V 54 in its Latin and Syriac versions. On the Evagrian authenticity of these versions, see Muyldermans, *Evagriana*, 209–14; also Bunge, "Origenismus," 32–33. For examples of Evagrius also admitting the possibility of the literal sense of the actual scriptural text, see the examples given by Géhin, SC 340, 26–27. This perspective would require a softening of Berthold's evaluation of Evagrius's exegesis. All the samples of this exegesis that Berthold collects and harshly evaluates are read by him outside the context of this presupposed correct doctrine. The main lines of Maximus's attitudes toward letter and spirit, which Berthold promotes in contrast to Evagrius, could likewise be subjected by our contemporary tastes to the same misunderstandings and criticisms he levels at Evagrius. It is true that with Maximus the whole issue of exegesis and doctrine makes new progress and reaches a needed precision, particularly in regard to the permanent significance of the Incarnation; but in the long run this is not best exposed by casting it into relief against the background of a too little nuanced understanding of the *exegesis* of Evagrius, in whose tradition Maximus obviously stands.

was aware that such a tripartite division of things was directly inspired by similar divisions within secular philosophy. Following in the tradition of both Clement and Origen, he was demonstrating his own position that the scriptures were meant to substitute for secular philosophy, that in them alone was found the true philosophy.[47] The structure of Evagrius's conception of this threefold division indeed owes much to secular philosophy, but the content he gives it is deeply scriptural. Like Clement and Origen before him, Evagrius in his theological positions represents another instance of the fruitful interchange of the classical philosophical tradition with the content of the Christian scriptures read with a deadly earnest, guided always by the church's rule of faith. *Praktikē*, natural contemplation, and theology were a sort of framework with which Evagrius received the scriptures—and no one receives them without a framework—but through assiduous meditation and study of the scriptures he suffuses this framework with what can be legitimately considered a profoundly biblical content.

For Evagrius, it is the knower (ὁ γνωστικός) who is prepared to interpret the scriptures in this way; and it is the knower's duty to do so for the good of others.[48] He finds in the language of scripture not only teachings that refer to the threefold division of the spiritual life but indeed "many names which name God and his angels and the mind and virtue and knowledge and evil and ignorance and the devil himself and his angels" (In Prov 1:9

---

[46] Thus, for example, many texts from the book of Proverbs reveal dimensions of *praktikē,* and this is the scope of many of the scholia on that book, though much of it also is seen to refer to dimensions of knowledge. The *Kephalaia Gnostica* could be described as fundamentally concerned with the levels of knowledge that precede knowledge of the Trinity, and many of its chapters are of a fundamentally exegetical nature. The *Scholia on Psalms* are in large part concerned with christology. No single work is wholly devoted to theology (i.e., theology of the Trinity), but many scriptural texts are explained throughout the Evagrian corpus as referring to this mystery. For a typical example, among many possible, see KG VI, 49.

[47] See Géhin, SC 340, 28–29.

[48] At least five of the chapters from the *Gnostikos* are devoted to the issue of exegesis, giving guidance as to how the knower is to refer texts either to *praktikē,* natural contemplation, or theology. See especially G 18 but also G 19, 20, 21, 34. Cf. In Prov 23:1 (G 250).

[G 7]).[49] Many texts in scripture are interpreted by awareness of the different names for mind and soul with which the scriptures speak. In one of the scholia on Proverbs Evagrius gives some twenty-four scriptural expressions for the mind and another twenty-five for the soul, finishing his list with the remark that there are many more which space does not permit his mentioning (In Prov 25:26 [G 317]). Yet this is not a simple word game arranged by God for our amusement or to test our ability to decode such language. The various expressions of scripture are "distinguishing signs of different actions worked on us by God through his angels and worked by us toward him; signs of what the demons do to us and what we do to them" (In Prov 1:9 [G 7]).

In this way of treating the scriptures Evagrius is obviously the heir of the rich exegetical tradition of Clement and Origen extended to him especially through the Cappadocians, through Rufinus and Melania, and practiced with other like-minded monks in his circle. Yet it is interesting to note a difference between the exegesis of Evagrius and that of Origen, as observed by Géhin.[50] For Origen, in each text of scripture there can be distinguished, theoretically at least, a literal, a moral, and a spiritual level. Evagrius instead shows little interest in the literal meaning. He finds three levels in the scripture that correspond to the latter two of Origen. In addition, Evagrius tends not to read a text across successive levels of meaning but rather to refer it to only one or another level. Thus, whereas Origen might comment on a text showing first the literal meaning, then the moral, then the spiritual, Evagrius would be more inclined to place a text within the realm either of *praktikē,* or of natural contemplation, or of theology, but not all three at once (see G 18).

This is not the place to attempt a full-scale apology for Evagrius's biblical exegesis and that of the monastic tradition he represents, and yet these preliminary remarks in preparation for our study of *Ad Monachos* would not be complete without requesting of the readers some openness to the exegesis they will encounter in the study that follows.[51] No age can read or should read the

---

[49] For a rich collection of examples, see Bunge, *Geistliche Vaterschaft,* 70.

[50] Géhin, SC 340, 30.

[51] That such a request is necessary is indicated not only by the sort of evaluations in Berthold's study but by the fact that at the end of his fine sketch of

scriptures apart from interpretive keys supplied to it by the church's rule of faith and a particular tradition that expresses this rule. And such a rule is shaped by categories at once biblical and extrabiblical. For us moderns the exegetical starting point tends to be "l'esprit du livre" to be commented on.[52] This is perhaps legitimate, but it is not exactly the starting point of the tradition to which Evagrius was heir, which, among other things, saw the entire Bible as one book, a book that by Evagrius's time could be commented on from the vantage point of the church's hard-won doctrinal formulations and through these applied (Evagrius's concern!) to the spiritual life of individual Christians. The criteria, then, for a proper evaluation of an ancient author's exegetical methods cannot be modern tastes or unrecognized prejudices in the methods that currently hold sway. For an honest and accurate assessment the criteria must always be a judgment of the content itself which the exegesis yields. Does it conform to the church's rule of faith? And, in the case of an exegesis with a spiritual aim such as that of Evagrius, does it represent a legitimate application—the occasion and tone of the application being some particular scriptural text—of the mysteries of the faith to the lives of individual Christians?[53]

This completes now five areas of Evagrius's teaching that I consider necessary in order to read the text of *Ad Monachos* with profit. In the study that follows we shall have ample opportunity to elaborate and deepen the understanding of the issues that have been but briefly sketched here. The strands of these five areas can perhaps be pulled together and focused for the present study by this simple set of remarks: in *Ad Monachos* Evagrius speaks of how a mind in a soul and body may reach the condition for which it was originally created by the path of *praktikē* and

---

Evagrius's exegesis Géhin cannot resist the following remark: "En généralisant la méthode allégorique, Évagre s'éloigne passablement de l'esprit du livre qu'il commente, et ce n'est pas la reprise de quelques thèmes spécfiquement bibliques comme celui de la crainte du Seigneur, ou encore celui de la pratique de la loi et des commandements, qui peut donner le change. L'Écriture sert trop souvent de caution à des doctrines qui n'ont rien à voir avec elle" (SC 340, 32).

[52] The expression is Géhin's, as cited in the previous note.

[53] In Part Three we shall return to the issue of Evagrius's relation to an exegetical tradition and see how the sort of exegesis he employed is part of a widely diffused practice among the desert monks.

knowledge; that is to say, by the path of doing battle with eight principal evil thoughts and by the path of a knowledge that moves progressively from corporeal realities to incorporeal realities to the Trinity itself. The guide for this journey of the mind is found in the deepest sense of the scriptures themselves, which reveal the mysteries of the journey's every phase and point the mind toward the Trinity.

The Relationship of Ad Monachos to Other Evagrian Texts

As mentioned in the Preface, in this study I follow the procedure of other commentators on Evagrius whose method is fundamentally commenting on Evagrius with Evagrius. This examination of the text of *Ad Monachos* thus becomes an occasion for contact with many other of Evagrius's works read from a particular angle. I suggested that the proverbs of *Ad Monachos* have an especially valuable role among the works of Evagrius in that they function as concise expressions of the already generally concise expressions of his other works. In what follows here I would like to indicate briefly what I see to be the relation of *Ad Monachos* to the other works of Evagrius, and I note the particular kind of contribution that each of these works has given to the present study.[54]

SCRIPTURAL COMMENTARIES IN THE FORM OF SCHOLIA[55]

Evagrius's *Scholia on Proverbs* and *Scholia on Psalms* are especially important for interpreting the language Evagrius uses. I have drawn attention to the intentionally biblical language in which the proverbs of *Ad Monachos* are written. Evagrius's explanations of this biblical language in his various scholia help us to

---

[54] For the references to the various editions of the texts discussed here, see the bibliography of primary sources. For a more general summary of the contents of these works, see Guillaumont, "Évagre le Pontique," in *Dictionnaire de spiritualité*, 1733–37.

[55] On this genre in Evagrius, see Géhin, SC 340, 13–18.

understand why he may have chosen a particular word or image in the composition of a proverb. In the scholia it can be seen how Evagrius finds in this biblical language constant references to the various divisions of the spiritual life; to the conditions of mind, soul, and body; to the actions of God, angels, demons, and humans. He sees hidden deep within some texts precious clues about Christ's work of salvation and about the Trinity itself. This biblical language is used in *Ad Monachos* to refer to the same things to which Evagrius sees it referring in the scriptures. For example, a word in the psalms that is understood as a reference to the mind and a certain of its conditions will be used in *Ad Monachos* in the same way.[56] We will see a number of instances of this in what follows.

The use I have made of the *Scholia on Proverbs* has been necessarily different from that of the *Scholia on Psalms,* and this for several reasons. In its imitation of biblical language the proverbs of *Ad Monachos* are especially modeled on the biblical book of Proverbs, and perforce more language parallels were found. Furthermore, these scholia are now available to us in the fine critical edition of P. Géhin, complete with an index of Greek words. This has greatly facilitated my study and has helped me to find many texts among these scholia that shed light on various proverbs of *Ad Monachos.*[57]

The situation is somewhat different for the *Scholia on Psalms.* The comments of Evagrius are extremely interesting in this text, but they have had to be used with greater caution for the lack of a critical edition. The text of Evagrius is found only with the help of a key provided by M. J. Rondeau, which guides the scholar painstakingly through four volumes of works attributed to Origen and Athanasius to pick out those portions that belong to Evagrius.[58] The journey is rewarding, but it yields results more slowly. In any case, particularly in commenting on some individ-

---

[56] See the commentary below on M 107.

[57] I hope that one of the values of this present study is that it will be among the first to be able to take advantage of this newly available Evagrian text.

[58] Rondeau, "Le commentaire sur les Psaumes d'Évagre le Pontique," 328–48.

ual proverbs, I have been able to find interesting texts from these scholia which help much with the interpretation.[59]

Evagrius's *Scholia on Ecclesiastes* is known through one manuscript (and portions of another), but it is unedited. However, six of the scholia were published in an article in 1979 by Géhin, and a few of them have been quite useful for interpreting some of the proverbs of *Ad Monachos*.[60]

THE *PRAKTIKOS*, THE *GNOSTIKOS*, AND THE *KEPHALAIA GNOSTICA*

This three-volume work of Evagrius is among the most valuable that we have for understanding his thought. All three works have critical editions and thus form an especially secure foundation for coming to know the thought of Evagrius. Each of the three, however, has figured differently in this study of *Ad Monachos*.

The *Praktikos* is available in Greek in its entirety and is a text on which the present study especially relies for understanding whatever in *Ad Monachos* is concerned with *praktikē*, the central theme of the *Praktikos*. As we shall see, a large portion of the text of *Ad Monachos* is devoted to *praktikē*, and I have turned often to the *Praktikos* to clarify what is said there. The relation between these two texts illustrates well my point about how *Ad Monachos* condenses what is expressed at greater length elsewhere.

Of the fifty chapters of the *Gnostikos* some thirty are extant in Greek, the rest only in Syriac. This smallest of the three works functions as a bridge between *praktikē* as it is treated in the *Praktikos* and the specific meditations on various aspects of knowledge as in the *Kephalaia Gnostica*. It describes the duties of the knower, particularly in regard to how one should teach others, in general in how one should relate to others. Another important theme of *Ad Monachos* is the bridge between *praktikē* and knowledge, and the *Gnostikos* proves useful in shedding light on this

---

[59] These texts too, of course, are made available here for the first time to English readers. In most cases it is also the first instance of bringing these texts from the scholia to bear on the particular texts from *Ad Monachos* which I think they help to illuminate.

[60] Géhin, "Un nouvel inédit."

theme. In the last part of this study the *Gnostikos* is used to form a picture of the teaching activity of Evagrius, which I think *Ad Monachos* illustrates especially well.

The *Kephalaia Gnostica* is the longest single work of Evagrius and certainly the most difficult to interpret. Unfortunately, the major part is extant only in several Syriac versions, though there are some seventy-five chapters that are still found in Greek. It is on the *Kephalaia Gnostica* that most studies of Evagrius's theoretical work are based, concerned as it is primarily with all those dimensions of knowledge that precede knowledge of the Trinity. Only a few of the proverbs of *Ad Monachos* touch on these various dimensions of knowledge. However, those few that do are especially important and particularly suggestive. Texts from the *Kephalaia Gnostica* have offered the necessary interpretive key for commenting on these. When available, I have used the Greek texts. In general I have found that the more difficult and enigmatic of the chapters are not helpful in interpreting *Ad Monachos*.[61]

OTHER WORKS DEVOTED TO *PRAKTIKĒ*

There are a number of Evagrian texts, available in Greek but not in critical editions, that in general are devoted to the concerns of *praktikē*. The lack of critical editions suggests that they should be used with a certain caution, but, used sparingly, they can contribute in various ways to clarifying different parts of *Ad Monachos*. Among these the most important is the *Treatise on Evil Thoughts*. This is a more extended analysis of the eight principal evil thoughts identified in the *Praktikos* and the way in which these thoughts are intertwined. Not infrequently the text seems suddenly to burst into talk about the realm of knowledge, and some especially inspiring texts are found among its pages. I have found it helpful to cite a fair number of these.[62]

---

[61] This is to say that, fortunately, the present study is not in the main affected by many of the scholarly controversies that surround the interpretation of various parts of this complex work.

[62] Other texts in this same category, that is useful but not quite as useful for understanding *Ad Monachos* as the *Treatise on Evil Thoughts,* include the *Bases of the Monastic Life, On the Eight Spirits of Evil, On Virtues Opposed to Vices,* and the *Treatise to Eulogium.* From time to time I have had occasion to refer to these.

The *Instruction to Monks* is a minor work that contains some interesting features that make a general comparison to *Ad Monachos* worthwhile. The text is composed of fifty-six separate little meditations resembling the biblical, proverb-like style of *Ad Monachos*. Many of these are in the style of comparisons similar to those found in the biblical book of Proverbs and which a number of the proverbs of *Ad Monachos* imitate.[63] Further, some of these individual proverbs are grouped together around certain themes, allowing one to be meditated on after the other. (Yet there is nothing so sophisticated here as the complex intertwining of themes that we shall see in *Ad Monachos*.) Finally, some of them have managed to encapsulate in just one short line some of the basic features of the teaching of Evagrius on one or another issue, and in this too they bear some similarity to *Ad Monachos*. Unfortunately, it is not possible to know with certainty whether the arrangements of the sayings as we have them is due to Evagrius or not. Presuming that it is, it is tempting to think of this work as a step along the way to Evagrius's own discovery of a possibility that clearly fascinated him; namely, what can emerge from grouping short, Bible-like proverbs together in certain patterns. Such possibilities are primitively developed in the *Instruction to Monks*. They are exploited to considerable advantage in *Ad Monachos*, as the present study will show.

THE *CHAPTERS ON PRAYER*

The whole of this text is extant in the Greek, but unfortunately it has not yet been critically edited.[64] It should be considered among the most important works of Evagrius, a text that contains one of the principal keys to his thought as a whole. In its 153 chapters it offers meditations which show that knowledge,

---

[63] This is the style, "Just as . . . , so . . . ." See M 10, 21, 36, 45, 46, 55, 83, 107, 109 and the Index of Biblical Citations and Allusions for these.

[64] I have, however, been able to use a text prepared by Simon Tugwell that is superior to the text available in Migne, which Simon Tugwell kindly shared with me. His text is based on the examination of eight manuscripts. It is available to students at Oxford through the Faculty of Theology. I base my English translations on this text, though I will cite Migne for the convenience of the reader who does not have access to Tugwell's text.

the goal of the spiritual life, is basically a knowledge received through prayer, which is defined in the treatise as "an intercourse of the mind with God . . . without intermediary" (Prayer 3 [PG 79:1168D]). This knowledge at its highest point is, as we have seen, knowledge of the Trinity; and this treatise makes it clear that such knowledge is gained through intratrinitarian prayer, that is, prayer to the Father through the Son and in the Holy Spirit. Such a goal in knowledge or prayer is not reached or even remotely approached, so the chapters stress, unless the monk is free from anger, unless he be gentle. The movement toward the Trinity and the importance of gentleness and freedom from anger in such a movement are fundamental points stressed by *Ad Monachos.* Thus, various citations from the *Chapters on Prayer* will help us to understand *Ad Monachos* in some of its most important dimensions.

EPISTULA FIDEI AND THE LETTER TO MELANIA

Though both of these texts are written in the style of letters, they are to be distinguished from the other letters of Evagrius for their extended treatment of doctrinal issues. Both texts are particularly valuable for their doctrinal content, and among the works of Evagrius they play a special role for the student of his thought in that in them he expresses himself in a genre different from his usual manner of short, condensed chapters. These two letters are what today would be called theological discussion.[65] His other works are designed more to provoke meditation. These two letters enter into details and face thorny questions in a way that the other works do not. Fortunately, *Epistula Fidei* is preserved in Greek and critically edited. It is concerned with both trinitarian and christological issues in the shape that these took in the latter quarter of the fourth century. The text exhibits the same complexity that generally accompanied discussions of these issues in the period, and in it Evagrius clearly shows himself to be the disciple of the Cappadocians. *Epistula Fidei* is distinguished from the *Letter to Melania* in that the latter is far more daring,

---

[65] *Theology* is a term that Evagrius reserves for the knowledge of the Trinity which comes through prayer.

suggestive, elusive, and enigmatic in the trinitarian discussion it promotes. The Trinity appears explicitly in *Ad Monachos* only toward the end of the text, but its appearance is critical for understanding everything that has preceded as well as the purpose of the whole. Passages from both of these letters will guide us in this portion of our study.[66]

THE LETTERS

Sixty-two other letters of Evagrius exist in Syriac translation with only some several pages of fragments existing in Greek. As Bunge notes in his fine introduction to his German translation of these letters, a letter has a special capacity to reveal the true life of a person, as it is a less self-conscious self-expression than might be found in more formal, theoretical works.[67] Bunge's introduction and notes to the letters seek to bring out these dimensions. More than shedding light on particular texts of *Ad Monachos,* these letters have been for me an occasion for developing a "feel" for the man Evagrius, a sense of his intentions, his tendencies, his reasons for stressing what he does. Thus, in ways that are difficult specifically to identify but which I feel required to acknowledge, the letters have contributed to the present study and to the way I treat different texts, to what I might choose to highlight. In his other writings the man Evagrius can be difficult to detect. But once given the clues to his personality that the letters offer, a real person is sensed in all of these texts. Knowing this person somewhat, as the letters make possible, can help the interpreter of Evagrius to develop a certain finesse in handling his texts.[68]

AD VIRGINEM

This work, available in Greek and critically edited, is the feminine companion text to *Ad Monachos.* It is composed in the same

---

[66] In addition, since *Epistula Fidei* is a text available in Greek and critically edited, it will sometimes offer clues to various issues of vocabulary.

[67] Bunge, *Briefe,* 18–19.

[68] In addition, there are occasions in what follows when a passage from a letter does shed light on some portion of *Ad Monachos.* Whenever possible I have dealt with these in the Greek fragments that are available.

proverbial style, and much of its language echoes that of *Ad Monachos*. Thus it could be expected to play a special role in the present study, but in reality what it offers, against high expectations, turns out to be somewhat disappointing. First of all, though the proverbs in *Ad Virginem* are grouped in definite patterns, the work does not exhibit nearly the sophistication in arrangement that is found in *Ad Monachos*. It has far less of the technical vocabulary of Evagrius, a less complete picture of the eight principal thoughts, far fewer references to knowledge in its various levels or in its relation to *praktikē*. The present study does benefit from attention to some of these proverbs that shed light on a given proverb of *Ad Monachos*, but it seems necessary to note that a text that might have been expected to play a special role has not in fact done so. The text certainly has an interest in its own right,[69] and its stylistic similarities to *Ad Monachos* help us to reach conclusions about the addressees of both texts, which will be taken up in the next section.

CONCLUSION

The above can suffice for orienting the reader among the other works of Evagrius as they will be employed here.[70] I would like to conclude this section by suggesting a caution about overemphasizing the categories into which we might place one or another of Evagrius's works. Scholars have been in the habit of dividing his ascetical works from his theoretical or speculative writings.[71] This is certainly justified, for it reflects the division

---

[69] Particularly interesting to me is the way in which it speaks of the virgin's special relation to Christ as her bridegroom and seems to substitute such talk for treatment of knowledge per se. This text is the subject of a study by S. Elm, "The *Sententiae ad Virginem* by Evagrius Ponticus." She studies the text not so much against the background of other Evagrian literature as for the information it contains about female monastic life at the end of the fourth century. Her methods would be interesting to apply as well to the text of *Ad Monachos*, but they would focus the study in a different direction from the present one.

[70] The study also occasionally quotes the so-called *Skemmata*, it too available in Greek and in some places particularly beautiful and suggestive.

[71] As, for example, Guillaumont in "Évagre le Pontique," in *Dictionnaire de spiritualité*, or "Evagrius Ponticus," in *Reallexikon für Antike und Christentum*.

between *praktikē* and knowledge, and it is generally the case that a particular work is more concerned with one than with the other of these. Yet pushing this division too strongly can be misleading in that it may cause us to overlook how often Evagrius establishes links between *praktikē* and knowledge throughout his writings.

For example, the *Praktikos* and the *Treatise on Evil Thoughts* are both certainly primarily ascetical works, but in both works there are swift and lofty passes into dimensions of knowledge. If we think of these as works written only for beginners, how are such passages to be explained? Or another example: How are the *Chapters of Prayer* to be classified? Some have considered it to be an elementary treatise, presumably because it does not treat the complicated issues found in the *Kephalaia Gnostica*.[72] But this is surely a misleading description, as will become clear throughout the course of this study.

---

[72] Thus O'Laughlin (*Origenism in the Desert,* 209) classifies it as "an elementary treatise" because it does not have in it what he calls the Evagrian doctrine of metempsychosis. Actually the *Chapters of Prayer* are relatively silent on this not because they are more elementary but because the movement of the text concerns pure prayer, which is a doctrine more lofty than the contemplations with which the *Kephalaia Gnostica* are concerned. Bunge (*Geistgebet*) comments on many of the chapters of this treatise, and the impression is that it is anything but elementary. O'Laughlin's treatment of the *Praktikos* is equally indicative of how classification of works can prejudice interpretation. He begins with the preconception that it too is an elementary treatise, and so he expresses surprise that the text begins by divulging information concerning the mind and its relation to the Trinity, and that "it is remarkable that something akin to the most elevated reflections of the *Kephalaia Gnostica* is also to be found in the beginning of the *Practicus*" (p. 226). But this is surprising and remarkable only if we begin the text with a set of preconceptions. It is preferable to take conceptions from the text itself. It is only at the end of his study that O'Laughlin is prepared to modify his preconceptions, though he continues to be "surprised" and suggests that the treatise may not be designed for neophytes (see p. 244). In his conclusion to the whole work, something similar happens. His observations on the texts studied are useful, but still he says, "Even rather esoteric subjects like that of the divine light seen in prayer are mentioned in all three of the more elementary treatises. The word gnosis, and its relationship to the contemplative life is also found in all the documents" (p. 246). What I wish to avoid here is a classification of a given work that suggests too much in advance what may be found in them. It is perhaps precisely this which has let *Ad Monachos* go too long unnoticed by serious scholars, it too being considered "an elementary treatise."

Drawing closer to the effect of these classifications on how *Ad Monachos* might be evaluated, one could ask how the division ascetical/theoretical would apply to the *Scholia on Proverbs* and the *Scholia on Psalms*. They are at once both ascetical and theoretical, depending on what the scripture verse in question suggests.[73] With its biblical language, *Ad Monachos* is best thought of as a text like these. It is neither purely ascetical nor purely theoretical but combines both dimensions. It is neither purely elementary nor wholly designed for those most adept in knowledge. It combines elements of both.[74] This will be borne out in the examination of the structure of the text, which is an actual image of the whole movement from *praktikē* to the very heights of knowledge. It will likewise be borne out in commentary on some of the individual proverbs, some of which are completely involved in *praktikē*, others of which are very deeply involved with knowledge, others of which speak of the connection between the two.

The Addressees of the Text

In order to try to determine to whom this text might have been addressed, the title given in several of the manuscripts and placed by Gressmann at the head of his edition is a good place to begin. That title reads, "To the Monks in Monasteries or Communities."[75] It is almost certainly from the hand of Evagrius himself, for the same expression occurs in a text from the *Praktikos*.

---

[73] Even so, it is the case that the *Scholia on Proverbs* treats more issues of *praktikē* than does the *Scholia on Psalms,* which deals more with knowledge. My point is that it is not a question of being wholly one or the other.

[74] Guillaumont's classification of *Ad Monachos* and *Ad Virginem* suggests little of these possibilities, saying that they can be connected to the elementary treatises the *Bases of the Monastic Life* and the *Treatise to Eulogium* (see SC 170, 33–34). A similar classification is offered some years later in his "Evagrius Ponticus" in *Theologische Realenzykolpädie,* 10: 566.

[75] Πρὸς τοὺς ἐν κοινοβίοις ἢ συνοδίαις μοναχούς. Gregory Nazianzus titles one of his poems Πρὸς τοὺς ἐν κοινοβίῳ μοναχούς (PG 37:642A). Perhaps Evagrius knew this title and it echoes somewhere in the back of his mind as he sets a title on this poetic piece.

Seeing the phrase in that context helps to determine what it might mean. Evagrius says,

> Against anchorites the demons fight straight out, without weapons [γυμνοί]; but against those who exercise virtue in monasteries or communities [τοῖς δὲ ἐν κοινοβίοις ἢ συνοδίαις], they arm the more negligent of the brothers. This second fight is much lighter than the first, for there are not to be found on the earth men more spiteful than demons or men who could take up all at once the whole of demonic evil-doings. (TP 5)

As Guillaumont's commentary on this chapter notes, ordinarily συνοδία has an abstract sense of designating a community of monks, while κοινοβίον generally refers to the monastery itself. Unfortunately in these two texts it is not possible to say exactly what difference, if any, Evagrius sees in the two terms.[76] Nonetheless, Evagrius does draw a distinction between two different types of the monastic life, namely, that of anchorites and that of monks in communities. The difference is clearly enough expressed in this text. In a community, negligent brothers can do the demons' dirty work; that is, they will agitate the brothers and stir up passions within them. But against the anchorite the demons themselves must do the fighting. They do this directly through thoughts (λογισμοί), which stir up the passions.

On the basis of this text Guillaumont suggests a sharp distinction between the type of monastic struggle that Evagrius conceives for these two different types of monks.[77] But this once again raises the problem mentioned above of how readers might classify *Ad Monachos* and what they may consequently be predisposed to see in it. There is no question that Evagrius does distinguish between the demons as they work through others and demons as they work directly through thoughts. Furthermore, rather obviously, the only means a demon would have of working against a solitary (while he is actually alone) would be through his thoughts. But the question may be raised whether or not Evagrius imagines that in actual fact anchorites are never likewise troubled by demons working through others, and vice versa,

---

[76] Guillaumont, SC 171, 504–5.
[77] Guillaumont, SC 170, 94–95; SC 171, 504–5; A. Guillaumont, "Un philosophe au désert," 36–37.

whether those in community are not likewise troubled directly through thoughts. In the text from the *Praktikos* cited here Evagrius may simply be drawing the contrast in order to make his point in the chapter.[78] In fact, throughout his writings there are many indications that the situation for anchorites and for those in community involves suffering mixed styles of demonic attacks; that is, passions may be stirred up through others or they may be stirred up immediately through a thought.

The title of *Ad Monachos* indicates that it is addressed to monks in communities, but the contents do not indicate that Evagrius imagines an audience not doing direct battle with the demons. For example, all eight of the principal thoughts or demons described in the *Praktikos* are found in *Ad Monachos*. The technical term used for this direct demonic attack, λογισμοί, is used on nine different occasions in the text. The word *demon* itself occurs six times, and the words *anachōrēsis* and *anchorite* are also found. According to the Evagrian conception, a monk may not enter into knowledge without having undergone this direct battle with demonic thoughts; yet there is indeed much talk about knowledge in *Ad Monachos* as well.

One may wish to draw attention to *Ad Monachos*'s stress on gentleness and other issues about brotherly relations as indications of a cenobitic addressee. To this can be added the texts that have to do with details of community life such as caring for the sick or handling carefully and distributing wisely the material goods of the monastery. A similar emphasis on gentleness is found in the *Chapters on Prayer,* and in fact in many of Evagrius's works. The conditions of community life about which the text yields information are not peculiar to cenobitic monasticism. They could equally well apply to the monastic arrangements of a group of semi-anchorites like the monks of Cells, where Evagrius himself lived.

I am not arguing here that *Ad Monachos* is not addressed to monks living in community. I think its title should be taken seri-

---

[78] The chapter precedes the listing of the eight λογισμοί and the chapters that describe these. These are λογισμοί, the *Praktikos* wants to say, with which the monk must do direct battle to reach the passionlessness that gives way to knowledge.

ously. My point is different. I am persuaded by the entire tone and content of *Ad Monachos* that Evagrius does not distinguish sharply between the way in which he addresses monks who live in communities and the way in which he addresses solitaries. In both kinds of communities the demons will attack indirectly through other people and directly through thoughts. In both communities a monk can hope to come to the heights of knowledge.[79]

Bunge, so far as I know, is the only scholar who has ventured a theory concerning the addressees of *Ad Monachos*.[80] His argument is constructed on the basis of a theme common to *Ad Monachos* and its feminine companion text, *Ad Virginem*. Both texts share a concern with false knowledge. To whom would Evagrius have directed texts with such a concern? Beginning with the examination of *Ad Virginem*, Bunge notes that there are four letters closely joined in content that can perhaps shed light on the origins of this text. The letters are numbers 7, 8, 19, 20.[81] Combining the information found in these various letters, he describes a situation in which a noblewoman living in Jerusalem apparently wanted to make a journey to visit the monasteries of Egypt. Evagrius strongly advices against such a journey, and his advice seems to have been followed. He is pleased about this and sends a gift to this woman instead, namely, a collection of proverbs, the text we know as *Ad Virginem*. Bunge identifies this woman as the deaconess Severa, a member of Melania's monastic community on the Mount of Olives. If he is correct in this reconstruction, it means that Evagrius wrote to a nun in the Jerusalem community warning her against teachers of false knowledge. But to whom in Jerusalem would Evagrius have been referring? It does not seem possible to say exactly.[82] It seems probable that Evagrius could have had personal experience with such false teachers both in Palestine and in Egypt.[83]

---

[79] See n. 84 below, for works with some of the most advanced teaching of Evagrius, addressed to monks living in community.

[80] Bunge, "Origenismus," 35–39.

[81] Bunge considers Lt 7 and Lt 20 to have been addressed to Rufinus, Lt 8 to Melania, and Lt 19 to a deaconess named Severa.

[82] Bunge notes that in a general way we know Evagrius to have been concerned about heresy on several fronts at once—Gnosticism, Apollinarianism, Docetism, and Arianism ("Origenismus," 35).

[83] Bunge, "Origenismus," 36.

In any case, the next step in Bunge's argument is to draw attention to the strict stylistic and thematic relationship between *Ad Virginem* and *Ad Monachos*. He suggests that *Ad Monachos* was addressed not to Egyptian but to Palestinian monks, more specifically to the brothers of Rufinus's monastic community on the Mount of Olives, with which we know Evagrius to have been in frequent contact and correspondence.[84] Again, without being able to identify exactly who the source of the problem was, Bunge brings forth evidence from a remark of Palladius about Melania that indeed these communities were threatened by a false knowledge. Melania is described by Palladius as being able, as a result of her assiduous study of the fathers, to have freed these communities from the danger of "false (so-called) knowledge."[85] Bunge raises the possibility that Evagrius's own contact with these communities might have given them a new orientation in their study of the fathers which helped them in the combat with false knowledge.[86] This for Bunge would have been the *Sitz im Leben* of *Ad Monachos*.

This theory is an attractive one and has much to recommend it, yet it cannot be established with certainty.[87] In terms of determining the addressees of *Ad Monachos*, the theory rests very much on associating *Ad Monachos* with *Ad Virginem*, particularly on the

---

[84] In all likelihood the trilogy of the *Praktikos*, the *Gnostikos*, and the *Kephalaia Gnostica* was also addressed to someone in this community. So say both Guillaumont (SC 171, 482–83) and Bunge ("Origenismus," 39). If this is so, it lends support to my point above about not stressing too strongly the distinction between the way Evagrius addresses anchorites and the way he addresses monks living in community. These three works represent virtually the core of Evagrian thought. Furthermore, it is likely that the *Chapters on Prayer* were addressed to Rufinus, presumably also not only for his personal benefit but for the benefit of his community. On letters between Evagrius and the Mount of Olives communities, see Bunge, *Briefe,* 179–81, 204 n. 61.

[85] Bunge, "Origenismus," 36–37. The reference in Palladius is LH 55:3.

[86] As the *Gnostikos* shows, interpretation of scripture is a major skill to be learned from the knower. The text from Palladius concerning Melania that Bunge cites indicates that scriptural interpretation may have been the concern. Evagrius's own scholia on the scriptures give ample evidence of his capacity to interpret them according to what he and the Mount of Olives communities would have considered "true knowledge." Furthermore, concern with the difference between true and false knowledge is a major theme in the *Scholia on Proverbs.*

[87] Bunge presents it as a possibility only. He does not claim its certainty.

theme of false knowledge. But these are not the only works of Evagrius where the theme is prominent; it plays a large role also in the *Scholia on Proverbs*. Although true versus false knowledge forms the theme of one of the most developed chains in *Ad Monachos* (123–31),[88] in an overall evaluation of the text it must take its place among other themes that are given equal prominence. Furthermore, the sophistication of *Ad Monachos* compared to *Ad Virginem* cautions against applying conclusions about one to the other.[89]

Maybe something like the following is the best that can be conjectured. There is firmer evidence (evidence from the letters) for thinking that *Ad Virginem* was written to a member of Melania's monastic community. In this text Evagrius tried a new twist in his style: Bible-like proverbs—short, pithy summaries of great insights from the tradition. We can imagine that the text would have been well received in the Jerusalem community. On the supposition that a text similar in style but far more sophisticated would have been composed later in time, we can imagine *Ad Monachos* being designed with much greater care (with a more effective and nuanced arrangement of these Bible-like proverbs) and perhaps, though not necessarily, being sent off to be shared with the companion monastic community in Jerusalem. If this was a community threatened by false knowledge, so much the better then to include that as one of its major themes.[90] Bunge suggests that *Ad Virginem* was a gift to a member of Melania's community, no doubt offered for the benefit of the whole community. *Ad Monachos* might be imagined in this same light. It would have been a fine gift to a monk familiar with this thought, received as a valued condensation of some of its major themes and their interrelations.[91]

---

[88] See comments below in the structural analysis.

[89] Only to focus on the question at hand, the theme of false knowledge is more carefully developed in *Ad Monachos* than in *Ad Virginem*. But is it therefore legitimate to conclude that it is directed to the same concerns that *Ad Virginem* addresses, particularly if, as Bunge claims, Evagrius may have had personal experience with false knowledge *both* from Egypt and from Palestine?

[90] Similarly, I suggested above that the *Instruction to Monks* perhaps represents a yet earlier stage in the process that led to the designing of a text the quality of *Ad Monachos*.

[91] I will return to this theme of the *Sitz im Leben* of *Ad Monachos* in Part

Perhaps the question that is more relevant to the present study is this: If *Ad Monachos* is addressed to Rufinus's community on the Mount of Olives, how would this affect a reading of the text? The answer is, not much. We know so little about that community that there could be but dim light shed on the text from knowing with certainty that it was addressed to them.[92] Things would be rather more interesting in the reverse direction; that is, it could perhaps contribute to shaping something of a more concrete picture of the monastic life in this Jerusalem community.[93]

Unfortunately, there is little that can be said with certainty on this question. Nonetheless, it is important to note at least this much: to whomever *Ad Monachos* was addressed, for whomever it was written, must have been someone capable of uncovering many hidden treasures in the text, someone who would be pleased by unexpected riches in levels of interpretation and surprise connections, someone familiar enough with the terminology and concepts of Evagrius's whole spiritual system to realize that this text was the carefully designed image of all the ins and outs of this spiritual way which leads at last to knowledge of the Holy Trinity. The present study of *Ad Monachos* is undertaken from the standpoint of such an addressee. I attempt to read the text in search of the treasures that Evagrius has hidden within. He himself is the principal guide. We can turn now to a reading of the text, presented here in Gressmann's Greek edition and my English translation.

Three, where I attempt to describe the relation between Evagrius's oral teaching and its written forms. I think this is the more fruitful direction to look for some sense of the situation that produced such a text.

[92] As we know from the prologue to the *Praktikos*, the trilogy was likely addressed to a certain Anatolius; but this fact did not influence the commentaries of Guillaumont in SC 170, 171 or SC 356; nor should it have. The same would apply to the *Chapters on Prayer*, most likely addressed to Rufinus. This fact did not influence Hausherr's classical commentary (*Leçons*) nor Bunge's more recent one (*Geistgebet*).

[93] Elm draws such conclusions for Melania's community from *Ad Virginem* ("The *Sententiae ad Virginem* by Evagrius Ponticus").

Part One

Ad Monachos
in Greek
and in English Translation

πρὸς τοὺς ἐν κοινοβίοις ἢ συνοδίαις μοναχούς

1. Κληρονόμοι θεοῦ ἀκούσατε λόγων θεοῦ,
   συγκληρονόμοι δὲ Χριστοῦ δέξασθε ῥήσεις Χριστοῦ,
   ἵνα δῶτε αὐτὰς καρδίαις τέκνων ὑμῶν,
   λόγους δὲ σοφῶν διδάξητε αὐτούς.

   Heirs of God, listen to the reasons of God.
   Coheirs of Christ, receive the sayings of Christ,
   so that you can give them to the hearts of your children,
   and teach them the words of the wise.

2. Πατὴρ ἀγαθὸς παιδεύει υἱοὺς αὐτοῦ,
   πατὴρ δὲ πονηρὸς ἀπολέσει αὐτούς.

   A good father trains his sons;
   an evil father will ruin them.

3. Πίστις ἀρχὴ ἀγάπης,
   τέλος δὲ ἀγάπης γνῶσις θεοῦ.

   Faith: the beginning of love.
   The end of love: knowledge of God.

4. Φόβος κυρίου διατηρήσει ψυχήν,
   ἐγκράτεια δὲ ἀγαθὴ ἐνισχύσει αὐτήν.

   Fear of the Lord guards the soul.
   Good temperance strengthens it.

5. Ὑπομονὴ ἀνδρὸς τίκτει ἐλπίδα,
   ἐλπὶς δὲ ἀγαθὴ δοξάσει αὐτόν.

   The perseverance of a man gives birth to hope;
   good hope will glorify him.

6. Ὁ δουλαγωγῶν σάρκας αὐτοῦ ἀπαθὴς ἔσται,
   ὁ δὲ ἐκτρέφων αὐτὰς ὀδυνηθήσεται ἐπ᾽ αὐταῖς.

   The one who enslaves his flesh, passionless shall he be;
   the one who feeds it, by it will he be pained.

7. Πνεῦμα πορνείας ἐν σώμασιν ἀκρατῶν,
   πνεῦμα δέ σωφροσύνης ἐν ψυχαῖς ἐγκρατῶν.

   A spirit of sexual impurity is in the bodies of the
   intemperate,
   but a spirit of chastity is in the souls of the temperate.

8. Ἀναχώρησις ἐν ἀγάπῃ καθαίρει καρδίαν,
   ἀναχώρησις δὲ μετὰ μίσους ἐκταράσσει αὐτήν.

   Anachoresis in love purifies the heart;
   anachoresis in hate agitates it.

9. Κρείσσων χιλιοστὸς ἐν ἀγάπῃ
   ἢ μόνος μετὰ μίσους ἐν ἀδύτοις σπηλαίοις.

   Better the thousandth in love
   than one alone with hate in inaccessible caves.

10. Ὁ ἐναποδεσμεύων μνησικακίαν ἐν ψυχῇ αὐτοῦ
    ὅμοιός ἐστι τῷ κρύπτοντι πῦρ ἐν ἀχύροις.

    The one who binds memory of injury to his soul
    is like to one hiding fire in chaff.

11. Μὴ δῷς βρώματα πολλὰ τῷ σώματί σου,
    καὶ οὐ μὴ ἴδῃς καθ᾽ ὕπνους φαντασίας κακάς.
    ὃν τρόπον γὰρ φλόξ καταναλίσκει δρυμόν,
    οὕτω φαντασίας αἰσχρὰς σβέννυσι πεῖνα.

    Do not give much food to your body
    and you will not see bad visions in your sleep.
    For in the way that a flame enkindles a forest
    so does hunger burn up shameful visions.

12. Ἀνὴρ θυμώδης πτοηθήσεται,
    ὁ δὲ πραῢς ἄφοβος ἔσται.

    An irascible man will be terrified;
    the gentle man will be without fear.

13. Ἄνεμος σφοδρὸς ἀποδιώκει νέφη,
    μνησικακία δὲ τὸν νοῦν ἀπὸ γνώσεως.

    A strong wind chases away clouds;
    memory of injury chases the mind from knowledge.

14. Ὁ προσευχόμενος ὑπὲρ ἐχθρῶν ἀμνησίκακος ἔσται,
    φειδόμενος δὲ γλώσσης οὐ λυπήσει τὸν πλησίον αὐτοῦ.

    He who prays for his enemies will be forgetful of injuries
    he who spares his tongue will not sadden his neighbor.

15. Ἐὰν παροξύνῃ σε ὁ ἀδελφός σου,
    εἰσάγαγε αὐτὸν εἰς τὸν οἶκόν σου,
    καὶ πρὸς αὐτὸν μὴ ὀκνήσῃς εἰσελθεῖν,
    ἀλλὰ φάγε τὸν ψωμόν σου μετ᾽ αὐτοῦ.
    τοῦτο γὰρ ποιῶν ῥύσῃ σὴν ψυχὴν
    καὶ οὐκ ἔσται σοι πρόσκομμα ἐν καιρῷ προσευχῆς.

    If your brother irritates you,
    lead him into your house,
    and do not hesitate to go into his,
    but eat your morsel with him.
    For doing this, you will deliver your soul
    and there will be no stumbling block for you at the
        hour of prayer.

16. Ὥσπερ ἡ ἀγάπη χαίρει πενίᾳ,
    οὕτω τὸ μῖσος τέρπεται πλούτῳ.

    Just as love rejoices in poverty,
    so hate is pleased by wealth.

17. Οὐκ ἐπιτεύξεται πλούσιος γνώσεως
καὶ κάμηλος οὐκ εἰσελεύσεται εἰς ὀπὴν ῥαφίδος,
ἀλλ᾽ οὐδὲν τούτων ἀδυνατήσει παρὰ κυρίῳ.

The rich man will not acquire knowledge
and the camel will not enter through the eye of a needle,
yet none of these things will be impossible with the Lord.

18. Ὁ φιλῶν ἀργύριον οὐκ ὄψεται γνῶσιν,
καὶ ὁ συνάγων αὐτὸ σκοτισθήσεται.

He who loves money will not see knowledge,
and he who amasses it will become dark in himself.

19. Ἐν σκηναῖς ταπεινῶν αὐλισθήσεται κύριος,
ἐν οἴκοις δὲ ὑπερηφάνων πληθυνθήσονται ἀραί.

In the tents of the humble the Lord will make camp,
but in the houses of the proud, curses will abound.

20. Ἀτιμάζει θεὸν ὁ παραβαίνων νόμον αὐτοῦ,
ὁ δὲ φυλάσσων αὐτὸν δοξάζει τὸν ποιήσαντα αὐτόν.

The one who transgresses God's law dishonors him,
but he who keeps it glorifies the one who made him.

21. Ἐὰν ζηλώσῃς Χριστόν, γενήσῃ μακαριστός,
τὸν δὲ θάνατον αὐτοῦ ἀποθανεῖται ἡ ψυχή σου,
καὶ οὐ μὴ ἐπισπάσηται ἀπὸ σαρκὸς αὐτῆς κακίαν,
ἀλλ᾽ ἔσται ἡ ἔξοδός σου ὡς ἔξοδος ἀστέρος,
καὶ ἡ ἀνάστασίς σου ὥσπερ ὁ ἥλιος ἐκλάμψει.

If you imitate Christ, you will become blessed.
Your soul will die his death,
and it will not derive evil from its flesh.
Instead, your exodus will be like the exodus of a star,
and your resurrection will glow like the sun.

22. Οὐαὶ ἀνόμῳ ἐν ἡμέρᾳ θανάτου,
    καὶ ἄδικος ὀλεῖται ἐν καιρῷ πονηρῷ.
    ὃν τρόπον γὰρ ἀφίπταται κόραξ ἐκ τῆς αὐτοῦ νοσσιᾶς,
    οὕτως ἀκάθαρτος ψυχὴ ἐκ τοῦ ἰδίου σώματος.

    Woe to a lawless man on the day of his death.
    The unjust man will perish at an evil hour.
    For as a crow flies away from its nest,
    so does the unclean soul from its own body.

23. Ψυχὰς δικαίων ὁδηγοῦσιν ἄγγελοι,
    ψυχὰς δὲ πονηρῶν παραλήψονται δαίμονες.

    The souls of the just, angels guide;
    the souls of the wicked, demons will snatch up.

24. Οὗ ἐὰν εἰσέλθῃ κακία, ἐκεῖ καὶ ἀγνωσία,
    καρδίαι δὲ ὁσίων πληρωθήσονται γνώσεως.

    Wherever evil enters in, there also ignorance;
    but the hearts of holy ones will be filled with knowledge.

25. Ἀνελεήμων μοναχὸς ἐνδεὴς ἔσται,
    διατρέφων δὲ πτωχοὺς κληρονομήσει θησαυρούς.

    The monk who gives no alms will himself be in need,
    but the one who feeds the poor will inherit treasures.

26. Κρείσσων πενία μετὰ γνώσεως
    ἢ πλοῦτος μετὰ ἀγνωσίας.

    Better poverty with knowledge
    than wealth with ignorance.

27. Κόσμος κεφαλῆς στέφανος,
    κόσμος δὲ καρδίας γνῶσις θεοῦ.

    An ornament for the head: a crown;
    an ornament for the heart: knowledge of God.

28. Κτῆσαι γνῶσιν καὶ μὴ ἀργύριον
    καὶ σοφίαν ὑπὲρ πλοῦτον πολύν.

    Procure knowledge and not silver,
    and wisdom rather than much wealth.

29. Δίκαιοι κληρονομήσουσι κύριον,
    ὅσιοι δὲ τραφήσονται ὑπ᾽ αὐτοῦ.

    The just will inherit the Lord;
    the holy ones will be fed by him.

30. Ὁ ἐλεῶν πένητας διαφθείρει θυμόν,
    καὶ ὁ διατρέφων αὐτοὺς πλησθήσεται ἀγαθῶν.

    He who is merciful to the poor destroys irascibility,
    and he who cares for them will be filled with good things.

31. Ἐν καρδίᾳ πραείᾳ ἀναπαύσεται σοφία,
    θρόνος δὲ ἀπαθείας ψυχὴ πρακτική.

    In the gentle heart, wisdom will rest;
    a throne of passionlessness: a soul accomplished
        in *praktikē*.

32. Τέκτονες πονηρῶν λήψονται μισθὸν κακόν,
    τέκτοσι δὲ ἀγαθῶν δοθήσεται μισθὸς ἀγαθός.

    Craftsmen of evils will receive a bad wage,
    but to craftsmen of good things, a good wage
        will be given.

33. Ὁ τιθεὶς παγίδα συλληφθήσεται ἐν αὐτῇ
    καὶ ὁ κρύπτων αὐτὴν ἁλώσεται ὑπ᾽ αὐτῆς.

    The one who lays a trap will himself be caught,
    and he who hides it will be seized by it.

34. Κρείσσων κοσμικὸς πραΰς
    μοναχοῦ θυμώδους καὶ ὀργίλου.

Better a gentle worldly man
than an irascible and wrathful monk.

35. Γνῶσιν διασκορπίζει θυμός,
    μακροθυμία δὲ συνάγει αὐτήν.

Irascibility scatters knowledge;
long-suffering gathers it.

36. Ὥσπερ νότος ἰσχυρὸς ἐν πελάγει
    οὕτως θυμὸς ἐν καρδίᾳ ἀνδρός.

Like a strong south wind on the sea,
so is irascibility in the heart of a man.

37. Ὁ προσευχόμενος συνεχῶς ἐκφεύγει πειρασμούς,
    ἀμελοῦντος δὲ καρδίαν ἐκταράσσουσι λογισμοί.

He who prays unceasingly escapes temptations,
but thoughts agitate the heart of the careless one.

38. Μὴ εὐφραινέτω σε οἶνος
    καὶ μὴ τερπέτω σε κρέας,
    ἵνα μὴ διαθρέψῃς σάρκας σώματός σου,
    καὶ λογισμοὶ αἰσχροὶ οὐκ ἐκλείψουσιν ἀπό σου.

Let not wine gladden you
and let not meat make you merry,
lest you nourish the flesh of your body
and shameful thoughts depart not from you.

39. Μὴ εἴπῃς· σήμερον ἑορτὴ καὶ πίομαι οἶνον,
    καὶ αὔριον πεντηκοστὴ καὶ φάγομαι κρέα,

διότι οὐκ ἔστιν ἑορτὴ παρὰ μοναχοῖς
οὐδὲ τὸ πλῆσαι ἄνθρωπον κοιλίαν αὐτοῦ.

Do not say, "Today is a feast and I'm drinking wine,"
and "tomorrow is Pentecost and I'm eating meat."
For there is not feast among monks
where a man can fill his stomach.

40. Πάσχα κυρίου διάβασις ἀπὸ κακίας,
πεντηκοστὴ δὲ αὐτοῦ ἀνάστασις ψυχῆς.

Pasch of the Lord: passing over from evil;
his Pentecost: resurrection of the soul.

41. Ἑορτὴ θεοῦ ἀμνηστία κακῶν,
τὸν δὲ μνησικακοῦντα λήψονται πένθη.

Feast of God: forgetfulness of offenses;
he who remembers injury, sorrows will grab.

42. Πεντηκοστὴ κυρίου ἀνάστασις ἀγάπης,
ὁ δὲ μισῶν τὸν ἀδελφὸν αὐτοῦ πεσεῖται πτῶμα ἐξαίσιον.

Pentecost of the Lord: resurrection of love;
but he who hates his brother will fall a mighty fall.

43. Ἑορτὴ θεοῦ γνῶσις ἀληθής,
ὁ δὲ προσέχων γνώσει ψευδεῖ τελευτήσει αἰσχρῶς.

Feast of God: true knowledge;
but he who courts a false knowledge will end shamefully.

44. Κρείσσων νηστεία μετὰ καθαρᾶς καρδίας
ὑπὲρ ἑορτὴν ἐν ἀκαθαρσίᾳ ψυχῆς.

Better a fast with a pure heart
than a feast in impurity of soul.

45. Ὁ διαφθείρων λογισμοὺς κακοὺς ἀπὸ καρδίας αὐτοῦ
    ὅμοιός ἐστι τῷ ἐδαφίζοντι τὰ νήπια αὐτοῦ πρὸς τὴν πέτραν.

He who completely destroys evil thoughts in his heart,
he is like the one who dashes his children against
    the rock.

46. Μοναχὸς ὑπνώδης ἐμπεσεῖται εἰς κακά,
    ὁ δὲ ἀγρυπνῶν ὡς στρουθίον ἔσται.

The sleepy monk will fall into evils,
but the vigilant one, like a sparrow shall he be.

47. Μὴ δῷς σεαυτὸν ἐν ἀγρυπνίᾳ διηγήμασι κενοῖς
    καὶ μὴ ἀπώσῃ λόγους πνευματικούς,
    ὅτι κύριος σκοπεύει σὴν ψυχὴν
    καὶ οὐ μὴ ἀθωώσῃ σε ἀπὸ παντὸς κακοῦ.

Do not give yourself during a vigil to empty stories,
and do not reject spiritual reasons;
for the Lord inspects your soul,
and he will not fail to punish you for every evil.

48. Ὕπνος πολὺς παχύνει διάνοιαν,
    ἀγρυπνία δὲ ἀγαθὴ λεπτύνει αὐτήν.

Much sleep thickens thought,
while a good vigil hones it fine.

49. Ὕπνος πολὺς ἐπάγει πειρασμούς,
    ὁ δὲ ἀγρυπνῶν ἐκφεύξεται αὐτούς.

Much sleep leads on temptations,
but these the vigilant one will flee.

50. Ὥσπερ πῦρ τήκει κηρόν,
    οὕτως ἀγρυπνία ἀγαθὴ λογισμοὺς πονηρούς.

As fire melts wax,
so the good vigil, evil thoughts.

51. Κρείσσων ἀνὴρ καθεύδων
ἢ μοναχὸς ἀγρυπνῶν περὶ λογισμοὺς ματαίους.

Better a man lying down to sleep
than a monk keeping vigil with idle thoughts.

52. Ἐνύπνιον ἀγγελικὸν εὐφραίνει καρδίαν,
ἐνύπνιον δὲ δαιμονιῶδες ἐκταράσσει αὐτήν.

An angelic dream gladdens the heart;
a demonic dream agitates it.

53. Μετάνοια καὶ ταπείνωσις ἀνώρθωσαν ψυχήν,
ἐλεημοσύνη δὲ καὶ πραΰτης ἐστήριξαν αὐτήν.

Conversion and humility have set the soul up;
compassion and gentleness have made it firm.

54. Μέμνησο διὰ παντὸς σῆς ἐξόδου
καὶ μὴ ἐπιλάθῃ κρίσεως αἰωνίας,
καὶ οὐκ ἔσται πλημμέλεια ἐν ψυχῇ σου.

In all things remember your exodus,
and do not forget the eternal judgment,
and there will be no transgression in your soul.

55. Ἐὰν πνεῦμα ἀκηδίας ἀναβῇ ἐπί σε, οἶκόν σου μὴ ἀφῇς
καὶ μὴ ἐκκλίνῃς ἐν καιρῷ πάλην ἐπωφελῆ.
ὃν τρόπον γὰρ εἴ τις λευκάνοι ἄργυρον,
οὕτως λαμπρυνθήσεται ἡ καρδία σου.

If the spirit of listlessness mounts you,
do not leave your house;
and do not turn aside in that hour from profitable
    wrestling.
For like someone making money shine,
so will your heart be made to glow.

56. Πνεῦμα ἀκηδίας ἀπελαύνει δάκρυα,
    πνεῦμα δὲ λύπης συντρίβει προσευχήν.

    The spirit of listlessness drives away tears
    and the spirit of sadness shatters prayer.

57. Ἐπιθυμῶν χρημάτων μεριμνήσεις πολλά,
    καὶ ἀντεχόμενος αὐτῶν πενθήσεις πικρῶς.

    Desiring riches, you will be divided by care;
    and cleaving to them, bitterly shall you mourn.

58. Μὴ χρονιζέτω σκορπίος ἐν κόλπῳ σου
    καὶ λογισμὸς πονερὸς ἐν καρδίᾳ σου.

    Do not let a scorpion linger on your breast,
    nor in your heart an evil thought.

59. Κτείνειν γεννήματα ὀφέων μὴ φείσῃ,
    καὶ μὴ ὠδίνῃς λογισμοὺς καρδίας αὐτῶν.

    Do not fail to kill the offspring of serpents,
    and you will not go into labor with the thoughts of
        their heart.

60. Ὥσπερ ἀργύριον καὶ χρυσίον δοκιμάζει πῦρ,
    οὕτως καρδίαν μοναχοῦ πειρασμοί.

    As fire tests silver and gold,
    so temptations, the heart of a monk.

61. Περίελε σεαυτοῦ ὑπερηφανίαν
    καὶ κενοδοξίαν μακρὰν ποίησον ἀπό σου.
    ὁ γὰρ ἀποτυχὼν δόξης λυπηθήσεται,
    ὁ δὲ ἐπιτυχὼν ὑπερήφανος ἔσται.

    Strip down pride from yourself
    and put vainglory far away from you.
    For the one who does not obtain glory will be sad,
    and the one who does obtain it will be proud.

62. Μὴ δῷς ὑπερηφανίᾳ σὴν καρδίαν
     καὶ μὴ εἴπῃς πρὸ προσώπου τοῦ θεοῦ·ᵗ δυνατός εἰμι,
     ἵνα μὴ κύριος ἐγκαταλίπῃ σὴν ψυχήν,
     καὶ πονηροὶ δαίμονες ταπεινώσουσιν αὐτήν.
     τότε γάρ σε δι᾿ ἀέρος πτοήσουσιν οἱ ἐχθροί,
     νύκτες δὲ φοβεραὶ διαδέξονταί σε.

     Do not give your heart to pride
     and do not say before the face of God, "Powerful am I";
     lest the Lord abandon your soul
     and evil demons bring it low.
     For then the enemies will flutter around you through
          the air,
     and fearful nights will follow you.

63. Πολιτείαν μοναχοῦ διαφυλάττει γνῶσις,
     ὁ δὲ καταβαίνων ἀπὸ γνώσεως περιπεσεῖται λῃσταῖς.

     Knowledge keeps guard over a monk's way of life;
     but he who descends from knowledge will fall among
          thieves.

64. Ἐκ πέτρας πνευματικῆς ἀπορρεῖ ποταμός,
     ψυχὴ δὲ πρακτικὴ πίεται ἀπ᾿ αὐτοῦ.

     From the spiritual rock, a river flows;
     a soul accomplished in *praktikē* drinks from it.

65. Σκεῦος ἐκλογῆς ψυχὴ καθαρά,
     ἡ δὲ ἀκάθαρτος πλησθήσεται πικρίας.

     A vessel of election, the pure soul;
     but the impure soul will be filled with bitterness.

66. Ἄνευ γάλακτος οὐ τραφήσεται παιδίον,
     καὶ χωρὶς ἀπαθείας οὐχ ὑψωθήσεται καρδία.

     Without milk, a child is not nourished,
     and apart from passionlessness, a heart will not be
          raised up.

67. Πρὸ ἀγάπης ἡγεῖται ἀπάθεια
πρὸ δὲ γνώσεως ἀγάπη.

In front of love, passionlessness marches;
in front of knowledge, love.

68. Γνώσει προστίθεται σοφία,
ἀπάθειαν δὲ τίκτει φρόνησις.

To knowledge, wisdom is added;
prudence gives birth to passionlessness.

69. Φόβος κυρίου γεννᾷ φρόνησιν,
πίστις δὲ Χριστοῦ δωρεῖται φόβον θεοῦ.

Fear of the Lord begets prudence;
faith in Christ bestows fear of God.

70. Βέλος πεπυρωμένον ἀνάπτει ψυχήν,
ἀνὴρ δὲ πρακτικὸς κατασβέσει αὐτό.

A flaming arrow ignites the soul,
but the man of *praktikē* will extinguish it.

71. Κραυγὴν καὶ βλασφημίαν ἀποστρέφεται γνῶσις,
λόγους δὲ δολίους φεύγει σοφία.

Clamor and blasphemy, knowledge turns aside;
cunning words, wisdom flees.

72. Ἡδὺ μέλι καὶ γλυκὺ κηρίον,
γνῶσις δὲ θεοῦ γλυκυτέρα ἀμφοτέρων.

Sweet is honey, its comb a delight;
but sweeter than both is the knowledge of God.

73. Ἄκουε, μοναχέ, λόγους πατρός σου
καὶ μὴ ἀκύρους ποίει νουθεσίας αὐτοῦ.
Ἡνίκα ἂν ἀποστείλῃ σε, ἐπάγου αὐτὸν
καὶ κατὰ διάνοιαν συνόδευε αὐτῷ.

τούτῳ γὰρ τῷ τρόπῳ διαφεύξῃ λογισμοὺς κακούς,
καὶ πονηροὶ δαίμονες οὐκ ἰσχύσουσι κατά σου.
ἐὰν πιστεύσῃ σοι ἀργύριον, οὐ διασκορπιεῖς αὐτό,
καὶ κἂν ἐπεργάσῃ, ἀποδώσεις αὐτό.

Listen, O monk, to the words of your father,
and do not make his admonitions something powerless
    in you.
Whenever he sends you, take him along;
and travel with him in thinking.
For in this way you will flee bad thoughts,
and evil demons will not prevail over you.
If he entrusts silver to you, do not throw it around;
and if you earn some, give it away.

74. Πονερὸς οἰκονόμος ἐκθλίψει ψυχὰς ἀδελφῶν,
    καὶ μνησίκακος οὐκ ἐλεήσει αὐτάς.

An evil steward will squeeze the souls of the brethren,
and the one who remembers injuries will not pity them.

75. Ὁ διασκορπίζων τὰ ὑπάρχοντα τῆς μονῆς ἀδικεῖ θεόν,
    καὶ ὁ ἀμελῶν αὐτῶν οὐκ ἀτιμώρητος ἔσται.

The one who wastes the goods of the monastery wrongs
    God,
and the one careless of them will not go unpunished.

76. Ἄδικος οἰκονόμος διαμεριεῖ κακῶς,
    ὁ δὲ δίκαιος πρὸς ἀξίαν δώσει.

The unjust steward distributes badly,
but the just one will give as is fitting.

77. Ὁ κακολογῶν τὸν ἀδελφὸν αὐτοῦ ἐξολοθρευθήσεται,
    ἀμελῶν δὲ ἀσθενοῦντος οὐκ ὄψεται φῶς.

The one who speaks ill of his brother will be utterly
    destroyed;
he who does not care for the sick will not see the light.

78. Κρείσσων κοσμικὸς ἐν ἀσθενείᾳ δουλεύων ἀδελφῷ
ὑπὲρ ἀναχωρητὴν μὴ οἰκτείροντα τὸν πλησίον αὐτοῦ.

Better a worldly man serving a brother in sickness
than an anchorite not pitying his neighbor.

79. Ἄφρων μοναχὸς ἀμελήσει ὀργάνων τέχνης αὐτοῦ,
ὁ δὲ φρόνιμος ἐπιμελήσεται αὐτῶν.

The foolish monk is careless of the instruments of his
   craft;
the prudent one takes care of them.

80. Μὴ εἴπῃς· σήμερον μενῶ καὶ αὔριον ἐξελεύσομαι,
ὅτι οὐκ ἐν φρονήσει λελόγισαι περὶ τούτου.

Do not say, "Today I will stay and tomorrow I will go out,"
for not with prudence have you reasoned thus.

81. Κυκλευτὴς μοναχὸς μελετήσει ῥήσεις ψευδεῖς,
τόν δὲ ἑαυτοῦ παραλογίσεται πατέρα.

The wandering monk will practice with lying sayings;
he will reason falsely with his own father.

82. Ὁ καλλωπίζων τὰ ἱμάτια αὐτοῦ καὶ πληρῶν γαστέρα αὐτοῦ
ποιμαίνει λογισμοὺς αἰσχροὺς
καὶ μετὰ σωφρόνων οὐ συνεδριάζει.

He who decorates his garments and fills his stomach
is shepherding shameful thoughts,
and he does not sit in council with the chaste.

83. Ἐὰν εἰσέλθῃς εἰς κώμην, μὴ προσεγγίσῃς γυναιξὶ
καὶ μὴ χρονίσῃς ἐν λόγοις πρὸς αὐτάς.
ὅν τρόπον γὰρ εἴ τις ἄγκιστρον καταπίοι,
οὕτως ἑλκυσθήσεται ἡ ψυχή σου.

If you enter a village, do not draw near to women
and do not pass time in words with them.

For like someone swallowing the hook,
thus will your soul be yanked away.

84. Μακρόθυμος μοναχὸς ἀγαπηθήσεται,
    ὁ δὲ παροξύνων τοὺς ἀδελφοὺς αὐτοῦ μισηθήσεται.

    The long-suffering monk will be loved,
    but the one who provokes his brothers will be hated.

85. Πραῢν μοναχὸν ἀγαπᾷ ὁ κύριος,
    τὸν δὲ θρασὺν ἀπώσεται ἀπ᾽ αὐτοῦ.

    A gentle monk, the Lord loves;
    but the rash one, he will banish from himself.

86. Ὀκνηρὸς μοναχὸς γογγύσει πολλά,
    καὶ ὑπνώδης προφασίσεται κεφαλαλγίαν αὐτοῦ.

    The sluggish monk will murmur much,
    and the sleepy type will seek excuses in headaches.

87. Ἐὰν λυπῆται ὁ ἀδελφός σου, παρακάλεσον αὐτόν,
    καὶ ἐὰν ἀλγῇ, συνάλγησον αὐτῷ.
    τοῦτο γὰρ ποιῶν εὐφραίνεις καρδίαν αὐτοῦ,
    καὶ θησαυρὸν μέγαν σωρεύσεις ἐν οὐρανῷ.

    If your brother is sad, console him;
    and if he is pained, share the pain.
    For doing thus, you will gladden his heart,
    and you will store a great treasure in heaven.

88. Μοναχὸς ἀπολειπόμενος φυλάξαι λόγους πατρὸς
    βλασφημήσει πολιὰν γεννήσαντος αὐτὸν
    καὶ κακολογήσει βίους τέκνων αὐτοῦ,
    ὁ δὲ κύριος ἐξουδενώσει αὐτόν.

    The monk who quits guard over the words of his father
    will blaspheme the grey hairs of the one who begot him
    and will speak ill of the life of his children.
    But him, the Lord will utterly destroy.

89. Ὁ πρόφασιν ζητῶν χωρίζεται ἀδελφῶν,
τὸν δὲ ἑαυτοῦ αἰτιάσεται πατέρα.

The one who seeks excuses is cut off from the brothers;
he will accuse his own father.

90. Μὴ δῷς ἀκοὴν λόγοις κατὰ πατρός σου
καὶ μὴ διεγείρῃς ψυχήν ἀτιμάζοντος αὐτόν,
ἵνα μὴ κύριος ὀργισθῇ ἐπὶ ποιήμασι σου
καὶ ἐξαλείψῃ σου τὸ ὄνομα ἐκ βίβλου ζώντων.

Do not lend your ear to words contrary to your father's
and do not stimulate the soul of one who dishonors him;
lest the Lord be angered by your doings
and rub out your name from the book of the living.

91. Ὁ ὑπακούων πατρὶ ἑαυτοῦ ἀγαπᾷ ἑαυτόν,
ὁ δὲ ἀντιλέγων αὐτῷ ἐμπεσεῖται εἰς κακά.

He who obeys his father loves himself,
but he who speaks contrary to him will fall into evils.

92. Μακάριος μοναχὸς ὁ φυλάσσων ἐντολὰς κυρίου
καὶ ὅσιος ὁ διατηρῶν λόγους πατέρων αὐτοῦ.

Blessed is the monk who guards the commands
of the Lord,
and holy the one who closely keeps the words of his
fathers.

93. Ὀκνηρὸς μοναχὸς πολλὰ ζημιωθήσεται,
ἐὰν δὲ θαρσύνηται καὶ τὸ σχῆμα αὐτοῦ προσθήσει.

The sluggish monk will be very much damaged;
and if he is encouraged, he will even lay his habit aside.

94. Ὁ φυλάσσων γλῶσσαν αὐτοῦ ὀρθοτομεῖ τὰς ὁδοὺς αὐτοῦ,
καὶ ὁ τηρῶν καρδίαν αὐτοῦ πλησθήσεται γνώσεως.

He who guards his tongue cuts his ways rightly,
and he who keeps his heart will be filled with knowledge.

95. Μοναχὸς δίγλωσσος ταράσσει ἀδελφούς,
    ὁ δὲ πιστὸς ἡσυχίαν ἄγει.

    The double-tongued monk agitates the brethren,
    but the faithful one brings stillness.

96. Ὁ πεποιθὼς ἐπὶ ἐγκρατείᾳ αὐτοῦ πεσεῖται,
    ὁ δὲ ταπεινῶν ἑαυτὸν ὑψωθήσεται.

    He who has relied on his temperance will fall,
    but he who humbles himself will be exalted.

97. Μὴ δῷς σεαυτὸν χορτασίᾳ κοιλίας,
    καὶ μὴ πλησθῇς ὕπνου νυκτερινοῦ.
    τούτῳ γὰρ τῷ τρόπῳ γενήσῃ καθαρὸς
    καὶ πνεῦμα κυρίου ἐπελεύσεται ἐπί σε.

    Do not give yourself to the trough of the stomach,
    and do not fill yourself with nightly sleep.
    For in this way you will become pure,
    and the spirit of the Lord will come over you.

98. Ψάλλοντος ἡσυχάζει θυμὸς
    καὶ μακροθυμοῦντος ἀπτόητος ἔσται.

    In the one singing psalms, irascibility is quiet;
    and the long-suffering one, fearless shall he be.

99. Ἐκ πραΰτητος τίκτεται γνῶσις,
    ἐκ δὲ θρασύτητος ἀγνωσία.

    Out of gentleness, knowledge is born;
    out of rashness, ignorance.

100. Ὥσπερ ὕδωρ αὔξει φυτόν,
     οὕτως ταπείνωσις θυμοῦ καρδίαν ὑψοῖ.

     As water makes a plant grow up,
     so humiliation of the irascible raises up the heart.

101. Ἰχνεύοντος συμπόσια σβεσθήσεται λαμπτήρ,
ἡ δὲ ψυχὴ αὐτοῦ ὄψεται σκότος.

The lamp will be extinguished in one who tracks down
    banquets;
his soul shall see darkness.

102. Στῆσον ζυγῷ τὸν ἄρτον σου καὶ πίε μέτρῳ τὸ ὕδωρ σου
καὶ πνεῦμα πορνείας φεύξεται ἀπό σου.

Weigh your bread on a balance and drink your water
    by measure;
and the spirit of fornication will flee from you.

103. Δὸς γέρουσιν οἶνον καὶ ἀσθενοῦσι πρόσφερε τροφάς,
διότι κατέτριψαν σάρκας νεότητος αὐτῶν.

Give wine to old men and carry food to the sick,
for they have worn down the flesh of their youth.

104. Μὴ ὑποσκελίσῃς τὸν ἀδελφόν σου
καὶ πτώματι αὐτοῦ μὴ ἐπιχαρῇς.
ὁ γὰρ κύριος γινώσκει σὴν καρδίαν
καὶ παραδώσει σε ἐν ἡμέρᾳ θανάτου.

You shall not trip up your brother
and concerning his fall you shall not rejoice;
for the Lord knows your heart,
and he will hand you over on the day of death.

105. Μοναχὸς φρόνιμος ἀπαθὴς ἔσται,
ὁ δὲ ἄφρων ἐξαντλήσει κακά.

The prudent monk shall be passionless,
but the foolish one draws up evils.

106. Ὀφθαλμὸν πονηρὸν ἐκτυφλοῖ κύριος,
τὸν δὲ ἁπλοῦν ῥύσεται ἀπὸ σκότους.

The wicked eye, the Lord totally blinds;
but the simple, he will rescue from darknesses.

107. Ὥσπερ ἑωσφόρος ἐν οὐρανῷ καὶ ὥσπερ φοίνιξ ἐν
      παραδείσῳ,
      οὕτως ἐν ψυχῇ πραείᾳ νοῦς καθαρός.

   Like a morning star in heaven and a palm tree in
      paradise,
   so a pure mind in a gentle soul.

108. Ἀνὴρ σοφὸς ἐρευνήσει λόγους θεοῦ,
      ὁ δὲ ἄσοφος καταγελάσεται αὐτῶν.

   The wise man will investigate the reasons of God,
   while the unwise man mocks them.

109. Ὁ μισῶν γνῶσιν θεοῦ καὶ ἀπωθούμενος θεωρίαν αὐτοῦ
      ὅμοιός ἐστι τῷ λόγχῃ νύσσοντι τὴν καρδίαν αὐτοῦ.

   He who hates the knowledge of God and rejects his
      contemplation
   is like to one who pierces his own heart with a spear.

110. Κρείσσων γνῶσις τριάδος ὑπὲρ γνῶσιν ἀσωμάτων
      καὶ θεωρία αὐτῆς ὑπὲρ λόγους πάντων τῶν αἰώνων.

   Better is knowledge of the Trinity than knowledge of
      the incorporeals;
   and the contemplation of it beyond reasons for all
      the aeons.

111. Πολιὰ γερόντων πραΰτης,
      ζωὴ δὲ αὐτῶν γνῶσις ἀληθείας.

   The gray hair of old men: gentleness;
   their life: knowledge of truth.

112. Νέος πραῢς πολλὰ ὑποφέρει
      ὀλιγόψυχον δὲ γέροντα τίς ὑποίσεται;

εἶδον ὀργίλον γέροντα ἐπαιρόμενον ἐπὶ χρόνου αὐτοῦ,
ἐλπίδα δὲ μέντοι μᾶλλον ἔσχεν ὁ νέος αὐτοῦ.

A youth who is gentle bears many things;
but a small-souled old man, who will be able to
    stand him?
I have seen the angry old man elevated in his time,
but someone younger than he had a greater hope
    than his.

113. Ὁ σκανδαλίζων κοσμικοὺς οὐκ ἀτιμώρητος ἔσται,
     καὶ ὁ παροξύνων αὐτοὺς ἀτιμάζει τὸ ὄνομα αὐτοῦ.

The one who scandalizes people in the world will not
    go unpunished,
and the one who irritates them dishonors his name.

114. Ταράσσοντα ἐκκλησίαν κυρίου ἐξαναλώσει πῦρ,
     ἀνθιστάμενον δὲ ἱερεῖ καταπίεται γῆ.

The one agitating the church of the Lord, fire will
    completely consume him.
The one resisting a priest, the earth will swallow him up.

115. Ὁ ἀγαπῶν μέλισσαν φάγεται κηρίον αὐτῆς
     καὶ ὁ συνάγων αὐτὴν πλησθήσεται πνεύματος.

He who loves honey eats its comb,
and he who gathers it will be filled by the Spirit.

116. Τίμα τὸν κύριον καὶ γνώσῃ λόγους ἀσωμάτων,
     καὶ δούλευε αὐτῷ καὶ δείξει σοι λόγους αἰώνων.

Honor the Lord and you will know the reasons of
    the incorporeals;
serve him, and he will unveil before you the reasons
    of the aeons.

117. Χωρὶς γνώσεως οὐχ ὑψωθήσεται καρδία,
καὶ δένδρον οὐκ ἀνθήσει ἄνευ ποτοῦ.

Without knowledge, the heart will not be placed on high;
and a tree will not flourish without a drink.

118. Σάρκες Χριστοῦ πρακτικαὶ ἀρεταί,
ὁ δὲ ἐσθίων αὐτὰς γενήσεται ἀπαθής.

Flesh of Christ: virtues of *praktikē;*
he who eats it, passionless shall he be.

119. Αἷμα Χριστοῦ θεωρία τῶν γεγονότων
καὶ ὁ πίνων αὐτὸ σοφισθήσεται ὑπ᾽ αὐτοῦ.

Blood of Christ: contemplation of created things;
he who drinks it, by it becomes wise.

120. Στῆθος κυρίου γνῶσις θεοῦ,
ὁ δ᾽ ἀναπεσὼν ἐπ᾽ αὐτὸ θεολόγος ἔσται.

Breast of the Lord: knowledge of God;
he who rests against it, a theologian shall he be.

121. Γνωστικὸς καὶ πρακτικὸς ὑπήντησαν ἀλλήλοις,
μέσος δὲ ἀμφοτέρων εἰστήκει κύριος.

A knower and one accomplished in *praktikē* met
each other;
between the two of them there stands the Lord.

122. Ὃς ἐκτήσατο ἀγάπην, ἐκτήσατο θησαυρόν,
ἔλαβε δὲ χάριν παρὰ κυρίου.

He who has acquired love has acquired a treasure;
he has received grace from the Lord.

123. Δόγματα δαιμόνων ἐπιγινώσκει σοφία,
πανουργίαν δὲ αὐτῶν ἐξιχνιάζει φρόνησις.

Wisdom knows about the dogmas of the demons;
prudence tracks down their crafty ways.

124. Μὴ ἀθετήσῃς δόγματα ἅγια,
ἃ ἔθεντο οἱ πατέρες σου,
πίστιν δὲ βαπτίσματός σου μὴ ἐγκαταλίπῃς
καὶ μὴ ἀπώσῃ σφραγῖδα πνευματικήν,
ἵνα γένηται κύριος ἐν σῇ ψυχῇ
καὶ σκεπάσῃ σε ἐν ἡμέρᾳ κακῇ.

Do not lay to the side the holy dogmas
which your fathers have laid down.
Do not abandon the faith of your baptism,
and do not thrust off the spiritual seal.
Thus can the Lord come into your soul,
and he will cover you on the evil day.

125. Λόγοι αἱρετικῶν ἄγγελοι θανάτου,
καὶ ὁ δεχόμενος αὐτοὺς ἀπολεῖ τὴν ἑαυτοῦ ψυχήν.

The teachings of heretics: angels of death.
The one who receives them looses his soul.

126. Νῦν οὖν, υἱέ, ἄκουέ μου,
καὶ μὴ προσέλθῃς θύραις ἀνδρῶν ἀνόμων
μηδὲ περιπατήσῃς ἐπὶ παγίδων αὐτῶν, ἵνα μὴ ἀγρευθῇς.
ἀπόστησον δὲ σὴν ψυχὴν ἀπὸ γνώσεως ψευδοῦς,
καὶ γὰρ ἐγὼ πλεονάκις λελάληκα πρὸς αὐτούς,
σκοτεινοὺς δὲ λόγους αὐτῶν ἐξιχνίασα,
καὶ ἰὸν ἀσπίδων εὕρηκα ἐν αὐτοῖς.
οὐκ ἔστι φρόνησις καὶ οὐκ ἔστι σοφία ἐν λόγοις αὐτῶν.
πάντες οἱ δεχόμενοι αὐτοὺς ἀπολοῦνται,
καὶ οἱ ἀγαπῶντες αὐτοὺς πλησθήσονται κακῶν.
εἶδον ἐγὼ πατέρας δογμάτων αὐτῶν
καὶ ἐν τῇ ἐρήμῳ συνέβαλον αὐτοῖς.
ἐχθροὶ γὰρ κυρίου ἀπήντησάν μοι
καὶ δαίμονες ἐν λόγοις ἠγωνίσαντο πρός με
καὶ οὐκ εἶδον φῶς ἀληθινὸν ἐν ῥήμασιν αὐτῶν.

Now therefore, son, listen to me:
do not approach the doors of lawless men
nor stroll into their traps, lest you be snared.

Keep your soul aloof from false knowledge.
For indeed I have often spoken with them;
their dark teachings I have tracked down,
and the venom of asps have I found in them.
There is no prudence and there is no wisdom in
    their teachings.
All who receive them will perish,
and those who love them will be filled with evils.
I have seen the fathers of these dogmas,
and in the desert I plunged in with them.
For the enemies of the Lord met up with me,
and demons—through their teachings—struggled
    against me,
and I did not see true light in their words.

127. Ἀνὴρ ψευδόμενος ἐκπεσεῖται θεοῦ,
    ἀπατῶν δὲ τὸν πλησίον αὐτοῦ ἐμπεσεῖται εἰς κακά.

The lying man will fall away from God;
he who deceives his neighbor will fall into evils.

128. Κρείσσων παράδεισος θεοῦ ὑπὲρ κῆπον λαχανίας
    καὶ ποταμὸς κυρίου ὑπὲρ ποταμὸν μέγαν ἐπισκοτοῦντα
    τῇ γῇ.

Better the paradise of God than a garden of herbs
and better the river of the Lord than the great river
    which darkens the earth.

129. Ἀξιοπιστότερον ὕδωρ οὐράνιον
    ὑπὲρ ὕδωρ Αἰγυπτίων σοφῶν ἀντλούντων ἐκ γῆς.

More worthy of faith is heavenly water
than water which Egyptian wise men draw up from
    the earth.

130. Ὃν τρόπον οἱ τοὺς τροχοὺς ἀναβαίνοντες κάτω εἰσιν,
οὕτως οἱ ὑψοῦντες λόγους αὐτῶν τεταπείνωνται ἐν αὐτοῖς.

In the same way that someone who mounts up round
a wheel would end up low again,
so those who exalt their words have been humbled
in them.

131. Σοφία κυρίου ὑψοῖ καρδίαν,
φρόνησις δὲ αὐτοῦ καθαίρει αὐτήν.

The wisdom of the Lord raises up the heart;
his prudence purifies it.

132. Λόγοι προνοίας σκοτεινοὶ καὶ δυσνόητοι κρίσεως θεωρίαι,
ἀνὴρ δὲ πρακτικὸς ἐπιγνώσεται αὐτούς.

The reasons of providence are dark,
and hard for the mind are the contemplations of the
judgment;
but the man of *praktikē* will know them.

133. Καθαίρων ἑαυτὸν ὄψεται φύσεις νοεράς,
λόγους δὲ ἀσωμάτων ἐπιγνώσεται μοναχὸς πραΰς.

He who purifies himself will see intelligible natures;
reasons of incorporeals, a gentle monk will know.

134. Ὁ κτίσμα λέγων τὴν ἁγίαν τριάδα βλασφημεῖ θεὸν
καὶ ὁ ἀθετῶν τὸν Χριστὸν αὐτοῦ οὐ γνώσεται αὐτόν.

He who says that the Holy Trinity is a creature
blasphemes God,
and he who rejects his Christ will not know him.

135. Κόσμων θεωρίαι πλατύνουσι καρδίαν,
     λόγοι δὲ προνοίας καὶ κρίσεως ὑψοῦσιν αὐτήν.

     Contemplations of worlds enlarge the heart;
     reasons of providence and judgment lift it up.

136. Γνῶσις ἀσωμάτων ἐπαίρει τὸν νοῦν
     καὶ τῇ ἁγίᾳ τριάδι παρίστησιν αὐτόν.

     Knowledge of incorporeals raises the mind
     and presents it before the Holy Trinity.

137. Μέμνησθε τοῦ δεδωκότος ὑμῖν ἐν κυρίῳ σαφεῖς παροιμίας,
     καὶ μὴ ἐπιλάθησθε τῆς ταπεινῆς μου ψυχῆς ἐν καιρῷ
     προσευχῆς.

     Remember the one who has given you in the Lord
       clear proverbs,
     and do not forget my lowly soul in the hour of prayer.

Part Two

The Structure of
Ad Monachos

An Overview

Discerning the structure and arrangement of the 137 proverbs of *Ad Monachos* is the first step in an accurate and complete assessment of the text. It is the task of Part Two of this study to discern that structure. This is a prerequisite for proper interpretation of any of the individual proverbs, which will be the task of Part Four of this study. Before viewing at close range the unfolding of the individual chains of *Ad Monachos*, it will prove useful to try to embrace the entire text in an overview.[1] There are several major movements in the text and a turning point. Keeping these in mind throughout is a means of catching Evagrius's meaning more securely.

M 1 and M 2 can be considered as introducing the whole collection, though in slightly different ways. M 1 is addressed directly to the readers of the text (in the second person plural) and is an invitation to listen. M 2 is a proverb contrasting a good (spiritual) father with an evil one. "A good father trains his sons." All the proverbs that follow are examples of precisely that, of a good father training his sons.

M 137 is the conclusion to the whole collection. It identifies the genre specifically as "proverbs" and asks the readers for prayers. The core of the proverbs is contained, then, between M1 and 2 and M 137. All these proverbs unfold within a perspective embraced in the two short lines of M 3: "Faith: the beginning of love. / The end of love: knowledge of God." As the commentary below will make clear, this proverb contains key terms that cover the beginning, the middle, and the end of the way Evagrius conceives of a monk's spiritual progress. The first line refers to the life of *praktikē*, which begins in faith and has love as its goal. The

---

[1] The word *chain* seems suitable for describing proverbs grouped together around a same theme, and there are many such chains in *Ad Monachos*. The term is, of course, not to be confused with the same term as used to describe collections of exegetical comments from different authors relative to a particular book of the scriptures.

second line refers to knowledge, which is a realm that the monk who has learned to love can hope to enter upon. In some senses, then, M 3 can likewise be considered an introduction to the whole, but it is also already part of the first chain of the text to be developed—namely, M 3 to M 7, which will be commented on below. Yet M 3 not only begins that particular chain; it suggests the two major themes of the whole: the life of *praktikē*, the life of knowledge, and their intimate interrelation.

In terms of an overview it is useful to conceive of all the proverbs as arranged in two large blocks, the first containing M 3 to M 106, the second containing M 107 to M 136. In general the sentences from M 3 to M 106 can be described as tending to concentrate on *praktikē*, and a number of themes related to *praktikē* are developed within these proverbs. At least two important general observations can be made here about this block. First, there is a strong emphasis throughout on the importance of love and gentleness. Second, *praktikē* is regularly—explicitly and implicitly—related to knowledge.[2]

At M 107 a turning point in the text can be discerned that could be described as an increased and growing concentration on knowledge. Several general observations can also be made about this second block. First, the emphasis on love and gentleness is maintained. Second, as in the first block *praktikē* is related to knowledge, in this second block knowledge is related to *praktikē*. No one can be maintained in knowledge without maintaining *praktikē's* virtues.

Keeping these broad outlines in mind, we can turn now to a closer examination of the unfolding chains. After treating the introductory proverbs, M 1 and M 2, the material can be treated in headings organized according to the two large blocks, from M 3 to M 106 and then from M 107 to the end. In order to help

---

[2]Only these general observations are made now to preserve the simplicity of the overview. It should not obscure the fact that many other themes are developed in the first block. It is also perhaps useful to observe here that this first block could further be subdivided into two sections: M 3 to M 72 and M 73 to M 106. But this will become more clear as the examination unfolds.

the reader keep hold of the thread, which becomes more complex as the text advances, I will periodically take up the chains that have been identified and view them in a glance. I name this procedure "Reprise."

In what follows I must ask the reader to be ready to refer as often as necessary to Evagrius's text, which has been presented now in its original Greek and in English translation. The proverbs are written and arranged for slow and careful examination and meditation, and this cannot be done without frequent reference to them.

The Introduction (M 1 and M 2)

M 1 is the introduction proper. The proverb reads like the opening verses of the book of Proverbs, and the identification of this whole collection as "proverbs" in M 137 helps the reader to know that such a scriptural echo is no accident. Evagrius expects his readers to catch his scriptural allusions, and in fact these allusions are a major clue to the fuller meaning of what he says. The biblical book of Proverbs opens with these words: "The Proverbs of Solomon son of David, who reigned in Israel; to know wisdom and instruction [γνῶναι σοφίαν καὶ παιδείαν], and to grasp words of understanding. . . . For by hearing these a wise man will be wiser, and the one who grasps will gain control; he will understand a parable and a dark speech, the sayings of the wise [ῥήσεις τε σοφῶν], and riddles" (Prov 1:1–2, 5–6). These scriptural verses help one to notice two key terms in M 1 and M 2: instruction or training (παιδεία), which occurs in verb form in M 2, and wisdom (σοφία). These two terms refer to the two major divisions of the monastic life, *praktikē* and knowledge, with which the proverbs of *Ad Monachos* are concerned. Evagrius's comments on these verses make this clear. Focusing on the words "to know wisdom and instruction" in Proverbs 1:2, he says, "It says he became king in Israel because he knew instruction and wisdom. And *wisdom* is knowledge of corporeals and incorporeals as well as the judgment and providence to be seen in them. *Instruction* is moderation of the passions which are seen in the passionate or irrational part of the soul" (In Prov 1:2 [G3]).[3] This moderation of the passions is the whole goal of *praktikē*. It must be reached in order to enter into knowledge, which is the ultimate goal of the monastic life. So M 1 and M 2 are about these two prongs of the monastic life, and all the language of M 1 shows that it is this ultimate goal of knowledge which is the more important, the more definitive.

Other terms in M 1 also indicate that knowledge is the definitive scope of the proverbs that follow. In order to interpret the terms "heirs of God" and "coheirs of Christ" they must first be recognized as a scriptural allusion. Romans 8:16–17 reads, "The Spirit himself bears witness with our spirit that we are children of God, and if children, then heirs, heirs of God [κληρονόμοι θεοῦ] and coheirs with Christ [συγκληρονόμοι Χριστοῦ], if only we suffer with him so that we may also be glorified with him." Interpreting M 1 first of all in line with this scriptural passage, being an heir of God means listening to his reasons.[4] According to the scriptural verse, we are coheirs with Christ provided we suffer with him so as to be glorified with him. Here also one can hear the two stages of the monastic life, suffering with Christ as the life of *praktikē*, being glorified with him as the life of knowledge.[5]

Yet catching the scriptural allusions does not exhaust the possibilities of interpretation in this proverb. The term "coheir of Christ" would have an especially suggestive resonance in the ears

---

[3] Emphasis mine. For a commentary on this scholion with many other references to Evagrius's use of these expressions, see SC 340, 93-95. As Géhin's comment makes clear, ἀπάθεια is Evagrius's more usual term for the controlling of the passions. The term παιδεία does not occur again in *Ad Monachos*, but words based on ἀπάθεια occur in six of the proverbs (M 6, 31, 66, 68, 105, 118).

[4] I have translated λόγων θεοῦ as "reasons of God" rather than "words of God" in order to help the reader hear the strong sense of λόγος (reason) that is contained in Evagrius's use of the word when it is employed in reference to knowledge. Ῥήσεις Χριστοῦ is a more concrete sense of words and sayings, more suited to Christ in his role as savior. In the fourth line λόγους σοφῶν is more appropriately translated "words of the wise," since the reference there is also to actual spoken words. In the deepest sense λόγοι θεοῦ are not spoken words but the very reason that lies in the depths of God. It is this that is expressed in the sayings of Christ and in the words of the wise. Knowing these deep reasons is what it means to be an heir of God.

[5] This interpretation of the scriptural verse is consistent with other proverbs of *Ad Monachos*. See especially M 21, M 118–20.

of someone familiar with Evagrian terminology. In fact, it is a term so precise in its meaning that it evokes virtually the whole christological system of Evagrius in all of its intricacies. To enter into its details here would be beyond the scope of the present project, and Evagrius's christology requires separate study in its own right.[6] Several texts, however, will serve to show the way in which "coheir of Christ" is a term connected with knowledge. In the *Kephalaia Gnostica* IV, 4 and 8 Evagrius distinguishes between an heir of Christ and a coheir of Christ. He first says, "The 'heir' of Christ is the one who knows the reasons for all created things subsequent to the first judgment" (KG IV, 4). Then he says, "The 'coheir of Christ' is the one who arrives in the Unity and who enjoys contemplation with Christ" (KG IV, 8). Thus, a coheir of Christ is someone who enjoys the same contemplation, the same knowledge of the Unity, as Christ. But first one must receive the lesser knowledge of created things. This is being an heir. "The inheritance of Christ is knowledge of the Unity; and if all become 'coheirs of Christ,' all will know the holy Unity. But it is not possible that they become his coheirs if before they have not become his heirs" (KG III, 72). Being separated from this knowledge is what characterizes the present human condition, and it is reacquiring this knowledge that constitutes salvation. One prepares to reacquire this knowledge, first of all, through a practice of the virtues, or as the scriptural verse has it, "provided we suffer with him [Christ]." We are coheirs with Christ provided we suffer with him.

Thus, when Evagrius begins this collection of proverbs—a collection that will speak much about the life of *praktikē*—by addressing his readers as heirs of God and coheirs of Christ, he is suggesting at the outset that the purpose of all that follows is to reach the knowledge of God. This is where wisdom aims. Evagrius has made his point with language that clearly echoes the

---

[6] For christology in the *Kephalaia Gnostica*, see A. Guillaumont, ed., *Les "Képhalaia Gnostica,"* 117–19, 151–56. For a study of the christology of Evagrius especially as it is found in the Commentary on Psalms, see Refoulé, "La christologie d'Évagre et l'Origénisme." But also important are many of the studies by Bunge, all of which are inclined to interpret Evagrius's christology as more orthodox than Guillaumont and Refoulé would consider it.

language of the beginning of the book of Proverbs as well as St.
Paul in his Letter to the Romans. Elsewhere, with language similar to the present proverb and to the mood of the whole collection, Evagrius says quite simply, "The wise will inherit knowledge,
but the impious have honored ignorance" (In Prov 3:35 [G 40]).[7]
    A certain progression downward can also be noted in the
proverb, from *God* to *Christ* to the *wise.* The monk's principal goal
is to arrive at knowledge of the *reasons of God.* This is done by
receiving the *sayings of Christ.* But the sayings of Christ are put in
relation to (that is to say, they will be known through) the *words
of the wise,* and the words of the wise are, among other things, the
proverbs presented here.[8]
    One final point concerns ἵνα of line 3, translated here as "so
that." Though throughout the writings of Evagrius there is always
a thrust forward toward knowledge (expressed here as toward the
reasons of God and the sayings of Christ), the one who reaches
knowledge, the knower (ὁ γνωστικός), is also bound to share his
knowledge with others. This is a major theme in Evagrius's work
the *Gnostikos.*[9] In M 1, one of the purposes for reaching toward
knowledge is so that knowledge can be shared with spiritual children. This idea, presented in the last two lines of M 1, opens
nicely onto the idea expressed in M 2 about a good father training his sons. The two proverbs together suggest that if one listens
carefully to the proverbs that follow, he will not only arrive at
knowledge but will also generate spiritual children.
    After these two introductory proverbs, the texts begin to
unfold in the various chains that we will now examine. We turn
now to the first major block, M 3 to M 106, and to the chains
within that block.

---

[7] Evagrius uses words like *heir* and *heritage* in reference to knowledge
throughout the *Kephalaia Gnostica;* see, for example, KG III, 65, 72; IV, 4, 8, 9, 78;
V, 36, 68. In *Ad Monachos,* see M 25, 29.

[8] For *sayings* and the related word ῥητόν as frequently referring to a scripture
passage, see many examples cited by Guillaumont, SC 356, 120. For the way in
which words of the fathers were thought to parallel the words of the scriptures,
see below, Part Three, "Stage Two: Evagrius and Scripture in Egyptian Desert
Monasticism."

[9] See, for example, G 3, 15, 22, 29, 36.

First Block: Praktikē *and Its Relation to Knowledge (M 3 to M 106)*

THE CHAIN OF VIRTUES (M 3 TO M 7)

As noted in the Overview, M 3 can be considered both as among the introductory sentences to the whole collection and as the first member of the first chain. The first line of M 3–"Faith: the beginning of love"–concerns the material contained in the proverbs from M 3 to M 106: its emphasis is on the life of *praktikē*. The second line of M 3–"The end of love: knowledge of God"–concerns the material contained in M 107 to M 136: its emphasis is on knowledge. Love is thus the crucial link in understanding the connection between the two major blocks of the collection, and this point is developed from many angles in what follows. Yet it is the first line of M 3–"Faith: the beginning of love"–that is developed in the several proverbs that follow. This first chain is a chain of virtues that appears in many places where Evagrius discusses the life of *praktikē*. Evagrius considers faith the first of the virtues of *praktikē* and love as its goal. Other virtues stand between faith and love. These virtues are expressed, among other places, in the prologue to the *Praktikos*. Evagrius says, "*Fear of God*, children, strengthens *faith*; and *temperance* in turn strengthens this fear; and *perseverance* and *hope* make this unshakeable; and from these *passionlessness* is born; and passionlessness has *love* as its child" (TP Prologue 8).[10] The italicized words in this text are the virtues, and they come in the same order in M 4 to M 6. The chain is constructed by following this

---

[10] Emphasis mine. Evagrius regularly associates fear of God and faith, but it is difficult to say which comes first. In the text cited here he says, "Fear of God strengthens faith," but in TP 81 he calls fear of God the offspring of true faith. The point seems to be that faith and fear of God work back and forth off each other. See Méhat, *Étude sur les 'Stromates' de Clément d'Alexandrie,* 314–17, for Clement's own ambivalence on this issue. For texts that associate the fear of God with knowledge, see In Prov 2:5 (G 20); 9:13 (G 113); 10:27 (G 122). For more on this chain of virtues in Evagrius and for his sources, see Guillaumont, SC 170, 52–55.

order. These virtues in the order found in M 4 to M 6 are the virtues that stand between faith and love.

The text cited from the prologue of the Praktikos continues: "and passionlessness has love as its child; and love is the gate to natural knowledge, and this knowledge gives way to theology, and then final blessedness" (TP Prologue 8).[11] The second line of M 3—"The end of love: knowledge of God"—is saying the same thing a little more briefly. That particular thought is not developed immediately here, but it slowly becomes one of the major impressions that *Ad Monachos* makes, as this study will make clear. Love is the goal of *praktikē*. It is the gate to knowledge.

The chain shows a particularly close relationship between passionlessness and love. M 6 speaks of passionless; but before love is developed in M 8 and the following proverbs, M 6 takes up again the issue of temperance mentioned in M 4. Part of the role played by M 6 is to complete the development from faith to passionlessness, but another role is played by the proverb in that it opens a little chain about evil thoughts, and it starts with the first of the thoughts: gluttony.[12] M 7 is a meditation on the second in Evagrius's list of thoughts: fornication.

LOVE AND HATE IN ANACHORESIS (M 8 TO M 10)

The mention of love in these next proverbs completes the development from passionlessness ("passionlessness has love as

---

[11] In this whole chain Evagrius is basing himself principally on Rom 5:3–4, as is clear from In Ps 24:20. But it is likewise a chain of virtues structured on faith, hope, and love; and "the greatest of these is love" (see 1 Cor 13:9–13, especially v. 13).

[12] M 6 has an immediate reference to gluttony in its use of the language of 1 Cor 9:27. This same biblical expression is used in G 37, where the reference is clearly concerned with food. See the comment by Guillaumont, SC 356, 159. The second line of M 6 uses ἐκτρέφων, likewise securing the reference to food. Yet the proverb can also be meditated upon more broadly to encompass a general enslaving of the flesh embracing not only gluttony but also fornication and love of money. This more extended meditation might come to mind for a monk less familiar with Evagrian vocabulary as the natural application of the Pauline allusion, but it would likewise be natural for the monk in Evagrius's circle, since gluttony, fornication, and love of money are all demons in the concupiscible part of the soul.

its child") in M 6 after the "digression" on temperance in M 6 and M 7. What in fact is happening is that Evagrius is weaving a strand with the themes of love and temperance. Finding love and temperance together in Evagrius is not unusual. The way in which he understands their relation is perhaps most simply expressed in this brief sentence: "Temperance cuts off the passions of the body, and spiritual love cuts off those of the soul" (TP 35). Or a little farther on in the same work he says, "and if love and temperance are present, the passions are not set in motion" (TP 38).

This chain is both a climax of a development and a summary of what has unfolded so far, the connecting link being the term *love*. M 8 and M 9 are proverbs about anachoresis as much as they are proverbs about love. *Anachoresis* is a technical term describing the withdrawal into the desert or into solitude that was considered a necessary base for the monastic life. In this chain love is emphasized as a crucial dimension of this withdrawal. Such an emphasis follows well after the proverbs on temperance and functions as a balance to that idea. Certainly Evagrius encountered monks who made too much of their rigorous asceticism. One could not accuse Evagrius of a lack of rigor in his own asceticism, but he knows that there is more to anachoresis than simply that. In one of his letters he puts the point rather strongly: "Let no one, I beg you, devote himself only to temperance. For not with only one stone is a house built, nor with only one brick is a house constructed. An irascible temperate person is a dried up tree, fruitless, twice dead, uprooted" (Lt 27:3).[13]

M 10 continues with the issue of love by introducing a theme that will be picked up and developed in M 13 to M 15. It warns against "memory of injury." This theme will appear in various ways throughout the text.

---

[13] Translated from a Greek fragment found in C. Guillaumont, "Fragments grecs," 220, lines 65–67. The words of Evagrius are constructed in part on Jude 12. An uncontrolled irascible part of the soul would be the opposite of love. This will be discussed more as the study unfolds. The text cited warns against the practice of asceticism without reference to love, but Evagrius also warned about asceticism without reference to knowledge. See, for example, In Prov 2:5 (G 20). In M 9 Evagrius appears to be citing a saying from Pachomius. See Lefort, "A propos d'un aphorisme d'Evagrius Ponticus."

RETURN TO TEMPERANCE (M 11)

Having made the point about love, the text comes back again to temperance. It does not mention temperance specifically, but that temperance is the issue is made clear by this simple description from the *Praktikos:* "[The role] of temperance is to reject with joy all the pleasures of the mouth" (TP 89). In coming back and forth to temperance like this the reader is never allowed to stray far from its requirements; nor, on the other hand, is he allowed to forget the demands of love. This intertwining of the proverbs of the text is the literary image of a deeper intertwining; namely, that of the virtues themselves. One falls without the other, different in focus though they be.[14]

GENTLENESS, IRASCIBILITY, AND MEMORY OF INJURY
(M 12 TO M 15)

M 12, though a simple little proverb, contains key terminology. The word *gentleness* appears for a first time. *Gentleness* and words associated with it will appear frequently throughout the collection. Its opposite, *irascibility*, is also presented here for the first time, and it and words associated with it will likewise appear throughout the collection. Gentleness and irascibility vie with each other, as it were, in the proverbs presented for meditation.

Gentleness is not abruptly presented here. It is a practical expression of the love mentioned in M 3, 8, and 9. It opens onto M 13, which takes up a specific problem for gentleness already mentioned in M 10, namely, memory of injury. Furthermore, M 13 presents memory of injury as a block to knowledge and thereby, typically for Evagrius, establishes a relation between gentleness and knowledge. M 14 is M 13's opposite. It speaks of prayer for enemies as a way to forget (as opposed to remember) injuries. M 15 is a fuller plan for achieving forgiveness or forgetfulness of injuries. It offers practical advice for establishing love

---

[14] For these same virtues intertwined again in the text, see M 93 to M 104 and the remarks on these below, pp. 118–24. This insistence on joining love to temperance is a widespread theme in the fight of mainline monasticism against the sort of asceticism practiced in gnostic sects. See Stroumsa, "Ascèse et gnose."

among the brothers and, if successful, opens a clear path to the
"hour of prayer," an expression that Evagrius regularly associates
with knowledge.[15]

POVERTY, WEALTH, AND KNOWLEDGE (M 16 TO M 18)

A new theme opens up in this chain: poverty and wealth. Yet
the connecting link with the previous theme is strong, established
around the contrasting terms of love and hate, sounding similar
to love and hate as they were used in M 8 and 9. But the link is
not only with M 8 and 9 but with all that precedes, since it all has
to do with love and hate.

M 16 associates love with poverty and hate with wealth. Then
in M 17 there is a direct connection with knowledge. This is
because knowledge is "the end of love." The logic is simple and
strict: if hate is pleased with wealth, then the rich man will not
acquire knowledge. M 17 states the connection bluntly. M 18 is
just as strong and likewise explicitly mentions knowledge.

HUMILITY AND PRIDE (M 19)

This proverb may seem to be a wholly new beginning, but it
does in fact develop with a certain logic out of the previous material. For Evagrius, poverty makes humility possible, whereas riches
make one proud. A scholion on Proverbs explains how. "The rich
man purifies his irascible part through almsgiving and thus
acquires love. The poor man through his poverty learns to be
humble" (In Prov 22:2 [G 234]). Géhin's comment on the verse
shows even more clearly the connection of M 19 with the preceding proverbs. He says, "La charité et l'humilité sont considérées comme les vertus du *thumos*. Par deux voies différentes, le
pauvre et le riche sont parvenus au même résultat: la guérison de
la partie irascible de leur âme."[16] Love and humility have the
same goal: the healing of the irascible. The expression "the Lord

---

[15] Cf. Prayer 11, 13, 19, 44, 45, 114, 117, 120, 128, 148. Prayer and knowledge are not exactly the same thing for Evagrius, but they are two aspects of a
same reality. We will return to this chain in Part Four.

[16] Géhin, SC 340, 329.

will make camp" should be considered an expression for knowledge. Thus, in those in whom the irascible is healed, knowledge can enter.

REPRISE (M 3 TO M 19)

In order not to lose the thread as the development becomes richer and consequently more complex, it will be useful now to pause for a moment and look back on what has unfolded so far. A chain of virtues from faith to love is exposed from M 3 to M 9, the connection to knowledge having been made at the outset. Love and hate are used to characterize a good and a bad monastic life in M 8 and 9, and in M 10 this focuses on the specific issue of memory of injury. In M 11 this idea is tied to temperance, which is woven through this whole development. M 10 opens onto a fuller development in M 12–15, which treats of gentleness and the memory of injury. The relation to knowledge is emphasized. The same theme of love and hate takes a new turn in M 16–18 on poverty and wealth and their relation to knowledge. M 19 adds a connection, not arbitrarily, to humility and pride.

GOD'S LAW, CHRIST'S "LAW," AND KNOWLEDGE (M 20 TO M 24)

A chain opens in M 20 with contrasting members: transgressing God's law or keeping it. These two different directions are set in opposition in the rest of the proverbs of this chain. Different terms for these two basic and contrasting ideas give the unit its structural unity. Starting with the negative expressions, there is transgressing God's law (M 20), then the notion of deriving evil from flesh (M 21), then the terms "lawless man," "unjust man," and "unclean soul" (M 22). Further, there is mention of the wicked and demons (M 23) and of evil itself (M 24). The positive expressions include keeping God's law (M 20), the notion of imitating Christ and dying his death (M 21). There is mention of the just and of angels (M 23) and of the holy ones (M 24).

M 21 is one of the more striking and suggestive proverbs of the collection. The soul's dying Christ's death and not deriving evil from its flesh is an expression that refers to the whole of *praktikē*. Dying Christ's death means also sharing in his resurrection.

This is to be associated with knowledge in Evagrius.[17] It is expressed with the beautiful image of a star and the glowing sun. M 22 stays with the idea of death, but speaks of a different kind of death, that of the lawless man. The image for this death is as ugly as the previous one is beautiful. M 23 shows how angels and demons are involved in these two contrasting ways. The proverb can be understood to have a sort of general sense of being guided or not through life, but the context also gives it a more specific sense in reference to death. Thus, when a soul is leaving its body in death, either angels guide it or demons snatch it up.[18] M 24 concludes the whole development with a specific reference to knowledge. The two contrasting ways are the difference between knowledge and ignorance. God's law, which is concerned with a life of *praktikē* that leads to love, finishes in a heart being filled with knowledge.

For a Second Time:
Poverty, Wealth, and Knowledge (M 25 to M 30)

It is typical of *Ad Monachos* to introduce themes, develop them a little, and then return to them strongly a second time. Such is the case with M 25 to M 30, which treats again, and this time in more insistent terms, the relation between poverty, wealth, and knowledge. M 16 to M 18 presented this specific idea and then the development from M 20 to M 24 spoke in more general terms that could apply to the struggle for all the virtues and the war against all the vices. But now the focus becomes specific again in M 25 to M 30.

---

[17] Resurrection is the condition necessary for reaching knowledge. This is discussed in Part Four in the particular commentary on M 21, where the thought of the proverb is also connected to the theme of love.

[18] This theme is common to desert literature. See A. Guillaumont, "Les visions mystiques," 120–21. For a vivid description of the ideas in M 22, 23, especially with the image of souls flying, see LH 21:16–17. Justice is virtue established in all the parts of the soul; cf. TP 89. Thus, the just are those who are ready to enter into knowledge. The reason angels guide these is that there is a special affinity between angels and the mind; cf. KG I, 68. For a development of the significance of this affinity and further texts, see Bunge, "'Nach dem Intellekt Leben,'" 101–2.

M 25 comes back to the theme of wealth and poverty with a new dimension, a more specific dimension: giving alms and feeding the poor. Giving alms is, of course, a practical expression of love. As the text from the *Scholia on Proverbs* cited above made clear, by means of almsgiving the irascible is purified and love is acquired.[19]

It is striking that every member of this chain mentions the connection with knowledge, either with an expression such as "inherit treasures" or "inherit the Lord," or with the word *knowledge* itself.[20] These terms, as well as the theme of wealth and poverty, hold this chain together. Moreover, since this discussion about poverty and wealth is at base concerned with love and the irascible, this whole chain can be considered as a specific and concrete treatment of the connection between love and knowledge.

The first and last members of this chain, M 25 and M 30, are similarly concrete in a way that the other members of the chain are not. In this way they form an inclusion around the proverbs they embrace. Both speak of the specific action of caring for the poor. Both mention that those who do so will inherit treasures or be filled with good things; that is, that they will reach knowledge. Finally, M 30 mentions specifically that being merciful to the poor destroys irascibility. This mention of irascibility prepares the way for the opening of the next chain on gentleness, irascibility's direct opposite.

FOR A SECOND TIME:
GENTLENESS AND IRASCIBILITY (M 31 TO M 36)

We saw above how by means of single proverbs on temperance (M 4, 6, 7, 11) Evagrius wove a strand on that theme through the chains on love and gentleness. We can now observe that chains on gentleness and chains on wealth and poverty are being woven together. M 12 to M 15 is about gentleness. M 16 to M 18

---

[19] See p. 79 above, citing In Prov 22:2 (G 234).

[20] On Evagrius's use of words like *inherit* in reference to knowledge, see pp. 72–73 above. For other instances of the term *treasure* associated with knowledge, see M 87 and M 122, both of which also concern love. See also Lt 47:1 and Lt 61 with notes by Bunge in *Briefe,* 365, 378.

is about wealth and poverty. Again, M 25 to M 30 is about wealth and poverty. Now with M 31 to M 36 the issue of gentleness winds its way back into the unfolding text. As mentioned, the immediate link in the construction of the chain is between M 30's *irascibility* and M 31's *gentle heart*. No monk trained in Evagrian vocabulary could fail to hear the connection. By this point in the text stronger echoes should also be sounding. In M 31's careful formulation they do.

M 31 is a strong proverb. In some ways it is a sentence that stands sparkling alone before it is noticed as part of a chain. It is a fine example of a feature characteristic of *Ad Monachos,* namely, that the single proverbs have a power and force in their own right apart from their presence in a chain. They are worthy of meditation in their own right as well as of meditation that considers their place in a chain.[21] M 31 can be considered a sort of summary of all that has gone before in the text. Irascibility, gentleness, wealth, poverty, knowledge, memory of injury, forgetfulness of injury, knowledge, love, hate, *praktikē,* gentleness, wisdom, passionlessness—all these words are swirling around together now in the mind of the careful meditator. Hearing one word can evoke another. Becoming used to hearing the words together helps the connection of the various concepts to sink down deeply into the mind.

M 31 acts as a summary of all this by bringing together in one proverb key words whose importance has already been highlighted. Gentleness is combined with wisdom, a word whose striking appearance in the first proverb set a tone for the whole collection. Passionlessness, which is the proximate goal of the life of *praktikē,* appears again. And for the first time in *Ad Monachos* the important Evagrian word πρακτική occurs, the technical term that sums up the whole first phase of the monastic life.[22]

M 32 and M 33 may seem at first glance not to fit especially well into the theme of gentleness and irascibility, but this difficulty

[21] M 31 will be commented on individually in Part Four.

[22] In M 31 πρακτική is used as an adjective for *soul,* a usage that occurs again in M 64. In *Ad Monachos* the feminine substantive ἡ πρακτική is not used, but it occurs frequently in the *Praktikos* (e.g., TP 1, 60, 78, 81, 87, 100). For other uses of the term in *Ad Monachos,* see M 70, 118, 121, 132.

disappears once they are recognized as scriptural allusions. M 32 is an allusion to Proverbs 14:22, a text that explains what characterizes both the craftsmen of evil and those of good. The biblical text reads, "The craftsmen of evils [κακῶν] do not understand mercy [ἔλεον] and truth, but compassion [ἐλεημοσύναι] and faithfulness are with the craftsmen of good." Both ἔλεος and ἐλεημοσύνη are terms associated with the irascible. The image of a bad or good wage keeps a connection, at least subliminally, with the previous chain on poverty and wealth and the true treasure and inheritance.[23] The image in M 33 of laying a trap is a biblical image for the activity of the irascible.[24] In the context of this chain it refers especially to the relations of the monks among themselves.[25]

M 34, 35, 36 finish the chain by contrasting again gentleness and irascibility. *Long-suffering* is a term closely associated with gentleness in Evagrius's writings, and in M 35 it is found in the proverb playing the same role as gentleness. Again, they are different aspects of a single all-embracing reality: love. M 35 once again explicitly mentions knowledge.[26]

THOUGHTS AGITATING THE HEART (M 37)

M 37 introduces an important word in the Evagrian vocabulary, λογισμοί, or *thoughts*. As we saw in the Introduction, *thoughts* is a word that quite vibrates with meaning for one who knows what Evagrius means by it, such that one might say, "Thoughts!

[23] Μισθός is a New Testament term used to signify the reward for the kingdom, as in Matt 5:12; 20:8; 1 Cor 3:8.

[24] See the many references under M 33 from the Psalms and Proverbs in the Index to Scriptural Citations and Allusions.

[25] This is in contrast to M 126, where the same image is used but the context gives it a different focus, namely, false knowledge.

[26] My continually drawing attention to the presence of the word *knowledge* and to other expressions that refer to it can seem repetitive, but I think it is part of the careful reading of the text, and I wish later to draw conclusions about the way in which Evagrius conceives the relation between *praktikē* and knowledge. Its continual recurrence is a way Evagrius has of pounding a point home. In my analysis I mention it often because Evagrius does, and the text is not well read unless it is noticed each time.

Oh no, not that!" The meaning of the term is pejorative in each of its nine occurrences in *Ad Monachos*.[27] Evagrius believes that thoughts are the principal means that the demons use to trouble an anchorite. Thus, to be troubled by a thought is to be troubled by a demon.

Evagrius's advice in M 37 for escaping these thoughts or temptations is unceasing prayer. It is good to be aware that Evagrius distinguishes between two types of prayer, one pertaining to *praktikē* and the other to contemplation.[28] Unceasing prayer pertains to *praktikē* and is designed to save the monk from being troubled by evil thoughts. Evagrius does not think that even the knower can maintain himself unceasingly in contemplation. The *Chapters on Prayer* speak of both types of prayer, but one short chapter gives an example of the sort of prayer being spoken of in M 37. Evagrius speaks of crashing sounds and roars and voices coming from the demons, and in the following chapter he advises, "At the time of such temptations, make use of a short and intense prayer" (Prayer 98 [PG 79:1189A]).[29] By continually directing short intense prayers against his thoughts, the monk can escape the demons.[30]

When M 37 refers to thoughts, and by implication to the work of the demons, it is a proverb that can swing both ways in the collection. Unceasing prayer would help in the temptations that have been mentioned so far, be they memory of injury,[31] amassing money, or irascibility in general. But likewise, unceasing prayer can be of help for the new issue raised in the chain

---

[27] In addition to M 37, see M 38, 45, 50, 51, 58, 59, 73, 82. For a text that shows that not all thoughts are bad, see KG VI, 83.

[28] Οὐκοῦν καὶ προσευχῆς διττὸς ὁ τρόπος. Ὁ μέν τις πρακτικός, ὁ δὲ θεωρητικός (Prayer, Prologue [PG 79:1165C]).

[29] As Hausherr points out in his commentary on this chapter, this is the method of *antirrhetikos* (*Leçons*, 134).

[30] For a useful study on continuous prayer as part of *praktikē* in Evagrius and in the whole desert tradition, see Bunge, "Betet ohne Unterlass" in *Das Geistgebet*, 29–43.

[31] It is to be remembered that prayer is precisely M 14's advice for this problem. The prayer of M 15 refers to the other type of prayer, the prayer of knowledge or contemplation. There the expression is "hour of prayer," not "unceasing prayer."

from M 38 to M 44. Before turning to that chain, another reprise will be useful at this point.

REPRISE (M 20 TO M 37)

This reprise can see in a glance now the development of three major steps. First, M 20 to M 24 offers two contrasting ways, one that leads through imitation of Christ to resurrection, that is, to knowledge; another that leads to death and ignorance. Next, for a second time (and a stronger time) poverty and wealth are related to knowledge. The third major development, closely connected through the issue of irascibility, is gentleness. It is a goal of the life of *praktikē*. It leads to knowledge. Evil thoughts will hinder one's coming to knowledge, but unceasing prayer as a part of *praktikē's* war against the demons will help the monk to escape them.

FOOD AND DRINK AND THE FEAST OF GOD (M 38 TO M 44)

These proverbs form a beautiful and subtle chain that begins with concrete remarks about wine and meat but climbs quickly under the metaphor of a feast to several especially striking proverbs about love and knowledge. First of all, in its concrete prescriptions about food and drink this chain develops a theme that has already been sounded in the thread on temperance, that is, in M 4, 6, 7, and 11.[32] M 38's formulations against wine and meat are similar to M 11, which reads, "Do not give much food to your body / and you will not see bad visions in your sleep. / For in the way that a flame enkindles a forest / so does hunger burn up shameful visions." Thus, this is to some extent a chain on temperance, though it is also more than that. Following as it does a chain on gentleness, it continues the interweaving of themes that was begun at the very start.

In addition, this present chain contains a smaller unit within it (M 40–43), which, *inside* the theme of temperance, transforms

---

[32] In the language of M 38 Evagrius is probably echoing the common expression known from Herodotus, πῖνε καὶ τέρπου. See Liddell-Scott, *Greek-English Lexicon* (Oxford: Clarendon, 1940), 1777B, s.v. τέρπω.

the chain into one that is more about love and knowledge than about temperance.[33] Let us see how this happens.

M 38 speaks against taking wine and meat; it is about temperance. It also makes use of the technical term *thoughts,* warning that shameful thoughts will not depart from one who takes wine and meat. We have seen that thoughts are really the work of demons, and noticing this makes the connection between M 38 and M 11 appear even tighter; for in M 11 if one eats too much, one sees bad visions in one's sleep, something that is also the work of demons.[34] The use of the word *thoughts* is the immediate hook to the preceding proverb, which was described as being able to swing in two directions. If when first read M 37 acts as a remark on the aforementioned temptations, in M 38 it shows that food and drink also affect whether or not one is beset with evil thoughts.

M 39 repeats the same idea but also introduces the theme of the feast, which will figure in the remaining proverbs of the chain. It is this image that forms the main structural component of the chain, actually enabling us to recognize it as a chain. A feast cannot be an excuse for monks to take wine and meat. For monks, *feast* cannot have a material meaning, something like filling one's stomach.

M 40 to M 43 builds on this idea and can actually be considered a chain within this chain. The reader is invited first to detect and then to enjoy the complexity of the construction at this point. If a feast is not filling the stomach, then these following proverbs (the chain within the chain) define what the real feast is. The real feast is spiritual. It is described in terms of Pasch and Pentecost. M 40, as the first member of the chain within the chain, presents once again in its two lines the two major divisions of the monastic life: *praktikē* and knowledge. *Praktikē's* image is the Pasch, and it is summed up as the passing over from evil.[35] Pentecost is the

---

[33] It is worth remembering Evagrius's plea from Lt 27:3: "Let no one, I beg you, devote himself only to temperance."

[34] Cf. M 52. For a study on the whole, see Refoulé, "Rêves et vie spirituelle." On p. 504 Refoulé remarks that M 11 is a good summary of Evagrius's teaching on the relation of food to demonic dreams.

[35] This language is similar to what has already been observed in M 21, where

image for knowledge, and here it is described as the resurrection of the soul.[36]

If M 40 introduces this chain with a statement of the two divisions of monastic life, then M 41 and M 42 develop a theme within *praktikē,* a theme that has appeared already and whose reappearance is beginning to leave some impression of its importance. M 41 describes the real feast of God as forgetting offenses. The second line expresses its opposite. Gloom is contrasted with feast. Remembering injuries is contrasted with forgetting them. M 42 is an expansion of the theme into more general terms, into the key terms of *love* and *hate.* So the chain that started with temperance, using an image suited to temperance (feasts), has become a chain about gentleness and love and how these are related to knowledge.[37]

M 43 is the last member of the smaller unit M 40 to M 43. Perhaps not surprisingly now, it directly associates knowledge with all that has been said, still using the image of the feast. The

---

the word *exodus* was used; and both are perhaps further clarified by a definition given in the *Scholia on Proverbs:* "Now he calls 'exodus' the soul which goes out from evil and ignorance" (In Prov 1:20 [G 12]). This is similarly expressed in In Prov 8:3 (G 99). For a slightly longer explanation, see KG VI, 64, which reads in part, "by the sensible exodus of the sons of Israel, he has shown us the exodus from evil and ignorance."

[36]In KG V, 22 we find a straightforward statement about the resurrection of the soul: "The resurrection of the soul is the return from the order of being troubled by the passions to the state of passionlessness." Thus, to speak more exactly, the image in this proverb is on the border between *praktikē* and knowledge, for from passionlessness, the monk passes to knowledge. For this passage "the resurrection of love" (M 43) is necessary. For more on resurrection, see the comments on M 21 in Part Four. Pasch and Pentecost are likewise discussed in a mysterious series of sentences in the *Kephalaia Gnostica,* where it is clear that both are symbols for knowledge (see KG II, 38–42).

[37] Gentleness is at issue not only in the proverbs in which that word is actually used but in all of the proverbs that use vocabulary associated with gentleness. This includes expression of its opposite as this is manifested in general in irascibility or specifically, as, for example, M 41's remembering injury or M 42's hating a brother. Thus, even though the word *gentleness* does not appear in this present chain, it can be identified through its content as a chain concerned with gentleness and love. Compare the chain extending from M 12 to M 15, which began with a specific mention of gentleness and then developed the theme of memory of injury and forgetting injury.

progress developed around this image has gone something like this: a feast for monks does not have to do with filling the stomach (M 39).[38] M 40 introduces terms of the Christian's feast, and we learn that the feast is forgetting offenses (M 41); it is the resurrection of love (M 42).[39] Indeed, the feast is true knowledge (M 43).[40] The true knowledge of God is contrasted with false knowledge, and the way it is placed here suggests a connection between false knowledge and hating one's brother.[41]

M 44 stands outside the immediate development of M 40 to M 43's movement from *praktikē* to knowledge, but it closes the larger chain that opened in M 38. It does so with a style that is becoming familiar, namely, in a "better . . . than . . ." form.[42] A feast is a good thing, the proverb suggests; but it is not good at all if the soul is impure. Better no food at all (a fast) with a pure heart.

AGAIN: EVIL THOUGHTS (M 45)

Once again we see the appearance of the technical term *thoughts,* its third appearance now since M 37. In fact, M 45 functions somewhat as M 37 does in the collection. It too is a sort of hinge sentence that swings both ways. The advice about banishing evil thoughts can be understood in reference to all that precedes and to all that is about to follow.[43] *Thoughts* function as the link, hooking on to *impurity of soul* in M 44 and on to *evils* in M 46.

[38] Here the link with temperance and the concupiscible is made.

[39] Here the link with love and the irascible is made. "The resurrection of the soul" in M 40 stands in relation to "the resurrection of love" in M 42, both being associated with Pentecost.

[40] Here the link between temperance, love, and knowledge is made.

[41] One of the reasons why Evagrius is at pains to intertwine love and temperance is in order to combat gnostics, whose ascetical feats, lacking in love, led to false knowledge as well as stemmed from it. See Stroumsa, "Ascèse et gnose."

[42] One of these sorts of comparisons is made for almost each major issue in the text. In M 9 we observed a better-love-than-hate proverb. In M 26 it is better poverty than wealth. In M 34 it is better gentleness than irascibility. In addition to M 44, see also M 51, contrasting sleep and vigils; M 78, contrasting the worldly caring for the sick with irascible anchorites; M 110, contrasting lower forms of knowledge with knowledge of the Trinity; and M 128, contrasting true and false knowledge.

[43] It is not difficult to catch the scriptural allusion of this proverb, which is

SLEEP AND VIGILS (M 46 TO M 52)

This chain introduces a new theme; it concerns not taking too much sleep but instead keeping vigil. In the *Praktikos* Evagrius cites the example of Macarius of Alexandria in this regard, and his words there offer some insight as to why a chain on sleep and vigils might be found to follow one that had in part to do with food and drink. When Evagrius went once to visit Macarius, Macarius told him, "During twenty years I never took my fill of bread or water or sleep. For my bread I ate by weight, my water I drank by measure, and, leaning against the wall, I snatched a little bit of sleep" (TP 94).[44] The advice of Macarius closely unites temperance and sleep.

The chain is striking for the many expressions about evil that it contains. These various expressions hold it tightly together. Beginning in M 45, which is a hinge sentence that swings into this, the expression "evil thoughts" is found, followed by "evils" (M 46), "empty stories," "evil" (M 47), "thickens thought" (M 48), "temptations" (M 49), "evil thoughts" (M 50), "idle thoughts" (M 51), and "demonic dream" (M 52). To all of these various expressions, keeping vigil is proposed as a solution. Each proverb explains a little of the reason. The concern throughout is the quality of the monk's thinking, that is, his avoiding evil thoughts and honing his thinking.

In one of his letters Evagrius advises his addressee to pray for the gift of discernment in order to learn the various strategies of the demons, and then he mentions a number of virtues that are necessary in order to receive this gift. The list is interesting not only in that it mentions vigils but also for the other virtues named in it. "These are," he says, "temperance and gentleness, vigils and anachoresis, and firmness in prayer" (Lt 4:5).[45] The mention especially of temperance, gentleness, and vigils together is a con-

---

to Ps 136:9. Evagrius's words in the second line quote the psalm verse exactly. For Evagrius's comment on this psalm verse, see In Ps 136:9. The rock is interpreted as Christ. See likewise In Ps 39:3 on faith in Christ and In Ps 60:3, citing 1 Cor 10:4, "and the rock was Christ." These texts are quoted below, p. 287 with n. 140.

[44] LH 18 shows that Macarius was famous for precisely these things.

[45] Translated from a Greek fragment found in C. Guillaumont, "Fragments grecs," 220, lines 44–46.

firmation of the pattern of the chains recognized here as they are unfolding in *Ad Monachos*. In the letter Evagrius mentions them as single words; here in *Ad Monachos* he unfolds and interlaces chains on these various virtues.

The core of the problem with taking too much sleep is expressed most clearly in M 48, where the expression is especially striking. "Much sleep thickens thought" (Ὕπνος πολὺς παχύνει διάνοιαν). The notion of thought being thickened or made heavier is one that can be understood in terms that are close to literal. A similar but more ample sentence in the *Chapters on Prayer* gives a clearer idea of what stands behind M 48's brief expression. The chapter reads, "Why would the demons want to produce in us gluttony, fornication, love of money, anger and memory of injury and the rest of the passions except that through them the mind becomes heavy [ἵνα παχυνθεὶς ὁ νοῦς ἐξ αὐτῶν] and is not able to pray as it ought" (Prayer 51 [PG 79:1177B]).[46] This text mentions some of the eight principal thoughts and shows that it is evil thoughts that make the mind too heavy to focus on its main purpose, namely, prayer. M 48 claims that too much sleep makes it impossible for the mind to avoid becoming heavier because, as M 49 goes on to say, much sleep leads to temptations, that is (as M 50 says), evil thoughts.[47]

---

[46] Here I follow a reading of the text different from that offered by S. Tugwell for reasons that the following note will make clear.

[47] It is worth pursuing these points for a moment in order to show how deeply involved the ultimate goal of knowledge is with these issues of *praktikē*. Behind M 48's expression of thought growing thicker stands the notion of the present condition of the mind as being placed in a body more or less heavy. When the mind in its original condition moves away from knowledge, it falls into a body more or less heavy, depending on the degree of its fall. Thus, "It is said that on high there are those who have light bodies, and below those who have heavy ones; and above the first there are those who are lighter than they; but below the second there are those that are more heavy than they" (KG II, 68). This receiving a body, described as a fall, is what Evagrius understands by the term "judgment." The weight of the body and the weight of the mind are virtually identical precisely because the body is the mind's instrument, given to the mind so that, the body becoming lighter by degrees, the mind may return to the union from which it fell. But if the monk does not make progress in virtue, then he in fact passes over into a yet heavier body, the mind becoming yet heavier. "The intelligible 'fat' is the thickness which accrues to the ruling principle [τὸ ἡγεμονικόν] as a result of evil"

Thus, the issue about sleep is directly related to the whole purpose of *praktikē*, namely, the mind's being able to raise itself toward contemplation. M 49 and M 50 build on the idea expressed in M 48 by using different terminology which shows the connection between thought growing heavier and temptations (M 49) and evil thoughts (M 50). Vigils help the monk to resist the demons working through all these.[48]

(In Ps 16:9–10 [PG 12:1220C–D]; cf. KG IV, 36). This passing to a lighter body is part of the work of *praktikē*, but it is precisely the monk's *praktikē* which the demons struggle against through thoughts. If the demons can cause the monk to sin, then "[t]he judgment of the impious will be the transposition from a body for *praktikē* into bodies dark and murky" (In Ps 1:5 [PG 12:1097D]; cf. KG III, 50). This sentence actually follows a positive expression of the same, which shows that the monk in *praktikē* who progresses in virtue passes over into a body that is more able to enter into knowledge. "The judgment of the righteous is the passage from a body for *praktikē* to an angelic one" (In Ps 1:5 [PG 12:1097D]; cf. KG III, 48).

This is not a notion reserved to the supposedly advanced monks to whom the *Kephalaia Gnostica* would have been directed. It is already clearly present in the earliest existing work of Evagrius, the *Epistula Fidei*, where he says, "But since our mind now become thick [ἐπειδὴ νῦν παχυνθεὶς ἡμῶν ὁ νοῦς] is joined to earth and is mixed with clay, it is unable to fix itself on naked contemplation" (Ep Fid 7, lines 31–33). In the same passage he speaks of resurrection as being when "our mind wakes up and raises itself toward a blessed height where it can contemplate the oneness and the singleness of the Logos [τὴν ἑνάδα καὶ μονάδα τοῦ Λόγου]" (Ep Fid 7, lines 30–31). This theme of the weight of the mind has been usefully studied elsewhere. For the most useful summary, citing many texts, see Hausherr, *Leçons,* 72–75, where he comments on Prayer 51, cited above. To the texts cited by Hausherr could be added G 37 and Inst ad mon 1. Also useful is A. Guillaumont, *Képhalaia Gnostica,* 107–8. For the same idea in Cassian and for Evagrius's influence on him, see Marsili, *Giovanni Cassiano ed Evagrio Pontico,* 48–49.

[48] The "Evagrian logic" of the placement of a chain on sleep and vigils at this point in *Ad Monachos* is clarified even further by several other texts which show that vigils is a monastic practice that is also concerned with the rational part of the soul. These texts shed further light on M 48's concern with thought growing thicker, but they also help the reader to see that the chains being interwoven here are concerned with all three parts of the soul, the irascible (in the chains on gentleness and love), the concupiscible (in the chains on temperance and on food and drink), and the rational in this chain on sleep and vigils. Evagrius says, "Reading and vigils and prayer make the wandering mind hold still." This shows that vigils is concerned with helping the mind to focus on its purpose, which the texts cited above have shown is ultimately prayer or contemplation. But Evagrius goes on in the same passage to speak of the other parts of the soul. "Hunger and pain and anachoresis quench a flaming concupiscence. Psalmody, long-suffering, and

The chain continues in M 51 with another proverb in the form "better/than." The form is used to show that a vigil is more than just staying awake. One could stay awake and the mind could still be involved with idle thoughts (again the use of λογισμοί), in which case it would be better to sleep. The chain concludes in M 52 in a suggestive way with a proverb on dreams, stating that an angelic dream gladdens the heart and a demonic dream agitates it. This proverb touches a theme that is well developed elsewhere in Evagrius in which he shows himself to be an acute observer of dreams. He shows how dreams can be used as a measure of one's spiritual health. In fact, if the monk is not dealing successfully in his waking life with the evil thoughts by which he is attacked, then this will also be revealed in an agitated dream.[49] So the logic of the present development is that if one does battle with temptations and evil thoughts by means of vigils, one can expect an angelic dream when one does sleep.

FOUR VIRTUES AS A HINGE IN THE COLLECTION (M 53)

M 53 stands free in the collection, at the end of the development on sleep and vigils, before the beginning of another development. It is a big sentence whose terms look in many directions. Four fundamental virtues are mentioned. All but one of these (conversion) have already occurred in the text. They set the

---

mercy set at rest an agitated irascibility" (TP 15). Similar remarks are dropped elsewhere in Evagrius's writings, showing the connection of vigils to the mind's true purpose. For example, "Reading the oracles of God pulls in the wandering mind [Πλανώμενον νοῦν συστέλλει ἀνάγνωσις λογίων Θεοῦ]–and so does a vigil with prayer" (Inst ad mon [PG 79:1236A]). (This sentence is found in a series of sentences that speak of temperance, poverty, and long-suffering.) Elsewhere, "Hunger and thirst quench evil desires [ἐπιθυμίας], and a good vigil purifies the mind [καθαίρει διάνοιαν]" (V 40). This is followed by a sentence that reads, "Love turns aside anger and irascibility. Gifts overthrow memory of injury" (V 41). It should be noted, however,that in TP 49 Evagrius associates vigils with curing the passionate part of the soul, that is, the irascible and the concupiscible.

[49] For a detailed description of the difference between a demonic dream and an angelic one, see Thoughts 4. For Evagrius's teaching about dreams, see Refoulé, "Rêves et vie spirituelle."

soul up, and they make it firm. And all that will be mentioned in the proverbs that follow does the same. Thus, the proverb is identified as a hinge.

REPRISE (M 38 TO M 53)

In this reprise we can draw into a single view two substantial developments, one on the true feast of God (defined as forgetting injuries and true knowledge) and another on sleep and vigils. Each development is surrounded by sentences of a more general application. M 37 and M 45 surround the feast-of-God series. M 45 and M 53 surround the sleep-and-vigils series. With this series we have now encountered interwoven chains that deal with each of the three parts of the soul. These relatively long and involved chains are now followed by several shorter ones.

LISTLESSNESS (M 54 TO M 56)

This is a chain about ἀκηδία, listlessness. Listlessness is one of the eight principal thoughts and one of the most dangerous and difficult for the monk to struggle against. Evagrius has long been valued among monastic writers for his descriptions of listlessness as well as for the various wise remedies that he proposes against it. In *Ad Monachos* only these three proverbs treat the theme explicitly; nonetheless, in them he has managed to express some of its most characteristic features. This chain illustrates well a claim that was made in the introduction, namely, that the proverbs of *Ad Monachos* are remarkable condensations of the already rather condensed writings of Evagrius. Thus, when one knows Evagrius's teaching on this central problem of the monastic life, these three proverbs can function as fine meditations and reminders of what is explained at greater length elsewhere. For the moment we observe only the structure of the chain, reserving commentary for later.

The placement of a chain on listlessness after one on sleep is no accident. Sleep is one of the ways that the demon of listlessness causes trouble.[50] Before even mentioning listlessness specif-

---

[50] See below, p. 267 for the passage from 8 Spirits 14 that shows this connection.

ically, as he does in M 55, Evagrius speaks in M 54 of one of his most important remedies against it, namely, remembering death, here expressed as "remember your exodus."[51] Thus, we can be certain that the chain begins with this proverb.

In M 55 Evagrius gives what is his most characteristic advice for the monk afflicted by listlessness. It is advice that he everywhere insists upon in his discussion of this evil spirit. He urges the monk to stay in his cell and face (wrestle) this demon head-on. As the discussion on listlessness below will make clear, the monk who stays and fights this demon can expect a deep peace to follow in his soul.[52] This is expressed in M 55 as the heart being made to glow, and in the expression we can notice again that Evagrius is once more directing the monk's attention to the goal beyond the monastic struggle, that is, to knowledge.

Several further dimensions of Evagrius's teaching about listlessness can be found in M 56, where it is said to drive away tears (of repentance), where it is connected with sadness, another of the eight principal thoughts, and where together with sadness it is said to shatter prayer. Sadness and listlessness are two demons that, according to Evagrius's observations and descriptions, work closely together.[53] In shattering prayer, they are conspiring against the highest goal of the monastic life.

SADNESS AND MONEY (M 56 TO M 57)

M 56 is not only part of a chain on listlessness; it is the first of a little series of two proverbs on sadness. The series shows how sadness comes from several directions: in the case of M 56 from listlessness, in the case of M 57 from desiring money. This notion of sadness coming from different directions is expanded upon elsewhere in Evagrius's writings. A good example is the treatise *On the Eight Spirits of Evil,* where sadness is treated after anger.[54] There Evagrius explains why sadness must be treated as coming

---

[51] See below, pp. 266–69 for the commentary on M 54.

[52] See below, pp. 269–71 for the commentary on M 55.

[53] See below, pp. 271–73 for the commentary of M 56.

[54] In the *Praktikos* the order of the eight principal thoughts is slightly different. There love of money (comparable to M 57's "desiring money") comes before sadness; then come anger and listlessness. Note that love of money leading

upon the monk from different directions. "Sadness has no power unless the other passions are present. . . . He who is fettered by sadness has been defeated by the passions, and he carries the fetters as evidence of the defeat" (8 Spirits 11 [PG 79:1156D]). In M 57 Evagrius manages rather suddenly to stab the reader again with the idea about money. The point has already been developed in two significant chains (M 16 to M 18, M 25 to M 30), and here the simple words "desiring money" should be enough to bring those chains back to mind. Now the proverb shows how the evil thought of loving money leads to the evil thought of sadness.

Sadness will arise from virtually any improper desire. "For sadness arises from a frustration of a fleshly yearning. A yearning goes with each passion. The one who has conquered a yearning has conquered the passions, and he who has conquered the passions will not be ruled over by sadness" (8 Spirits 11 [PG 79:1156D]). M 57's desiring money is a case in point.[55] But the full point is not grasped unless the careful reader has made the connection to the chains about poverty and wealth. This little proverb greatly enhances the material of those chains by its warning that the lover of money will fall prey to sadness. And "sadness is the partner and schoolmate of listlessness" (cf. Vices 3, 4 [PG 79:1141D, 1144C]), the most difficult demon of them all (cf. TP 28). The chains on poverty and wealth have warned against the pleasures of this world, and "he who flees all the worldly pleasures is an inaccessible fortress against the demon of sadness" (TP 19). A proverb from another work of Evagrius expresses this same thought in an order that follows exactly that of M 56 and M 57 taken together, a further confirmation of the identification of the two proverbs as a little unit. "Perseverance checks listlessness, and so do tears. Hatred of pleasures makes worldly sadness quiet" (Inst ad mon [PG 79:1236A]).

---

to sadness is the same order of thoughts expressed in M 57. The analysis of these thoughts in the *Praktikos* shows how they are intertwined and work off of each other. Concerning sadness Evagrius explains, "Sadness follows sometimes from the frustration of desires and sometimes it comes after anger" (TP 10).

[55] M 61 will make the same point concerning the desire for glory.

ADVICE ON EVIL THOUGHTS AND TEMPTATIONS (M 58 TO M 60)

We have seen several free-standing proverbs that deal with thoughts (λογισμοί) (M 37, 45) and several others in which thoughts and temptations figured significantly and built an understanding of how Evagrius uses the term λογισμοί (M 38, 45, 49, 50, 51). Now here are three such proverbs in which this is the main structural component of the chain.

The chain is held tightly together with some key words. In all three proverbs the place of the battle with the evil thought is the heart. In all three there is a striking image for the evil thought and a strong verb suggesting what to do about it. M 58 speaks of not letting the scorpion linger; M 59 urges the killing of the offspring of serpents; and M 60 speaks of the purifying fire of silver and gold.

Like the free-standing proverbs, this series of three can swing both ways in the collection, since through many texts it has become clear now that *thoughts* is a generic term for various demons. By this point in the collection any number of demons have been named or encountered in the course of the meditation. The advice here is to cut the thoughts off immediately when they attack. As Evagrius explains in the *Praktikos*, the monk has no choice about whether or not a thought will trouble his soul, but he does have a choice about how long it will linger and about whether it will move his passions or not (TP 6).[56]

As the collection slowly works its way toward more and more talk about knowledge, this particular series about ridding the heart of evil thoughts becomes crucial advice; for the mind that is attacked by thoughts and perhaps allows them to linger is also the mind that is to be used for contemplation. This connection appears clearly in a passage from one of the letters: "For the scope of the monk is not to lose the mind to these or those thoughts and then to join it again to some others, but rather

---

[56] The text in TP 6 uses χρονίζειν for lingering thoughts, as does M 58. The word is used frequently in reference to thoughts in *On Evil Thoughts;* see Thoughts, 11, 14, 16, 20, and especially 22. The word is also used in the same way in In Prov 5:20 (G 68); 6:27–28 (G 82); 9:18a (G 115, ἐγχρονίζειν). The opposite of thoughts lingering would be lingering in contemplation; see, for example, In Prov 31:21 (G 377) Ἀπάθειαν δὲ κτησάμενος χρονίσει τε ἐν τῇ θεωρίᾳ.

wholly to present the mind, freed from all impure thought, before Christ" (Lt 52:6).[57]

A series of three proverbs on thoughts that can swing both ways in the collection is well placed here; for as the following analysis will show, there is a sort of dividing line among types of thoughts between listlessness and the next two thoughts to be considered in M 61, 62—namely, vainglory and pride. That little series is followed by a long, complex chain on the interrelation in general of *praktikē* to knowledge. *Thoughts* refers to all of this; but this series, placed as it is, signals the division between the nature of the thoughts leading up to listlessness and those that follow upon listlessness being defeated. Yet no kind of thought should be allowed to linger. "As it is inexplicable that a man struck by an arrow not be weakened, so it is impossible for a monk who accepts evil thoughts not to be wounded" (Inst ad mon [PG 79:1237B]).

Vainglory and Pride (M 61 to M 62)

This short chain treats vainglory and pride, the last two demons in the list of eight principal demons about which Evagrius teaches. It was mentioned above that a deep peace and joy follow in the soul after the defeat of listlessness, yet it is a constant feature of Evagrius's teaching about vainglory and pride that they can slip in very quickly after the defeat of listlessness, coming as a sort of self-satisfaction at the state of virtue that has been reached. "Alone of all the thoughts, the thoughts of vainglory and pride survive after the defeat of the rest of the thoughts" (Skemmata 57).[58] The two demons are found working closely together, much like sadness and listlessness. Thus once again, because of Evagrius's consistent teaching elsewhere, M 61 and M 62 can confidently be identified as a short series.

In its language the series links up well with the preceding chain on evil thoughts. The "strip down" and "put away" of M 61

---

[57] Translated from a Greek fragment found in C. Guillaumont, "Fragments grecs," 219, lines 27–29. For the biblical sense behind the notion of "presenting" the mind, see the commentary on M 136 below.

[58] Muyldermans, *Evagriana* (1931), 44.

are only a more specific way of saying what M 58 to M 60 said in their urging that evil thoughts not be allowed to linger. In fact, this shows why M 58 to M 60 can be described as able to swing both ways in the text. When first read, the proverbs naturally would be meditated on with reference to the aforesaid evil thoughts. Now, as the last two evil thoughts are mentioned, the same advice of getting rid of them is given.

M 61 is a proverb that shows the way in which three evil thoughts—pride, vainglory, and sadness—work in conjunction. M 62 speaks only of pride and shows its essence. Though pride is not mentioned frequently in *Ad Monachos,*[59] M 62 is a powerfully constructed proverb and is powerfully placed.[60] It is the last proverb to precede the extended and intricately developed chain that stands at the center of the whole collection, the chain that will speak so eloquently of the relation between *praktikē* and knowledge. Pride will always be a temptation for a monk who has entered into knowledge. If the monk gives way to it, he will fall from knowledge; the evil demons will bring him low. With this severe warning and its powerful images, the reader now comes upon the beautiful proverbs that show the intricate connection between *praktikē* and knowledge.

THE CENTER OF THE TEXT:
PRAKTIKĒ AND KNOWLEDGE INTERTWINED (M 63 TO M 72)

Now at the very middle of the entire text a relatively complex chain made of up ten proverbs deals with the relationship between *praktikē* and knowledge. Positioned thus in the middle of the whole, and of such striking length, it will evoke a sustained meditation on a connection that has been made at almost regular intervals throughout. In terms of the number of proverbs involved, this is one of the longest chains of the text. It is intri-

---

[59] Apart from M 61 and M 62, it is mentioned explicitly only in M 19, though it is also at issue in M 130.

[60] See Part Four for the analysis of M 62 and all that is contained in it. See also p. 283 for the way in which this proverb is likewise related to M 107, one of the most dense proverbs of the collection and the collection's turning point.

cately constructed, and its analysis here requires that we dwell at some length on its structure.[61]

This long chain is sandwiched between M 61–62 and M 73. M 61–62 treated pride, the last in the list of the eight principal demons and the one into which the knower can most easily fall again. Thus, heretofore having treated many of the demons with which a monk must do battle and arriving at the last demon, the text now offers a long development on how the whole of *praktikē* (where the demons are fought) is intimately related to knowledge. The chain is followed by M 73, which is a fresh invitation to listen, similar in many ways to the opening proverb of the entire collection, M 1.[62]

Every proverb in this chain is two lines long, and in almost every one there is both a term referring to *praktikē* and a term referring to knowledge.[63] This fact gives the chain its coherence and enables its being identified as a chain. Furthermore, there are units within the chain, and the one in the very middle on passionlessness (M 66 to M 68) is especially significant. It will be best to note these structural elements now proverb by proverb.[64]

In M 63 the term denoting *praktikē* is the expression "monk's way of life [πολιτεία μοναχοῦ]." The word *knowledge* itself is used in this first proverb. Both expressions occur in the first line, signaling strongly the relation that the entire chain treats. In the second line it becomes clear that the series is not introduced without links to what immediately precedes. Knowledge is said to guard the monk's way of life, that is, all his effort in *praktikē*. But

---

[61] The only chain of comparable length is M 123–31 on true and false knowledge. Thus, of the two longest chains of the text one is about *praktikē*'s relation to knowledge and the other is about true and false knowledge. One is in the first block of the text; the other is in the second.

[62] Compare M 1's opening line, Κληρονόμοι θεοῦ ἀκούσατε λόγων θεοῦ with M 73's, Ἄκουε, μοναχέ, λόγους πατρός σου.

[63] It is either this or, as in M 69, 70, 71, two proverbs refer to *praktikē* and one to knowledge, all three standing in tight relation to each other. This is explained below.

[64] For the moment the discussion involves only the structural elements of this chain. The contents of the proverbs in this chain are the subject of further study in Part Four. The specific claims made now about various elements of the proverbs (only those necessary for uncovering the structure of the chain) will be justified in Part Four.

when a monk has entered into knowledge, he can become proud and, as M 62 warned so vividly, will thus fall among the demons. M 63 says the same thing, if more briefly, in speaking of descending from knowledge and falling among thieves.

The second proverb in the chain, M 64, opens with a biblical image for knowledge: a spiritual rock from which a river flows. The term for *praktikē* is clear enough, namely, a soul accomplished in *praktikē*. But close attention should be paid to the Greek construction, ψυχή πρακτική. This is a good example of what Guillaumont points out about Evagrius's tendency in using the term πρακτικός and its derivatives. He says, ". . . le plus souvent . . . c'est [le pratique] celui qui l'a accomplie [la πρακτική] et qui a atteint les frontières de l'impassibilité; en ce sens, il est à peu près synonyme de 'impassible.'"[65] Thus, the ψυχή πρακτική is especially the soul that has come far in the life of *praktikē* and is ready to drink of knowledge, and it is the *soul* that is specified as doing the drinking.

Noticing this nuance tightens the connection with the next proverb, M 65, where *praktikē's* terms are the contrast drawn between a pure and an impure soul. Another biblical image for knowledge is given: vessel of election. The first line of the proverb, even leaving a verb out of the construction, could not have expressed the relation between *praktikē* and knowledge any more economically, any more tersely. One who has reached *praktikē's* goal, here expressed as "pure soul," is virtually the same as one who can enter the realm of knowledge. Thus, "A vessel of election, the pure soul."

M 66 introduces passionlessness, another term virtually synonymous with *praktikē's* goal. We begin to see that the expressions in these proverbs which refer to *praktikē* are not simply making a vague reference to the life of *praktikē* in general; they are referring much more precisely to the *goal* of *praktikē*. It is from this point in the life of *praktikē* that the link with the life of knowledge can be made. To note the terms in the Greek causes this point to fall into clearer relief. We have in this order (in M 64, 65, 66) the terms ψυχή πρακτική, ψυχὴ καθαρά, and ἀπάθεια. The expression for knowledge in M 66 is "a heart is [not] raised up."

---

[65] Guillaumont, SC 170, 50.

M 66 not only introduces the term *passionlessness;* it likewise opens a unit within the chain made up of three members joined together by this term. A close look at the positioning of this chain as well as its content reveals the extraordinary care with which Evagrius joined all the proverbs of *Ad Monachos* into patterns that offer further clues to their fullest meanings. It has already been mentioned that the chain M 63 to M 72, which beats away at some length on the relation between *praktikē* and knowledge, is positioned in the middle of the whole collection. The theme of this chain, then, can be considered a key to the whole; and this will certainly be borne out when we enter more deeply into discussion of some of the individual proverbs. But now in M 66 to M 68 we find the center of the center, and we might reasonably expect to find in its center proverb a major clue to the entire text or a proverb, which somehow manages or comes close to "saying it all."

M 67 is precisely that. It is constructed around three terms: passionlessness, love, and knowledge.[66] The way in which this proverb joins these terms manages to summarize what all the proverbs of *Ad Monachos* are about. The word *love* occurs in both lines. In the first line it appears as the goal of *praktikē*. In the second line it appears as the door to knowledge. Subsequent comments on the various proverbs of the collection will show the extent to which the individual proverbs elaborate in various directions this one fundamental insight: that love is *praktikē's* goal and that love leads the way to knowledge.

M 68 likewise speaks of passionlessness and thus concludes the little unit of M 66 to M 68. But it also introduces two more terms that appear together for a first time in this proverb: wisdom and prudence.[67] These two virtues coupled together are interwoven in an upcoming chain,[68] but each of the two virtues is

---

[66] It should be noted that M 67 is very much like M 3 in the way that it places love as the hinge between *praktikē* and knowledge. M 3 reads, "Faith: the beginning of love. / The end of love: knowledge of God." M 67 reads, "In front of love, passionlessness marches; / in front of knowledge, love." Thus, at the very beginning of the collection in M 3 (M 1 and 2 are considered introductory) and halfway through, love and knowledge are tightly joined.

[67] Wisdom has already been seen in M 28, 31. This is the first occurrence of prudence.

[68] For prudence and wisdom together, see M 68, 123, 126, 131. It can be

treated singly in the proverbs that immediately follow. In M 68 wisdom is a virtue connected with knowledge, whereas prudence is a virtue that looks toward *praktikē*. This is consistently Evagrius's teaching on these two virtues. Of the several proverbs that follow, M 69 and M 70 speak of prudence, M 71 of wisdom. Thus, in this ten-member chain whose theme is the relation between *praktikē* and knowledge, Evagrius has placed proverbs that deal with one of the key virtues of *praktikē* and one of the key virtues of knowledge.

M 69 picks up on the term *prudence*. It says that fear of the Lord, the first of the virtues of the life of *praktikē*,[69] begets prudence, which Evagrius defines as a virtue in the rational part of the soul that directs all the operations against the demons (cf. TP 89). M 70 can be considered a development of the theme of prudence, making this the third proverb in a row to touch on this theme. The flaming arrow is an image of the attacks of the demons, and since it is the role of prudence to direct operations against the demons, this proverb expresses these operations against the demons as the sum of *praktikē*. "The man of *praktikē* will extinguish it."

If M 69 and M 70 are a development of one half of the couplet prudence/wisdom, M 71 is the development of the other half. It treats specifically of wisdom. Wisdom's role is defined elsewhere by Evagrius as "the contemplation of the reasons of the corporeals and incorporeals" (TP 89). As such, it is clearly concerned with knowledge. M 71 puts wisdom and knowledge in a close parallel; and the whole proverb, in its talk against clamor, blasphemy, and cunning words, is the first announcement of a theme that will be developed in subsequent chains.[70]

The intricacy of the way this chain has unfolded is worth noticing and enjoying. The whole chain is about *praktikē* related to knowledge. In the middle of the whole is a unit of three

---

noted now (discussed later) that M 123, 126, and 131 are all part of the other major chain of the text (M 123 to M 131) on true and false knowledge.

[69] Cf. M 4 and the chain begun there.

[70] These would be the chain on listening to one's spiritual father in M 88 to 92, but already picked up on in M 73. But further, wisdom and prudence figure significantly in the most developed chain of the second half of the text, M 123 to M 131, on true and false knowledge.

proverbs on passionlessness, and its center member is one of the
most important and characteristic proverbs of *Ad Monachos*. The
three proverbs (M 63, 64, 65) that precede this center unit (M 66,
67, 68) seem to look backward to themes that have already been
opened in the collection. In each of the proverbs up to and
including the central three, there have been terms clearly referring respectively both to *praktikē* and to knowledge. The three
proverbs (M 69, 70, 71) which follow this center unit unfold out
of M 68's mention of wisdom and prudence into specific proverbs
on prudence and wisdom, which look forward to themes now to
be developed in the proverbs that follow. The proverbs on
prudence refer to *praktikē;* the proverb on wisdom refers to
knowledge.

This intricacy comes to an especially poetic conclusion with
a final proverb that is based on an allusion to the biblical image
of honey as knowledge. This proverb does not make specific mention of *praktikē*. It is as if following the chain through to this point,
the reader arrives at the goal of all *praktikē*, the very knowledge
of God. This is the last specific mention of knowledge for the
moment, and thus M 72 signals the conclusion of the chain that
began with its specific mention.

REPRISE (M 54 TO M 72)

In general terms we could describe the development up to
the last reprise at M 53 as one that has taken place in several large
portions, even if it had a number of minor developments. There
were large portions on various aspects of gentleness and irascibility, several more on poverty and wealth. However, beginning at
M 54 we found a number of shorter developments which touched
on ideas important to Evagrius but not receiving extended
emphasis in this text. The first (M 54–56) concerns listlessness;
the second (M 56–57) connects listlessness to sadness and sadness
to money. Then a series of three (M 58–60) gives advice on evil
thoughts and temptations, which is followed by yet another little
series on vainglory and pride (M 61, 62). After these four short
developments there follows one of the longest and most complex
series of the text, M 63–72. It is a series that insists from various

angles on an important theme of the entire text—the connection between *praktikē* and knowledge. Located as it is in the middle of the whole collection, this long chain functions as a summary of all that has preceded, but it also signals more clearly a theme that will slowly come to dominate in the second half, namely, knowledge itself.

A New Invitation to Listen (M 73)

The text continues with a new invitation to listen, similar to the way the entire collection opened. Here the admonition is to listen to the words of the father. In this way the sentence links by contrast with the preceding "cunning words" of M 71.[71] The mention of father sounds for the first time (except M 2) a theme that will sound again in M 81 and then be developed in a substantial chain from M 88 to M 92. But more on that below. Here it is sufficient to observe that M 73 is a longer proverb, effecting a transition between the long chain M 63–72 and a number of shorter chains that follow.[72]

The proverbs that follow until M 107 are grouped together in briefer chains. In the whole of the text it is these more than others that illustrate the capacity of each proverb to stand in its own right. This is to say that the identification of chains in these proverbs must avoid artifice, avoid forcing the issue. On the other hand, the proverbs do continue to be grouped together according to themes, and the themes are interwoven with one another. The careful reader moves back and forth between the impression that the arrangement here is loose and the impression that the arrangement is a complicated combination of many short chains. Themes

---

[71] In M 62 and M 73—that is, in the two proverbs immediately preceding and following the central chain—demons are a concern. Pride and failure to listen to a father will bring the demons on. Their opposites protect against them. The cunning words of M 71 likewise come from demons; cf. M 123.

[72] This technique of "starting over" again with the invitation to listen is one of the ways in which Evagrius consciously imitates the writer of the biblical book of Proverbs. For example, a fresh invitation to listen starts each of the sections of chapters 2–7 of the book of Proverbs. For further examples, see the Index of Scriptural Citations and Allusions.

that have been developed earlier in the text are hinted at again with only one or two proverbs, and all is driving toward the turning point of M 107, after which the theme of the excellence of knowledge sustains itself to the end. A surprise slowly emerges from the arrangement of the proverbs up to the turning point. There are thirty-three proverbs in the text after the new beginning of M 73 until the turning point in M 107. These proverbs are grouped symmetrically around the five proverbs that form a chain on spiritual fathers (M 88 to M 92), such that fourteen proverbs precede the chain and fourteen follow it. It is within this very precise structure that the text unfolds into a number of shorter themes. M 73 urges the monk to listen carefully.

TEMPORAL AND SPIRITUAL STEWARDSHIP (M 74 TO M 76)

The theme that holds these proverbs together is that of the steward of the monastery and care for the goods of the monastery. These are some of the proverbs, along with M 77 and M 78 on the care of the sick, that could lead some observers to claim that the material of *Ad Monachos* has especially to do with monks who live in cenobitic monasteries. However, there is nothing in the advice of these proverbs which suggests that they are applicable only to the cenobitic situation. On the contrary, they all apply well to the semi-anchoritic life as lived at Nitria and Cells, and stories from the *Lausiac History,* the *Apophthegmata Patrum,* and even from Cassian all illustrate that they are proverbs Evagrius could have developed as advice for the semi-anchorites living in the circumstances in which he himself lived, even if this same advice is shared with cenobites.

These three proverbs have a meaning that immediately strikes the reader as referring to the material goods of the monastery and the role of the steward concerning these. The use of the term *steward* in the *Lausiac History* indicates that it has this reference to material things, but it likewise provides evidence that the position is not one limited to cenobitic communities. The story is told of the visit of Melania to Pambo, where she arrives with a gift of a large amount of silver. Pambo receives it rather nonchalantly and immediately hands it to his steward (τῷ οἰκονόμῳ αὐτοῦ) with the directions to distribute it among the more needy brethren (LH 10:3).[73]

So much for the identification of the chain and its applicability to both cenobitic and semi-anchoritic life. It remains necessary, however, to enter into some of the details of how these proverbs might be interpreted in order to understand why proverbs on this theme are placed at this particular point in the text. Evagrius's own use of the term *steward* suggests that these sentences are susceptible of a spiritual interpretation as well. The first evidence is in M 74 itself. It speaks of squeezing the *souls* of the brethren, and in the second line it moves immediately to the issue of remembering injuries, something that is a major block to knowledge (cf. M 13 and 41). Furthermore, the expression in M 76 of a steward distributing is surely a deliberate allusion to scripture. Titus 1:7 speaks of the bishop as God's steward (θεοῦ οἰκονόμον) who "must be above reproach, not headstrong or angry, not a drunkard, not quarrelsome, and not shamelessly greedy." The text goes on in verse 9 to say that he should be "able to encourage with solid teaching and refute those who oppose it." In 1 Corinthians 4:1–2 St. Paul says, "This is how you should think of us: as Christ's servants and stewards of God's mysteries. And further, it is to be expected of stewards that they be trustworthy."[74]

These scriptural verses accord well with the sentiments expressed in M 74 to M 76, especially when interpreted in reference to distributing spiritual goods. In at least two places Evagrius cites the passage from 1 Corinthians and understands the

---

[73] Cassian in *Institutes* V, 40 mentions "abbati Iohanni oeconomo in heremo Sciti." He too is distributing generously. The position of steward is likewise mentioned in Evagrius's circle of monks in the *Coptic Life*, 115; and once again it is a question of generous distribution. In M 75 I have translated μονή as "monastery." The term is derived from μένω and its basic meaning is a dwelling place. Thus, though the term can be used for monastery in a cenobitic sense, it could also be used for individual cells. So G. W. H. Lampe, *A Patristic Greek Lexicon* (Oxford: Clarendon, 1961), 880. Significantly, Palladius uses the term to mean individual cell in LH 7:5. Thus, neither does M 75 exclude a semi-anchoritic application.

[74] The other scriptural verses that are likewise carefully echoed here all lean the interpretation to a spiritual level, without discounting also the material application. See Luke 12:42; 16:8; Acts 2:45; 1 Pet 4:10.

word *steward* to have a spiritual reference. In one of the scholia on Proverbs, Evagrius speaks of a man who has been able to dominate the demons by means of the virtues and then he says, "Such a man becomes a steward of the mysteries of God, giving spiritual knowledge to each of the brothers according to his condition [for receiving it]" (In Prov 17:2 [G 153]). This teaching of others according to their capacity is a frequent theme in Evagrius's writings. One of his terms for the one who does so is οἰκονόμος. In a scholion on a verse from the Psalms he refers again to the passage from 1 Corinthians, basing himself on the vocabulary of the psalm verse, in the same context of appropriately adapting teaching. "The righteous man 'will distribute [οἰκονομήσει] with judgment.' One can use this saying against those who without care or without distinguishing capacities expound the mysteries of holy scripture. Thus Paul says, 'One should regard us, as servants of Christ and stewards of the mysteries of God'" (In Ps 111:5 [PG 12:1572A]). Thus, when M 76 speaks of a just steward distributing as is fitting, on the level of physical needs the meaning is distributing as each has need.[75] On the spiritual level, the distribution is according to one's capacity for knowledge. The adjectives for the steward—*just* and *unjust*—are not merely vague uses of a biblical word. Such distribution is specifically the work of justice as described in one of the chapters of the *Gnostikos*. "The function of justice is to hand over to each one a word adapted to his capacity (τὸ κατ' ἀξίαν ἑκάστου λόγον ἀποδιδόναι),[76] announcing some things obscurely, expressing others enigmatically, showing others things more clearly for the benefit of the more simple" (G 44). Or as is said elsewhere in the same work, "It is said that the steward is an intelligible purse" (G 30).[77]

By drawing attention to this possible spiritual level of proverbs in addition to their more obviously mundane level, I would not wish to distinguish too sharply between them. Actually, presumably even the physical needs of the monastery all have a

---

[75] Cf. Acts 2:45. The distribution spoken of in Acts is expressed with the same word (διαμερίζω) as is used in M 76.

[76] Compare with M 76's πρὸς ἀξίαν.

[77] The theme of proper distribution of teaching is found frequently in the *Gnostikos*.

relation to the monk's ultimate goal of reaching knowledge. A good steward could actually distribute physical things in such a way that he imparts thereby a spiritual teaching.

I have spent some time establishing this point because unless it is noticed the presence of M 74 to M 76 might seem a rather abrupt descent to a merely mundane level after the extended meditation on knowledge in M 63 to M 72. Instead, it flows nicely out of it. It accords well with the introductory proverb of M 73, which urges listening to the father. Indeed, it would be legitimate to think of the good steward as a good father. It leads the meditation toward the chain that anchors this section as its center, M 88 to M 92, on spiritual fathers.

CARE FOR THE SICK (M 77 AND M 78)

These two proverbs flow out of the previous one in that they also deal with some of the practical dimensions of life in the monastic community, be that cenobitic or semi-anchoritic. Care for the sick is reported in the desert literature as an important expression of practical charity. In M 77 Evagrius sees it in this same perspective and lays it alongside another theme important to *Ad Monachos*—not speaking ill of a brother. In the formulation of both lines of the proverb, the issue of knowledge is once again at stake, though the expressions are negative. If the monk neglects these practical forms of charity, he will be utterly destroyed. He will not see the light; that is, he will not enter into knowledge.[78]

In teaching thus, Evagrius stands in the line of his own great teachers in the desert. Macarius the Great, so renowned as a model of the gnostic life, left a firm impression of the importance of care for the sick. The story was told of his remarkable charity in satisfying the rather inappropriate desires of a sick brother. The brother had mentioned that some sherbet would taste good to him. No sooner had the sick brother said that than

---

[78] Light is an image for knowledge very frequently found in Evagrius's writings. For a study of this with many references to Evagrius's own writings, see Bunge, *Briefe*, 85–93.

Macarius set off all the way to Alexandria to fetch him some! (Macarius 8).[79] Evagrius's own monastic training was based on examples of this quality. He knew that love for the brethren had so indispensable a role to play in coming to knowledge that he could say, "Better a worldly man serving a brother in sickness than an anchorite not pitying his neighbor." Once again, then, in the unfolding proverbs of *Ad Monachos* the connection between love and knowledge is made. When the monk makes the effort to love, knowledge will be the reward. As Evagrius says in another place, playing, it seems, on a double (physical and spiritual) understanding of sickness and health, "Without knowing it the one curing others by (the power of) the Lord also heals himself, for the medicine which the knower applies cures his neighbor insofar as is possible, but it cures him necessarily" (G 33).[80]

Though M 77 and M 78 certainly belong together as having to do with the sick, it is to be observed that there are several firm verbal links with the preceding chain. The word *brother* or *brothers* occurs in M 74, 77, and 78. The theme of being careless or not caring (ἀμελέω) occurs in M 75 and M 77, and it will occur again in M 79.[81]

---

[79] For other stories of the importance of care of the sick, see Arsenius 20 and the story of Apollonius in LH 13. In this latter, his care for the sick is called his form of ἄσκησις. It is said to have worked for the good of his soul.

[80] It seems to me important to maintain both the physical and spiritual levels of understanding care for the sick both in M 77 and in G 33, even if in the former the most obvious meaning concerns the physically sick, while in the latter it concerns the spiritually sick. To insist, as does Guillaumont in SC 354, 150, on only one or the other possible meaning is to fail to catch the deep correspondence Evagrius sees between acts of charity carried out on the physical plane and the same on a spiritual plane. Evagrius never chooses his images arbitrarily. If he speaks of "medicine" for the spiritually "sick," it is because physical sickness reveals (corresponds to) something about the nature of the fallen condition of the mind. Charity in regard to the physical reveals something about charity in regard to the spiritual. By means of the needs of the physical, one discovers the needs of the spiritual. It is this correspondence which the wisdom literature of the scriptures explores, which surely explains in part why Evagrius imitates it. For more on these correspondences and wisdom literature influencing Evagrius, see below, Part Three, Stage One: Proverbs in Human Culture and the Bible.

[81] Cf. the use of the same term in M 37. Caring for the sick is also probably an indirect way in which the monks can help each other in the fight against the demon of gluttony, who, among other things, suggests to the monk that if he does not eat enough, he will grow sick and no one will take care of him. See TP 7.

PRUDENCE, WANDERING, AND GLUTTONY (M 79 TO M 83)

Several little chains and the way in which their themes overlap are viewed together here. M 79 and M 80 are held together by the theme of prudence. In M 79 prudence is defined by contrast with the foolish over the issue of being careless or not, thus linking up with the theme of carelessness already observed in M 75 and M 77. The expression "instruments of his craft" is evidence once again of the precision with which Evagrius uses his language. Prudence has a very specific role, that of "directing the strategy against the enemy powers [i.e., the demons]" (TP 89). This involves observing closely how the demons operate. "If a monk would like to know the cruel demons through experience and to understand the state of their craft [τῆς αὐτῶν τέχνης ἑξίν λαβεῖν], then let him observe his thoughts [τηρείτω τοὺς λογισμούς]" (TP 50). The monk who observes his thoughts and rules over his evil thoughts by his life of virtue is employing the instruments of his own craft against the craft of the demons.[82]

In M 80 prudence is connected with going out from one's cell, and this is developed (without further specific mention of prudence) in M 81. Thus M 80 is the second of two proverbs on prudence and the first of two proverbs on wandering. The weave of the proverbs is showing a fine attention to detail! The issue of wandering is to be connected with the theme already sounded in the chain on listlessness, where we saw that Evagrius's principal advice for the monk afflicted by this demon was that he should stay in his cell.[83]

The same polyvalence noted above between a literal understanding of the proverbs in this section and a more spiritual understanding can also be observed in these proverbs on wandering. Certainly Evagrius is speaking of the importance of the monk staying in his cell. But the mind of the monk can wander as well, and these proverbs likewise warn against that. The wan-

---

[82] Compare also τηρείτω τοὺς λογισμούς of TP 50 with ὁ δὲ φρόνιμος ἐπιμελήσεται αὐτῶν (i.e., the instruments of his craft) of M 79.

[83] The identification of M 81's wandering monk (Κυκλευτὴς μοναχὸς) with the problems in the area of listlessness is secured by 8 Spirits 13, a chapter on listlessness in which Evagrius speaks of the Κυκλευτὴς μοναχὸς. In the same passage he also mentions problems with women, as is suggested in M 83. See PG 79:1160A.

dering monk is said to be pursuing false sayings, that is, a false teaching.[84] Elsewhere Evagrius says, "The mind begins to wander [κυκλεύει γὰρ ὁ νοῦς] when it is immersed in the passions . . . and it stops wandering when it becomes passionless" (KG I, 85).[85] Wandering into the passions on the physical level produces wandering in the mind.

M 82 introduces a new theme into the present development: the concern with clothing and food. In M 83 the topic flips back again to wandering. This arrangement bears out my remark that the impression created by the flow of proverbs here is that they are at once loosely joined and carefully combined. This concern with clothing and food is but briefly sounded here, yet it has already sounded before, especially in the chain that concerned eating and the true feast (M 38–44). And the connection between intemperance and chastity was made in M 7.

M 83 develops the theme of leaving the cell around the specific topic of what to do about meeting women. The monk should not draw near them or linger in conversation with them.[86] In one of his letters Evagrius advises his correspondent of the way the demon of fornication observes a monk, watching for his weak point. His remarks there show that for Evagrius there is a definite connection between the thoughts expressed in M 82 and 83, for he notes that this demon will watch a monk closely when he meets a woman to see if the meeting is merely happenstance or if it was somehow arranged under some pretext. The same demon will examine the monk's clothing, to see if he tends to be well dressed or not (cf. Lt 16:3).[87]

A battle with a demon is always a battle with thoughts, and this special Evagrian term occurs again in M 82's expression of "shepherding shameful thoughts." For Evagrius "the mind is a

---

[84] Compare M 81's ῥήσεις ψευδεῖς with M 1's ῥήσεις Χριστοῦ.

[85] Translated from the Greek in Muyldermans, *A travers la tradition manuscrite*, 50.

[86] On the significance of the word *linger* (χρονίζειν), see n. 56 above.

[87] This is wisdom about the demon that Evagrius probably learned from personal experience. Evagrius's amorous affair in the city of Constantinople is well known, but he fell a second time during his stay in Jerusalem. Palladius remarks that this return to his old way of life involved a change of clothes and a change in the way he spoke; he became intoxicated with vainglory; see LH 38:8.

shepherd and the sheep are the concupiscible impressions that are in it, and if he [the shepherd] nourishes these [impressions], then 'he dishonors God by transgressing his law.' For passionate thoughts developed by use of the body—this is the dissoluteness of the soul" (In Prov 28:7 [G 344]).[88]

GENTLENESS (M 84 TO M 87)

The theme of caring for the brothers and not speaking ill of them has been recently sounded in the proverbs from M 74 to M 78. Now in M 84 and 85 a couplet is created using the basic vocabulary that usually expresses this issue for Evagrius. The proverbs are constructed around the closely associated terms of long-suffering and gentleness (cf. M 34, 35 and 98, 99), and in both proverbs these words are used as adjectives for the word *monk*. Each of the proverbs is designed with antithetical formulations between the first and second lines. Thus, in M 84 there is an antithesis between long-suffering and the one who provokes. The verbs *love* and *hate* shape the antithesis with even sharper clarity. In M 85 the antithesis of the gentle monk is the rash one, and the verbs in this proverb likewise draw the contrasts sharply: the Lord *loves* the gentle monk and *banishes* the rash one. Between the two proverbs there is the movement from the monk being loved by his brothers to the monk being loved by the Lord.

M 87 can be considered to be moving in the same vein of gentleness, though the word itself is not mentioned in that proverb. However, before readers arrive at M 87, they are first given a different theme for meditation in M 86. With its message about sluggishness and sleepiness it may seem another instance of a free-standing proverb that intrudes into the orderly grouping of several other proverbs that clearly share themes. I repeat my position that each proverb can and deserves to be meditated upon singly and in its own right. Yet once again when we notice the weave of themes through each other, the single proverbs do yield a richer meditation. M 86 is a case in point.

---

[88] Compare In Prov 29:3 (G 358B): "The good shepherd is the mind which has passionless thoughts, and the bad shepherd is the mind that has passionate thoughts." The image of the mind as shepherd is more extensively developed in Thoughts 17.

The sluggish and sleepy monk is a monk afflicted by the demon of listlessness.[89] This theme was seen to be operative also in the formulations of M 80, 81, and 83. So without specific mention of the demon's name, some angle of listlessness has been moving through the text for some time; it continues here in M 86; and it will keep moving, as it shows up again in M 93. It has already been observed that listlessness and sadness are "partners and schoolmates." In this way M 86 bends rather nicely into the first line of M 87, which speaks of a brother being sad. The proverb urges helping such a brother, sharing his pain. Among his many tricks, the demon of listlessness inspires the thought that "love has disappeared from among the brothers" (TP 12). M 87 and M 84 and 85 show that this demon can be chased away for others by gentleness.[90] In its mention of a great treasure in heaven, M 87 connects once again the issue of gentleness and knowledge.[91] So various angles of listlessness have been moving in the text now and have been alternating with various angles on care for the brothers.[92]

THE SPIRITUAL FATHER (M 88 TO M 92)

This is a chain about the spiritual father and the brotherhood that is created around him. The theme of father has been noted as being positioned at key points in the text, in M 2 as part of the introduction to the whole and in M 73 with a new invita-

---

[89] See 8 Spirits 14, Ἀκηδιαστὴς μοναχὸς, ὀκνηρὸς εἰς προσευχὴν (PG 79: 1160B). The same passage speaks of the way in which sleep afflicts the monk under the influence of this demon. Evagrius's comments on sluggishness in In Prov 18:8 (G 177) and In Prov 22:13 (G 242) could also be compared, where in both cases the sluggish [monk] is afraid before the attacks of the demons. In the description of listlessness in TP 12, the demon convinces the monk to "leave his cell and flee the stadium." The biblical text Prov 22:13 is quite close in language to M 86.

[90] Lt 50 speaks of how a kindness done for Evagrius chased listlessness away from him. The prologue to the *Chapters on Prayer* (also cast in the form of a letter) expresses a similar sentiment.

[91] For other instances of the term *treasure* associated with knowledge, see M 25 and M 122, both of which also concern love. See also Lt 47:1 and Lt 61 with notes by Bunge in *Briefe*, 365, 378.

[92] For a description of Evagrius's own concern for the brothers, particularly for those who are troubled, see the *Coptic Life*, 114–15.

tion to listen following the long chain on the relation between *praktikē* and knowledge.[93] Now for the first time in the text the theme is developed in a chain.

The chain is held together by strong verbal links. The word *father* is contained in each of the five. In each there is some expression, either negatively or positively expressed, that concerns following the father. Thus, the monk should not quit guard over the father's words (M 88); he should not seek excuses (M 89), nor lend his ear to contrary words (M 90). He should obey the father (M 91) and keep his words (M 92). M 88 and M 89 in their talk of children and brothers show that a brotherhood is created around a father.[94]

The proverbs indicate that there is a close association between the father and the Lord himself. In M 88 the Lord destroys the one who does not keep guard over the words of the father. In M 90 the Lord becomes angry at someone who does not follow the father, and he rubs his name out of the book of the living; that is, he does not grant him the gift of knowledge.[95] Finally, the last proverb of the chain puts the commands of the Lord and the words of the fathers in tight parallel.[96]

This notion of the father's commands really being the Lord's is closely associated in Evagrius with the idea of brotherhood. Understanding this relationship helps not only to grasp the proverbs of this chain but also to see that a chain on fathers is

[93] The term was also noticed at M 81.

[94] This chain is viewed from the perspective of the disciple. Evagrius also gives advice to those qualified to be fathers in the *Gnostikos* and in *Masters and Disciples*. Especially interesting in terms of the present chain is G 32, which speaks of the need for the father to remain calm in the face of being run down by others. There is a sense of personal experience standing behind this, especially in the last phrase, "even if you don't want to" (cf. KG III, 90).

[95] For this interpretation of "book of the living," see In Ps 68:29: "The book of the living is the knowledge of God" (PG 12:1517B).

[96] This should be compared with M 1 and the relationship established there between *reasons of God*, *sayings of Christ*, and *words of the wise*. That the commands of the Lord have knowledge as their aim Evagrius says explicitly in In Prov 2:9 (G 21) and In Prov 9:10a (G 109). Μακάριος in M 92 also means to allude to knowledge, as does its use in M 21, following the meaning given to it in TP Prologue 8, where it is the term for the highest form of knowledge at the end of a long list of virtues. Cf. Prayer 118–23.

appropriately fitted in among the themes in this part of the text. The various concerns of gentleness that have been noted in the immediate vicinity all have to do with keeping unity in a brotherhood.[97] But brothers are brothers in the first place because they have a common father, and for Evagrius this common father is ultimately Christ himself. The spiritual father acts in his name. The relationship between brotherly accord and Christ's fatherhood is nicely expressed in Evagrius's comment on a text from the book of Proverbs. The biblical text reads, "An unjust witness kindles falsehoods, and brings on quarrels between the brethren." Evagrius comments,

> Brothers are those who have the grace of adoptive sonship (Rom 8:15) and who depend upon the same father, namely, Christ. They are the ones whom "the witness of injustice" tries to divide by throwing into their midst agitations and "quarrels." I think the word "kindles" has been used because of the passionate thoughts which inflame the irascible [part of the soul] toward anger and hatred and because of those which inflame the concupiscible [part of the soul] to shameful actions. (In Prov 6:19 [G 78])[98]

This text shows clearly that monks familiar with this kind of teaching would likely catch the significance of a chain on fathers standing in the midst of proverbs that warn against remembering injuries or provoking brothers or neglecting the sick or decorating garments and filling the stomach (referring to the concupiscible). Not to follow the father is just one more item in the list of things that could divide the brethren among themselves and thus keep them from finding their names in the book of the living, keep them from knowledge itself. Everything in the meditation keeps moving toward knowledge. Yet the text also keeps insisting that knowledge depends on love. The present chain and its placement in the whole show that both love and knowledge depend on having a father and on following his commands.

---

[97] Note how frequently the word *brother* has been used in the proverbs in question: M 74, 77, 78, 84, 87, and now M 89. To this can be added the word *children* in M 88. Amidst all this talk about brothers, the text turns to what holds the brothers together, that is, a father. It should be remembered that also in M 1 and M 2 the talk was of children, father, and sons.

[98] This same theme occurs with some frequency in the *Scholia on Proverbs* and in the *Scholia on Psalms*. See the note and references in Géhin, SC 340, 179.

Reprise (M 73 to M 92)

M 73 offered a fresh invitation to listen to the words of the father, and as such it signaled a new movement in the text. The previous long and intricate chain (M 63 to M 72) was a sort of climax in the text to that point. Then, imitating the invitations to listen by which new movements in the biblical book of Proverbs are begun, Evagrius himself makes a kind of new beginning.

The proverbs in this new section were seen to have something about them that enabled them to stand alone. Indeed, a rapid view of the text would leave a reader with the impression that there is really very little order or grouping of the proverbs in question. However, a closer examination reveals considerable care in the arrangement. Evagrius has linked them together in subtle but very firm ways, and in these proverbs, more so than previously, an overlapping of themes is observed.

Thus M 74 to M 76 dealt with stewardship in the monastic community, but these proverbs also connected stewardship with the issue of relation among the brothers and even with spiritual fatherhood. M 78 and M 79 spoke of a special dimension of care for the brothers, namely, care of the sick. M 79 to M 83 represented an interlacing of prudence, wandering, and issues of food and clothing. Concern with listlessness was seen to underlie these, and M 81 keeps the theme of father (begun in M 73) alive in the movement.[99] The issue of gentleness again appears in M 84 to M 87. It has appeared in many ways now throughout the text, and it will continue to the very end. Within this chain, the theme of listlessness remained present in M 86.

All of this led up to a tightly constructed chain on the spiritual father and the importance of heeding his teachings. The father's commands lead the monk to knowledge, but they do this by establishing a brotherhood in which love, the door to knowledge, must be ever more firmly established.

In the proverbs that remain up to the turning point in the text at M 107, the relation of one to the other continues in the

---

[99] If one takes proverbs M 74 to M 87 (i.e., the fourteen proverbs that precede the developed chain on fathers), then M 81 stands at the midway point in the development.

same style we have observed in this section. That is to say, they are short chains of two and three members with overlapping themes. However, stopping at this point for a reprise has not been arbitrary. We stop after the five-member chain on the father, which is surrounded by fourteen proverbs preceding it and fourteen following it. The structure itself of the text underscores the points that the proverbs themselves are making, namely, that a spiritual father must stand at the center of the monk's journey through the virtues as he makes his way toward knowledge.

SLUGGISHNESS AND GUARDING THE TONGUE (M 93 TO M 95)

M 93 is concerned with listlessness, and as such it continues a theme that occurs periodically in this part of the text. The proverb warns that the sluggish monk may well give up his whole monastic life, symbolized in his laying the habit aside.[100]

The next two proverbs form a couplet around the theme of the tongue, but M 94 with its emphasis on guarding the tongue and keeping the heart can also be considered good advice to a sluggish monk. The language of M 94 is strongly biblical.[101] Since for Evagrius the biblical language is filled with many levels of meaning, it is by means of this language that with just a few short words, he is able to make a firm and precise connection with knowledge. As the meditation moves toward the turning point at M 107, there are increasing references to knowledge. In order to observe at what these increasing references aim, it is worth establishing more precisely how Evagrius understands knowledge in the advice that he delivers in M 94.

Guarding the tongue probably means to refer to more than just keeping control over one's speech. Evagrius explains that *tongue* is a biblical code word for the soul (In Prov 25:26 [G 317]),[102] and thus the proverb can suggest to the monk familiar

---

[100] In TP Prologue, lines 45–46, the habit is called a symbol of the monastic life and its various virtues. Thus, to lay it aside would be to lay aside the virtues it symbolizes, that is, to give up the struggle, which is precisely what the demon of listlessness encourages the monk to do.

[101] See Index to Scriptural Citations and Allusions.

[102] That Evagrius rather automatically understands the tongue to refer to

with this use of biblical language that the whole soul is to be guarded. *Ways* refers to the monastic life, much as the word *habit* did in the previous sentence.[103] Thus the first line of M 94 is meant to be the direct antidote to the danger that the sluggishness of M 93 posed to the whole monastic life. The second line of M 94 directs the reader's attention to knowledge. Though the word *heart* is a biblical code word that generally refers to the soul (In Prov 25:26 [G 317]), in this proverb it probably refers to the mind.[104] The phrase "keep his heart" is a direct quotation of an expression found in Proverbs 4:23, a text Evagrius cites in the *Kephalaia Gnostica* in a context that shows how keeping the heart is related to knowledge. He says, "Many passions are hidden in our souls, which are revealed by the sharpness of the temptations when these passions slip out of us. So, it is necessary 'to keep the heart with the utmost care' (Prov 4:23), lest when the object [for which we have a passion] appears, we be won over to the passion, carried off suddenly by demons and do something abhorrent to God" (KG VI, 52).[105] This is to lose control of the mind for what it is meant to focus on, namely, knowledge.[106]

M 95 stays with the image of the tongue and relates it to the agitation of brothers.[107] Agitating the brothers is opposed to another expression for the realm of knowledge, bringing stillness (ἡσυχία). Ἡσυχία is a technical term for Evagrius, used in one of

---

the soul is shown in his comment on Prov 18:21, where he explains the text "Life and death are in the power of the tongue" by simply saying, "Here he says that the soul is susceptible of life and death" (In Prov 18:21 [G 186]).

[103] Cf. In Prov 4:10 (G 45), where in commenting on the biblical expression "many ways," Evagrius says, "These many ways lead to the one way of him who said, 'I am the way.' For by 'many ways' he means the virtues which lead to the knowledge of Christ." For other instances of *way* referring specifically to the monastic life, see In Ps 94:11 (1): "The ways of the Lord are the virtues of *praktikē*, which lead into the Kingdom of heaven" (PG 12:1556B). See also In Prov 6:8 (G 72); TP 91; Lt 16:1; 17:1.

[104] For other examples of heart meaning mind, see KG VI, 52, 84, 87. This is probably also its sense in M 117.

[105] Translated from the Greek in Hausherr, "Nouveaux fragments," 231.

[106] See also Lt 11:3 for a charming and lengthier description of what it means to keep the heart. There the monk is to question each and every thought that comes into his mind to see if it be friend or foe.

[107] This is now the seventh mention of brothers since M 74.

two ways. First, he considers it a precondition for the monastic life. Stillness is required precisely so that, once removed from people and objects, the movements and passions of the monk's mind may be set in motion and war with the thoughts begun.[108] Yet at other times he associates it closely with passionlessness, the goal of *praktikē,* and with the readiness of the mind for knowledge. A text from the *Praktikos* helps us to see that the "stillness" of M 95 closely parallels the keeping of the heart in M 94. Evagrius says, "It is a sure sign of passionlessness when the mind begins to see its own proper light and when it remains still [νοῦς . . . διαμένων ἥσυχος] before the visions seen in sleep and when it looks at objects indifferently" (TP 64).[109]

Thus, three simple proverbs have unfolded into insights that lead in many directions. The remedy for the threat that listlessness poses to the whole monastic life is guarding the whole soul, which especially includes guarding the tongue. This is a prerequisite for keeping the mind still for knowledge. Anyone who agitates the brothers cannot hope to enter into this knowledge or lead others there.

TEMPERANCE AND GENTLENESS INTERTWINED (M 96 TO M 104)

The proverbs succeed each other here in several sets that alternately treat temperance and gentleness. M 96 and M 97 are concerned with temperance; M 98 to M 100 with gentleness. M 101 to M 103 return to temperance, and M 104 comes back to the theme of gentleness. This is the second time in the text that gentleness and temperance have been joined in intertwining chains. It was noticed that M 4, 6 and 7, and M 11 were intertwined with themes of love and gentleness developed from M 3 to at least M

---

[108] Evagrius devotes an entire work to explaining these preconditions in his treatise the *Bases of the Monastic Life.*

[109] "It looks at objects indifferently" (λεῖος βλέπων τὰ πράγματα) should be compared with the expression in KG VI, 52, cited just above, "lest when the object appears" (μήποτε παραφανέντος ἐκείνου τοῦ πράγματος). See also In Prov 1:33 (G 17), "The passionless one lives in stillness, unafraid of any evil thought." Likewise M 98, "irascibility is still."

15. A similar intertwining occurs in the text now, and it is significant that this is the last theme developed before the text takes a major turn at M 107 to the various levels of knowledge. Evagrius is offering a clue here to how the monk himself can hope to pass a turning point in his own spiritual journey and enter into knowledge. Yes, one will enter knowledge by means of the temperance which is so characteristic of monastic asceticism, but not unless this temperance is accompanied by gentleness and love.

M 96 introduces the theme of temperance by noting that of itself it is not enough: "He who has relied on his temperance will fall." The second line of the proverb shores up the sentiment with the gospel authority of the words of the Lord himself: "He who humbles himself will be exalted" (Matt 23:12; 18:4; Luke 14:11; 18:14). That point having been made about relying on temperance, M 97 says that temperance is nonetheless extremely important. It leads to purity, the goal of *praktikē*;[110] it means that "the Spirit of the Lord will come over you," that is, that one is led into knowledge (cf. M 115).[111]

M 98 to M 100 can be considered a little chain on the irascible and gentleness. Each proverb mentions either the irascible or rashness. Each speaks of the opposite, either as long-suffering, gentleness, or humiliation of the irascible. Concern with the irascible is often the way Evagrius raises his concern about not relying on temperance alone, as he is doing at this point in *Ad Monachos*. It is worth citing again his plea: "Let no one, I beg you, devote himself only to temperance. For not with only one stone is a house built, nor with only one brick is a house constructed. An

---

[110] This is so consistently and frequently Evagrius's understanding of purity that reference to it is not necessary. Let it suffice here simply to note the theme in *Ad Monachos*: M 8, 44, 65, 97, 107, 131, 133. *Puritas cordis* is how Cassian, who knows Evagrius well and in many ways reproduces his system, renders in Latin the controversial ἀπάθεια. For more on this, see Marsili, *Giovanni Cassiano ed Evagrio Pontico,* 114–15; J. Driscoll "*Apatheia* and Purity of Heart in Evagrius Ponticus," in *Purity of Heart in Early Ascetic and Monastic Literature,* ed. H. A. Luckman and L. Kulzer (Collegeville, 1999), 141–59.

[111] On Evagrius's precise and consistent use of the word *spiritual* to refer to the Holy Spirit and the Holy Spirit as the revealer of knowledge, see Bunge, *Geistliche Vaterschaft,* 37–38, and "The 'Spiritual Prayer,'" 194–98.

irascible temperate person is a dried up tree, fruitless, twice dead, uprooted" (Lt 27:3).[112]

M 99 is the middle member of this three-member chain, and it directly associates gentleness with knowledge. This placement means to say that the association of these two is the key point to the whole development of this part of the text.[113]

The proverbs from M 101 to M 103 swing the meditation back once again to the issue of temperance. A monk's interest in banquets, as mentioned in M 101, is typical of the type of attack the demons make on the concupiscible part of the soul (cf. TP 54). M 102 opposes two practices to the thought of a banquet: weighing one's bread and drinking water by measure. This assures that the demon of fornication will flee the monk. The connection between temperance and the demon of fornication was made in M 7 as part of the other chain that wove temperance and gentleness together. The idea is a commonplace in Evagrian

---

[112] Translated from a Greek fragment found in C. Guillaumont, "Fragments grecs," 220, lines 65–67. It seems worthwhile to quote the passage again in order to draw attention to the way in which Evagrius is concerned that a quieting of the irascible must accompany temperance. This theme is frequently insisted upon in the writings of Evagrius, particularly in his letters. This particular letter goes on to say that temperance controls the body, but gentleness makes the mind into a seer (Lt 27:4). Lt 28:1 speaks of temperance together with long-suffering and love. Lt 52:5–6 speaks of how fasting alone is not sufficient for knowledge, and then speaks of the importance of concentrating on ridding the soul of a number of other evil thoughts, including memory of injury and anger. Lt 56:5 is quite strong: "Accept no temperance that chases away gentleness" (μηδὲ ἀποδέχου ἐγκράτειαν, διωκομένης πραότητος). Translated from a Greek fragment found in C. Guillaumont, "Fragments grecs," 218, lines 11–12. See also TP 38, which speaks the importance of temperance and love going together.

[113] It was noted above that in the proverbs extending from M 74 to M 106, fourteen proverbs precede the chain on fathers (M 88–92) and fourteen follow it. The center point of the first set of fourteen is M 81, a proverb on the importance of the father. In the second set of fourteen (M 93–106) M 99's statement about knowledge born from gentleness is the midway point. It can further be observed that these three proverbs constructed on the contrast between gentleness and irascibility echo both in content and in placement three proverbs found earlier in the text which did the same, M 34, 35, and 36. M 97, 98, and 99 are roughly equidistant from the end as are M 34, 35, and 36 from the beginning. In both chains the contrast is between irascible and gentle. In both the center member makes an explicit connection with knowledge.

teaching, and he himself notes that it is something he had learned from Macarius of Alexandria.[114]

M 103 also nicely manages to encapsulate another dimension of Evagrius's teaching on temperance. A certain letting up of the rigors of asceticism of the body can be granted to the old and the sick. There comes a point in the life of *praktikē* when the passions of the body no longer trouble the monk, that is, when fleshly appetites no longer agitate the concupiscible part of the soul. This is a first major hurdle in *praktikē*. On the other hand, the passions of the soul, which afflict the irascible part, require a much longer struggle. In the *Praktikos* Evagrius explains, "Those [demons] which rule over the passions of the soul last until death, while those who rule the passions of the body depart more quickly" (TP 36). "The irascible part [of the soul] has need of more remedies than the concupiscible" (TP 38). It is the long-lasting power of the troubled irascible that causes Evagrius to keep coming back to the theme of gentleness when he talks about temperance. It may be expected that an old monk would be temperate, but he will still need to be exhorted to gentleness. Generally a young monk will need to be exhorted to both, though temperance is a starting point for the young. Thus, "Exhort the old to master the irascible and the young to master the stomach" (G 31).[115] Yet if M 103 is about temperance, it is a proverb that also manages to touch on the irascible in its advice to carry food to the sick.[116]

M 104 focuses squarely on the issue of the irascible and gen-

---

[114] See TP 94, where Evagrius quotes Macarius in words close to M 102. The phrase in question is τὸν μὲν γὰρ ἄρτον μου ἤσθιον σταθμῷ, τὸ δὲ ὕδωρ ἔπινον μέτρῳ . . . . Evagrius develops this in TP 16, 17, where in SC 171, 543–45 Guillaumont comments at length on the teaching in Evagrius and in other monastic teachers. To the texts cited there could be added In Prov 21:19 (G 227) and In Prov 31:27 (G 380). In Thoughts 43 temperance in bread and water is connected with memory of injury and the desire for pure prayer.

[115] M 103 is well meditated on with M 111 and 112.

[116] In TP 91 Evagrius cites a monk who spoke of how "a dry and regular diet quickly" leads the monk "into the harbor of passionlessness." This is followed by telling how this same advice once freed a brother from nighttime fantasies (see M 11 for the connection between temperance and such fantasies) by "bidding him serve the sick with fasting." For, "nothing extinguishes such passions like mercy does."

tleness again, not by specific mention of these but by a warning against tripping a brother or rejoicing over his fall. This is one of many proverbs in the collection that is to be associated with the text's emphasis on gentleness. The association is established by warnings against attitudes and ways of acting that are inimical to the spirit of love and gentleness.[117] In M 104 the word *brother* is used for the eighth time in the section from M 74 to M 106. We could say that *father* is the center of this section while *brother* is a thread woven throughout. This concentrated used of the term *brother* is peculiar to this part of the text.[118]

Finally, it should be noted how many allusions there are to the realm of knowledge in these proverbs which interweave temperance and gentleness. Attention has already been drawn to these allusions in the couplet preceding this section, M 94 and M 95. The reference to knowledge in M 96 is the notion of being exalted. M 97 speaks of being overshadowed by the Spirit. M 98 speaks of irascibility being still. M 99 specifically mentions knowledge. M 100 speaks of raising up the heart.

PRUDENCE, PASSIONLESSNESS, RESCUE FROM DARKNESS
(M 105 AND M 106)

These two proverbs complete what I have called a major movement of the text, namely, various interrelated expressions for *praktikē* and its relation to knowledge. Each of these two proverbs expresses with simple bluntness the two opposing ways that a monk can move in life: toward virtue or toward vice. In M 105 it is the prudent monk (i.e., the monk who has "directed successful strategies against the demons" [cf. TP 89]) who will acquire the virtues, summarized in the expression that denotes the goal of *praktikē,* passionlessness.[119] The imprudent one will draw up evils. In M 106 the Lord blinds the wicked but rescues the simple from darkness.

---

[117] Other proverbs that should be similarly associated are M 8, 9, 16, 42, 74, 75, 76, 77, 78, 84, 113, 114, 127.

[118] There are only two other instances: M 15 and M 42.

[119] This same idea was expressed in the important chain that stands in the center of the text. See M 69, "Prudence gives birth to passionlessness."

Both proverbs prepare for the turning point of M 107 in a way that is perhaps inauspicious but nonetheless precisely formulated according to Evagrius's understanding of what is necessary to reach knowledge. Prudence is virtue in the rational part of the soul. It must be established there for the mind to turn itself to knowledge, for it is the rational part of the soul that is used for knowledge. But this part cannot turn toward knowledge unless the other parts are passionless. Then the mind turns toward knowledge by means of another virtue in the rational part of the soul, wisdom.

The image of being either blind or rescued from darkness is likewise suitable to knowledge as Evagrius conceives it. Virtues blind the mind to evil and prepare it to see. "Both virtues and vices make the mind blind: virtues so that it does not see vices, vices so that it does not see virtues" (TP 62).[120] M 106 speaks only of the kind of blindness that wickedness brings. Evagrius speaks similarly in a scholion on Proverbs that is likewise connected with prudence. "For it is said . . . 'He who acquires prudence loves himself (Prov 19:8).' But the impious prevent this acquisition when they persuade the just to do something abhorrent to God, so that blinded by the sin, the mind fall from its holy acquisitions" (In Prov 1:12 [G 8]).[121]

Being rescued from darkness, of which M 106 speaks, is the Lord's doing. It is entering into knowledge. As the next proverb begins the whole text's increasing emphasis on knowledge, it does so with a beautiful image of light: the morning star in heaven. It is this morning star which rescues from darkness.

---

[120] See Guillaumont's commentary in SC 171, 644–45 for Evagrius on the vices that blind the mind. TP 62 initiates a series of chapters that treat of spiritual blindness viewed in the favorable understanding of the term as defined in TP 62.

[121] The expression "something abhorrent to God (τι τῶν ἀπηγορευμένων παρὰ θεῷ) was seen in a context similarly involving knowledge in KG VI, 52, cited above, p. 119. For another example of the image of sin blinding the intellect and causing it to fall, see the expression in TP 24, ". . . so that the mind, being darkened and falling from knowledge, become a traitor to the virtues." Evagrius quotes the Lord himself as his authority for interpreting *eye* to mean *mind*. "Christ in the gospels names the soul 'body,' when he says, 'The lamp of the body is the eye (Matt 6:22),' calling the mind a lamp, for it is made for receiving knowledge" (In Prov 11:17 [G 127]).

Before turning to that proverb—and by means of it into further meditations on knowledge—another reprise will help us to collect and see in a glance how the text has unfolded to this point.

REPRISE (M 93 TO M 106)

This reprise collects the fourteen proverbs that follow the chain on the spiritual father and the brotherhood that is created around him (M 88–92). The first three proverbs in this section (M 93–95) suggested the importance of keeping guard over the whole of one's monastic practices and of not agitating the brothers. Then there followed an interlacing of chains on temperance and gentleness (M 96–104), the development concluding with proverbs mentioning prudence, passionlessness, and the image of being rescued from darkness as a metaphor for knowledge.

The understanding of what is developed in these proverbs can be more tightly focused by the observation that all of them are being unfolded by means of an interlacing of virtues in the three parts of the soul as Evagrius conceives these. For Evagrius, passions in the concupiscible and irascible parts have to be defeated for virtue to be established in the rational part. An image of this fact is created in the arrangement of the proverbs here. M 94 and M 95, especially in the mention of agitating the brothers, belong to the irascible. M 96 and M 97 on the issues of the stomach and sleep (i.e., temperance) belong to the concupiscible. M 98 to M 100 return to the irascible and do so with specific mention of it and of the most important virtue in that part of the soul, gentleness. M 101 to M 103 flow back to the concupiscible. M 104 returns to the irascible. This movement back and forth between these two parts of the soul creates an image of what virtues must be established there for the rational part of the soul to turn its attention to knowledge. M 105 with its mention of passionlessness marks the end of this particular development by speaking of that condition being at last established. With its mention of prudence it introduces a technical term for virtue in the rational part of the soul. M 106, with negative and positive expressions, turns toward the vision of knowledge. If the proverbs of this section have dwelt especially on the concupiscible and irascible parts, the section concludes with mention of the rational part and will be followed by more proverbs concerned with the rational part. The concern now will increasingly be that of knowledge. The only issues of *praktikē* that will continue to receive mention in this focus on knowledge are those that concern gentleness and love.

Second Block: Levels of Knowledge Leading to the Trinity (M 107 to M 136)

Beginning with M 107 the proverbs of *Ad Monachos* sustain a concern with knowledge which carries through to the very end of the text. The issue of knowledge has been present from the start, but heretofore in the text it was joined to other issues of *praktikē*; it was a part of other chains; it was something pointed toward. Now knowledge itself (and various expressions for its various levels) is the main structural component of the chains. We have noticed in the structuring of previous portions of the text that the tightness of the identified chains has tended to vary from "quite tight" to "fairly loose," with intermediary levels between these two poles. The same can be said for this portion of the text. Some of the proverbs are extraordinarily suggestive and beautiful. In their individual power they bear out the importance of taking them one at a time and meditating on them one at a time. Yet here too, as before, there is a richer meaning that emerges when the placement of the proverbs is noticed and meditated upon as well. Continuing the thrust of this part of the present study, the comments that follow focus on this aspect of the text, attempting to determine the movement of the whole.

I have called M 107 a turning point. This is a strong expression. Is it justified for describing what happens at M 107? Again, at first glance, perhaps not. Certainly the structure at this point in the text is not so immediately evident as in a more tightly constructed chain, for example, M 63 to M 72. M 107 is a seemingly simple (if slightly more poetic than usual) proverb of only two lines which perhaps comes upon a reader by surprise. Yet something happens in the text here for the careful reader after which the flavor of the whole is never quite the same. This is true not least of all for the extraordinary range of meditation that M 107 itself evokes.[122] Yet it is but the first of a number of rich and beautiful meditations.

Perhaps the image of a musical symphony can help us to understand what happens in the text at this point. M 107 is like some fine, remarkable, "quick" moment (turn) in the symphony, after which it is never quite the same, for a new energy has come into the piece which sustains it to the end. To be sure, the shift is subtle—or, better said, gentle. Yet it is nonetheless firm for all that. It is like a sound, an instrument, which enters and is heard before it is noticed entering. Yet once it is there and noticed, it drives the piece forward. Some themes already heard are heard again, but they are heard in a new way, with new, richer variations of the theme. There are some intense moments of remarkable beauty and complexity (M 118–20, 133, 135), some others of extreme tension and even fear (M 123–31, especially 126). Yet something is driving the whole piece forward toward its climax, and the listener is caught up in the drive. Gentleness, love, and right doctrine are leading the mind before the very presence of the Holy Trinity! This is the turn in the text.

KNOWLEDGE, VARIOUS TERMS AND VARIOUS LEVELS
(M 107 TO M 110)

The turning point in the text is accomplished with what I have called one of the most beautiful and suggestive of all the proverbs in the collection. This claim will be justified in the specific examination of M 107 later in this study. Several observations here will serve our present purposes. First, it should be noticed that the first line of the proverb (and thus of this whole new section) presents the reader with two bright and striking images. Simply from a poetic point of view, this alone signals some turn in the text. As mentioned, the bright image of the morning star is the rescue from darkness spoken of in M 106.

The second line of the proverb speaks of two important realities, of which the morning star and the palm tree were offered

---

[122] This is the subject of special commentary in Part Four.

as images—they are mind and soul. The language is careful and precise. It speaks of mind *in* a soul, which is consistent with Evagrius's understanding of the relation of these two realities. The adjectives for mind and soul are critical. He speaks of a *pure* mind and a *gentle* soul. The mind is what is used for contemplation and knowledge, of which the following proverbs will speak. For contemplation and knowledge it must be pure. A human being's mind is found in a soul. That soul must be gentle for the mind to be pure. Thus, *gentle* here serves as the term that summarizes the whole of *praktikē*. Its position here at the text's turning point images the absolutely critical importance of gentleness in the monk's coming to knowledge.

M 108 speaks of the wise man. It has been observed that wisdom is a partner virtue with prudence and that their work is in the rational part of the soul. Prudence's work is directed toward *praktikē*, whereas the role of wisdom is directed toward knowledge. Likewise, it was observed that M 105 introduces prudence (and thus the rational part of the soul) into the text at the end of a development that intertwines the concupiscible and irascible parts of the soul. M 108's mention of the wise man picks up on all of this. The other virtues have been established, and this fact has been summarized in the expression "gentle soul." Now the mind can benefit from the virtue of wisdom, whose role is "the contemplation of the reasons of the corporeals and incorporeals" (TP 89). M 108 says that the wise man will search the reasons of God. "The reasons of God" were mentioned in the very first line of *Ad Monachos,* "Heirs of God, listen to the reasons of God." The meditation on the text has taken the reader along the road of many virtues that are necessary in order for one truly to contemplate the reasons of God. That road having been traveled, the text returns now to the expression "reasons of God" as if to make a new beginning or really to enter onto a new level, the level that was promised in the very first proverb. It is this new level that is offered in the proverbs that follow.

M 109 introduces two terms that belong to this new level: *knowledge* and *contemplation.* Knowledge, of course, has already been mentioned at many points, but this is the first appearance of *contemplation,* a word that Evagrius uses frequently in his

writings.[123] The significance of the present proverb is the introduction of the terminology at this point in the text. With negative
expressions, the proverb speaks of their vital importance. In the
style of the biblical author of Proverbs, Evagrius makes a comparison that shows the absurdity of someone who thinks knowledge and contemplation unimportant.[124]

M 110 expresses the hierarchy of types of knowledge so characteristic of Evagrius's understanding of this dimension of the
monastic life. The proverb presents knowledge of the Holy Trinity as being beyond all other forms of knowledge. Again in the
style of biblical proverbs, the first line says that it is better than
knowledge of the incorporeals; the second line, that contemplation of the Trinity is beyond the reasons for the aeons. Thus two
types of knowledge are ranked lower than the Trinity here, knowledge of the incorporeals and knowledge of the worlds to which
they are assigned.

The progress of the movement of these first four proverbs of
the new section is worth observing. M 107 presents strong poetic
images for the mind. M 108 adds the virtue particularly suited for
the realm of knowledge: wisdom. M 109 introduces the terminology of contemplation and knowledge. M 110 uses this terminology
to express the hierarchy in levels of knowledge, focusing on the
supreme value of knowledge of the Trinity. The levels of knowledge that lead up to knowledge of the Trinity are the subject of
many of the following proverbs, but the last proverb of the movement, M 136 (M 137 being considered a conclusion to the whole),
leaves the reader with what has been suggested in these opening
four, namely, the mind presented before the Holy Trinity.

---

[123] Evagrius tends to distinguish the terms *knowledge* and *contemplation* even
while closely associating them. A. Guillaumont observes that when it is a question
of knowledge of created things, the preferred word is *contemplation,* reserving
knowledge for knowledge of God himself ("Un philosophe au désert," 50). Yet this
is a tendency more than a hard and fast rule. In M 109 the terms seem to be used
synonymously, and in M 110 *contemplation* is used both for the Trinity and for the
incorporeals. M 136 likewise speaks of knowledge of the incorporeals. This tendency is not reserved to *Ad Monachos;* see also In Prov 1:1 (G 2).

[124] See Index to Scriptural Citations and Allusions. For comparisons very
similar to the present, see Prayer 64 and G 5, where in both cases the sort of comparison is made of someone who wishes to enter knowledge but is still troubled
by anger.

BLOCKS TO KNOWLEDGE:
GENTLENESS VERSUS IRASCIBILITY (M 111 TO M 114)

The dividing line between M 110 and M 111 is not sharp. M 111 could be well pondered in conjunction with the movement identified from M 107 to M 110. The text comes back to gentleness from M 107 and presents a different image in association with it: the gray hair of old men. With this return to gentleness M 107 and M 111 can be seen as forming inclusions based on gentleness around the three proverbs in between. Then the beautiful language of wisdom, contemplation, and knowledge is seen surrounded by the images of morning star, palm tree, and (very concretely now!) the gray hair of old men. All of these are images of gentleness. And because they are, they are likewise "knowledge of truth."

Yet M 111 also signals the start of a new development which concerns gentleness and expressions of its opposite. In the text of *Ad Monachos* up to the turning point many different dimensions of *praktikē* were touched on in the various proverbs. In those that remain, only the theme of gentleness (treated by means of the various expressions that have been noted for it) and the theme of true versus false teaching are interlaced among the other proverbs that are meditations on knowledge itself. It is to be noted that the first strand woven here is with gentleness. It is one more indication of the critical position in which Evagrius holds it. The issue is critical for Evagrius because gentleness will make the difference in whether the monk will arrive at true knowledge or fall into false knowledge.[125]

M 112 moves this theme forward by contrasting a youth with the old men mentioned in M 111. An old man is not automatically gentle (cf. G 31). And so important is gentleness that a gentle youth—one might not expect much from a youth—would be

---

[125] True versus false knowledge is the subject of the major chain in this portion of the text, M 123 to M 131. This position on gentleness and its relation to knowledge is a major theme in the *Gnostikos*. A number of its chapters stress its importance; see G 4, 5, 8, 10, 31, 32, 47. In two chapters Evagrius explains that the sin of the knower, false knowledge, does not come about from a failure in intelligence but from being subject to anger and the irascible or some other passion. Cf. G 4, 43.

better than an old man. The old man spoken of here is small-souled and angry. He is the opposite of gentleness itself, which was described in the gray hair of the previous proverb. The proverb is tightly constructed and finds its links to M 111 by means of the language of old versus young, and small-souled and angry versus gentleness.[126]

M 113 and M 114 develop the theme of anger in the direction of several specific issues: scandalizing others, agitating the church, and resisting a priest. Strong verbs (scandalize, irritate, agitate, resist) tie the single lines of the proverbs tightly together into a same mood. Placing these specific manifestations of being small-souled or angry at this point in the text is Evagrius's way of indicating that there can simply be no access to knowledge for persons who commit such offenses.

Only the first of the four proverbs considered here mentions knowledge specifically, but it should be clear that the label of this section, "Blocks to Knowledge," is justified, and this for three reasons. The first concerns the point of placement of these proverbs in the text. The talk all round is talk of knowledge. Second, the talk here is also of gentleness and its opposites; and by this point in the text it is clear that gentleness has a very special relation to knowledge.[127] Its opposites have the capacity to block knowledge. "Irascibility scatters knowledge" (M 35). Third, the punishments mentioned here in Evagrius's warnings are typical of the language he uses when he speaks of someone who will not enter into knowledge, a language strong and vivid.[128]

THE SWEETNESS OF KNOWLEDGE (M 115 TO M 117)

M 115 presents the pleasing image of honey, an image of knowledge, in contrast to the rough images of M 113 and M 114.

---

[126] The language here closely echoes Prov 14:29–30, where μακρόθυμος and πραΰθυμος are contrasted with ὀλιγόψυχος. Evagrius would expect the unspoken μακρόθυμος and πραΰθυμος to be heard in the meditation.

[127] The connection has been suggested in M 12, 31, 34, 53, 85, 99, 107, not to mention the many other proverbs that do the same in language closely associated with gentleness.

[128] Many examples are possible from Evagrius's writings. To take examples only from *Ad Monachos* see M 10, 12, 22, 25, 42, 43, 62, 63, 75, 77, 88, 90, 106.

Honey has appeared in the text already in M 72 as the final proverb in the important development of ten proverbs at the center of the text. In M 72 the image of honey followed a proverb that spoke of clamor and blasphemy. That is, it followed a concern similar to the material found in M 114. Noticing this helps us to realize that M 115 offers more than some nice but vague biblical image for knowledge. The clamor and blasphemy of M 71 have a specific reference to doctrinal error.[129] It is similar to M 114's "agitating the church" and "resisting a priest." Honey, and particularly its comb, is Evagrius's image for correct doctrinal knowledge, which is the antidote to blasphemy or agitation in the church.[130] This meditation, which moves back and forth between M 114 and M 115, is already sounding the theme that is going to be taken up in earnest a few short proverbs hence in the major chain of this portion of the text, M 123 to M 131, which is very much concerned with true versus false knowledge. That concern is already unfolded here. The second line of M 115 adds to this a connection between knowledge and the Spirit himself. For Evagrius the Spirit is the revealer of knowledge.[131]

M 116 speaks of what is necessary to come to true knowledge, here identified at two of its levels, reasons of the incorporeals and reasons for the aeons. In each of its two lines the whole distance between the beginning of *praktikē* and the entry into knowledge is spanned. With a beautiful swiftness, the meditator passes from terms appropriate to *praktikē* (honor and serve) to terms within the realm of knowledge. The formulation "Honor the Lord," comes from the book of Proverbs, and Evagrius definitely associates the expression with *praktikē*. "If it is 'by breaking the law that one dishonors God' (Rom 2:32), then it is clear that

---

[129] See below, pp. 303–4.

[130] See below, pp. 304–7, where this is developed in a more detailed examination of M 72. For understanding how *comb* in M 115 has the dimension of right doctrine, the most important text in the discussion is In Prov 24:13 (G 270), discussed below at p. 307 n. 172 where the distinction between honey and comb is between those who simply know how to derive some profit from the scriptures and those who know how to derive doctrine from the things spoken of there.

[131] On Evagrius's precise and consistent use of the word *spiritual* to refer to the Holy Spirit and the Holy Spirit as the revealer of knowledge, see Bunge, *Geistliche Vaterschaft*, 37–38, and "The 'Spiritual Prayer,'" 194–98.

by doing the law one honors God" (In Prov 7:1a [G 87]). In the scholion Evagrius does not develop the second part of the verse, but it seems to have inspired him in the composition of M 116. The verse reads, "My son, honor the Lord and you will be strong" (Prov 7:1). In M 116 this being strong is understood to be knowing the reasons of the incorporeals.

If M 115 showed that the Spirit has the role of revealing knowledge, M 116 shows that Christ likewise has the role of revealer. A scholion on a verse from Psalm 22 pictures the movement from *praktikē* to knowledge as a movement from being Christ's servants to being his friends. "At one time Christ pastured the sheep as a shepherd. Now, henceforth as a friend he calls them friends and calls them to his table. For he says, 'I no longer call you servants but friends.' Fear of God makes someone a servant, but knowledge of the mysteries makes someone a friend" (In Ps 22:5 [PG 12:1264C]).[132] This is the same movement of M 116, from serving the Lord to the unveiling of mysteries.

M 117 is a proverb that speaks of knowledge as the purpose of life, here expressed as the heart being placed on high. The image of a tree flourishing (or not) is used in the second line. For Evagrius, tree is a biblical word for the rational nature. He says this clearly in a chapter that moves in the same perspective as M 117. "If rational natures bear the sign of trees and if trees grow in water, then rightly is knowledge said to be the spiritual water which flows from 'the source of life'" (KG V, 67).[133] Thus, without knowledge (water) the rational nature (tree) does not flourish.[134] The knowledge with which the rational nature flourishes is M 116's reasons of the incorporeals and of the aeons. It is M 115's honey and its comb. It is being filled by the Spirit.

---

[132] Recall that "fear of God" is the very beginning of *praktikē* for Evagrius.

[133] Evagrius also interprets tree as rational nature in In Ps 21:7. It is presumed in KG V, 69. See below, pp. 314–15 for the interpretation of palm tree in M 107.

[134] Water and drink are images of knowledge also in Lt 2:2; 31; KG V, 67, 69; In Prov 4:21 (G 51); 25:25 (G 316, with mention of gentleness) 30:4 (G 284); M 129.

Christ in *Praktikē* and in the Various Levels
of Knowledge (M 118 to M 120)

These three proverbs are often cited as an example of the
way in which Evagrius divides the monastic life into *praktikē,* contemplation, and theology. They form a good text for illustrating
that. But there is much more. These three proverbs are absolutely
dense with possible directions for meditation. They manage to
express with admirable succinctness so much of Evagrius's teaching, not least of all his teaching about Christ, though this often
goes unremarked by those who draw attention to this chain. For
our present purposes, we shall observe how the chain itself is
constructed, leaving for later in the study an examination of its
contents.

The proverbs could be described as being carefully and precisely built. Virtually every word in each of the proverbs has its
exact correspondence in the other two. Thus *flesh of Christ* corresponds to *blood of Christ,* and these together correspond to *breast
of the Lord.* Next, *virtues of praktikē* corresponds to *contemplation of
created things,* and these together correspond to *knowledge of God.*
Then there are the verbs. *Eats* corresponds to *drinks,* and these to
rests against. Finally, there are the "conditions" that each proverb
describes. *Passionless* corresponds to *wise,* and these in turn to *theologian.*

Within the single proverbs a correspondence is likewise
established, no less precisely expressed. In each proverb the guid-
ing image is some dimension of the Last Supper scene. In M 118
Christ's flesh is identified with the virtues of *praktikē.* This being
established, the second line speaks of the condition one reaches
if this flesh (these virtues) is eaten. One becomes passionless,
Evagrius's term for one of the goals of *praktikē.* In M 119 Christ's
blood is identified with the contemplation of created things. This
being established, the second line speaks of the condition one
reaches if this blood (this contemplation) is drunk. One becomes
wise, Evagrius's term for this level of contemplation. In M 120 the
breast of the Lord is identified with the knowledge of God, that
is, with the very highest level of knowledge. This being established, the second line speaks of the condition one reaches if he

rests against this breast (this knowledge). One becomes a theologian, Evagrius's term for the goal of all knowledge.[135]

Not only is there correspondence in the terminology of the proverbs; a progress is also marked, a progress expressed with each of the terms. Thus, as Evagrius consistently teaches, the virtues of *praktikē* lead to the contemplation of created things, and this contemplation leads to the knowledge of God. Passionlessness opens the way to wisdom, and this leads on to theology. The movement from flesh to blood to breast or from eating to drinking to resting against is a movement toward an ever greater intimacy with Christ.

Perhaps no other chain in *Ad Monachos* is as tightly packed as this and so rich with meaning. Perhaps no other proverbs exhibit quite such economy in expression. In three two-line proverbs every major phase of the journey to the knowledge of God is offered for meditation. Each phase is expressed in its most basic terminology. And each phase is placed in the tightest possible relationship with Christ, more specifically, with some particular dimension of the incarnate Lord. Not even a verb is used to express this relationship, simply "flesh: virtues," "blood: contemplation," "breast: knowledge." The role of Christ is placed squarely in the process from beginning to end. He himself *is* the life of *praktikē*. He himself *is* contemplation. He himself *is* the knowledge of God. The beginning of the monastic life is dependent on Christ. Its final goal is equally dependent on him, indeed on intimacy with him. The whole timbre of the chain is sounded in a eucharistic key, which is to say that Evagrius is guided by symbols from the church's central mystery in his understanding of the role of Christ in his own monastic journey and in that of his fellow monks. The mystery of the Eucharist itself may account for

---

[135] We have had ample opportunity in this study to become used to the idea that passionlessness is Evagrius's expression for the goal of *praktikē* and that wisdom is an expression suited to the contemplation of corporeals and incorporeals. We are less used to what the terms *theologian* and *theology* mean for Evagrius. However, we have at least encountered the term in a text that is consistent with the way in which Evagrius uses the term. Theology is the goal of knowledge. See TP Prologue, 8; cf. TP 1, 84 and Prayer 60. For more on this, see the extended commentary on M 120 in Part Four.

the tight conjunction expressed between Christ and the phases of the monastic life as well as accounting for the tone of intimacy in which the chain finishes. Only by resting against the breast of the Lord can one know God, can one be a theologian.

PRAKTIKĒ AND KNOWLEDGE WITH LOVE AS THE LINK (M 121 TO M 122)

These two proverbs add a sort of flourish to the strong and beautiful chain on Christ that has just finished. The three proverbs of that chain moved from *praktikē* to the very knowledge of God. M 121 adds to this meditation the concrete image of actual monks (γνωστικὸς καὶ πρακτικὸς) embodying these stages of the monastic life. Their meeting each other has a wonderful sense of mystery in the thought that between the two of them, the Lord himself is found.[136] This repeats from a different perspective a key idea of the previous chain—the presence of Christ in every phase of the monastic journey. Thus, there are two links by which M 121 is joined to M 118–20: the same joining of *praktikē* and knowledge, the same presence of the Lord. Now the presence of the Lord is mediated through accomplished monks.

M 122 continues in this same vein of bringing together the two principal parts of the monk's journey. Love is the goal of *praktikē* and the way to knowledge.[137] Treasure refers to knowledge.[138] What is significant is finding at this point once again the term *love*. The proverb virtually equates love with knowledge, not by losing the distinction between them but by putting them in so

---

[136] Much of the literature of the desert is marked with a sense of the presence of God in the meeting of monks one with another. It is tempting to wonder if in composing this proverb Evagrius might have had two of his most important monastic fathers in mind: namely, Macarius of Alexandria, who was for him a model of *praktikē;* and Macarius the Great, who was for him a model of knowledge. In any case, this proverb stresses strongly once again the close relation between *praktikē* and knowledge, and Evagrius owes this stress to his desert masters. On the whole theme, see Bunge, "Évagre le Pontique et les deux Macaire."

[137] Cf. M 3 and M 67 and the significant positioning each receives in the text.

[138] For other instances of the term *treasure* associated with knowledge, see M 25 and M 87, both of which also concern love. See also Lt 47:1 and Lt 61 with notes by Bunge in *Briefe,* 365, 378.

close a relation that it is clear that one leads naturally to the other. The proverb attributes this to the grace of the Lord, and this is precisely the other dimension of the theme that is being brought to the fore again and again now. Christ is the author of the monk's progress in *praktikē* and in knowledge.[139]

M 123 opens a new theme and is the first member of a long, carefully constructed chain. Before going on to that, a reprise will help us to keep our bearings in the text.

REPRISE (M 107 TO M 122)

M 107 was identified as a definite turning point in the text. It presented striking images for a pure mind in a gentle soul. By using this kind of language in such an important proverb Evagrius wished to accent the critical importance of gentleness in the mind's turning itself toward knowledge. There followed several proverbs (M 108 to M 110) in which a number of terms associated with the realm of knowledge were introduced. This is what characterizes the turning point. It is a turn toward meditation on knowledge, which will be sustained until the end of the text. Knowledge was ranked in a hierarchy, with knowledge of the Trinity placed in the uppermost position (M 110).

Significantly, after this "introduction" of knowledge and the terminology associated with its various levels, the first theme to unfold is the relationship of gentleness to knowledge (M 111–14). Things that are opposed to gentleness (anger, irritation, agitation, etc.) were presented as blocks to knowledge. Having warned against these, the text turned back to a meditation on the excellence of knowledge and expressed again several of its dimensions (M 115–17). The relation between *praktikē* and knowledge is introduced here as well as the Lord's role in both (M 116).

There followed a dense and intricate chain showing Christ's role in the progressive movement from *praktikē* through lower

---

[139] In addition to the presence of Christ in M 118–20 and the observation of the way in which this leads into the Lord's presence in M 121 and M 122, it should also be noticed that M 116 speaks of the Lord's role in unveiling the reasons for the aeons and this after the admonition to honor and serve him.

forms of knowledge to the highest form of all (M 118–20). Meditation on this chain is meant to leave the reader with a deep sense of the intimacy with Christ that the monastic journey brings. Though these three proverbs definitely form a unit in their own right, the proverbs that follow do not abruptly present some new theme. Rather, they spring out of it, as it were, with the image of two monks meeting, one representing *praktikē* and the other knowledge. The Lord is standing between them. M 122 finishes the movement by representing love (once again!) as the hinge between *praktikē* and knowledge.

WISDOM AND PRUDENCE VERSUS FALSE KNOWLEDGE (M 123 TO M 131)

This lengthy chain is a stinging indictment of false knowledge. It is the longest single chain of the whole text, containing as well the longest proverb. Its length and its position here in the last major movement of the text, virtually bringing it to a conclusion, are an indication of the importance of Evagrius's concern against false knowledge. The reader has just completed a meditation on the way in which grace from the Lord leads from the virtues of *praktikē* to theology. The meditation has been rich, beautiful, and dense. Now the reader is warned. Between *praktikē* and the heights of theology (here understood as the highest union with God, no longer involved with any sort of discursive thinking), there are many ways in which the monk can go astray. In general, the first movement of the text often warned against the ways in which one can go astray in the practice of the virtues. But there are also false paths in what concerns knowledge, and the present chain is warning against these.[140]

To examine the movement of this carefully designed chain, it is helpful to first observe that there is an overarching structure to the whole. Noticing this makes it easier to follow the flow of the proverbs one by one.

---

[140] I have already suggested, for example, that Evagrius's concern to join love to temperance can in part be seen to stem from the failure of gnostic ascetics to join these two virtues. This failure both stems from false doctrinal positions and gives rise to them. See Stroumsa, "Ascèse et gnose."

The central beams around which this chain is built are the partner virtues of prudence and wisdom.[141] M 123 introduces the two terms, devoting one line to wisdom, the other to prudence. M 131, the last proverb in the chain, does the same. It is this, in fact, that enables the identification of these and the intervening proverbs as a unit. Especially interesting from the structural point of view is the mention of these two virtues in M 126 in the statement against false teachers: "There is no prudence and there is no wisdom in their teachings." This statement falls in the exact middle of that long proverb, there being seven lines on either side of it. It also falls at the exact middle of the whole chain, counting the total lines of the member proverbs. So, it can be said in a quite literal way that the *central* message of this chain is that "there is no prudence and there is no wisdom in their teachings." The structure is a perfect chiasm. Around these central beams of the structure other specific ideas are made to rest. We turn to the unfolding of themes in the proverbs one by one. As heretofore in this part of the study, our task at this point is only to identify the way in which these ideas are interlaced in the chains.[142]

As already mentioned, M 123 introduces the two terms with which the central message of the chain will be formed—wisdom

---

[141] The significant role that these two virtues played in the important chain at the very center of the text (M 63–72) has already been observed.

[142] I have not chosen any of the proverbs of this chain for particular comment in Part Four for reasons of space and because this theme has already been well studied by Bunge. His "Origenismus-Gnostizismus" is directly relevant to the material found in M 123–31, especially pp. 28–32, which comment on some of these proverbs. In this study Bunge shows that "false knowledge" (see M 126 but also M 43) is a watchword in Evagrius with a very specific focus of doctrinal concerns. He interprets the proverbs of this chain against the background of specific occurrences in Evagrius's life in which he was involved in refuting a false gnosis among the monks of the Egyptian desert and in the Jerusalem Mount of Olives community to whom he thinks *Ad Monachos* is likely addressed. In addition to this important article, Bunge's *Briefe* as well as his *Geistliche Vaterschaft* are useful for forming a picture of Evagrius's thoroughgoing concern against false knowledge and false teachers. The Evagrian text that especially shows this is the *Scholia on Proverbs*. In my remarks on this chain I will amplify my notes somewhat in order to guide the reader to particularly useful parts of Bunge's work, and I will also draw attention to other Evagrian texts that would be useful in further study of the proverbs of this chain.

and prudence. Further, it introduces the image of demons and speaks about their dogmas and crafty ways. Demons are another key thread to this chain. After being mentioned here, they are designated as "angels of death" in M 125. They can be associated with the "lawless men" of M 126, which also speaks explicitly of demons and calls them enemies of the Lord. Wisdom and prudence must know all about the demons and their ways. Various demons specialize in causing particular types of problems, and wisdom and prudence would know about them all. "Among the demons some are opposed to the practice of the commandments; others are opposed to the reasons of nature, and others are opposed to the reasons which concern the divinity, because also the knowledge of our salvation is made up of these three things" (KG I, 10).[143] Thus, in M 123 Evagrius opens a chain in which he wishes to speak of false knowledge. He does this by mentioning demons and the two virtues that most protect against the demons, who will be shown, as the chain unfolds, to be the real authors of false knowledge.

M 124 returns to the theme of fathers, which was developed and located in so central a position above (M 88–92). It speaks of their dogmas and calls them holy, contrasting them thereby with the dogmas of the demons mentioned in M 123. Then these dogmas of the (monastic) fathers are put in direct relation to baptismal faith, indicating that Evagrius thought of his and other monastic teachings as a way of life that develops out of this baptismal faith.[144] The monk is advised neither to abandon the faith

---

[143] For another example of demons specializing, see G 31.

[144] An important contribution that Bunge has made to Evagrian studies concerns the many places where he draws attention to Evagrius's concern for the faith of the church. If the goal of monastic life as conceived by Evagrius is knowledge, there is no knowledge for him that does not rest on the faith of the church, often called by him "right faith." And right faith means especially correct doctrine concerning the Trinity. So Bunge, *Geistliche Vaterschaft*, 57, citing many texts in support of this. For Evagrius's spirituality as coming from the grace of baptism, see Bunge, *Das Geistgebet*, 62-73. That Evagrius puts the teaching of the monastic way in relation to baptismal faith is taken for granted in virtue of his being a part of the desert tradition. So Bunge, *Briefe*, 126, citing M 124 along with V 54, TP 81, and Lt 17. Faith, put at the base of the ladder of the virtues, as in M 3, means for Evagrius the faith of baptism. See Bunge, *Briefe*, 128.

of his baptism nor to thrust off the spiritual seal (σφραγίς). This refers to the sealing that occurs at Christian initiation, and with this expression Evagrius wishes to refer specifically to the Holy Spirit (cf. M 115).[145] This faith and the Holy Spirit are necessary for the monk to come to true knowledge, here expressed as the Lord coming into the soul. They are necessary to protect the monk from the demons, this protection here expressed as being covered on the evil day.

Up to the turning point in M 107 there has been much talk about demons of various kinds.[146] Given the fact that, according to KG I, 10 cited above, there are demons who make trouble for true knowledge, it is not surprising that Evagrius should express his concerns about orthodox faith interwoven with images of demons. In the first line of M 124 Evagrius has closely followed the biblical text of Prov 22:28, "Do not lay to the side the boundaries of this age (ὅρια αἰώνια) which your fathers laid down." His comment on that text is much in the same line as M 124, and it is worth quoting here, for it demonstrates that Evagrius's concern with right faith cuts across the issues of the life of *praktikē* and into specific doctrinal concerns. He says,

> He who lays aside the boundaries of piety changes them either into superstition or into impiety, and he who lays aside the boundaries of courage turns them into either rashness or cowardice. One should think the same about the other virtues and the dogmas and the faith itself. This should be especially observed concerning the Holy Trinity. For he who does not recognize the divinity of the Holy Spirit undoes his baptism. And he who gives to others the name of God introduces gods, in the plural! (In Prov 22:28 [G 249])

The dogmas of the demons about which Evagrius is speaking now in *Ad Monachos* are quite specifically heretical doctrines, as the following proverb makes clear.

---

[145] On Evagrius's precise and consistent use of the word *spiritual* to refer to the Holy Spirit, see Bunge, *Geistliche Vaterschaft,* 37–38, and "The 'Spiritual Prayer,'" especially 194–98.

[146] Demons are mentioned explicitly in M 23, 52, 62, and 73; but it is to be remembered that talk of evil thoughts is talk about demons, and the mention of any specific evil thought is also talk about demons.

M 125 specifies that the teaching being spoken of is that of heretics, and these are called angels of death, another term for demons.[147] Another of the scholia on Proverbs shows how the work of these death-dealing demons spans the whole movement from the trouble demons cause in *praktikē* to the trouble they cause in regard to heresy. The biblical text upon which Evagrius is commenting is, "War is carried out by knowing how to pilot" (Prov 24:6).[148] He says,

> Those who shipwreck in what concerns the faith make war against spirits adverse to theology [i.e., demons] without knowing how to pilot. It is possible to say the same about each virtue, for there are shipwrecks in chastity and in love and in generosity. Likewise there is a shipwreck for each dogma of the catholic and apostolic Church. So, if war with the adversaries is carried out by knowing how to pilot, then our life on earth is a naval battle. (In Prov 24:6 [G 266])[149]

This is the kind of battle to which Evagrius is summoning the monk here in *Ad Monachos* in urging upon him the virtues of wisdom and prudence as a means of avoiding the death which the teaching of heretics brings. Having prudence and wisdom is "knowing how to pilot."[150] As the next proverb shows, the heretics are those who offer "false knowledge." Such teachers are a concrete and specific concern for Evagrius.[151]

M 126 is the longest proverb of the entire collection, and it is a relentlessly sounded warning against such teachers and their false knowledge. Like M 1 and M 73, it begins with the invitation to listen to the advice of the father. Strong words and images are

---

[147] Cf. Prayer 95, which speaks of demons appearing as angels and trying to convince the one to whom they appear into thinking that they are holy angels. The expression "angel of death" comes from Prov 16:14.

[148] The Greek text reads, μετὰ κυβερνήσεως γίνεται πόλεμος.

[149] Géhin cites other texts where shipwreck is an image for false doctrines and heresies (SC 340, 360–61). See also TP 84 and In Ps 141:4.

[150] Recall also the "war" imagery with which Evagrius defines prudence in TP 89, namely, as a virtue in the rational part of the soul that directs all the operations against the demons.

[151] See Bunge, "Origenismus-Gnostizismus," 30, where the flow of *Ad Monachos* at this point is studied and many references to Evagrius's writings are offered which help to identify his specific concern.

used for the false teachers and their false knowledge. These images are strung together one after another, giving the proverb momentum. The tension builds in it throughout; from one line to the next this strong vocabulary flows: lawless men, traps, snares, false knowledge, dark teachings, venom of asps, no prudence and no wisdom, evils, enemies, demons, no light.[152]

A more personal note than usual sounds in this proverb. In the invitation to listen, Evagrius, borrowing his text from Proverbs 5:7, says, listen to *me*. Then he appeals to his personal experience with such false knowledge and its teachers. He has spoken with them often. He has tracked down their dark teaching.[153] He has visited them in the desert. There is evidence elsewhere in the monastic literature to give us a fuller idea of the kind of experience Evagrius may be referring to in this proverb. Palladius tells stories of his former teacher such that one can think that Evagrius appealed to his personal experience with good reason.[154] Palladius praises Evagrius for his discernment of spirits, and by

---

[152] These images are all scriptural and are used by Evagrius elsewhere. For example, the meaning of "lawless men" is clarified by In Ps 118:15, where Evagrius refers the term to those who promise to teach the knowledge of God from a worldly wisdom. In In Ps 141:4 Evagrius speaks of enemies laying traps through heresy. "False knowledge" comes from 1 Tim 6:20, and wherever he mentions this, there is always implied the knowledge of the truth spoken of in 1 Tim 2:4. For the way in which these verses from 1 Timothy stand behind all of Evagrius's talk about true and false knowledge, see Bunge, "Origenismus-Gnostizismus," 31. The image of snares comes from Ps 139:4, that of the venom of asps from Ps 13:3; 139:3.

[153] Note that the expression "track down" is the same as was used of prudence in regard to the demons in M 123.

[154] See Bunge, "Origenismus-Gnostizismus," 26ff., where Bunge examines M 126 in conjunction with the story in LH 38:11 in which three demons who are heretics appear to Evagrius and are confounded by him. Bunge especially focuses on this story as it is recounted in a longer version in the *Coptic Life*. He thereby draws three conclusions from M 126. First, the teachers of a false knowledge were threatening the monks to whom Evagrius addressed the work. Second, Evagrius himself met and argued with such teachers. Third, the real fathers of such teachings are demons. On Evagrius's attitude to the heretical strife in his time and on his involvement with Origenism at the end of the fourth century, see also, Bunge, *Briefe*, 59, with n. 166 as well as the suggestive remarks with which he concludes his study, "Évagre le Pontique et les deux Macaire," 359–60.

this he means not only the evil spirits who excite the passions but also those which lead into doctrinal error.[155]

The image of demons with which the proverb concludes can recall the strong demonic images of M 62, the proverb on pride, which spoke of demons bringing the soul low and fluttering around the monk in the air. To be reminded of this image of the demon of pride as M 126 closes is no accident. This demon, according to Evagrius, stands behind much theological strife.[156] In any case, this long and forthright proverb leaves no doubt about where Evagrius stands on teachings different from those of the monastic fathers and the faith of the church.[157]

After this long proverb, the chain completes itself with five more proverbs of two lines each. The first of these, M 127, acts as a two-line summary of the fifteen lines of M 126. Having stated his warnings so vividly and at comparative length in M 126, Evagrius can now simply say that the liar falls away from God and into evils. The image of the fall renders specific now the fall mentioned in M 62, which I suggested could be brought to mind at the end of M 126. The Greek verbs in each line draw the contrast strongly between falling *away* (ἐκπεσεῖται) and falling *into* (ἐμπεσεῖται). One falls away from *God* and into *evils*.[158]

---

[155] See Bunge, *Geistliche Vaterschaft*, 29–30 with references. Note especially the fact that Palladius specifically says that he himself was saved from false knowledge by Evagrius (see p. 30 n. 24).

[156] Cf. Ant VII, 17, 25, 56, on the relation between pride and false knowledge.

[157] These remarks on M 126 cannot close without specific attention being drawn to V 54 in its longer and authentic Latin version. The various studies of Bunge to which the notes above refer take this text frequently into account. I simply wish to mention its importance here, especially as the closest parallel in the works of Evagrius to M 126 and the other surrounding proverbs. The text extant in the Greek version reads, "I have seen men corrupting virgins in dogmas / and rendering vain their virginity. / But you, daughter, listen to the dogmas of the Church of the Lord, / and let nothing else persuade you. / For the just shall inherit light, / but the impious shall dwell in darkness." Then in the Latin and Syriac versions there follows a list of the dogmas which Evagrius thinks important. The Latin text is found in Wilmart, "Les versions latines des sentences d'Évagre pour les vierges," 150. For the authenticity of the Latin and Syriac versions and for an analysis of their contents, see Bunge, "Origenismus-Gnostizismus," 32–33.

[158] The use of the term *neighbor* also suggests that the issue of love is at stake

M 128 and M 129 are proverbs that contrast true knowledge with worldly knowledge. They would likely seem mysterious and strange to someone unacquainted with the way in which Evagrius thinks scripturally, but someone familiar with this procedure would either recognize the allusions and their meaning or be challenged to find them. By using scriptural language Evagrius can evoke much in few words. These two proverbs evoke Deuteronomy 11:10–11, which is meant to guide and promote the meditation. The passage reads, "For the land into which you enter to inherit is not as the land of Egypt, from which you came out, where they sow the seed, and water it with their feet, as a garden of herbs [κῆπον λαχανείας]: but the land into which you enter to inherit is a land of mountains and plains; it shall drink water of the rain of heaven [ἐκ τοῦ ὑετοῦ τοῦ οὐρανοῦ πίεται ὕδωρ]."

Once again using the construction "better . . . than . . . ," these two proverbs contrast images from Egypt with images meant to refer to knowledge. In line with the exegetical tradition to which he is heir, Evagrius consistently interprets Egypt as an image of the evils of this world and its ignorance.[159] Thus, in the first line of M 128, based on the Deuteronomy passage, ignorance is symbolized as Egypt's garden of herbs; knowledge is the paradise of God.[160] In the second line two rivers are contrasted. The great river here is the Nile, which Evagrius also understands —not surprisingly—as a symbol of evil and ignorance on account of Jeremiah's instruction not to drink its waters.[161] The river of the Lord, an image for knowledge, is contrasted with this.[162]

---

here. Recall M 43, which spoke of true and false knowledge in a context of love and hate.

[159] KG I, 83; IV, 64; V,6, 88; VI, 49; In Ps 104:22; 135:6. For more examples of Evagrius's applying this interpretive principle to the psalms, see Bunge, *Geistliche Vaterschaft,* 70.

[160] Hausherr (*Leçons,* 185) interprets M 128's paradise as an image of gnosis and the herb garden as an image of the joys of this world. My remarks do not differ much from his but perhaps permit the precision of seeing that the real contrast presented in M 128 is between true and false knowledge. This precision is made possible by interpreting the proverb within its chain! Hausherr brings M 128 and M 129 together with many other Evagrian texts in order to comment on Prayer 153, which speaks of counting prayer a greater joy than all others.

[161] Cf. Jer 2:18 as alluded to in KG I, 83; cf. Lt 7:2.

[162] The image of the river is one of the richest with which Evagrius describes

M 129 stays with this water image and the Nile and contrasts it with heavenly water, which alludes to the water of the rain of heaven in the Deuteronomy text, likewise an image for knowledge.[163] The specific mention of "wise men" continues the theme of "no wisdom in their teachings" of M 126. It may also indicate a subtle shift or addition in what this proverb is offering for meditation, namely, not only a contrast of true knowledge with the false teachers of the desert, but also a contrast with worldly wisdom. Such a contrast is drawn not infrequently in Evagrius, and one of its expressions is structured rather like M 128 and M 129. "The life of man is holy knowledge, and the mercy of the Lord is the contemplation of created things. Many of this age [πολλοὶ τοῦ αἰῶνος τούτου, cf. 1 Cor 2:8] have promised us knowledge, but 'the mercy of the Lord is better than life'" (In Ps 72:4 [PG 12:1488C]; cf. KG VI, 22). In a way significantly similar to another major theme of *Ad Monachos,* when the *Gnostikos* draws this contrast between worldly knowledge and true knowledge, it is likewise pointed out that there can be no true knowledge with trouble in the irascible (G 4, 45).

M 130 comes specifically again to the issue of pride. The allusion here is to the Lord's own words, "He who exalts himself will be humbled" (Matt 23:12 and parallels; cf. M 96). This dominical saying is applied to the false teachers spoken of in this chain. Pride, defined in M 62 as saying "Powerful am I," in the presence of God, can be a source of such false teaching. It is a desire to exalt oneself. The image of being brought low as if on a wheel is a variation of the falling away from God mentioned in M 127 and of the image of being brought low mentioned in M 62.

M 131 signals the close of the chain by its mention again of the virtues of wisdom and prudence. As they are stated in this proverb and consistent with how these virtues are discussed in Evagrius, prudence looks toward *praktikē* and is thus said to *purify* the heart. Wisdom looks toward knowledge and so is said to *raise* the heart up.

---

knowledge. His use of this biblical image is discussed below in Part Four in the commentary on M 64.

[163] On water and drink as images of knowledge, see above, p. 134 n. 134.

VARIOUS LEVELS OF KNOWLEDGE LEADING
TO THE HOLY TRINITY (M 132 TO M 136)

After the long and perhaps even strenuous meditation on true and false knowledge, the whole collection comes to a quiet and awesome finish with five simple, rich proverbs of two lines apiece, each of which repeats for one final time some point related to various levels and terms for knowledge that have appeared elsewhere in the text.

M 132, after the diatribe on false knowledge, seems now willingly to admit that true knowledge is not an easy thing to reach, not only because of false teachers but because of the difficult and mysterious nature of the questions themselves.[164] These are dark and hard for the mind to reach, but the proverb also offers a promise: the man of *praktikē* will know them. Thus, as the text comes to its conclusion, it repeats here a theme that has occurred frequently throughout and was literally located in the center of the text (M 63 to M 72), namely, the relation between *praktikē* and knowledge.

By speaking of purifying oneself, M 133 builds on this theme of *praktikē* in talk particularly suited to its goal.[165] The one who purifies himself will see intelligible natures. Then unable, it seems, to resist saying it one last time, Evagrius comes back to gentleness and its relation to knowledge. The turning point in the text at M 107 turned on the issue of gentleness. The first specific development in a chain after the opening chain of the block (M 107–10) concerned itself with gentleness (M 111–14). The theme has been touched on at regular points throughout the whole text, and now the text concludes with one final mention of it. The construction of the Greek text forms a chiasm (producible at least in part in the English translation) in which "intelligible natures" and "reasons of the incorporeals" lie immediately side

---

[164] Bunge's discussion of the specific concerns of Evagrius when he uses the watchword "false knowledge" indicates that among his concerns are the issues that M 132 mentions, namely, providence and judgment. See "Origenismus-Gnostizismus," 33–35.

[165] This understanding of purity is so consistent and frequent in Evagrius that reference to it is not necessary. Let it suffice here simply to note the theme in *Ad Monachos:* M 8, 44, 65, 97, 107, 131.

by side, sandwiched between the first and last words of the proverb, "purifies himself [καθαίρων ἑαυτόν]" and "gentle monk [μοναχὸς πραΰς]." It is as if to say that gentleness and purity must always surround knowledge.

M 134 is a proverb directed against two specific doctrinal errors, such as would have been the reference in the previous chain on false knowledge. It is not surprising to see Evagrius place a proverb like this toward the end of his text. We saw above that if it is generally important to follow the teachings of the fathers and the church, "this should be especially observed concerning the Holy Trinity" (In Prov 22:28 [G 249]).

M 135 offers the beautiful image of the heart growing larger under the influence of the various contemplations.[166] The reasons of providence and judgment, that is, knowing the why of God's creations and his intricate plan of salvation—these lift the heart up. When the reader savors the proverb by lingering with it some time, the sense it offers is one of a wonderful expansiveness. There are *worlds* and *contemplations* and *reasons*, all these in the plural. They seem to invade the heart and in their greatness cause it to grow wider so that the meaning can be contained there. The movement in this invasion is ever upward.

In M 136 this raised-up heart is now explicitly named *mind*, the original creation and the definitive object of salvation. The other levels of knowledge, the lesser contemplations, raise the mind to its last and greatest goal, the Holy Trinity itself. Of the Trinity, Evagrius is here characteristically lacking in details and silent, content just to mention it.[167] These five proverbs in their progression have mounted upward twice toward the Trinity, each time mentioning a movement from the reasons of providence

---

[166] The image of being enlarged is a favorite of Evagrius, occurring here in *Ad Monachos* for the only time. Cf. In Prov 1:20 (G 12); 18:16 (G 184); and especially In Prov 22:20 (G 247), which reads, "He who has enlarged his heart by purity will understand the reasons of God, reasons which concern *praktikē* and natural contemplation and theology." Géhin in his notes on In Prov 1:20 cites many references to the same theme in the *Scholia on Psalms* (see SC 340, 105). For Evagrius, heart is a scriptural code word not only for the soul, as in In Prov 25:26 (G 317), but also for the mind; see KG VI, 52, 84, 87.

[167] On the significance of this silence, see the commentary in Part Four on M 136.

and judgment to reasons of the incorporeals to the Trinity. The first mounting upward (M 132–34) warns of the difficulty with heresies and the importance of gentleness. The second (M 135–36) is a clean movement with the difficulties and dangers no longer mentioned. In this double movement passing twice through meditations on the reasons of providence and judgment Evagrius has built into the finish of the meditation advice he received from Didymus the Blind. Evagrius reports Didymus as saying, "Exercise within yourself constantly the reasons concerning providence and judgment . . . , for almost everybody trips up on these" (G 48).

M 136 and the whole collection end with an openness to a great mystery. In 136 proverbs the reader has circled and climbed through many levels of *praktikē*, passed dangerous demons, and heard of wonderful and mysterious contemplations. There has been a continual movement upward in the meditation. But at the summit of the climb, the reader is left now with a sense of things just beginning. The mind is presented before the Holy Trinity. And what might that mean!

THE COLLECTION CONCLUDED (M 137)

The whole collection is concluded simply and humbly. Evagrius places his effort "in the Lord." He identifies the genre as proverbs. He asks for prayers for his lowly soul.

REPRISE (M 123 TO M 137)

The dominant chain of the second block is the longest chain of the entire text and is a vigorous meditation on true versus false knowledge (M 123–31). Prudence and wisdom are the virtues that protect against false knowledge, something that in fact is ultimately the work of demons; and these virtues are the main structural components of the chain. After this extended warning on the dangers of false knowledge, the text's final movement is an upward ascent through various levels of knowledge culminating in knowledge of the Trinity (M 132–36). This is the point toward which the whole meditation drives. It finishes, it could be said, almost silently. The mind is presented before the Trinity, but of the Trinity itself nothing is said. At this point, it is hoped, the meditating monk simply stands there in its presence. As he does, Evagrius asks that he be remembered in this "hour of prayer."

Conclusion to Part Two

It may be useful in a sort of general reprise to pass in review briefly now the structure of the whole text that has been uncovered in the foregoing examination. We have seen that *Ad Monachos* is a text constructed with very careful attention to the order of the proverbs it presents for meditation. Having followed it through from beginning to end, we can see that this order follows the order of a monk's spiritual progress as Evagrius conceives it. It begins with the first of the virtues, faith (M 3), and ends with the mind presented before the Trinity (M 136). This is a movement that passes from the practice of virtue in the life of *praktikē* to the enjoyment of knowledge across the various levels that lead to the Trinity. The bridge of passage between one realm and the other is love (M 3, 67).

If knowledge of the Trinity is the goal of monastic striving, there is no way to reach this goal apart from the way that passes by love. *Ad Monachos* is an arrangement of proverbs whose order helps the monk to pass along this only way that leads to knowledge. The other virtues are important because they lead the monk to the supreme virtue of love. Within the first block, the meditation can be conceived in its first broad movements as attempting to interlace temperance and love, that is, virtue in the concupiscible part of the soul and virtue in the irascible part. It does this from a number of different angles. Regarding the concupiscible, it speaks of amounts of food and sleep, chastity, attitudes toward money. Regarding the irascible, it speaks of love, gentleness, forgetting injuries. These kinds of exercises can be considered as extending from M 3 to M 53.

From M 54 to M 62 the text follows more closely for a while the last several evil thoughts in Evagrius's list of eight principal thoughts. Thus, progressively, there are meditations on listlessness, vainglory, and pride. It is only by constantly guarding against the dangers presented by these evil thoughts that a monk can hope to enter into the realm of knowledge. But having said so, Evagrius moves the reader into that realm with a sustained meditation placed at the center of the text (M 63–72). The center of the text images what the center of the spiritual life is: the inextricable relation between *praktikē* and knowledge. At the center of this center is the key to the whole: virtue leading to love and love leading to knowledge (M 67). The chain finishes with a barely veiled reference to where the whole text will end: knowledge of God (M 72), knowledge of the Trinity (M 136).

A new start in the text (M 73) begins a section symmetrically organized around the theme of the spiritual father. Fourteen proverbs (M 74–87) precede a central chain on fathers (M 88–92), and fourteen (M 93–106) follow it. The proverbs that surround the center speak of various angles of a brotherhood created around a father, and the second set of fourteen intertwines once again virtues in the concupiscible and irascible parts of the souls. The final two proverbs in the second set of fourteen (M 105–6) exercise the rational part of the soul and prepare the meditator for the text's turning point.

This turning point (M 107) is characterized by a shift in the type of meditations, all of which are now concerned with one or another dimension of knowledge, a concern that sustains itself to the very end. One virtue from *praktikē* continues to receive emphasis, a virtue introduced in the proverb that is the turning point. This virtue is gentleness, love's most practical expression. After meditations on the basic terminology of the realm of knowledge (M 108–10) and warnings against not being gentle (M 111–14), the text develops the role of Christ in the journey toward knowledge in two closely related chains (M 118–20 and M 121–22). Then a long, strong chain insists on guarding against false knowledge and speaks of the wisdom and prudence that raise the heart up and purify it (M 123–31). This prepares the meditation for its final upward ascent through the various levels of knowledge climaxing in knowledge of the Trinity (M 132–36).

This evidently intended and carefully designed structure does not emerge with a rapid reading of the text. Yet with slow meditation it does. Once a scent is found and followed, more and more secrets in the text begin to reveal themselves. Slowly the reader comes to realize the nature of the work that lies before him. It is an invitation to listen deeply, as deeply as possible, "to the reasons of God." It is a summons to practice, to the exercise of virtue. It is a road map that offers invaluable guidance through what otherwise may be uncharted territory, showing the paths that go around the crafty ways of demons and lead to the passionlessness that has love as its child. With continued meditation it emerges as offering yet more. Its structure offers images of values that must be held in careful balance: temperance and love, practice of virtue and enjoyment of the knowledge of God. The various centers around which parts of the text are organized suggest that their counterpart need be found in actual life: love and gentleness form a center of all the monk's striving for knowledge, and no monk should ever imagine that he can come to knowledge without the guidance of a father. The text's turning point and the tone that it thereafter maintains to the end is an image of what every monk who practices virtue may hope for: the beautiful contemplations that will enlarge the heart of the monk who is gentle. The text finishes with what is the monk's last and best hope: the mind presented before the Trinity.

I hope in this part of the study to have thrown these dimensions of *Ad Monachos* into clear relief and thereby to have indicated what is surely one of its most characteristic features. Discovering this structure is a major moment in hearing what Evagrius is saying in this text. The structure itself is his message. Yet it is not the whole message. There remain the rich contents of each of the individual proverbs and the range of the meditations that these provoke. We turn to the individual proverbs in Part Four, but it should be clear now that an individual proverb is meant to be interpreted in part by the position it has in the text. This position adds to each proverb's richness and leads the meditations in directions that might not otherwise be traveled.

Part Three

Situating This Kind of Christian Literature

Introduction

I have wanted in this study to focus squarely on the text of Evagrius, trying to read it carefully in the context of the meditative environment in which it was designed to be read. The study to this point has, I hope, revealed a text remarkable for its capacity to evoke wide-ranging meditations in the monks to whom it was addressed. This is a range achieved both by the effective ways in which the proverbs are positioned in the text as parts of chains and by the power of the individual proverbs themselves.[1]

Focusing immediately on the text itself, as opposed to a lengthy preliminary effort to establish its more general context, was a methodological move designed to avoid a preclassification of the text. I wanted, for example, to avoid labeling it in advance as an elementary treatise among the Evagrian works or classifying it—another example—with writings devoted to *praktikē* as opposed to works devoted to knowledge. I did not want its evident imitation of biblical proverbs to suggest that this work necessarily somehow stood outside the mainstream of Evagrius's thought.[2] Free from such preconceptions, I think we have been in a position to discern that *Ad Monachos* is a text designed to let its reader discover deep levels of meditation within it, eventually to detect in its emerging structure an image for the whole journey of spiritual ascent from the first of the virtues to the heights of union with the Trinity. In all that lies hidden for discovery within it, it is hardly an elementary treatise. It is the mnemonic summary in biblical language of Evagrius's entire vision of the spiritual life. The method of proceeding here has let this fact fall into relief.

Now we are in a position to ask further questions about the nature of *Ad Monachos*. Where did such a text come from? Is

---

[1] In Part Four we will meditate on individual proverbs, focusing more on the particular content than on the position in the whole.

[2] On cautions about classifying the works of Evagrius, see the section in the Introduction entitled, "The Relationship of *Ad Monachos* to Other Evagrian Texts."

Evagrius unique in what he has created here? Is he the originator of a genre? How much has he relied on former precedents? Answering these questions will enable us to situate the text in its broader environment and can thereby offer further clues about the attitudes that are appropriately brought to the text if it is to be read as Evagrius would have intended.

I propose to answer these questions in three stages, which from three different perspectives attempt to evaluate the precise nature of the sort of literature we find in *Ad Monachos*. The first stage considers the phenomenon of proverbs in human culture in general and in the biblical culture in particular, locating Evagrius broadly within this cultural stream. The second stage looks at the way in which this biblical culture functioned in fourth-century Egyptian monasticism, again locating Evagrius within this stream. This monastic tradition goes a long way toward explaining especially the style and the effect of the individual proverbs Evagrius composed. The third stage looks in a different direction and attempts to draw closer to the structure of the whole text. It looks toward the spirit of ancient philosophy, the classical tradition in which Evagrius had been educated, and it finds there both attitudes and literary genres that for their part also go a long way toward explaining the literary shape of the text Evagrius created in *Ad Monachos*.

Stage One:
Proverbs in Human Culture and in the Bible; Evagrius in This Stream

In this first stage we want to take account of the fact that *Ad Monachos* is a text written in the style of *proverbs*. The questions to be examined can be organized in three steps that proceed toward an ever closer focus on the nature of the proverbs in *Ad Monachos*. In the first step we look at proverbs in general; in the second, at proverbs in the Bible; in the third, at proverbs in *Ad Monachos*.

1. PROVERBS IN HUMAN CULTURE

The basic genre of the text we have been studying is that of a collection of proverbs. *Proverbs* is Evagrius's own word for what he has written (M 137), but even were it not, there could be no doubt that the sentences of *Ad Monachos* fall under such a classification. It may be presumed that this form is no accident to the content Evagrius wishes to present. First, therefore, a basic question in assessing this sort of literature must be, What is the nature of a proverb and how does it function? Scholars of the biblical book of Proverbs likewise begin here. In order to locate Evagrius within both this general human phenomenon and its biblical shape, I follow here the work of one biblical scholar, J. M. Thompson, who approaches the question of biblical proverbs from the perspective of proverbs in general. His work is a solid digestion of a vast literature on the topic.[3]

Thompson's discussion of the general phenomenon of proverbs in human culture begins with a definition, noting that we must content ourselves with a very general description.[4] He cites Lord Russell's concise and useful description: "The wisdom of many, the wit of one." This points to three common features found in proverbs: (1) an arresting and inspired form (one); (2) a wide appeal and endorsement (many); and (3) content that commends itself to the hearer as true (wisdom).

Thompson surveys the proverbs of many European cultures and finds that although forms vary considerably, there are certain aspects of form that continue to reappear and that also characterize the proverbs of other civilizations. Some of these are the

---

[3] Thompson, *Form and Function of Proverbs in Ancient Israel.* Obviously here it is not possible or even desirable to enter at length into the questions posed by a study of biblical proverbs in their own right. Our purpose is more simple: a summary of the issues in order to see broadly how Evagrius is located among them. Following Thompson for both the human and biblical shape of the phenomenon has the advantage of profiting from the continuity his presentation offers. For other useful studies, see Williams, *Those Who Ponder Proverbs: Aphoristic Thinking and Biblical Literature;* and Neumann, ed., *Der Aphorismus: zur Geschichte, zu den Formen und Möglichkeiten einer literarischen Gattung.*

[4] Thompson, *Form and Function,* 17. For what follows, see pp. 17–34.

simple declarative statement or question, rhyme and meter, repetition, alliteration, assonance, similes, and metaphors. He notes that it would not really be useful to study proverbs on the basis of this or that particular form,[5] but he finds it significant that all these forms are forms typical of poetry. This suggests that the power of a proverb is akin to the power of the poem.[6]

Poetry always places the interpreter on shaky ground. Yet if the text is poetry, the interpreter must enter on that ground. Authors turn to poetry when the nature of the content they wish to deliver requires it.[7] A given content asks a certain rapport with the reader, and poetry has the capacity of establishing a particularly suggestive rapport. Thompson's description of this is both accurate and suitably cautious: "It is impossible to state exactly what it is that happens in the human mind when it perceives the 'truth' of a poem or of a 'poetic proverb', but that it happens few would deny. It is as though, within the depths of human consciousness, we perceived the proverb's content to be true, not because of logical demonstration or even just its appeal to 'common sense', but by the way in which it says what it has to say."[8]

---

[5] That is, there does not seem to be a connection between the use of one or the other particular form and the delivery of some particular content. In general all these forms are given free play.

[6] This is an important and suggestive connection. I agree with Thompson's observation, and I have tried in many of my comments on the individual proverbs (Part Four) to treat their distinctive effect from the perspective of their poetic impact. See, for example, the comments on M 31, 53, and 107, but this perspective has affected many more.

[7] S. Langer, in her masterful work on a philosophy of aesthetics, *Feeling and Form*, claims that the nature of the content that inspires any art form, poetry included, is some insight and understanding about the emotional content of the world. In the case of poetry in particular, she suggests that the inspiration has to do with insight into the *emotion* that accompanies *thought*. To grasp the implications of her claim requires a close following of her carefully developed arguments. I feel required to acknowledge here, however, that I am persuaded by her claims and in my interpretations of the various proverbs have tried to remain sensitive to the dimensions of the text that her approach throws into relief. In this part of the study, we face a more general question: What is it about the nature of Evagrius's content that causes him to turn to a form closely akin to poetry? For Langer's general theory, see *Feeling and Form*, 24–68. For the theory applied to poetry, see pp. 208–35, 280–305.

[8] Thompson, *Form and Function*, 23–24.

Thompson has put his finger here on the secret of the power of both poetry and proverbs: the *way* they say what they have to say. The range of a poem's or proverb's impact is impossible to predict precisely because of a power that seems to emerge ("impossible to state exactly . . . but that it happens few would deny") in a successful joining of form and content. In the good poem there is always a sense of "there is no other way to say it." If there are metaphors, they needed to be these metaphors. If there are rhyme and meter, they needed to be these rhymes and this meter. If there is alliteration or assonance, the feeling and idea delivered would be different without them.

Yet for all their similarities, proverbs and poetry cannot simply be identified one with the other. The proverb is generally a nonliterary form, and this too is significant. It is a significance which, Thompson notes, we Westerners are inclined to overlook. We tend to overevaluate books and the printed page and are not particularly sensitive to the spoken word, particularly the sententious word.[9] In cultures more sensitive to the spoken word, an oral form, easily remembered and transmitted, could carry great weight. These oral forms—proverbs in their various shapes— embody and make it possible to pass on the wisdom of a people. They are forms which by their use of poetic devices "convince the hearer in much the same way as poetry does. And also, like poetry, they must be spoken and heard in order to be fully appreciated."[10]

Thompson then goes on to discuss the *function* of the proverb in human culture.[11] He contends (appropriately, I think) that a proverb's function is that of bearing philosophical insight. By philosophy he intends more than only the developed *systems* of Western thought. He means "the attempt of man to describe and understand the world in which he lives,"[12] which includes issues of life and death, ethics, the gods, nature, and so on. Proverbs ought not be seen as only a primitive culture's attempts to deal with the meaning of life, a culture incapable of abstract thought.

[9] Ibid., 25.
[10] Ibid., 27.
[11] Ibid., 27–34.
[12] Ibid., 28.

This would be a mistaken preconception about both primitive culture and abstract thought. Based on his examination of proverbs in many cultures, Thompson claims, "any consideration of proverbial material, even that of primitive peoples, displays what cannot but be seen as abstract thinking."[13]

This understanding of proverbs is developed following a classic study by W. O. E. Oesterley and T. H. Robinson.[14] These authors speak of the aim of philosophy as "the unification of experience . . . the discovery of a single fact or principle with which all the varied manifestations of the universe can be brought into accord."[15] They see the proverb as an effort of this aim for unification. A proverb, a wise man's formulation, brings together into a single expression a host of observed interrelations between the human world and nature, between these and God. In doing so it may embody some law of nature or a rule of conduct or even (more deeply) cut to the very nature of reality in a way that can only be classified as metaphysical.

Thompson adds to these insights of Oesterley and Robinson a consideration of the way in which creative insight comes into play in a proverb's reaching its final form. Philosophy's aim, as described by these authors, requires speculation and careful observation; but, Thompson maintains, that moment in which a collection of insights "gels" into a proverb is more than the end process of a particular line of thought. There must come a creative and intuitive moment, and in this the creation of a proverb is once again like the creation of a poem. On this process, he cites J. F. Genung, who wrote at the beginning of the century:

> In a sense this manner of statement [the proverb's] may be regarded not as a contrast to, but a vigorous condensation of, the typical line of reasoning; something like the enthymeme as distinguished from the full syllogism. The conclusion is affirmed with uttermost emphasis; the process by which it is arrived at is left out. Between the analogy or sign which furnished the occasion and the full-orbed truth affirmed there is a gap for the reader or hearer to

---

[13] Ibid., 28.

[14] W. O. E. Oesterley and T. H. Robinson, *Hebrew Religion* (New York, 1930).

[15] Ibid., 334, cited by Thompson, *Form and Function*, 29.

fill in; and so the latter is compelled to furnish the contribution of his own thought to the solution.[16]

This for me is a very convincing description of both the nature and function of a proverb. Its nature is a "vigorous condensation" of a line of reasoning. Viewing the matter in this way helps us to avoid treating proverbs as merely primitive expressions of the capacity of the human mind. On the contrary, a proverb requires considerable ability to abstract. Its function, by means of this vigorous condensation, is not only to embody the truth but to provoke hearers to fill in a gap, to furnish their own contribution to the wisdom process.

I think the foregoing discussion can lend valuable insight into the nature of Evagrius's *Ad Monachos;* but before turning to that, I would like to follow briefly Thompson's own application of this discussion to the biblical book of Proverbs. Evagrius is a creator of proverbs, but he does so in the biblical style. Therefore, following Thompson's discussion one step further before turning to Evagrius will prove useful for accurately assessing the nature of *Ad Monachos.*

2. PROVERBS IN THE BIBLE

The comments of Oesterley, Robinson, Genung, and Thompson on proverbs in general have all been made with a view toward discussing proverbs in the Bible. The same general drive toward the embodiment of a culture's wisdom in such forms seems to stand behind Israel's wisdom literature as well.[17] However, a distinction is to be drawn between the popular proverb in its oral form and the more polished literary aphorisms typical of the biblical book of Proverbs. In these latter there is an abundance of forms typical of Hebrew poetry, whose distinctive feature is the use of various types of parallelism.[18]

---

[16] J. F. Genung, "The Development of Hebrew Wisdom," *The Biblical World* 42 (July–December, 1913): 19, cited by Thompson, *Form and Function,* 31.

[17] For what follows, see Thompson, *Form and Function,* 59–84.

[18] The parallelism in Hebrew poetry is generally classified as antithetic, synonymous, synthetic, or comparative. These forms are discussed in any handbook

In discussing the function of Hebrew proverbs, Thompson is persuaded to describe it also as philosophical. He suggests, in fact, that in Hebrew proverbs there is an even more profound connection between content and form. The truth value of the Hebrew proverb is intimately connected with its poetic structure. In this he follows the studies of G. von Rad on wisdom literature, who observes that "[e]mpirical and gnomic wisdom starts from the unyielding presupposition that there is a hidden order in things and events—only, it has to be discerned in them, with great patience and at the cost of all kinds of painful experience."[19] This is basically a reasoning by analogy, which presupposes a profound order and coherence in the universe such that wisdom proceeds by discerning in the order of nature a correspondence with the order of human relations and that, in their structures, these bear relationship to the divine order. The proverb-maker is telling us that order in one realm has some mysterious correspondence to order in another.

The proverbs of the biblical book are distinguished by their polished literary nature. This observation is certainly applicable to the majority of the proverbs in the book, but scholars do not agree on how polished the structure of the book is, that is, its entire literary shape. Nevertheless, the book, at least in some of its parts, is more than a haphazard collection of individual proverbs. Some scholars, for example, Oesterley, see in chapters

on the topic, and Thompson does not repeat what is generally known about it. Concerning the book of Proverbs, however, he does point to four particular types that frequently appear: (1) a couplet in which two synonymously parallel parts of the first stich stand in comparative parallelism with the climactic second stich (example from Prov 10:26: "Like vinegar to the teeth and smoke to the eyes, so is the sluggard to those who send him"); (2) the comparative type of *better A than B;* (3) the numerical proverb characteristic of Prov 30, which begins by stating one number less than the total number to be considered; (4) the second person form of address. All except the third type are represented in *Ad Monachos.* When Gressmann first published his critical addition of *Ad Monachos,* in his most brief introductory remarks he at least made the observation that the text was characterized by "die Neigung zum Parallelismus membrorum and zur antithetischen Formulierung, wie in der hebräischen Spruchliteratur" (Gressmann, "Nonnenspiegel und Mönchsspiegel," 152).

[19] Von Rad, *Old Testament Theology,* 2:421, cited by Thompson, *Form and Function,* 70.

1–9 "short sections approximating to a miniature essay form."[20] Thompson himself observes that in chapters 10 to 22:16 practically no arrangement is to be noted.[21] P. Skehan claims that the book is arranged in groups of proverbs, the groups varying in length in such a way that when written out on a scroll, they would have created a visual image of the temple, Wisdom's house of seven columns.[22]

Without needing to solve the many particular questions that a scholarly assessment of the book of Proverbs poses, our following of Thompson's discussion of these various themes enables us to make a few simple observations about biblical wisdom literature that will help to locate Evagrius in relation to it. The proverbs of the Bible share in the same dynamic as proverbs in other cultures. They are, however, a particular instance of this dynamic, an instance characterized by an especially profound relation between form and content. This form, which promotes a reasoning by analogy, has now in many cases a polished literary shape. Yet the function remains philosophical in the broadest sense of the term, requiring the reader's own contribution to the process.

3. EVAGRIUS: AN IMITATOR OF BIBLICAL PROVERBS

Evagrius drank deeply from the springs of the Bible's wisdom literature.[23] The foregoing remarks on the expression of

---

[20] Cited by Thompson, *Form and Function,* 84.

[21] Ibid., 84.

[22] Skehan, "Wisdom's House." The theory relies on rearranging the placement of many verses. Prescinding from the debate over the value of this theory, for our purposes it is evidence that there is at least some structure in portions of the book. Evagrius, of course, could not have been influenced by such an alleged structure since he would not have known of Skehan's rearrangement of verses! However, it is true that Evagrius created a sort of architectural image in the shape of his text, not of a visible temple with seven columns but nonetheless a sort of house for wisdom and knowledge. I must personally confess that though I was not convinced by Skehan's argument, it did cause me to look in *Ad Monachos* for a sort of "architectural" structure, and it was such a search that helped me to detect many of the details of structure that I exposed in the examination of the various chains.

[23] The evidence has been presented throughout this study. It is no accident

wisdom in the form of a proverb, both in its general human dimensions and in its biblical shape, open certain perspectives that help us to evaluate the kind of text Evagrius created in *Ad Monachos* and to gain some sense of what he intended in creating such a text.

General Dimensions

Regarding the general dimensions of the phenomenon found across cultures, it is not too difficult to signal Evagrius's place within this dynamic. He is a successful creator of proverbs with an effective poetic touch. His proverbs express "the wisdom of many, the wit of one." His is the creative intuition that produces the arresting and inspired form (one). Yet he is formulating a teaching already traditional among the desert fathers (many). The content commends itself to the hearer as truth (wisdom).

In all three of these dimensions Evagrius makes his own contribution to the process of seeking out and expressing wisdom. Of the first dimension it could be said that in the creation of the form he is carving out a new path for a sort of Christian wisdom literature. Or, at least, he certainly has given an effective example of using biblical language to suggest in only a few words whole realms of detailed teachings on virtue and doctrine. Proverbs often rely on this capacity of a single word to evoke a host of associations. Evagrius has relied heavily on this approach and maintained a very consistent vocabulary in order to promote it. To the extent that he relies on this, he is distinguished from previous Christian authors.

Concerning the second dimension it could be said that in expressing the traditional wisdom learned from his desert masters, he makes his own contribution as well. Like the gifted pupil who quickly becomes the pride of a school and soon after is

---

that the present study quotes extensively both from the *Scholia on Proverbs* and the *Scholia on Psalms.* The reader need but glance briefly at the Index of Scriptural Citations and Allusions to see that many come from the book of Proverbs and other wisdom writings. We know also that Evagrius composed scholia on Ecclesiastes, Job, and perhaps also the Canticle of Canticles, to mention only the wisdom literature on which he commented.

teaching and extending that school's insights into new fields of research, Evagrius formulates and teaches, for example, the desert's wisdom about demons in a way that certainly is the product of his own speculation and careful observation, even while being founded in an indispensable way on a teaching that preceded him. This would be true, *mutatis mutandis*, for all the teaching that Evagrius formulates, whether in the realm of *praktikē* or of knowledge.

Of the third dimension, content that commends itself as truth, Evagrius's formulations ring with the sound of a hard-won wisdom, gained through personal battle with evil thoughts and personal experience in the heights of prayer. There is an authority here, attractively exercised. This teaching's power to attract comes from the *way* it says what it has to say. This is not to suggest that the way Evagrius expresses himself in *Ad Monachos* is some clever and seductive clothing for an otherwise dull teaching. Quite the opposite. The power of *Ad Monachos* is that power which emerges from a successful joining of form and content. There was no way of saying it other than this proverb's way. There was no better simile. There was no other metaphor. "It is as though, within the depths of human consciousness, we perceived the proverb's content to be true, not because of logical demonstration or even just its appeal to 'common sense', but by the way in which it says what it has to say."[24]

Biblical Dimensions

Regarding the biblical shape of the phenomenon of proverb making, Evagrius must be considered a conscious imitator of biblical proverbs. His are polished literary aphorisms that employ the same forms of poetry that are found in the biblical books. Virtually every proverb of *Ad Monachos* is constructed in some way or other out of the several styles of parallelism that characterize the biblical proverbs. Evagrius has a penchant for comparisons. Many others are in the style of *better A than B*. And many employ the second person form of address. His language is biblical through-

---

[24] Thompson, *Form and Function*, 23–24.

out. When these various biblical styles are used, Evagrius often alludes strongly to or actually cites a biblical proverb or other biblical text.[25] Yet he does not hesitate to use these biblical techniques to create a proverb of his own mint.

The proverbs of *Ad Monachos* ought also to be considered from the perspective of the *function* of the biblical proverbs. Those of *Ad Monachos* are likewise appropriately labeled philosophical, in the broad sense described by Thompson and the scholars whom he follows.[26] Evagrius has entered into that vast effort of the human and biblical family which aims, on account of its love for wisdom, for that "unification of experience . . . the discovery of a single fact or principle with which all the varied manifestations of the universe can be brought into accord."[27] He takes aim in a form that is a "vigorous condensation of the typical line of reasoning."[28]

In *Ad Monachos* Evagrius has managed to formulate some of the various dimensions of the unity of reality that his own tradition and experience have taught him. What is "faith: the beginning of love" if not a vigorous condensation of the unity among a host of necessary virtues? Formulated thus, it leaves a gap for the reader to fill in. All of the proverbs are shaped by this same drive

---

[25] See Index of Scriptural Citations and Allusions.

[26] This is, of course, not the first time that the teaching of Evagrius has been labeled philosophical; but the usual reference is to the influence of his training in classical philosophy on the shape of his thought. That influence is not to be denied, but even the nature of that influence perhaps needs reconsideration, as I shall suggest below in Stage Three of this discussion. The point I make at present is that Evagrius ought also to be considered philosophical in the sense in which the term describes the Bible's wisdom literature. Thompson himself feels it necessary to conduct a defense of wisdom literature. There is a prejudice against its significance among some which runs something like this: Hebrew thought is active, concrete, and nonspeculative. Therefore, wisdom is not Hebrew. This prejudice is spawned from the dubious assumption that primitive people are incapable of thinking speculatively and that Hebrew contrasts sharply in its capacities with the speculative thought of the Greeks. But the wisdom tradition, which was operative in Israel long before the postexilic editing of the books as we have them, puts the lie to these facile contrasts. Similar prejudices could accuse Evagrius of not being biblical, but only if the wisdom literature is excluded from what is counted for biblical. For Thompson's discussion, see *Form and Function,* 96–99.

[27] Oesterley and Robinson, cited by Thompson, *Form and Function,* 29.

[28] Genung, cited by Thompson, *Form and Function,* 31.

for condensation, a drive motivated by the desire to discover relations and unity: the unity among the virtues, an interrelationship among the vices, the effect of these on the knowledge of the way things are, and the relation of this knowledge to the knowledge of God himself. Evagrius's proverbs leap across these various levels of reality, drawing connections among them all. "Irascibility scatters knowledge" is a leap from a vice to its unmentioned counterpart among the virtues, gentleness, to the unifying goal at which that virtue aims. "Do not give much food to your body / and you will not see bad visions in your sleep" is a connection discovered and formulated. "Reasons of the incorporeals, a gentle monk will know" is not only a leap from *praktikē* to knowledge, but it also crosses levels within knowledge, from knowledge of the corporeals to knowledge of the incorporeals. "Knowledge of the incorporeals presents the mind before the Holy Trinity" is a connection discovered and formulated. All of these formulations challenge the reader to fill in the gap. The reader "is compelled to furnish the contribution of his own thought to the solution."[29] This study of *Ad Monachos* has tried to indicate that the very nature of the text is that there are gaps to be filled in. In the commentary on individual proverbs we will offer examples of how such gaps can be filled, but we do not pretend to offer definitive ways of interpreting proverbs, which because of their affinity to poetry have a very wide range of possible effects on any given reader.

If part of the dynamic that lends impulse to the drive to create proverbs is the search for some "single fact or principle" with which the variety at work in the universe can be brought into accord, this seems nonetheless to be a goal that often lies just beyond the reach of even the most effective formulations. Thus are many proverbs produced that circle around the meaning of all reality from various angles. Yet in *Ad Monachos* Evagrius must be credited with some formulations that come close indeed to expressing in a few short lines the unity that underlies many various dimensions of the monastic culture for which he has become proverb-maker. These are the proverbs that he has used to anchor

---

[29] Genung cited by Thompson, *Form and Function*, 31.

his arrangement. "Faith: the beginning of love. / The end of love: knowledge of God" (M 3). This is the principle that lends unity to all of the ins and outs of the struggles of *praktikē*. It is the principle which lends unity to what are certainly different realms and different dimensions of a journey, namely, the difference between *praktikē* and knowledge. It is the principle that expresses the end (the τέλος, M 3's word) of everything: knowledge of God. The whole collection appropriately opens with such a formulation.

"In front of love, passionlessness marches; / in front of knowledge, love" (M 67). This is that same single underlying principle of unity expressed in terms suitable to the midway point of a monk's journey. "Knowledge of incorporeals raises the mind / and presents it before the Holy Trinity" (M 136). This is the same single underlying principle with its most distinctively Christian shape rendered explicit. All of reality comes together and finds its unity in the presence of the Trinity. The other proverbs of the collection move within the overarching framework provided by these especially effective formulations. The study of the structure has, I think, indicated this framework and shown how the other proverbs move within it.

Evagrius is likewise working within the biblical wisdom literature's "unyielding presupposition that there is a hidden order in things and events—only, it has to be discerned in them with great patience and at the cost of all kinds of painful experience."[30] Biblical proverbs reason by analogy. Evagrius's imitation of this biblical technique needs to be considered as much more than a merely surface imitation. A large number of the proverbs of *Ad Monachos* use analogy as the path of insight into the invisible dimensions both of *praktikē's* struggles and knowledge's various mysteries.[31] This is a trait of all of his writings, and it occurs with such frequency that it cannot be dismissed as simply a decorative flourish.[32]

---

[30] Von Rad, cited by Thompson, *Form and Function*, 70.

[31] Classifying only very strictly on the basis of a formula of comparison, the following could all be cited: M 10, 11, 13, 17, 21, 22, 27, 33, 36, 45, 46, 50, 55, 58, 59, 60, 66, 70, 72, 83, 100, 107, 109, 115, 130. This is not to mention the many other images employed that likewise form part of the dynamic of reasoning by analogy.

[32] This position differs from that of Guillaumont (SC 170, 438–41), who

We moderns are inclined to sit down and read a text through, Evagrius's texts included, in one or two sittings. There is really little hope of understanding Evagrius if he is read in this way. A one- or two-sitting reading of *Ad Monachos,* even if it is done very carefully, cannot even approximate how the text was designed to be used. Especially the metaphors, the reasonings by analogy so extensively employed in this text, are lost unless the reader will live for some time with each metaphor and work with it, allowing it to speak. For the analogies have their own gaps to fill, the gap between the physical order and the spiritual order, of which something in the physical is used as an image. This gap takes time to cross. The analogy is meant to be a *means* of crossing. If we, by reading too rapidly, simply arrive at the naked content that is expressed, we have reached that content only by what we would call an intellectual grasp, but not experientially. The analogy, when taken seriously, offers the reader a way to come to the content experientially; for by their very nature the images offered have the power to unlock levels within human consciousness that must be unlocked if wisdom is to be experienced in the depths of one's being.[33]

I am convinced on other grounds that there is evidence that the proverbs of *Ad Monachos* were meant to be meditated on very slowly, perhaps a day at a time, a week at a time, even longer.[34] It is in this kind of situation that we must take account of that reasoning by analogy which *Ad Monachos* employs. To gauge the effect of a given analogy, it is necessary to imagine the proverb in which it stands as being meditated on over a period of time. For example, the "naked content" of M 13 would be that someone

---

explains Evagrius's use of metaphors as a means of giving color to his otherwise abstract, logical style. Evagrius's use of analogy would be an interesting dimension to pursue in the whole of Evagrius's thought. I limit myself here to examples from *Ad Monachos.*

[33] For a further discussion of the power of images, particularly biblical images, to promote a more than intellectual grasp of spiritual realities, see my article, "The Psalms and Psychic Conversion."

[34] In Stage Two I will put these proverbs in relation to a word given by a desert father to his disciple. Such words were meant to be taken, pondered, and worked with until the next visit. In Stage Three I will discuss these proverbs in relation to ancient philosophy's notion of the spiritual exercise of meditation.

who remembers an injury cannot have knowledge. Anyone can be
told that and grasp intellectually what is being said. But the kind
of teaching we are dealing with here is one in which such a content is intimately joined to the *way* in which the content is delivered. "A strong wind chases away clouds." This is the analogy for
understanding just how memory of injury keeps the mind from
knowledge. It "chases" it from knowledge. The meditation on this
proverb involves actually looking up at the sky and watching
clouds race along. They are driven by the force of the wind. The
wind is in control. The cloud could not remain still no matter how
hard it may try. The wind blows and blows, and the sky is eventually cleared of all clouds. Then the meditating monk must say
something like, "This is how it is within me. I may want knowledge of God, but if I remember injuries, some force is set loose
within me over which I no longer have control." And as the meditation lingers, he can begin to put together instances from his
past in which this very connection was borne out. He harbored
the memory of an injury; and before he knew it, his mind was far
from knowledge; indeed, it was all wrapped up in the injury and
its various emotions. "Like a strong south wind on the sea, / so is
irascibility in the heart of a man" (M 36). This storm at sea must
be discovered within. This takes time. It means each individual
must make the connections for himself. Images like these, used as
a means of entering one's interior recesses, unlock a power latent
within for making such connections.

Several more examples can strengthen the point I am making. The "naked content" of M 21 involves a concept that Christians hear perhaps too often for its profundity to strike them any
longer: dying the death of Christ in hopes of sharing his resurrection. But M 21's *way* of speaking of this is content joined to
form. This proverb's meditation involves searching the night sky
for a shooting star. When at last one is seen bursting into light
and falling through the darkness, then this becomes the image
for how the life of Christ suddenly emerges from the death the
monk shares with him. Again, this image must be taken within.
And it can suggest to the monk that this is an experience that he
perhaps in part already knows, that there is a sudden bursting
into light that occasionally brightens the night sky of his struggle
with the flesh. Would the monk be able to detect this interior

movement in himself without the metaphor? At least it has certainly helped. And what of when the meditation continues, watching the sun rising and the way in which it glows? The proverb suggests that the monk's future is comparable to this, that he will glow as brightly and as strongly as the sun. This kind of analogy stems not from a simple desire to add a bit of flourish to a time-worn concept. It stems from the biblical wisdom literature's "unyielding presupposition that there is a hidden order in things." This order is discerned at the cost of all kinds of painful experience, the painful experience of each meditating monk finding the connections within himself of that which Evagrius's proverbs suggest.

It is tempting to pursue this point, to underline this too-little-noticed dimension of Evagrius's thought.[35] I think it explains much of the power of his teaching to attract and the kind of encouragement it offers. Every monk is supposed to know that a vigil helps him fight evil thoughts, but let that monk watch fire melt wax as an image of what a vigil does to evil thoughts (M 50), and he is encouraged to keep vigil in a way that he might not otherwise be. Every monk knows that he ought not let an evil thought linger, but let him imagine how quickly he would react to the sudden appearance of a scorpion on his breast (M 58), and he might trust more readily the time-worn advice that evil thoughts can do him a far more serious kind of damage than a scorpion. Every monk knows that he ought to be gentle, but he may feel that his efforts are getting him nowhere, until one morning he looks up and sees the morning star beautifully placed against the brightening blue vault of the sky and remembers that his teacher once told him, "so is a pure mind in a gentle soul" (M 107).

CONCLUSION TO STAGE ONE

Evagrius as a creator of proverbs in the biblical tradition has found that key to wisdom which the biblical proverbs themselves offer, namely, the coherence between the order of nature and the order of human relations, the coherence between these and the

---

[35] It is this dimension that I would suggest is worthy of extended study throughout the Evagrian corpus.

divine nature which all human beings long to know. This is the analogy of nature used for the "contemplation of the commandments" (TP 79).[36] It is the contemplation of corporeal things used for the contemplation of incorporeal things. It is the contemplation of all things related to the knowledge of God, the Holy Trinity. Proverbs are the genre that promotes this contemplation.

Stage Two:
Evagrius and Scripture
in Egyptian Desert Monasticism

When Evagrius, the talented writer and skilled theological dialectician, came to the deserts of Egypt to be a monk and to submit himself to the desert's already established spiritual traditions, a change was worked in him such that there would henceforth never issue from his pen works of a theological polemical nature that employed the flourish of rhetoric and argument in which he had been trained and by which he had already distinguished himself with Basil and Gregory in the imperial capital of Constantinople.[37] In his monastic conversion Evagrius renounced the sort of theological literature that rhetoric and argument could produce.[38] Yet his pen and literary talents were not to lie

---

[36] Compare G 1's "the reasons of *praktikē.*"

[37] Thus, from Evagrius we have nothing like, say, Basil's *Against Eunomius* or Gregory's *Orations.* Nor do we have collections of homilies like Basil's *On the Hexaemeron* or *On the Psalms.* We have no poems like those Gregory has left us.

[38] My point here focuses on literary genre. The influence of rhetorical training on the new kind of literature that Evagrius was to produce is not to be denied. See, for example, Guillaumont, SC 170, 433–46, for the influence of Evagrius's classical training on his language and style. There is rhetoric in his language naturally, the way it would be found in the language of any well-educated person. What I wish to emphasize here is that Evagrius's use of rhetorical devices is not rhetoric employed for polemic or for preaching or for some desire to impress or for any theological exploration of doctrinal subtleties. Rather, I think it can be considered a well-educated poet's instinctive choices. This is similar to what W. Lackner suggested concerning Evagrius's letters: unintentionally the influence of his education impresses itself on the style of his letter writing (see Lackner, "Zur profanen Bildung des Euagrios Pontikos," 20–21). For this renouncing of rhetoric as a dimension of Evagrius's conversion to monastic life, see Bunge, *Briefe,* 82-85.

idle in the desert. He would turn them to a new purpose and thereby create for his fellow monks (and for the posterity of the spiritual tradition that was to extend from this milieu) new literary forms suited to the monastic spirituality. This was a spirituality in which wisdom was passed on from master to disciple by means of a "word" from the master on which the disciple was to meditate and which the disciple would put into concrete practice in his life. By many such "words" being practiced over the years, monks would make progress in their spiritual journey and come at last to enjoy that for which they had come to the desert: constant prayer, knowledge of God. It is to this desert milieu and its way of passing on wisdom that more than anywhere, I think, are to be sought the explanations for the kind of text we have in Evagrius's *Ad Monachos.*

Any scholar of Evagrius grants the influence on him of both the monastic culture and his classical education. The question is, Where does the weight of the influence fall? Guillaumont, in facing this question for the *Praktikos* places it strongly on the side of Evagrius's classical background.[39] This is a judgment that carries through his other studies, always substantiated with citations of classical texts and traditions that have shaped a given formulation. It could be noted that in general the work of Bunge assigns the influence rather more in the direction of the monastic tradition. The question of these two categories of influence can be posed again regarding *Ad Monachos.* Hopefully what follows here can contribute to the shaping of the whole picture regarding Evagrius, which must be formed by attention to all his works. What we find in *Ad Monachos* is the strong influence of both environ-

---

Evagrius frequently declares himself against profane knowledge (G 4, 27, 41, 45; KG IV, 90; Lt 52: 5; M 128–29), but Lackner accuses him of not following this ("Zur profanen Bildung," 19). However, I think it is important to distinguish between the influence of an education and the kind of actual literary works that Evagrius the monk produced. That is the distinction I am drawing here. When he declares himself against profane knowledge, Evagrius is not speaking against an intelligent and skilled use of language. He is instead warning that knowledge of God is reached not by exercising the mind in the way it must be exercised to pursue worldly knowledge. Knowledge of God comes from "grace, justice, absence of anger, and mercy" (G 45).

[39] Guillaumont, SC 170, 123–25.

ments. Yes, Evagrius brought his education to the desert with him, and with it he reinterpreted and rethought and reexpressed the monastic tradition he received.[40] But he was likewise strongly influenced by this tradition, and *Ad Monachos* clearly bears the signs.

What Evagrius has done in this text is to take the kind of words delivered orally in the desert from master to disciple and put those words together into a literary structure. As such he is an innovator in Christian literature. Few of the desert fathers were writers, but there were many skilled masters who could formulate and deliver words. For a complete assessment of the nature of this text it is necessary to highlight both these dimensions, the oral roots and the literary structure.

That Evagrius writes in short chapters is well known as a characteristic feature of his writing. It has also been frequently observed that there is an order to these chapters.[41] The nuance I wish to add here is that such "chapters" as we have them in *Ad Monachos* stand very close to the spirit of the oral sayings, even while at the same time a new dimension is given them by the order of their presentation in the final literary shape.

Thus, there are two dimensions to be considered: first, the nature of the individual proverbs as words from a master to a disciple, their oral dimension. Second, the proverbs must be considered in their polished form and in the arrangement in which they stand, their literary structural dimension. Roughly, these two dimensions are represented here by Stage Two and Stage Three. For the moment we remain within the desert tradition, (Stage Two) in order to determine the relation of this tradition to the oral dimension that I am suggesting for Evagrius's text.[42] For

---

[40] See ibid., 124.

[41] Such chapters also have precedents in classical literature, as E. von Ivánka shows in "ΚΕΦΑΛΑΙΑ: Eine byzantinische Literaturform und ihre antiken Wurzeln." But the study likewise shows that Christian use of this form arises out of circumstances particular to Christianity. More on this below in Stage Three.

[42] In some ways these two stages correspond to two of the major divisions of this study, namely, an examination of the structure of the whole and a commentary on individual proverbs. Only now the order of treatment is reversed, and the focus is not on what Evagrius is saying as much as it is on his inspiration for composing such proverbs and for so arranging them.

the oral dimension I look mainly to the influence of desert monasticism. For the literary dimension I look mainly to Evagrius's classical education. In what follows now (Stage Two) we shall first examine the desert tradition's attitude to and use of scripture. Second, we shall attempt to see how Evagrius relates to it.

1. THE DESERT "WORDS" FROM A FATHER AND THEIR RELATION TO SCRIPTURE

In examining the desert's style of teaching I propose looking to one of its major dimensions, namely, the role of scripture in this teaching style. I choose this focus on the basis of my claim in Stage One that Evagrius is a conscious imitator of biblical proverbs and chooses his language from the scriptures.

The desert fathers' use of scripture is the theme of a major study by D. Burton-Christie which examines the question on the basis of the *Apophthegmata Patrum*.[43] Though the textual and critical questions concerning the *Apophthegmata Patrum* are extremely complex, it is still possible to use them, as does Burton-Christie, as a privileged witness to monastic life in Egypt in the fourth century. They offer a vast field for fruitful study of the spirituality of the desert, in the case of Burton-Christie's study, of scripture as it forms a part of this spirituality.[44]

The sayings of the *Apophthegmata Patrum* originated in the relationship between master and disciple and in particular from the disciple's request for a word of salvation.[45] The contribution of Burton-Christie's study is to show the extent to which scripture is the foundation of the spiritual world of the desert fathers. He convincingly demonstrates how the interpretation of scripture is at issue in all levels of the *Apophthegmata Patrum*. In an examination of the final form of the redaction of the *Apophthegmata Patrum* the evolution can be traced from the oral to the written

---

[43] Burton-Christie, *Word in the Desert: Scripture and the Quest for Holiness in The Apophthegmata Patrum.*

[44] For a summary of the critical situation of the text, see Burton-Christie, *Word in the Desert,* 76–103.

[45] This situation is usefully described by Guy in "Les Apophthegmata Patrum," in *Théologie de la Vie Monastique,* 74–75. See also Regnault, *La vie quotidienne des pères du désert en Égypte au IV siècle,* 139–51, especially 143–44.

stage of the sayings they contain, though it is argued just how neatly the development can be traced.[46] However that may be, Burton-Christie is probably correct in suggesting that much of the appeal and interest of the *Apophthegmata Patrum* is that it hovers between the worlds of oral and written discourse.[47] For our purposes it is not necessary to enter into the details concerning how to treat the *Apophthegmata Patrum* as *literature* and how to read it as such. This is an important part of the method of Burton-Christie's study.[48] I am more interested in the results this method yields. The distinction must be clearly established: my comparison is not a literary one between the final redaction of the *Apophthegmata Patrum* and *Ad Monachos* or any of the other written works of Evagrius. Such a comparison is really not appropriate.[49] My comparison is rather in what can be detected behind the *Apophthegmata Patrum* and *Ad Monachos* about the use of scripture and attitudes toward it in the oral dimension of desert teaching. Thus, the *Apophthegmata Patrum* show the evolution from the oral to the written stage of the desert teaching. Burton-Christie focuses on the literary level for his discussion of the role of scripture across all the stages of the teaching. I am interested principally in what the text tells of the oral dimension of this teaching.

Following a study by G. Gould, Burton-Christie concludes with him that the interpretation of scripture is a major responsibility of a father and can be discerned in the earliest strata of the material in the *Apophthegmata Patrum*.[50] Across all the levels of the text, oral and literary, Burton-Christie's study reveals how

---

[46] Guy offers a rather orderly explanation identifying three stages which move from simple pronouncements to longer speeches, narratives, or discussions. Regnault was the first to caution against this view, followed by C. Gould and then by Burton-Christie's own contribution. The arguments with their bibliography are found in Burton-Christie, *Word in the Desert*, 81–85. We will come to this point again below.

[47] Burton-Christie, *Word in the Desert*, 84–85.

[48] Ibid., 79–81.

[49] So Guy, "Les Apophthegmata," 73; and also Burton-Christie, *Word in the Desert*, 93.

[50] Gould, "A Note on *The Apophthegmata Patrum*"; see also Burton-Christie, *Word in the Desert*, 82.

"patterns of biblical events and phraseology were transformed into the structure and language of monastic experience."[51]

After having discussed the critical issues concerning the text and outlining the method of his study, Burton-Christie examines the overall orientation to scripture revealed in the *Apophthegmata Patrum*.[52] How and where, he asks, did the monks encounter the scriptures and incorporate them into their lives? For the monks of the desert, scripture was not only a written word but also (and especially!) a spoken and lived word. There were certainly copies of the scriptures in the desert, and many monks had them and made use of them, though certainly not all. But that the text be *lived* as opposed to simply *read* was certainly where the emphasis fell. Thus, the famous statement of the monk who sold his copy of the scriptures and said, "I have sold the book which told me to sell all I have and give to the poor" (TP 97).[53]

The Word of God was appropriated especially through hearing, and this would have happened for monks in three different contexts. First, scripture would have been heard during the public reading of the Sunday synaxis. Second, there was a daily recitation of psalms and other scripture which the monk would perform in his cell, usually alone, sometimes with others. Third, the monk would meditate on scripture, one or two verses at a time, usually reciting it aloud, often while he worked, repeating a verse over and over, digesting it.[54] In these three ways, over many days and weeks and years, the monk slowly became saturated in the language and the spirit of the scriptures.

In very close relationship with this oral/spoken dimension of the Word of God stand the words of the spiritual father. When a monk requested a word from an elder, the words were received—

---

[51] The expression is taken from Burton-Christie, *Word in the Desert,* 90. It serves to sum up much of his study.

[52] For what follows, see Burton-Christie, *Word in the Desert,* 107–29.

[53] This story was to appear in many of the collections of apophthegmata. The recounting by Evagrius in TP 97 is the oldest testimony. (TP 97 will be discussed below).

[54] For details of all three types of oral exposure to the scripture, see Burton-Christie, *Word in the Desert,* 117–29; Regnault, *La vie quotidienne,* 115–21; Davril, "La Psalmodie chez les pères du désert," 132–39. For this in Evagrius, especially as it concerns psalmody, see Bunge, "Psalmodie und Gebet," in *Geistgebet,* 13–28.

orally, person to person—as carrying the same weight and authority as the scriptures. This is because the father's words were seen as being an extension of the scriptures in virtue of the fact that by the purity of his life the father was a living embodiment of the scriptures. Indeed, he was a living text.[55]

A father was a father precisely because he was a living text, because by his way of life he expressed the meaning of scripture. Asking a father for a word was asking him how *the* Word could save the disciple in the concrete circumstances in which he stood asking, how it could save him and change his life. If a father was a father because he embodied the Word, then the word he delivered to a disciple was delivered with the expectation that it too be embodied, that it be put into concrete practice in the disciple's life. One of the principal values of Burton-Christie's study is that it highlights and documents the fact that the exchange between master and disciple was very often an exchange based on the meaning of some part of the scriptures. And "meaning" was especially concerned with how the scriptures were to be embodied. In essence the disciple was asking for a word from scripture that fit his life. The master was giving such a word and giving it with the requirement that if this scripture was to be understood, it must in fact be practiced.[56]

Burton-Christie's reading of the *Apophthegmata Patrum* is a careful listening for evidence of this pattern. He finds it in many ways: in stories that show monks reading or meditating on scripture, in situations where biblical figures function as models, in encounters where a father is asked the meaning of a particular text, in instances in which an allegorical explanation of a biblical passage explains the meaning of some monastic practice, in responses to a request for a word where the father simply offers a verse from scripture, even in the refusal on certain occasions to speak about the scriptures or to own a copy, or also in the refusal to give a word when a father perceives that it will not be prac-

---

[55] For these attitudes, see Anthony 19, Amoun 2, Poemen 187; Burton-Christie, *Word in the Desert,* 108–11. Guy, "Educational Innovation in the Desert Fathers." This same point is made by Hadot in *Exercices spirituels et philosophie antique,* 67. I will come back to Hadot's point in Stage Three.

[56] Demonstrating this is the work of chapter 5 of Burton-Christie's study, "Words and Praxis," 134–72.

ticed.[57] In all these types of evidence there is found among the fathers a reluctance to speak about scripture in a theoretical way and instead a desire to explore the practical implications of the text.

One of the striking impressions that the material in the *Apophthegmata Patrum* leaves—Burton-Christie does not quite express it in this way, though it is an effect of the evidence he produces—is of the liberty with which the fathers altered the scriptural text to fit particular circumstances. This was not for them a betrayal of the sense of the text but rather a deepening of its spirit and an extension of its wisdom to an ever widening range of experience. Indeed, the alteration seems virtually unconscious and is in many cases difficult to detect without careful comparison of the text of the *Apophthegmata Patrum* and the scriptural text. The fathers themselves would not have called this "alteration." This is the result of the scriptures being for the desert monks an oral, living experience more than a written one. This is how the scriptures are cited in such a culture, not *verbatim* but as remembered in a particular moment and as understood in that moment, as given in that moment as a word of salvation for this particular monk.

2. EVAGRIUS IN THE DESERT'S SCRIPTURAL TRADITION

I wish to suggest now that it is to this milieu with its attitudes toward scripture that we ought to look for much of the explanation of the kind of literature Evagrius has produced in *Ad Monachos*. The proverbs of *Ad Monachos* are certainly polished literary aphorisms, and yet at the same time I think it is possible still to hear in them their oral roots, that dimension of their being delivered as a living word of scripture that was expected to be put into practice. This is the appeal of the text, its power to attract. It is similar to the appeal Burton-Christie claimed for the *Apophthegmata Patrum* with its way of hovering between the worlds of oral

---

[57] For the many ways in which the attitude toward scripture is revealed in the *Apophthegmata Patrum,* see Burton-Christie, *Word in the Desert,* 181-291. These pages are filled with examples.

and literary discourse. The difference is that Evagrius's text hovers more on the literary end of the spectrum, while the *Apophthegmata Patrum* hover more on the oral end. And there is a further difference. The *Apophthegmata Patrum* are the resultant literary shape of a collected memory of *oral* traditions. Evagrius's literary productions are *written* responses to requests.[58] But the important point of connection is that the proverbs of *Ad Monachos* are a father's response to a request for a word. In responding to such a request, Evagrius stayed within the style of desert teaching: he delivered short words that extended the biblical text toward those who received his word. He did this orally as well.[59] But when he needed to respond to a request in writing, he took care—natural writer that he was—to give form and structure to his writing, to take advantage of the possibilities latent in form and structure.

The oral and written dimensions of Evagrius's teaching can be presumed to have worked off each other, as they would naturally in anyone. With the proverbs of *Ad Monachos* it is not difficult to imagine this process. A monk comes to the cell of Evagrius, shares a problem, and asks for a word. Evagrius, steeped in the scriptures, offers a word, and the monk departs to practice it. Evagrius returns to what he was doing before the monk arrived, perhaps to chanting a psalm, perhaps to continuing work on proverbs he is writing. The disciple's problem stays in his mind as well as the word he gave him. A psalm verse gives him a further insight or a key word. He sits down to his writing and refines the word he gave the disciple. He polishes it. It suits the larger work he is writing. He includes it.[60]

---

[58] Thus, the Prologue of the *Praktikos*, which indicates that it, along with the *Gnostikos* and the *Kephalaia Gnostica*, are written in response to a request. So also the prologues to the *Chapters on Prayer* and the *Antirrhetikos*. In connection with this latter, see also Lt 4. On the possible circumstances that gave rise to *Ad Monachos* and *Ad Virginem*, see the section in the Introduction entitled "The Addressees of the Text."

[59] There is ample evidence for this, which I shall come to shortly.

[60] Bousset (*Apophthegmata*, 285) suggests a similar process for the composition of the structure of the *Kephalaia Gnostica*, though he does not distinguish oral and written dimensions as sharply as I am doing here; nor does he draw the conclusions I am preparing to make about Evagrius's relation to a wider tradition. On

This process can be imagined as continuing this way over time. Polished proverbs are taking their place one by one in the text Evagrius is shaping. Again, a disciple comes to the door of his cell and asks for a word. Evagrius discerns that one of the proverbs he has recently written exactly suits the situation. He offers it. The disciple departs to practice. He has much in the two or four lines he has received. He has words that echo the scriptures, and he will catch these echoes the more he ponders the proverb. He has metaphors extremely suggestive, which can lead his thinking down paths more varied than he may at first have expected. He has a rhythm and an assonance in the word that make it easy to repeat and remember. He has much to practice.

It was mentioned above that the stages of evolution in the sayings of the *Apophthegmata Patrum* as suggested by J. C. Guy ought not perhaps to be considered as happening quite so neatly as he has outlined them.[61] What I am describing here is further evidence that tells against his argument. The first two stages Guy suggests involve a movement from (1) the saying given to a disciple in a determined circumstance to (2) that saying remembered by the disciple and then generalized and perhaps elaborated and combined with other sayings about the nature of the monastic life in situations more widely applicable than the original word.[62] Guy thinks that stage two is the first step toward using the material for purposes other than that for which it was originally intended, namely, for constructing systematic doctrine on the spiritual life.[63] But what I am describing here for Evagrius shows both of Guy's stages under the control of one father; that is, not only is a word shaped in response to a particular circumstance (1), but it is also used in a more general way (2) and fitted into a systematic written work—or vice versa. Evagrius would thus be *one* father controlling *both* stages of a word's evolution, and it does not seem to me possible to distinguish the oral stage as somehow more authentically, more primitively monastic than the written stage.

---

p. 75 he observes, "Euagrios hat fast seiner ganzen literarischen Hinterlassenschaft . . . die Form der Apophthegmen-Literatur aufgeprägt."

[61] See n. 46 above.
[62] Guy, "Remarques sur le texte des *Apophthegmata Patrum*," 252–58.
[63] Guy, "Les Apophthegmata," 77–78.

In advancing a different kind of caution against too easy an acceptance of the neatness of Guy's stages one and two, Gould speaks of how a father was at liberty to reuse the saying of another father and adapt it to use in a new situation. Thus, in response to a request for a word, a father might respond by saying, "Father So-and-So used to say . . . ."[64] Gould remarks that surely this use of a remembered word does not represent a less authentic stage of monastic teaching. I would like to add here an observation along the lines of Gould's remark, namely, that surely the *same* father would be at liberty to remember his own words and reuse them in differing but appropriate circumstances. The direction of reuse could be either from oral to written or from written to oral.[65]

In summary, it can be noted that I am making several suggestions here. The first is that Evagrius's words as we have them in *Ad Monachos* can be understood as words like the words of other fathers that are reported to us from the *Apophthegmata Patrum*, namely, extensions of scripture, applications of scripture to determined situations. Second, I suggest that both an oral and a written dimension are to be discerned in *Ad Monachos* and that the text has its power, its dynamic of interpretation, because it hovers between the two.

I wish now to firm up these suggestions by substantiating them from several different directions. First, I will look to direct evidence in the text of *Ad Monachos* for this particular understanding of the relation between scripture and the words of a father, and I will draw some conclusions about the scriptural allusions and citations in *Ad Monachos*. Second, I would like to widen the circle by indicating evidence in some of Evagrius's other writings that shows him to be the kind of teacher I am suggesting here.

Evidence in Ad Monachos

At least eleven proverbs in *Ad Monachos* refer to the role of the spiritual father. The introductory and concluding proverbs

---

[64] Gould, "A Note," 135.

[65] It is not uncommon for Evagrius to use a portion of a text he has written as a part of a letter addressed to a specific concern. Evagrius also reuses the words of other fathers in his writings, and there is no reason to think that he would not have done the same orally.

fall into this category, making the theme a framework for all the teaching that is contained within. The very first point established, in M 1, is to invite the disciples to listen to the proverbs that follow, which are called "reasons of God, sayings of Christ, words of the wise." Here scripture and these "words" are put in strict relationship. This is "a good father training his sons" (M 2). The final sentence of the collection (M 137) labels all that has preceded with the biblical word "proverbs." These proverbs have been given "in the Lord," and the father himself asks the listening disciples for prayers.

Though all the proverbs that come between this beginning and end thus fall into the category of a word between master and disciple, the theme comes to the surface of the text a fair number of times. M 73, for example, a proverb slightly longer than usual, begins, "Listen, O monk, to the words of your father." It continues by asking for an obedience "which travels with him in thinking." Shortly after this a five-member chain on fathers (M 88–92) stresses listening to the father's word and not listening to the words of others. In M 92, the final proverb of this chain, the commands of the Lord are put in strict parallel with the words of the father: "Blessed is the monk who guards the commands of the Lord, / and holy the one who closely keeps the words of his fathers." In M 124 the holy dogmas of the fathers are put in direct relation to the church's baptismal faith and in the following proverb are opposed to the teachings of heretics. In M 126 Evagrius speaks with an explicit reference to himself as father: "Now therefore, son, listen to me." He goes on to tell the story of his experience with heretics, of whom he says, "There is no prudence and there is no wisdom in their teachings." Theirs are not "the words of the wise" (M 1). Theirs are not "clear proverbs" (M 137).

These eleven proverbs draw specific attention to the relationship between the words of this text and the words of scripture, a relationship founded in the disciple's expectation that this father is able to give him a saving word. The positioning of these eleven proverbs is significant. The point is made at the very beginning (M 1 and 2) and the very end of the text (M 137). It is made again in M 73 as the text passes its halfway point and makes a new beginning. It is the subject of a chain (M 88–92) located exactly in the middle of the development from this new beginning up to the text's turning point, that is, in the middle between M 73 and M 107. M 124 and 126 are part of the important chain on true and false knowledge (M 123–32), and M 126 with its "Now therefore, son, listen to me" is the middle member of that chain. "There is no prudence and there is no wisdom in their teachings" is the exact middle line of all the lines in the ten-member chain. This is telling evidence, I think, that in *Ad Monachos* Evagrius is consciously aware of teaching in the style that characterizes the monastic practice of master giving disciple a word that at base is always God's Word.

The eleven proverbs mentioned above are explicit in their reference to the relationship between scripture and the words of the father as Evagrius understands it. But the same relationship is expressed implicitly in virtually every proverb of the text. I have already drawn attention to Evagrius's desire to imitate the style of biblical proverbs. But why would he do this? I think that such imitation could have no purpose apart from extending the scriptural word to specific situations in the monastic life, the various situations of which the many proverbs speak.

Consulting the Index of Scriptural Citations and Allusions, however, shows that Evagrius was not only imitating biblical proverbs but also alluding to many portions of the scriptures, Old Testament and New. Throughout this study and especially in my commentary on the individual proverbs, I have tried to give some examples of the lines of thought into which this scriptural language is meant to lead the meditating monk. These are but a sampling; yet combined with this index, they can serve to show how saturated the text of *Ad Monachos* is with the vocabulary, style, and spirit of scripture.

The *Apophthegmata Patrum* show that this way of teaching characterized the teaching of the desert. *Ad Monachos* shows that Evagrius was a master of this style of teaching.

Evidence from Other Evagrian Texts and Other Monastic Literature

The picture I am trying to describe, the *Sitz im Leben* of the creating of a text, can likewise be substantiated by evidence beyond the text itself of *Ad Monachos,* both in other Evagrian writings and in monastic literature from other hands. This, of course, opens a vast area of possible investigation: Evagrius's relationship to the rest of the desert monastic tradition, a topic that is appropriately explored only by a careful confrontation of Evagrian texts with other texts that give evidence of this tradition. Such a confrontation is complicated by the fact that some of this evidence comes to us in forms that are friendly to Evagrius, others that are not.[66] A friendly text is not necessarily an unreliable witness, nor is an unfriendly one to be either uncritically accepted or rejected. A method is required that reaches behind these texts in their present form, friendly or unfriendly, and tries to reconstruct the actual relationship Evagrius had with the rest of the monastic traditions of fourth-century Egypt.[67]

One thing is certain: the style of teaching in *Ad Monachos* stands squarely within the desert tradition; indeed, *Ad Monachos* is a precious example of such teaching. The picture of Evagrius revealed there is confirmed by others of his works and by those who have written about him.

For example, the most extensive information we have on the life of Evagrius is in a biography written by Palladius and extant only in Coptic and a brief Greek fragment of the same. Scholars consider it authentically the work of Palladius and a generally trustworthy account of Evagrius's life.[68] The account tells us much about the kind of spiritual father and teacher Evagrius was, and it is a text that becomes especially interesting when allowed to echo off one of Evagrius's own, namely, the *Gnostikos,* in which Evagrius addresses the issue of the qualities a teacher, a knower, ought to have. In these echoes one hears a teaching like that found in *Ad Monachos.* The clues that can be gathered from the *Coptic Life* fall roughly into three categories: information about

---

[66] See Guillaumont, SC 170, 125.

[67] I think three models of the kind of study I am describing are found in Bunge's "Évagre le Pontique et les deux Macaire," his "Origenismus-Gnostizismus," and his "Introduction aux fragments coptes."

[68] Butler, *Lausiac History of Palladius,* 1:137, 145. A. Guillaumont, ed., *Les Képhalaia Gnostica,* 76 n. 118. Bunge, "Évagre le Pontique et les deux Macaire," 324–25; idem, "Origenismus," 26–28; and Bunge and de Vogüé, *Quatre ermites égyptiens,* 18–80. O'Laughlin, *Origenism in the Desert,* 55–56. Bunge begins his book

Evagrius's relationship to scripture, descriptions of his teaching activity, and comments about the nature of his writing.[69]

Palladius begins his account by claiming Evagrius as his personal teacher and specifies that it was a teaching that involved reading the scriptures in a certain way: "It was he who taught me the life which is in Christ, and he who made me know the holy Scripture in spiritual wise" (*Coptic Life*, 105).[70]

Later in the text Palladius associates Evagrius's knowledge of the scriptures not with his intellectual strength but with his purity (i.e., *praktikē* opening a way to knowledge). After describing his ascetical regime, Palladius says, "His mind became very pure, and he was worthy of the grace of wisdom and knowledge and judgment, discerning the works of demons. He was accurate in the Scriptures and the orthodox traditions of the Catholic Church, and the books which he wrote testify to his knowledge and excellent mind" (*Coptic Life*, 113). This statement should be understood in connection with what was observed of fathers from the *Apophthegmata Patrum,* namely, that a capacity to speak a word that was considered a word extended from scripture came only from purity of life. Palladius's text is interesting also for the way in which it puts orthodox tradition in relation to scripture. In the fourth century's theological controversies the difference between orthodoxy and heresy often turned on a scriptural text being rightly interpreted or not.

There are several places in Palladius's story that give indications as to how Evagrius became saturated in the scriptures in so spiritual a way. We are told that he prayed one hundred prayers a day (*Coptic Life*, 112). Further we learn that Evagrius slept but a third of the night and spent the rest of the time meditating, praying, and contemplating the scriptures (ibid., 113). Evagrius's meditation on the scriptures during the night is described in another place as well, as a part of a vision that Evagrius himself

---

Akedia with a brief biography of Evagrius that relies heavily on Palladius (pp. 9–16).

[69] These same three categories will be used to organize the material contained in the *Gnostikos.*

[70] References to the *Coptic Life* are given according to the pages of Amélineau's published text. The English is the translation provided by Butler, *Lausiac History,* 116–17, 132–35, 143–45.

recounts. He begins the story with the circumstances in which the remarkable vision came about: "I was seated at night in my cell with the lamp burning, reciting one of the prophets." The hour is given as midnight (ibid., 117).[71]

When all this information is combined, it goes a long way toward explaining how naturally scriptural language came to the pen of Evagrius. It is on the basis of this information, together with the fact that it is known that many monks came to his cell to receive a word, that I proposed my own reconstruction of how a text like *Ad Monachos* came gradually to be composed: Evagrius at prayer or at work, the scriptures ever on his mind, and a monk coming for a word.

From Palladius's biography we can also glean some sense of the actual conditions in which Evagrius was sought as a teacher and in which he conducted his teaching. There is a fine description of the brothers gathering around him on Saturday night. "During the night they would discuss their thoughts with him and listen to his words of comfort" (*Coptic Life,* 114). Next Palladius turns to the fact that during the week as many as five or six visitors a day came to his cell. He is said to have loved strangers. They for their part came to him because they were "attracted by his wisdom and asceticism" (ibid., 115). A kindness and gentleness must have suffused his reception of visitors and his manner of teaching. "It was impossible to find a worldly word in the mouth of abba Evagrius, or a quarrelsome word; nor would he hear such from another" (ibid., 118).

Palladius also speaks of Evagrius as writer. It was mentioned above (by Palladius) that among the ways in which one can see Evagrius's knowledge of scripture there are the books he has written, which in turn testify "to his knowledge and his excellent mind." These books teach all "to live profitably according to the traditions of the Church" (*Coptic Life,* 113). Later Palladius tells us why Evagrius wrote: so that those who read "might be comforted," for "he taught us by what methods different thoughts are overcome" (ibid., 116). Palladius's text mentions that this work bears witness to Evagrius's personal experience standing behind

---

[71] We will have the occasion to examine this vision below. See the commentaries on M 53 and M 107.

that which he wrote. "If you wish to see all the temptations he suffered, read the book . . . and you will see all his power and different temptations" (ibid.).

This is a brief but valuable witness about what motivated Evagrius's writing activity. The way in which it is mentioned and the context of the passages indicate that the teaching embodied in his writing is of a piece with his oral teaching. Both were expressions of his love. Evagrius himself says so explicitly in another place, in a letter responding to a request for "words" on prayer: "I am sending them [the words] to you in the basket of love" (Prayer, Prologue [PG 79:1165B]).

This Palladian picture of Evagrius's use of scripture, his teaching, and his writing activity finds its echo and confirmation in Evagrius's own work, the *Gnostikos*, which treats the theme of how and what a father should teach. And not only does it confirm this picture, but it colors it a little more with a sense of the quality and tone of his teaching.

Seven of the fifty chapters of the *Gnostikos* are devoted to exegesis (G 16-21, 34), and in these Evagrius explicitly expresses himself on how central right understanding of scripture is to true knowledge and to teaching it. Thus, he explains, the teacher must be prepared to have at hand the material necessary for the explanation of scripture and at least to attempt to face every issue that presents itself (G 16). He must know how to determine if a passage is speaking of *praktikē*, natural contemplation, or theology (G 18). Evagrius speaks of the need to become familiar with the scripture's habitual way of speaking, and to establish any understanding of this on the basis of examples drawn from the scriptures themselves (G 19).

These concerns and this advice about exegesis give us a fuller sense of what Palladius would have meant by "he made me know the holy Scripture in spiritual wise," and "he was accurate in the Scriptures and the orthodox traditions." On the other hand, *Ad Monachos* shows us the fruit of a teacher who had learned well the scripture's habitual way of speaking and had drawn together many examples of it. Thus, when he wants to compose a proverb about *praktikē*, he uses scripture's language and scripture's images for *praktikē*. If it is a proverb about theology, he knows scripture's habitual way of speaking about that. And so on.[72]

In the *Gnostikos* Evagrius also expresses himself on the qualities a teacher ought to have, and he leaves evidence of some of the sorts of situations in which he found himself teaching. In a touching way he speaks of the importance of the father's being approachable, an approachability that will be expressed in his very countenance and which stems from his genuine concern for the salvation of others. "It is necessary for the knower to be neither sullen nor hard to approach. For sullenness comes from ignorance of the reasons of created things, and being hard to approach comes from not wanting 'all men to be saved and to come to knowledge of the truth' (1 Tm 2:4)" (G 22).[73]

The *Gnostikos* leaves evidence that Evagrius taught both in groups and individually, just as Palladius has reported, and also that he taught anchorites as well as laity. Of the five or six visitors who came to his cell each day, certainly some were lay pilgrims.[74] It is striking how frequently Evagrius stresses the importance of a father's sensitivity to the capacity of the person receiving instruction. The advice he gives on this lets us believe that he himself would have had such a sensitivity. "Become acquainted with the reasons and the laws of times, lifestyles, and occupations so that you can easily have something profitable to say to everyone" (G 15).[75] This and related kinds of advice can serve to fill in Palla-

---

[72] This would extend to the details of the three parts of the soul and to the various levels of contemplation, to true and false knowledge. Scripture has its way of speaking about each, and the proverbs of *Ad Monachos* have employed this way of speaking, which is demonstrated in the individual commentaries and is further indicated by the Index of Scriptural Citations and Allusions.

[73] This can be compared with G 46, which speaks of "eagerly nourishing those who present themselves" to the teacher for help. The church historian Socrates reports of Macarius of Alexandria, whom he specifically mentions as Evagrius's teacher, that he was always cheerful (ἱλαρός) to his visitors and that "he used to joke with the young men whom he introduced to asceticism" (Socrates, *Church History,* 4.23 [PG 67:516A]). For this portrait discussed, see Guillaumont, "Les problèmes des deux Macaire," 53–54.

[74] For the variety of the types of people Evagrius taught, see G 13, 36.

[75] Many other chapters speak about the importance of adapting teaching to

dius's description of the Saturday night teaching sessions, the individual interviews that followed, and the five or six visitors who came each day. For each Evagrius shaped a word suitable to particular circumstances. It was this same capacity for adapting to the individual that I suggested was involved in the process of shaping *Ad Monachos*.

The *Gnostikos* does not give any direct information about Evagrius's writing activity, other than the too obvious fact that it is itself a piece of writing! Yet two clues in Evagrius's own words confirm Palladius's statement that the reason he wrote was "for the comfort of others." We heard Evagrius speak of a "desire for all men to be saved" and of "eagerly nourishing" those who come for teaching. This is why Evagrius wrote. He wrote works suited for people across all stages of the spiritual journey, that is, he adapted himself to the capacities of those receiving instruction. Great care went into the making of *Ad Monachos*. To those who would not know how to understand the scriptures "in a spiritual wise" the text could appear harmless and flat. But to those acquainted with "the scripture's habitual way of speaking" it would be a text that gradually could unveil itself as a beautiful image of the whole upward ascent toward the Holy Trinity. This is the work of someone who desires all to be saved, who eagerly nourishes those who come to him, someone who easily has something profitable to say to everyone.

Apophthegmata are a genre of monastic literature particularly suited to passing on the teaching that was usually given in face-to-face encounters between masters and disciples. Evagrius plays an important role in the growth of this genre, and some attention now to his influence there will help us to measure from a different perspective where he stands in relation to the broader tradition of desert monasticism. In addition to the fact that, as W. Bousset observed, Evagrius "hat fast seiner ganzen literarischen Hinterlassenschaft . . . die Form der Apophthegmen-Literatur aufgeprägt,"[76] he also leaves us with three series of his own collected apophthegmata: at the end of the *Praktikos* (TP 91–100), at

---

the capacity of those to be instructed: G 6, 23, 25, 31, 35, 36, 40. For chapters that may be advice for teaching groups, see G 26, 29, 31, 35.

[76] Bousset, *Apophthegmata*, 75.

the end of the *Gnostikos* (G 44–48), and two-thirds of the way through the *Chapters on Prayer* (Prayer 106–12). These are the oldest examples we have of this literary genre. Though it is not possible to determine if Evagrius is the first to make such a written collection, he is certainly among the first to have done so.[77] His having done so was a critical step in the eventual flourishing of such literature among monks. Indeed, I. Hausherr remarks, "Si nous avons cette inappréciable collection des *Apophthegmes des Pères,* c'est certainement pour une bonne part à son exemple et à sa doctrine que nous le devons."[78]

These apophthegmata, which are strategically placed in each of the three works, should be understood as Evagrius's explicit avowal that the teaching of each work is dependent on and in the line of the fathers mentioned, indeed on the fathers in general. They, for their part, are the guarantee of his teaching. For his part, he is their disciple, himself now become a teacher. Thus, at the end of the *Praktikos* he seals, as it were, his teaching with a series of apophthegmata which concern *praktikē,* some of which also make the connection with knowledge. At the end of the *Gnostikos* he seals his teaching with a series meant especially to guarantee Nicaean orthodoxy. In the *Chapters on Prayer* he relates his doctrine on prayer to stories of some of its great monastic exemplars.[79]

There are striking similarities between the teachings of the fathers that Evagrius cites, some of whom are the most renowned of the desert, and the teaching found in *Ad Monachos.* The fathers' influence can be noticed both in the content of individual proverbs and in structural elements. In addition, these fathers teach in memorable sayings that condense large amounts of teaching. Evagrius has become their imitator, both orally and in writing. Furthermore, in writing down these oral teachings of the fathers as he does here, Evagrius is shaping a new literary genre (whether he be its originator or not) that will have a great future

---

[77] See ibid., 75–76; Guy, "Les Apophthegmata," 77.

[78] Hausherr, *Leçons,* 141.

[79] On the apophthegmata of the *Praktikos,* see Bunge, "Évagre le Pontique et les deux Macaire," passim. On those in the *Gnostikos,* see his "Origenismus-Gnostizismus," 41–44.

as a means of embodying and passing on monastic doctrine. This is the genre that we find in the *Apophthegmata Patrum*, so revered as a witness to fourth- and fifth-century Egyptian monasticism.[80]

CONCLUSION TO STAGE TWO

I have dwelt at some length on Evagrius's relation to the rest of the desert tradition of monasticism because it seems to me that it is a dimension of his thought not frequently enough examined. More precisely, I have done so because *Ad Monachos* provides the occasion and new evidence of the strength of the links between Evagrius and this desert tradition. Indeed, I do not think we can understand the nature of the text unless we locate it within that tradition. The place where an author lived and wrote is the first place to look for the influences that shaped his work. In Evagrius's case the desert tradition is not the only influence on the shape of his writing. In Stage Three we turn to other influences. Yet it is in looking to the desert tradition that we begin to see *Ad Monachos* for what it is: Evagrius's experiential understanding of the monastic journey expressed in memorable biblical words given to disciples to be practiced and given for their comfort.

With the help of Burton-Christie's study we saw that scripture is a fundamental dimension of the teaching that a desert father gave to his disciple in face-to-face encounters. Evagrius feels this same commitment to the sense of scripture in the teaching he gives when he meets a disciple. These kinds of encounters influenced also the manner of his writing. In reverse, his writing can be presumed to have affected the style and quality of the teaching he delivered orally.

Ad Monachos is a text that lets us sense both these oral and written dimensions, and as such it is a precious witness to the

---

[80] In other studies I have compared the teaching of Evagrius with the teaching represented in the *Apophthegmata Patrum*. My purpose has been to show that Evagrius should be considered as belonging to the mainstream of the Egyptian monastic tradition and not, as some scholars would have it, to some nonrepresentative portion on the sidelines. See Driscoll, "Exegetical Procedures in the Desert Monk Poemen"; idem, "Evagrius and Paphnutius on the Causes for Abandonment by God"; idem, "The Fathers of Poemen and the Evagrian Connection."

quality and nature of his teaching effort. Though it is a written text very carefully constructed, it is a text in which one still feels the steep price of personal experience in the construction. Evagrius's own experience stands behind the formulation of each individual proverb as well as behind the structure of the whole text. There is also a steep price expected from those who receive this text. It is the price of practicing the words that are given. This is the price that every disciple must pay to his father for a word received.

These claims about the nature of *Ad Monachos* have been supported by evidence drawn from different sources. First, we listened to Evagrius's own words both from *Ad Monachos* and from some of his other works in which he himself witnesses to his reliance on the teaching of the monastic fathers both in style and in content. The biography of Evagrius by his disciple Palladius presented us with a picture of a teacher who both speaks to disciples and writes to them, and this picture converged with both the style and content of *Ad Monachos*. This picture was more firmly verified by Evagrius's own words about the nature of teaching as expressed in the *Gnostikos*. All this is evidence, I think, that can contribute to the shaping of a more accurate picture of fourth-century Egyptian monasticism and Evagrius's place within it.

If it is generally granted less grudgingly that Evagrius's teaching on *praktikē* is a representative instance of the general monastic teaching on the same, then it becomes important to listen especially closely to that teaching; for Evagrius teaches a *praktikē* inconceivable without its reference to knowledge. And he teaches a knowledge inconceivable without its roots continually in *praktikē*. This is the *whole* desert's teaching on *praktikē*. *Ad Monachos* is the image of how tightly conceived is this relation. If one wants to continue to maintain that it is simply a text addressed to beginners,[81] then still the more than forty proverbs in this text concerned with knowledge must somehow be explained, concluding at the very least that the attention of beginners is certainly directed rather frequently toward knowledge.

---

[81] As does Guillaumont (SC 170, 33–34; also "Evagrius Ponticus," *Theologische Realenzyklopädie* 10:566). Most other students of Evagrius follow Guillaumont's classification.

Stage Three:
Evagrius and Ancient Philosophy

In the fifth century when the church historian Socrates introduces Evagrius into his account, he describes him as the disciple of Macarius the Great and Macarius of Alexandria, and he says of him that "he acquired from them the philosophy of deeds, whereas formerly he had been a philosopher only in word" (*Church History* 4.23 [PG 67:516A]). Evagrius himself speaks even before his having gone to the desert of "a certain longing which stole into me for the divine dogmas and for the philosophy concerning these." He continues, asking rhetorically, "Who would become a Laban for me, free me from Esau, and guide me [παιδαγωγῶν] to the highest philosophy?" (Ep Fid 1, lines 11–14).[82] In the text from Socrates, there is succinctly expressed, perhaps unwittingly, what I think is the core of the way in which the tradition of ancient philosophy makes its influence felt on Evagrius, that is, as a philosophy of deeds and not of words only.[83] In Evagrius's own words we hear him speak of philosophy in a way that clearly means to rely on the etymological sense of the word, love of wisdom. He longs for a wisdom that would understand divine dogmas. He desires a teacher who will train him (παιδεία) to reach the highest wisdom, the highest philosophy.

With these two texts the question of Evagrius's relation to ancient philosophy can be posed. I noted above in comparing the scholarly project of Guillaumont with that of Bunge that the

---

[82] In what immediately follows in the text, Evagrius points to his having found Gregory Nazianzus to help him in his desires. He calls Gregory "a vessel of election." On the significance of this term, see its use in M 65 and the commentary on that proverb below. Evagrius clearly owes much of what he knows of ancient philosophy to Gregory; see TP 89, TP epilogue, G 44. The theological influence of Gregory on Evagrius is even more thorough and certainly needs further investigation.

[83] I say "perhaps unwittingly" because probably Socrates wishes to contrast more strongly than I will here the "philosophy" Evagrius learned from his desert masters and the philosophy that he knew before he came to the desert. What we shall see here is that ancient philosophy was meant to be "a philosophy of deeds" and not of words only.

former tends to assign a stronger role to Evagrius's classical background than to his monastic teachers, whereas Bunge's tendencies are in the opposite direction. In so observing I wanted to approach the question again on the basis of *Ad Monachos*. It seemed to me that the desert was the first most obvious place to look for influences on a monk who wrote in the desert; and looking there, we found considerable influence from Evagrius's desert masters on the text that he composed. But clearly this was not the only influence on Evagrius. His mind was well formed in the classical philosophical tradition, and there is no doubt that this tradition continued to influence the theology and spirituality of this monk. Every scholar grants this, and it need not be demonstrated anew. I want to ask a more specific question here: What has been the influence of ancient philosophy on *Ad Monachos?*

E. von Ivánka has shown that the chapters (κεφάλαια) in which Evagrius wrote, following one after another and not linked together in the line of an unfolding discourse, are not a genre unique to him but one that existed already in the philosophical tradition. Among the Stoics he especially draws attention to the *Meditations* of Marcus Aurelius; among the Neoplatonists, to Porphyry's collection of excerpts from Plotinus. Such chapters had for their purpose to aid the meditation of the reader.[84] Evagrius seems to have been among the first to employ this literary form in Christianity.[85] Von Ivánka notes that these collections of philosophical chapters could not have but influenced Christians when

[84] Von Ivánka, "ΚΕΦΑΛΑΙΑ," 285–91.

[85] In *Ad Monachos* Evagrius does not simply create another set of chapters but chapters that carefully imitate the scripture's wisdom literature. There are several other examples of Christian wisdom literature, and two such texts serve to some extent as literary precedents for the text Evagrius has created, namely, the *Teachings of Silvanus,* found among the Nag Hammadi codices, and the *Sentences of Sextus.* For the former, see the titles in the bibliography by Zandee and Peel. For Sextus, see Chadwick, *Sentences of Sextus.* As other examples of Christian wisdom literature in gnomic style, the texts merit being compared. Though such a comparison would yield a number of similarities among the texts, more than anything, I think, it would throw into greater relief the uniqueness of Evagrius's text. It would especially show Evagrius as singular (to date) in the creation of a very carefully designed order to his chapters and in the evenness of the composition of his literary product.

they came to do the same, yet he likewise insists on what is unique in the Christian use of this genre. "Es wäre falsch zu sagen, dass die christlichen Literaturgattungen aus der Antike einfach übernommen sind. Sie entstehen aus eigenen Wurzeln, eigenen Bedürfnissen."[86] Our study of Evagrius as a spiritual father within desert monasticism showed what some of these particular roots and needs were. As Evagrius met those needs, it seems to me that he could not have remained uninfluenced by his philosophical background.

Great minds—Evagrius is one—are able to see the relation between two distinctive expressions of wisdom in two distinctive cultures. If the wisdom is genuine, then the connection is not to be wondered at. If it is truth, then it is truth valid for all. It is this that explains Evagrius's synthesis between the wisdom of the Greek philosophical tradition and the wisdom in desert monasticism. If wisdom from the Greeks is seen as no real wisdom, then what Evagrius has done is reprehensible. This age-old question of what has Athens to do with Jerusalem has received many different answers through the centuries, but it remains the case that we still will evaluate Evagrius today on the basis of an implicit or explicit position on this question. It is between Athens and Jerusalem that the synthesis he has created must be viewed. I think the wisdom of the Greek philosophical tradition is a genuine one, even if from the standpoint of Christian theology it stands in need of completion by the wisdom proclaimed in the

---

[86] Von Ivánka, "ΚΕΦΑΛΑΙΑ," 291. Apophthegmata also had a classical precedent (see Klauser, "Apophthegma"); likewise for gnomic literature (see Spoerri, "Gnome"). Ancient philosophy and these ancient forms already influenced the Christian authors who influenced Evagrius, making the question more difficult to unravel. There is much field for fruitful study yet to be done on more exactly how Clement, Origen, and Gregory Nazianzus influenced Evagrius. A small sampling in Clement's regard can be found in A. Guillaumont, "Le gnostique chez Clément d'Alexandrie et chez Évagre le Pontique." Clement's seemingly rambling approach in the *Stromata,* often called his esoterism, seems to have had primarily a pedagogical purpose. See Mondésert, *Clément d'Alexandrie,* 47–62; also Méhat, *Étude sur les "Stromates" de Clément d' Alexandrie,* 492–99. For Origen, see Kline, "Christology of Evagrius and the Parent System of Origen." If Evagrius is not an originator of chapters, apophthegmata, or gnomic literature, he does seem to be the originator of "Centuries," that is, chapters collected in groups of one hundred (see Hausherr, "Centuries").

cross of Christ. Evagrius viewed Greek wisdom in this way. When he read the Christian scriptures and sought, for example, to understand the wisdom contained therein according to the Greek philosophical division of ethics, nature, and contemplation, this was his way of claiming Christian faith as the only true philosophy. When he applied a similar schema to help understand the desert's ascetical tradition and the nature of the experience of prayer to which such ascetical practices led, this was the same claim: monasticism as true philosophy.

When Christians in the early centuries made claims like these, they were not necessarily aware that they had in fact achieved a synthesis. It may have seemed to them that they had simply successfully wrested wisdom from ineligible claimants. Christians, particularly educated Christians, could not be completely aware of how much they had absorbed from their culture. A person's very ability to think and the language in which thinking is done is so thoroughly saturated with cultural presuppositions that it is impossible to let them go even when on a conscious level the decision may be made to reject fundamental directions of that culture, to claim, for example, that Athens ought not to have anything to do with Jerusalem. I do not pretend to know Evagrius's awareness or lack of it in terms of how the Greek philosophical tradition influenced him. Yet conscious or not, it is there; and it shows itself in a particularly interesting and subtle way in *Ad Monachos*. The influence is there, of course, in the content; but it emerges especially in a certain attitude, a certain set of expectations, which it would seem Evagrius wanted his reader to bring to the text. These are attitudes that any lover of wisdom in antiquity was expected to bring to the philosophical school to which he adhered. It is what P. Hadot has called "spiritual exercises."[87] Ancient philosophy was, more than anything, Hadot claims, an *exercise* for the human *spirit: Exercise*—because philosophy was more than an abstract theory; it was an art of how to live. *Spirit*—because it concerns the whole of the human person, the entire inner life of the person raised up to the life of the Spirit.[88]

---

[87] Hadot, *Exercices spirituels et philsophie antique.*
[88] Ibid., 14–15.

I want to follow now some of Hadot's study indicating how the perspectives he opens on ancient philosophy in general can help us to view *Ad Monachos* in the context of the Christian continuation of that philosophical tradition. First I will summarize his notion of "spiritual exercise"[89] and use it to develop a more complete feel for what Evagrius was attempting in *Ad Monachos*. Then I will observe with Hadot how this notion from ancient philosophy was continued in a certain strand of Christian spirituality and theology and indicate where Evagrius fits into this strand.

1. THE NOTION OF SPIRITUAL EXERCISE

It is impossible, Hadot argues, to understand ancient philosophy without taking into account the very concrete perspectives, the existential attitude, on which the dogmatic edifice of ancient philosophy is constructed. These perspectives are described by him as philosophy's purpose of exercising those who love wisdom in the practices of learning to live, learning to dialogue, learning to die, and learning to read. He demonstrates this with detailed references to the texts of many different philosophical traditions. Evagrius's text has, I think, a similar purpose. Some attention to what Hadot exposes will show how.

Concerning the rubric, "Learning to Live,"[90] Hadot begins by showing that philosophy was an art of living that involved a conversion that effected a passage from unauthentic living to authentic living. It was not something purely in the order of knowledge. It involved the order of self and the order of being. Passions were seen as the principal cause of suffering and disorder. Thus, in the first place philosophy was therapy for the passions. Here arises the need for exercises, for a transformation worked little by little.[91]

---

[89] Ibid., 13–58.

[90] Ibid., 15–29.

[91] On pp. 18–19 Hadot offers two lists of exercises given by Philo that offer some sense of what is meant by the term. The first list, taken from *Quis rerum div. heres.*, 253, mentions inquiry (*zētēsis*), deep examination (*skepsis*), reading, listening, attention (*prosochē*), mastery of self (*enkrateia*), indifference to indifferent things. The second list, taken from *Leg. Alleg.*, 3.18, includes readings, meditations

The fundamental spiritual exercise for the Stoic was attention (*prosochē*). The exercise was a continually awakened consciousness of oneself, a concentration on the present moment. This is, Hadot says, the secret of spiritual exercise; for concentration on the present delivers from the passions provoked by past or future. It permits an immediate response to events, which are like questions suddenly posed. By attention we have answers ready to hand, not simply by means of an intellectual knowing of a proper response but a knowing that has involved imagination and affectivity. This kind of knowing and this readiness for events have been accomplished by means of meditation and memorization. The one exercising imagines the difficulties of life in advance, and striking maxims aid in the process.

This understanding of spiritual exercise can profitably be brought to Evagrius's text. His proverbs are designed for a meditation and memorization that will prepare a monk in advance for the questions life suddenly poses. And the answers they provide to life's questions extend beyond mere intellectual grasp of a situation. They promote *prosochē*. The preparation is by means of striking maxims and metaphors that involve affectivity and engage the imagination.

In commenting on the second rubric, "Learning to Dialogue,"[92] Hadot points to the figure of Socrates as standing at the root of the emergence of the practice of spiritual exercise in Western consciousness. In observing his lasting influence as a figure who awakens the moral conscience, it should not go unnoticed that it is an appeal which is made in the form of a dialogue. In the Socratic dialogue the key question is not that about which one speaks but rather *who* speaks. Socrates knew how to pose questions that continually caused others to question themselves. This kind of dialogue should be considered a spiritual exercise practiced in common with the scope of leading the interlocutor into an interior dialogue in which one comes to know oneself.

Evagrius's *Ad Monachos* can be considered a model dialogue in a similar sense. In their own way the various proverbs pose the

---

(*meletai*), therapies of the passions, memory of what is good, mastery of self (*enkrateia*), the accomplishment of duties.

[92] Hadot, *Exercices spirituels,* 29–37.

challenge "Know thyself." They ask for authentic presence to one-self, to others, and to God. The text is not a theoretical or dog-matic exposé of either *praktikē* or knowledge. It is an attempt to persuade souls to dialogue. In each proverb the reader is chal-lenged to find the truth of the proverb in himself and for himself. The challenge is issued by a master who has dialogued with him-self by means of challenges posed by his own masters.

The theme of "Learning to Die"[93] was widespread across the various philosophical traditions, and once again it is the figure of Socrates who especially clarifies its meaning. Socrates died for his fidelity to *Logos;* that is, he preferred the Good to being; he preferred conscience and thought to the life of his body. This is the fundamental philosophical choice: choosing the life of the mind over the life of the body. Thus does philosophy become the spiritual exercise of the practice of death.

The practice of death had as its purpose the separation of the soul from the body for acquiring independence of thought. It was a dying to individuality and to the passions so that one could see things from the perspective of universality and objectivity. It was precisely the body and the passions, which are so intimately joined to the body, that prevented this objective seeing; and so "death" to the body and to the passions became the price for true knowledge.

Obviously the theme of spiritual death expressed in physical asceticism and in perspectives on this world is a major theme in Christian spirituality. Its fundamental roots lie in the death of Jesus. This theme could not help but be a major point of contact between Christianity and ancient philosophy. Here two wisdoms meet, and a synthesis could not help but be worked out. The influence of philosophy on the Christian understanding was widespread.[94]

The subject is directly broached in *Ad Monachos* in a chain that will be examined below, M 54–56 on listlessness. Remem-bering death is one of the major solutions which Evagrius pro-poses for listlessness precisely because doing so has the ability to

---

[93] Ibid., 37–47.

[94] Hadot cites a number of Christian authors in the second of the three stud-ies (*Exercises spirituels*, 71–72) we will examine here.

put things in perspective. As his source for this teaching Evagrius cites monastic fathers (TP 29, 52). Here we see again the difficulty of unraveling the roots of the formative influences on Evagrius, for the fathers he cites seem influenced by philosophy's wisdom on this point. The difficulty is characterized by a chapter from the *Praktikos* in which Evagrius says, "Our fathers called practicing death [μελέτην θανάτου] and flight from the body [φυγὴν τοῦ σώματος] 'anachoresis'" (TP 52). The expressions "practicing death" and "flight from the body" strongly echo the philosophical tradition.[95] "Our fathers" and "anachoresis" place the thought squarely within the monastic tradition, and in the same chapter Evagrius uses another expression strongly within the philosophical tradition: "separating the soul from the body."[96] So, which is it, philosophy or the fathers? Do we not have to answer that it is both?

It is not only in the proverbs on listlessness that this part of the philosophical tradition has made its mark on *Ad Monachos.* All the sentences that are concerned with temperance, with "not deriving evil from the flesh" (M 21), are exercises in which the monk practices death. Further, there is also a type of "physics" practiced in *Ad Monachos.* It is the movement from corporeals to incorporeals, a mounting upward to a more complete perspective. Here the Neoplatonic stress on progress comes into play. In Neoplatonism the progress of the spiritual journey is toward an experiential knowing of the immateriality of the soul. In Evagrian thought this is a progress by means of the death of *praktikē* in which eventually, in pure prayer, the mind, created as the image of God, "goes immaterially to the Immaterial" (Prayer 67 [PG 79:1182A]).[97] *Ad Monachos* is a spiritual exercise designed to promote this progress, and the very design of the exercise is saying that in order to know it is necessary to transform oneself; more specifically, it is necessary to die to the passions, to the flesh, and to this whole material world. Here once again two wisdoms meet. Two traditions are saying that to know it is necessary to transform

[95] See Guillaumont, SC 171, 620.
[96] Ibid., 619.
[97] See the commentary on M 136 for the discussion of the condition of the mind as it is presented before the Holy Trinity.

oneself. This is *praktikē*'s indissoluble relation to knowledge. It is a wisdom at once Greek and Christian.[98]

When he comments on the fourth rubric, "Learning to Read,"[99] Hadot changes his perspective and speaks not so much of how the ancients read as how we ought to read the ancients. It is impossible for us, Hadot argues, to read the written texts of ancient philosophy properly unless we take into account the concrete perspectives in which these texts were born. These texts were produced always in the context of a school in which a master was forming disciples and trying to lead them to the transformation and realization of self. Thus, even though there is a sense in which any written work is a monologue, these texts are always implicitly a dialogue, and they cannot be interpreted properly without awareness of this dimension. In such a text, more important than the master philosopher to whom the work is attributed is the interlocutor for whom the text is destined.

Ad Monachos, and for that matter all the works of Evagrius, must be read in the context of the concrete circumstances that gave rise to such texts. Our location of these texts in the desert monastic tradition has already prepared us to see that they are writings in which, as Hadot would put it, the interlocutor is always implicitly present. Evagrius's words are not a systematic treatise. I have suggested that we can hear in them still the questions that stand behind them, questions posed by disciples who stood in concrete circumstances. Evagrius's answers are always adapted to the needs of his disciples, and they enlist, especially by means of the metaphors, the emotional energy needed for the long journey toward wisdom's heights.

The same danger that has tripped up modern interpreters of ancient philosophy stands lurking to snag modern interpreters of Evagrius. Modern interpreters may be tempted to expose this man's "fascinating" or "peculiar" thought and then take positions in its regard by evaluating where it stands in relation to some systematic and orthodox exposure of the faith.

---

[98] I wish to argue in the next section that the Evagrian synthesis of these notions ought to be considered authentically Christian. For the moment I only want to point to the ways in which the philosophical tradition has worked its influence.

[99] Hadot, *Exercices spirituels,* 47–58.

History has shown that Evagrius does not hold up well under this type of scrutiny. Few mystics do. Hadot helps us to see why. Texts promoting spiritual exercise must be evaluated with a standard different from that by which texts involved in doctrinal questions are evaluated. It is these latter that may be expected to provide a reader with a clearly expressed systematic presentation on some given position, but spiritual exercises do not offer this same kind of clarity.

In *Ad Monachos* or in other works of Evagrius we do not have a systematic exposure of what could be called "his thought."[100] This is not to say there is no system. As Hadot says of the words of Plato, "Chaque *logos* est un 'système', mais l'ensemble des *logoi* écrits par un auteur ne forme pas un système."[101] In *Ad Monachos* each word is a system because each word invites participation in a coherence based on what Evagrius calls the reasons of providence and judgment, the reasons of corporeals and incorporeals. This is the system, these reasons. Ultimately each word is a system because each word is a stage in an exercise that prepares the mind for that for which it was made: knowledge of the Trinity. Evagrius's thought is systematic not in the way it is exposed but in the fact that it is designed to help his interlocutor "fit into" God's economy, God's "system." Fitting into this system is to reach grandeur of soul; it is "contemplations of worlds which enlarge the heart" (M 135). It is the grandeur of knowing an overarching and profound coherence that exists between mind, world, and God himself. This coherence, like Plotinus's demonstration of the immateriality of the soul, cannot be proven or known in a theoretical exposé. It must be known by exercising, an exercising in which knowledge itself becomes the spiritual exercise.

I have already pointed to the risk that *Ad Monachos* runs of seeming banal, pious in an unattractive way, confused in its pre-

---

[100] It may be objected that the *Letter to Melania* would be an exception. It is true that the letter is a frank and open discussion of material that from a certain perspective could be considered "theoretical." However, the letter is meant as a private sharing of his thinking with a friend whom he judges to be equal to its contents. Evagrius in general does not teach this way because in his teaching he always takes account of his interlocutors. This letter likewise takes account of that, and for that reason must also be considered as intending to provoke spiritual exercise.

[101] Hadot, *Exercices spirituels,* 52.

sentation. Here enters the need for knowing how to read! Here reading means practice; it means exercise; it means living with the text; it means rereading. To read *Ad Monachos* well, to read it for what it is, requires spiritual exercise. I would like to use Hadot's own words to make this point: "nous passons notre vie à 'lire', mais nous ne savons plus lire, c'est-à-dire nous arrêter, nous libérer de nos soucis, revenir à nous-mêmes, laisser de côté nos recherches de subtilité et d'originalité, méditer calmement, ruminer, laisser les textes nous parler. C'est un exercice spirituel, un des plus difficiles."[102]

In another part of his study Hadot offers a key for reading the *Meditations* of the Stoic emperor Marcus Aurelius. He makes an observation about this work that could well be made about *Ad Monachos* or most of the other works of Evagrius, namely, that the mode of composition escapes the reader, that the sentences seem to follow without order, following at whim the impressions and moods of the author.

Hadot's study shows that underneath this apparent disorder there is hidden a rigorous law that explains the contents of the *Meditations*. He demonstrates that each individual meditation is an exercise on one or another (or several together) of the three *topoi* of Stoic philosophy as described by Epictetus. Hadot says of Marcus Aurelius that each time he wrote a sentence he knew with precision what he was doing: he was exercising himself in the discipline of one of the three *topoi*. In each proverb Evagrius likewise knew with precision what he was doing. His proverbs are spiritual exercises on one or another (or several together) of the following "*topoi*": the relation between mind, soul, and body; the three parts of the soul; the eight principal evil thoughts and their order; the divisions of the spiritual life between *praktikē* and knowledge; and various levels of knowledge distinguished.

The kind of commentary I have been able to make in this study on the structure of the whole text and on the individual proverbs is possible only on the basis of recognizing the text as containing precise meditations on one or another of these

---

[102] Ibid., 58. It is worth recalling that in the ancient world reading always meant reading aloud, and meditating on a text always involved repeating the text aloud.

dimensions of the spiritual life. My commentary recognizes the proverbs as very concentrated formulations of a rich and multi-faceted teaching in these various realms, and it seeks to show how the details of this teaching have been condensed into the order of the whole text and into the carefully chosen language of the individual proverbs. The very act of creating the kind of text Evagrius made in *Ad Monachos* is itself an act of philosophy, for it requires an extremely careful meditation on each subject penned and requires that actual living stand behind and in front of the text he creates. As Hadot said of Marcus Aurelius in the act of writing his meditations: "Ce faisant, il philosophe."[103]

It is not possible, nor is it necessary, to claim that Evagrius would have known the *Meditations* and further would have known this key for reading them. This comparison, I think, has a different purpose. It means to help us catch the spirit with which ancient philosophers (here I include Evagrius) wrote proverbs, wrote meditations. It means to help us catch the "why" of the kind of intricacy Evagrius hid in his text. He was in love with wisdom. He was philosophizing. He wanted to share this love and provoke it in others. He created a spiritual exercise. In it he created a literary shape that mirrored the shape of the divine economy whose outlines he had come slowly to discern in his own search for wisdom. He trusted this shape to take his disciples where it was taking him. It is the shape of faith leading to love and love leading to knowledge of the Holy Trinity.

2. SPIRITUAL EXERCISES AND CHRISTIAN PHILOSOPHY

Hadot's description of this spirit of ancient philosophy puts us in a position to catch the significance of the fact that Christianity was presented by a part of the Christian tradition as a philosophy.[104] Christianity was a way of life; and if it could be presented to its contemporaries as a philosophy, it was because philosophy too was perceived as a way of life. The relation between ancient philosophy and this part of the Christian tradi-

---

[103] Ibid., 153.
[104] Ibid., 59–74.

tion is the subject of the second study in Hadot's book.

The Christian tradition which identifies itself as a philosophy begins with the apologists and extends from Justin Martyr to Clement to Origen to the Cappadocians to Chrysostom. All these are conscious heirs of a philosophical tradition. When monasticism appears in the fourth century as the realization of Christian perfection, it too can be presented as a philosophy. Here Hadot identifies as the architects of this synthesis the two Gregorys, Chrysostom, and "concretely," he says, Evagrius.[105]

For Hadot, Christianity's assimilation of ancient philosophy must be carefully understood. It does not mean that the strong assimilation would in the end compromise the incomparable originality of the Gospel. This does not happen. But what the assimilation does mean is that through philosophy the notion of spiritual exercise is introduced into Christianity. With it comes a certain style of life, a certain spiritual attitude, a certain spiritual tonality that was not originally there.

Prosochē, attention to self, can serve to summarize the fundamental attitude of both Stoic and Platonic philosophy. This had both a *moral* and a *cosmic* dimension. It involved yielding in both dimensions to the will of universal Reason. *Prosochē* becomes also the fundamental attitude of monasticism. It involves control of thoughts, accepting the divine will, the perfection of intentions in regard to others. The focus was not simply moral conduct. It was a question of coming to know one's true being, known only in relation to God.

In philosophy, *prosochē* supposed meditation and memorization of the rule of life, principles to be applied in each particular circumstance. It is necessary always to have ready to hand the principles of life, the fundamental dogmas. Hadot notes that the same thing is found in the monastic tradition. In this tradition the principles are the words of Christ in the Gospel commands, as well as the words of the elders. Both were presented in the form of short sentences which, as in the philosophical tradition, could be memorized and easily meditated upon.[106]

---

[105] Ibid., 62.

[106] Hadot (*Exercices spirituels,* 67) refers to the study by E. von Ivánka cited above. We see here the point at which the form of short sentences used in the philosophical tradition is taken over by Christians for their own needs.

It is here, of course, where Evagrius fits in. His proverbs are meant to be fundamental principles ready to hand. The use of such principles in philosophical tradition shows us how they were meant to be used also by Christians who loved wisdom. Hadot observes that there was a sort of "conspiracy" between the formulated principle (memorized and meditated upon) and life's actual situations, such that when one found oneself in a particular circumstance, one would know the proper course of conduct and face it with accurate understanding.

Meditating on the proverbs of *Ad Monachos* means to be a similar conspiracy. Evagrius's disciples in their actual living are meant to know that faith is the beginning of love and that the end of love is knowledge of God (M 3). These disciples will come to various circumstances prepared in advance by a memorized principle to face that situation untroubled by the passions. They will know, for example, what to do "if a brother irritates you" (M 15). They will know what to do about wine and meat (M 38, 39), about bread and water (M 102). They will know how fast to react when faced with a temptation (M 58, 59). They will be concerned both to care for the poor and to be poor themselves (M 16–18, M 25–30). They will have imagined in advance, with the help of vivid images, how dangerous is the irascible part of the soul when out of control (M 10, 13, 36). They will have been impressed with the importance of trying in every circumstance to be gentle, since they will know that only a gentle monk will be loved by the Lord, only a gentle monk will see reasons of the incorporeals (M 85, 133).

These examples from Evagrius stand in the line of the sort of preparation in advance of which Hadot speaks, but this idea can be extended further in *Ad Monachos*. These proverbs do not only supply a preparation for the realm of *praktikē*. Evagrius has also formulated principles for knowledge, and I think these too are designed for the monk to have ready to hand especially as he prays, to help him recognize the realm of knowledge and how to move within it when grace brings him to its borders. Certainly in the entire arrangement of *Ad Monachos* a fundamental principle is articulated, namely, *praktikē's* continual drive toward knowledge. As the monk enters knowledge, he will know in advance, having been prepared by the spiritual exercise of *Ad Monachos*, that he can only stay there "if he keeps guard over his way of life," his *praktikē* (M 63). He will know that "knowledge of the Trinity is better than knowledge of the incorporeals" (M 110). Knowing this develops a sensitivity in his mind and soul, a sensitivity to the subtle movement from one kind of knowledge to another. He will know to cling to no knowledge less than the knowledge of the Trinity. Yet by the same token he will have been prepared in advance to mount up toward the Trinity by the only path that leads there: by contemplations of worlds, by reasons of providence and judgment, by knowledge of the incorporeals (M 135, 136). In the same way that a memorized principle meditated upon with a certain image taught the monk to look to Christ to nourish him in the struggles of *praktikē* (M 118), he has been prepared also to look to Christ's very blood for the secrets of all created things (M 119), and indeed to rest intimately in Christ in order to know God as Trinity (M 120). This is spiritual exercising.

Hadot notes that in this strain of Christianity influenced by philosophy the goals proposed for the spiritual life are strongly colored by Stoicism and Neoplatonism. He especially notes passionlessness as an example, but the same could hold good for the goal of knowledge. Nonetheless, Hadot continues, even if what Christianity assimilated from this tradition is indeed very much, it must equally be recognized that the final synthesis is essentially Christian.

Evagrius's own teaching on passionlessness would be an example of a synthesis essentially Christian. And here I would like to suggest shifting slightly a remark Hadot makes about Evagrius in this regard. This shift, which concerns Evagrius on passionlessness, can serve *mutatis mutandis* as a demonstration of how deeply Evagrius managed to render authentically Christian much of what he borrowed from ancient philosophy. Hadot is discussing Evagrius's chapter from the *Praktikos* in which he says, "The kingdom of God is passionlessness of the soul with true knowledge of beings" (TP 2). Concerning this Hadot says, "Une telle formule, si on essaie de la commenter, montre quelle distance sépare ces spéculations de l'esprit évangélique."[107]

To this I say both yes and no. If one compares Evagrius's for-

---

[107] Hadot, *Exercices spirituels*, 70.

mulation here with the language in which Jesus himself preached about the kingdom, then obviously, yes, some considerable distance lies between the two. Clearly Evagrius takes from philosophy a term that philosophy proposed as a goal, and he uses it himself to describe an (intermediary) goal in the Christian spiritual journey. But the most basic question here is not the term and not even how much of philosophy's influence is found in Evagrius's understanding of passionlessness. To these questions everyone can answer that the term is Stoic and Neoplatonic and that the influence of these schools is strong in Evagrius. But this is not enough to understand *Evagrius's* notion of passionlessness. Evagrius is using the philosophical tradition, and here this particular term in it, to help reach to the deepest core of the Gospels' message about the kingdom.

Any angle of study on Evagrius's notion of passionlessness would reveal how deeply Christian is its final synthesis, but here let us use *Ad Monachos* as an example. *Ad Monachos* is an architecture that uses passionlessness as a principal beam in its structure, but it is not the whole structure. In this structure at its front door (M 3–6) and in its very center (M 67) passionlessness is inextricably joined to love. And love is the only door that leads to knowing God. This is because God is Love, and he cannot therefore be known apart from love.[108]

Evagrius's notion of passionlessness is not accurately understood without reference to this particular understanding of love and this particular understanding of knowledge. Then when we locate philosophy's term "passionlessness"—or for that matter, the term "knowledge"—in such an architecture, we have discovered the place where a synthesis is worked between the spiritual exercise of philosophy and the same in its Christian strain. In this synthesis the statement "the kingdom of heaven is passionlessness of the soul" is a vigorous condensation, a condensation based in the discovery of the congruence between all of Jesus' teaching about the kingdom and philosophy's wisdom about passionlessness. But an even more ample congruence stands behind this particular formulation about passionlessness. It is the congruence between

---

[108] "Through like we know like. Thus, through love we know love" (In Ps 17:2–3 [PG 12:1224D]). See the commentary on M 67 in Part Four.

passionlessness and knowledge, which, yes, also is philosophy's term but in Evagrius's Christian synthesis is vigorously condensed like this: "The Kingdom of God is knowledge of the Holy Trinity" (TP 3).

Two wisdom traditions meet when the Christian Gospel encounters ancient philosophy. Their wisdoms are not mutually exclusive. Indeed, historically the message of the Gospel maintains its purity on an intellectual plane and deepens its understanding only with the help of this philosophical tradition. Yet Christ himself, God incarnate, crucified, and risen, remains Christianity's distinctive core and distinguishes it from all other wisdoms. Something similar is true on the spiritual plane when philosophy's notion of spiritual exercise meets and contributes to monasticism's search for spiritual perfection. Philosophy's contribution has become a virtually inextricable part of the Christian monastic heritage. Evagrius himself is witness, however, to how at base this monastic heritage has a distinctive Christian face which distinguishes it from all other traditions of spiritual exercises, from all other cultural manifestations of monasticism. This distinctive face, again, is the face of the Incarnate Lord who is with the monk in every stage of his exercises, the Incarnate Lord to eat whose flesh is to become passionless (M 118), to drink whose blood is wisdom (M 119), to rest against whose breast is knowledge (M 120).

Hadot concludes this part of his study with the suggestion that in order to grasp well the Christian version of ancient philosophy's notion of spiritual exercise it is necessary to look to the general spirit with which Christians practiced spiritual exercises. This is a practice with a distinctively Christian tone—presupposing the grace of God, stressing humility, penitence, and especially obedience. In the end the transcendent dimensions of the love of God and of Christ transfigure all the exercising. The practice of death becomes participation in the death of Christ. The renouncing of one's own will becomes adherence to divine love.

What Hadot says here of the whole Christian tradition is certainly true likewise for Evagrius. One of the proverbs of *Ad Monachos* has made this point explicitly and memorably. In M 21 what is both a notion from ancient philosophy and from Christianity, that of "not deriving evil from the flesh," is explicitly joined to "imitating Christ" and "dying his death." This is the spirit and this is the tone in which Evagrius understands all the exercising of the monastic life, no matter how much his understanding of exercising owes to ancient philosophy. It is an exercise in which the monk wants *to die* with Christ *so that he may know* Christ and the power of his resurrection, so that his "resurrection will glow like the sun."[109]

CONCLUSION TO STAGE THREE

I think this look at some of the material in Hadot's study of ancient philosophy enables us to hear the special overtones in the description of Socrates the historian about Evagrius: "he acquired the philosophy of deeds." I looked to Hadot's study not so much in search of an explanation for the philosophical background in the content of Evagrius's teaching as for a way of catching how philosophy influenced the spirit of Evagrius's work and how philosophy can suggest an attitude with which it should be read.

Ad Monachos is a philosophical text in the ancient sense of spiritual exercises. It is a text profoundly shaped by a dialogue between master and disciple, a dialogue that seeks to learn by means of authentic dialogue itself how to live and how to die. If we are to understand the text, we ourselves must learn a new way of reading that takes into account the concrete perspectives in which the text was born.

Ad Monachos is a Christian text that is consciously the heir of a philosophical tradition. Its content and the spirit it breathes, in so many ways similar to the content and spirit of ancient philosophy, must ultimately be considered authentically Christian. Such a text is produced not so much by a Christian "borrowing" certain things from another cultural tradition. Such a text is produced by someone who is a part of that "other" cultural tradition. That culture's wisdom is assimilated inseparably into the author. The real question before us is whether or not with that other culture's tools the Christian author has managed to stay true to what is

---

[109] Cf. Phil 3:10–11; and see the whole discussion of the theme of the death of Christ in Evagrius in the commentary on M 21 below.

essentially a Christian wisdom. The touchstone for this is found in the mysteries of Incarnation, crucifixion, and Trinity. This is the bedrock of the philosophy Evagrius teaches.

The structure of *Ad Monachos* is a structure that expresses an attitude about spiritual exercises. Like the *Meditations* of Marcus Aurelius, the proverbs find their order by means of various *topoi*.

For Evagrius, Christianity itself became his philosophy. In it he "found a Laban who freed him from Esau and guided him to the highest philosophy."[110] In the last sixteen years of his life, his philosophy was Christianity as it took shape in Egyptian monasticism. He was a Christian, a theologian, and then a monk because "a certain longing for philosophy" stole into his heart. He longed for "the highest philosophy." On the feast of Epiphany in the year 399 Evagrius received Holy Communion and departed this life (LH 38:13). It might be hoped that on that day his longing was satisfied: that eating the Lord's flesh he became passionless (M 118), that drinking his blood he received the wisdom he loved (M 119), that resting on the breast of the Lord, he became a theologian (M 120) and was presented before the Holy Trinity (M 136).

---

[110] Formulated according to Evagrius's words in Ep Fid 1, lines 11–14.

Part Four

Commentary on
Individual Proverbs

Overview

In this part of the study I wish to examine another dimension of the richness of *Ad Monachos:* the proverbs considered individually. Each proverb deserves to be meditated upon in its own right. Each one offers much food for thought; some offer extraordinary richness. In what follows I would like to offer commentary on some selected proverbs in order to demonstrate this point. Perforce this can only be by way of demonstration as opposed to a proper commentary on each of the 137 proverbs.[1]

It would be difficult to organize the various themes found in *Ad Monachos* into a systematic presentation and still be faithful to the text Evagrius has designed. The themes have an order, and they are the order of the proverbs of this text. So, though it is not possible to comment on every proverb, it does seem best to treat the selected proverbs in the order in which they appear in the text. In that way this study will at least roughly follow the themes as they unfold in the text.[2]

If it is not possible to explain each of the proverbs, it is at least possible to explain the reason for the choice of the proverbs I have selected to comment on here. This explanation can serve as an overview of this part of the study. M 3 is the first proverb commented on here. It is, as the analysis of the structure showed, the first proverb of the text after the introductory proverbs. It contains in its two lines a summary of the whole text and of much of Evagrius's whole teaching. This is followed by commentary on M 12, the first proverb to mention gentleness, which was seen to be a recurring theme throughout. Next, M 13 to 15 are com-

---

[1] The comments offered here will show that a commentary on all of the proverbs could require a study of considerable proportions. It seems best to limit this study to some of those proverbs I consider especially important or interesting.

[2] This is not to say that in commenting on a proverb it is necessary to avoid reference to proverbs that come later in the text. On the contrary, it is often necessary to do just that in order to explain a given proverb. My point here is simply to explain the reason for the choice to treat the proverbs in their order rather than according to selected, organizing themes.

mented upon in sequence. These proverbs are one example among many in the text that speak of the importance of the relations among the brothers and the relation of this to knowledge. M 21 is a beautiful and weighty proverb which shows the relation of Christ to the major phases of the monk's spiritual progress. M 31 is a proverb literally freighted with meaning, in which each word offers a precise, if not immediately apparent, meaning. It is a fine example of how much Evagrius manages to suggest with an economy of words, of how much he manages to "hide" for discovery by the careful reader. M 53 will serve as an example of what I have called "hinge" proverbs in the text. By examining its terms carefully, we can see how strong a hinge it is.

It will also be worthwhile to comment on several of the different types of chains that were observed in the text, taking them proverb by proverb and showing how the chain's meaning builds when each proverb is understood well. Thus, M 54 to 56 is a little chain on listlessness. Though by comparison not much space is devoted to this theme in *Ad Monachos,* the commentary here will show that in these few proverbs Evagrius has expressed the major features of this characteristic aspect of his spiritual teaching. M 61 and M 62 are worth examining for a similar reason. They treat vainglory and pride and are the last development in the text before the large chain on *praktikē* and knowledge, which forms the center of the whole.

This central chain, M 63 to 72, will likewise be examined here. We observed that its message can be literally considered the central message of the whole. The proverbs of this chain, each formed of only two lines, are filled with rich meaning. Uncovering what lies there proverb by proverb will enable us to enter more deeply into the ideas Evagrius is, we could say, insisting on here.

If choices have to be made, it would be impossible not to select M 107, which I have argued is a turning point in the whole text. Its terminology is crucial, precise, and wide-ranging all at once. The commentary can further justify my labeling the proverb a turning point. From this point on in the text, Evagrius focuses the reader's attention on issues of knowledge. Several of those meditations can be commented on here. M 118 to 120 is a tightly constructed chain that returns again to the role of Christ in every phase of the spiritual progress. It is a different angle on the christological issues that appear in M 21. Finally, we can conclude with a commentary on M 136, which is the culminating proverb of the whole. And it culminates by offering for meditation what is for Evagrius the culmination of the spiritual journey: the mind in the presence of the Holy Trinity.

The method of commentary here necessarily remains what it has been heretofore in the study, namely, commenting on Evagrius with Evagrius. There is simply no better way to understand his meaning. Further, in the comments on some of the proverbs it will be necessary to fix with care Evagrius's understanding of various of the terms encountered. This cannot always be done briefly. Thus, sometimes within the context of an individual commentary, it may be necessary to digress into broader considerations of some issue that the proverb presumes is understood. Yet it is hoped that such digressions can function as an image and a strong reminder of the very way in which a proverb ought to be meditated on, namely, with the mind moving off in many directions to ponder the meaning of the proverb's various terms. For the meditative mind, such digressions and the discovery of the interconnections they yield are meant to be part of the value and pleasure of meditating on proverbs. In any case, the comments that follow are an attempt to imitate the directions followed by a meditating mind, a mind trained to hear the many allusions to scripture and to the desert monastic tradition as these were lived and understood in the circle of Evagrius.

Commentary on M 3

3.   Faith: the beginning of love.
     The end of love: knowledge of God.

Πίστις ἀρχὴ ἀγάπης,
τέλος δὲ ἀγάπης γνῶσις θεοῦ.

The first line of this proverb describes the whole of the life of *praktikē*, whose beginning is faith and whose goal is love. The second line describes the whole of knowledge, whose beginning is love and whose goal is the knowledge of God himself. Love is clearly the critical link between these two prongs of the spiritual life. To understand all that is implied in these two short lines, the proverb is best meditated upon in conjunction with another to which it stands in special relation, namely, M 67: "In front of love, passionlessness marches; / in front of knowledge, love." In the examination of the chains both were seen to be located in especially significant positions. After the introductory proverbs, M 3 is the actual beginning of the whole text as well as the beginning of a chain on virtues. M 67 was seen to be at the exact middle of the whole text.[3] This positioning is a clue to the importance of their contents. In each love is placed as the link between *praktikē* and knowledge. The position of each suggests that understanding this—that love links *praktikē* to knowledge—is a key to understanding the whole text. Much is implied in these two proverbs. Much is left unsaid and presumed understood. These unspoken implications can be uncovered by attention to some other key Evagrian texts.

FAITH

Not only in M 3 but throughout his writings Evagrius places faith at the very beginning of the monastic journey. It introduces the monk into the life of *praktikē*. By faith is meant first of all believing in the existence of God. This in turn causes one to fear God; and if one fears God, one observes God's commandments. Thereby does one enter the life of *praktikē*. This chain of logic is spelled out (in descending order) in the *Praktikos,* where we read, "Love is the child of passionlessness; passionlessness is the flower of *praktikē*; keeping the commandments is what constitutes *praktikē*; these have the fear of God for guard, which is the child of right faith. Faith is an interior good which exists naturally even in those who have not yet believed in God" (TP 81).[4] This text shows

---

[3] It is the middle of the central chain of the whole text (M 63–72), as well as the middle of a chain within the chain on passionlessness (M 66–68)!

[4] See Guillaumont, SC 171, 670–71, for a fuller comment on this text, especially on the sense of the last sentence about faith as an interior good. The same chain is found already in TP Prologue 8.

that faith, standing at the beginning of *praktikē*, leads on through different virtues, culminating twice, as it were: first in passionlessness, since "passionlessness is the flower of *praktikē*," and second in love, because "love is the child of passionlessness." So to say "faith: the beginning of love" in the Evagrian system is to say a considerable amount. It is to say that faith begins a whole series of successive virtues whose acquisition follows logically one from another and whose goal is love. It is to imply the movement from faith to fear to keeping the commandments to passionlessness to love.[5]

LOVE

The text from the *Praktikos* indicated a tight relation between passionlessness and love—"love is the child of passionlessness"—a relation that is clearly in line with M 67's assertion, "In front of love, passionlessness marches." Passionlessness is Evagrius's term for the health of the soul (see TP 56).[6] It exists when all the parts of the soul are healed and act according to their proper nature (see TP 86). Thus it is a term for describing the results of the whole life of *praktikē*, which is concerned with the firm establishing of various virtues in the various parts of the soul. If faith is the beginning of *praktikē*, passionlessness is its proximate aim, its "flower," as TP 81 puts it. But passionlessness is by no means the end of the journey for the monk, for "love is the child of passionlessness."[7]

---

[5] This succession of virtues is developed in the proverbs immediately following M 3. This same order of virtues is found also in In Ps 24:20; 129:4-5; 137:7. Faith, as it is described in all these texts, is the same, that is, the beginning of the life of virtue. But Bunge notes that there is also another dimension of faith for Evagrius, namely, as a concrete act (see Bunge, *Geistliche Vaterschaft,* 56, citing In Ps 115:1 and KG III, 83).

[6] See the commentary by Guillaumont on this sentence in SC 171, 631, where he cites KG I, 41; II, 48; III, 46; VI, 64.

[7] It is perhaps worth observing that love (ἀγάπη) is a word that has its difficulties in any language. It is a wide-ranging term, difficult to pin down exactly, and yet a term that everybody seems to use with some sort of understanding. This same wide sense is certainly present in Evagrius's use of the term, though, of course, it is narrowed by Greek's capacity to distinguish types of love, in this case ἀγάπη. It means loving others, being charitable to them, with all that that might

KNOWLEDGE

Another text from the *Praktikos* makes it clear how dynamic the process undertaken is: "and passionlessness has love as its child, and love is the gate to natural knowledge, and this knowledge gives way to theology, and then final blessedness" (TP Prologue, 8). This text, as well as M 3 and M 67, indicates that love leads on to yet another realm; namely, knowledge. The end of love, its τέλος, is knowledge of God, the highest of knowledge's various levels. It is true that knowledge, not love, is Evagrius's expression for the final goal of the monastic life. This has led to some misunderstanding of his teaching.[8] It can be thought less than Christian for this emphasis, but this is to fail to notice another emphasis, equally as striking, namely, the insistence throughout *Ad Monachos* and throughout all of Evagrius's work on love as the indispensable passageway to the realms of knowledge as well as that which must always be present to maintain the monk in knowledge. It is also to pose the question in the wrong way, that is, love or knowledge? For Evagrius, it is not a question of one or the other. These proverbs show love and knowledge to be dynamically united. Knowledge of God is knowledge of a God who is love.[9] And love is not merely a passageway; it must remain a permanent part of the life of one who has entered into knowledge. Love's being a permanent part of knowledge has contributed in a fundamental way to the structure of *Ad Monachos,* not only in the way this concept finds expression in the beginning and middle of the text but also in the way in which gentleness remains an emphasis of the text to the very end. This is not mere lip service paid by Evagrius in order to give his "gnostic" teaching a Christian appearance. Love remains a permanent part of

---

suggest or imply. Much of the text that follows has to do with what love suggests and implies: gentleness, forgetting injuries, care for the poor, and so on.

[8] Typical in this regard would be Chitty, *Desert a City,* 50; he says, "Some of Evagrius' speculations did fall wide of the Christian balance of truth. And one is suspicious at his seeming to set Knowledge above Love." In answer one could refer to Bunge, *Briefe,* 127ff. A concern similar to Chitty's has attached itself also to Clement's thought. See n. 10 below.

[9] Cf. Lt 56:3, cited in the commentary on M 67.

knowledge for a necessary reason: because knowledge means knowledge of a God who is love.[10]

Thus, at the very beginning of the meditation, M 3 summarizes and characterizes the whole of the spiritual journey as conceived by Evagrius. M 67 does the same midway through the text. In each love leads to knowledge. Yet there is a difference between one proverb and the other that is appropriate to their respective positions in the text. At the *beginning* of the text M 3 begins with faith, which is the *beginning* of the whole Christian and monastic life. At the *middle* of the text M 67 starts the meditation at the *"middle"* of the spiritual journey, namely, at that point where one moves from passionlessness to love. Each proverb implies the whole life of *praktikē* and its chain of virtues. Each places love as the goal of this life of *praktikē* and the gate of entry into knowledge. Each places knowledge as the goal of the whole.

---

[10] In this position Evagrius shows himself to be the disciple of Clement, who explicitly treats in many places the relation between love and knowledge. Some scholars have felt required to "defend" Clement's thought from seeming too gnostic by claiming that knowledge is subsumed into love in his thinking. But A. Méhat summarizes this effort and then demonstrates that for Clement love and knowledge are two faces of a single reality (Méhat, *Étude sur les "Stromates" de Clément d'Alexandrie*, 475–88). After examining a number of texts, he suggests, "Il vaut mieux renoncer à cette vaine question de la primauté [love or knowledge]. Visiblement il y a des rapports réciproques entre la gnose et la charité. C'est la seule chose que Clément ait voulu marquer. Il y a des rapports au niveau des progrès à accomplir. Il y en a dans l'état final. Sans essayer de distinguer les deux, retenons seulement d'abord que la gnose est un amour. . . . Inversement, charité est connaissance: car elle se meut dans le cercle de la Vérité" (p. 482). Clement's reflections on this relation are designed to show what the qualities of a *Christian* gnosis would be, and it is precisely love's relation to knowledge that gives Clement's ideas their distinctively Christian shape. Evagrius's thinking is likewise distinctively Christian within this same tradition. On the suitability of comparing Clement and Evagrius on this point, see A. Guillaumont, "Le gnostique chez Clément d'Alexandrie et chez Évagre le Pontique," 199–200.

Commentary on M 12

12. An irascible man will be terrified;
     the gentle man will be without fear.

     Ἀνὴρ θυμώδης πτοηθήσεται,
     ὁ δὲ πραῢς ἄφοβος ἔσται.

This is the first occurrence in the text of a very important word and concept: *gentle*. Gentleness is one of love's most concrete expressions.[11] Certainly one of the most significant impressions *Ad Monachos* leaves with the reader is of the importance of gentleness in the monk's journey to knowledge. It is the subject of a number of different chains, either directly or indirectly. It is a theme spread evenly throughout the text;[12] it appears in the proverb that functions as the turning point of the whole text (M 107); it is among the last thoughts offered for meditation as the text comes to a close (M 133). By the way in which Evagrius has made this theme to sound throughout his meditation, he creates an image of gentleness penetrating every portion of the monk's life, every stage of his progress.

This first appearance of the term in M 12 introduces a dimension of the issue that is fundamental for understanding how Evagrius conceives its importance. The proverb contrasts the gentle man with the irascible man. A number of other proverbs in *Ad Monachos* do the same,[13] and the contrast is a basic point in Evagrius's teaching. Understanding him on this point is necessary in order to grasp the significance of M 12 and the other proverbs which likewise draw the contrast. It will explain why gentleness is so frequently associated with knowledge.

[11] For the close identity between love and gentleness in Evagrius and for the influence of Clement on this thought, see A. Guillaumont, "Le gnostique chez Clément d'Alexandrie et chez Évagre le Pontique," 199.

[12] Observing the numbers of the proverbs in which the word *gentleness* occurs shows this relatively even distribution: M 12, 31, 34, 53, 85, 99, 107, 111, 112, 133.

[13] See M 34–36 and M 98–100. In some of these proverbs *long-suffering* and *rashness* also occur as virtual synonyms for gentleness and irascibility respectively. This is demonstrated shortly in what follows.

The irascible (ὁ θυμός) is a technical term for one of three parts of the soul. Gentleness is proposed as the opposite of irascibility, which is said to scatter knowledge (M 35). Evagrius does not think that it is the irascible part of the soul as such that scatters knowledge or drives it away; it is when this part of the soul is aroused in an inappropriate way that trouble occurs. In many, many places throughout his writings Evagrius speaks of establishing virtue in this part of the soul. Gentleness is not the only virtue that must be established there, but it is one of the principal ones.

The aim is to have the irascible part of the soul actually help in the war against the demons. A text from *On Evil Thoughts* explains how this works:

> As sheep to a good shepherd the Lord has given to man conceptions (νοήματα) of this present world, for it is said, "The world he has placed in his heart." And he has joined to man the irascible and the concupiscible to help him so that through the irascible he may make flee conceptions that come from the wolves and through the concupiscible he may love the sheep. (Thoughts 17)

The images of this text and the ideas presented here, perhaps difficult to follow for one not familiar with Evagrius, fall neatly into place when it is noticed that they are organized around the three parts of the soul. Conceptions of this world (and conceptions of other worlds as well) are the work of the rational part of the soul. They are to be guarded (as sheep guarded by a good shepherd) with the help of the other parts of the soul. The irascible part of the soul, when it is functioning as it ought, drives away conceptions of the wolves, which would be false ideas that come from the demons. The concupiscible part of the soul, where desire lies, when it is functioning properly, can desire these conceptions given by the Lord, that is, it can "love the sheep."

Shortly after the passage quoted here, Evagrius gives examples of the sheep being caught by wild beasts, which should have been made to flee by a proper use of the irascible. Among the examples is one related to the issue of gentleness. It describes a "conception" (νόημα) of a brother coming to mind, but he is thought of with hatred. This is something going wrong in the irascible part of the soul. That is where gentleness should reside, and then the wolflike conception of regarding a brother with hatred would be driven away by the activity of this healthy part of the soul. In other words, gentleness is health in the irascible part of the soul.[14]

Trouble in the irascible part is extremely dangerous for the soul. One of the main ways in which trouble shows itself there is through anger and hatred. "Anger and hatred make the irascible grow; compassion and gentleness diminish that which is there" (TP 20). The reason irascibility is so dangerous is that "the irascible part predominates in the demons, for it is said, 'Without pity is the irascible; and anger is sharp' (Prov 27:4)" (In Prov 5:9 [G 60]).[15]

Long-suffering appears contrasted with irascibility in two proverbs, M 35 and M 98.[16] It plays a role very similar to that of gentleness. In M 35 it stands opposite irascibility and gathers the knowledge that irascibility scatters. In M 98 it stands alongside psalmody as a means of quieting the irascible, which will mean that the one practicing it can be without fear, in the same way that M 12 claimed that a gentle man would be without fear.[17] Thus, "The gentle man will be without fear" (M 12). Or, "The

[14] Gentleness is not the only indication of health in the irascible part. For example, courage and perseverance are also virtues in the irascible. Their role is "not to fear the enemies and to stand firm, eagerly [προθύμως], in the face of dangers" (TP 89). Other texts that speak clearly of putting the irascible to this kind of use are found in TP 24; Eulog 10; In Prov 29:11 (G 363)—this last text speaking of destroying a part of the irascible and saving a part. The part saved would be for doing war with the demons.

[15] Other texts showing the predominance of the irascible in demons can be found in KG I, 68; III, 34; V, 11.

[16] The term also occurs in M 84. In that proverb the word *irascibility* is not used, but the issue is certainly that.

[17] Psalmody is regularly cited by Evagrius as a means for quieting the irascible. In TP 15 he distinguishes it from other monastic practices that are concerned with other parts of the soul. "Reading, vigils, and prayer make a wandering mind stand still. Hunger and pain and anachoresis quench a flaming concupiscence. Psalmody, long-suffering, and mercy set at rest an agitated irascibility." In his commentary on this chapter, Guillaumont gives references showing an analogous role for psalmody in Origen, Basil, and Gregory Nazianzen (Guillaumont, SC 171, 537–38). To the other Evagrian texts which he cites could also be added the interesting passages in Thoughts 27 (SC 438, 250), Eulog 9 (PG 79:1106A–C), and Inst ad mon (PG 79:1236A), this latter being brief enough to quote here: "Long-suffering softens a raid from the irascible—and so does psalmody." For a study of psalmody in Evagrius, see Bunge, "Psalmodie und Gebet" in *Geistgebet,* 13–28.

long-suffering one, fearless shall he be" (M 98). Long-suffering being associated with gentleness and calming the irascible is not uncommon in Evagrius's writings. In Greek, long-suffering is μακροθυμία, a word especially suited for the point Evagrius wishes to make. In its two parts, μακρο and θυμος, it implies a sort of stretching or enlarging of the irascible, so that it will be, we could say, less tight and prone to explosion.

If long-suffering closely approaches gentleness in its meaning, a virtual synonym for irascibility is rashness, as M 99 shows, a sentence where rashness stands opposite gentleness.[18] These terms are defined opposite each other in one of the scholia on Proverbs: "In the same way that death is born out of rashness, so out of gentleness, life; for gentleness is the opposite of rashness" (In Prov 18:6 [G 176]).[19]

Gentleness, long-suffering, humiliation of the irascible, singing psalms—all these quiet the irascible and, as M 12 (as well as M 98) expresses, cause us to be without fear. This being without fear is a mark of passionlessness and refers to being without fear before the demons; for by ridding ourselves of that part which makes us most like the demons, we have nothing to fear from them.[20] Another text from the *Scholia on Proverbs* explains why gentleness and like virtues take away fear. "Compassion takes away the terrifying visions that come over us by night. The same for gentleness and absence of anger and long-suffering and all the things that check the agitated irascible, since it is from the agitation of the irascible that terrifying apparitions usually come" (In Prov 3:24–25 [G 36]).[21]

M 12 and the other proverbs from *Ad Monachos* noted here

[18] This is true as well in M 85.

[19] See also In Prov 17:9 (G 157), cited just below.

[20] See In Prov 1:33 (G17): "The one who is passionless lives in stillness, unafraid of any evil thought." It is to be remembered that *thought* and *demon* are virtually synonymous.

[21] The expression "agitated irascible" is significant. The word *agitate* (in Greek ταράσσειν, ἐκταράσσειν) carries some technical force in Evagrius. In TP 21, 22, 46, 54, it refers specifically to a troubled irascible part of the soul; and in TP 21, 22, 54, 99, it refers to a monk who is not making progress. In M 8, 37, 52, it refers to an agitated heart. See also In Ps 31:9: οὐδέν οὕτω σκοτεῖ διάνοιαν ᾧ θυμὸς ταρασσόμενος (PG 12:1301A).

show gentleness contrasted with irascibility. They show that without gentleness there can be no health in the soul. And they show that without health in this part of the soul, there is no knowledge. This line of thinking is based on a principle that covers the whole of *praktikē*, namely, that each virtue casts out a vice.[22] In a text from the *Scholia on Proverbs* Evagrius explains rather straightforwardly how this works. "Through justice we hide injustice; through chastity, licentiousness; and again, through love, hate; and through lack of greed, greed. And we hide pride through humility and through gentleness, rashness. Thus do we seek spiritual friendship, that is, holy knowledge" (In Prov 17:9 [G 157]). Characteristically this explanation ends with the connection to knowledge rendered explicit. Vice drives knowledge away. Virtue prepares for it. Thus, "Irascibility scatters knowledge; / long-suffering gathers it" (M 35). Or beginning on the positive end: "Out of gentleness, knowledge is born; / out of rashness, ignorance" (M 99).

The connection these texts make between irascibility, gentleness, and knowledge may suggest something about the level of the audience for whom *Ad Monachos* is intended. In his writings Evagrius distinguishes between an imperfect and a perfect passionlessness. An imperfect passionlessness is one in which the monk is no longer troubled by the concupiscible part of his soul (see TP 68). From this imperfect passionlessness the monk can pass to a certain level of knowledge, but he has yet to continue battling the irascible in order to make further progress in knowledge. When Evagrius refers to the knower (ὁ γνωστικός) and addresses advice to him, it is usually to the monk who stands between imperfect and perfect passionlessness.[23] It is because such a monk's principal battle is with the irascible that Evagrius so frequently stresses gentleness to him.[24] The way in which gentleness is stressed in *Ad Monachos* and the frequent connection with knowledge suggest a reader who stands between the two

---

[22] This is the subject of a short work of Evagrius, *Vices Opposed to Virtues*.

[23] On these two kinds of passionlessness, see A. Guillaumont, "Le gnostique chez Clément d'Alexandrie et chez Évagre le Pontique," 198. Also SC 356, 26–27.

[24] Cf. G 4, 5, 8, 10, 32. See also Guillaumont, SC 356, 26–28, 94–95 (with many more references).

degrees of passionlessness, that is, a reader who to some extent has become a knower.

Perhaps no text brings all these ideas together into one development as successfully as does a passage from *On Evil Thoughts*. The text shows the relationship between the irascible and the demons. It puts forward gentleness as the means for mastery over the irascible. It mentions Moses and David as examples of gentleness, and then cites Christ's own command that we imitate his gentleness. It concludes by urging use of the irascible to destroy evil thoughts and guard good ones.

> If someone has mastery over the irascible, that one has mastery over the demons, and if someone is a slave to that passion, that one is a complete alien to the monastic life and a stranger to the ways of our Savior. Indeed our Lord himself said that he would teach the gentle his ways. Thus, the mind of the anchorites becomes difficult to catch when it flees to the field of gentleness. Hardly any of the virtues do the demons fear like they fear gentleness. Moses had it, being called gentle beyond all men. And the holy David frankly claimed that it is worthy of the memory of God, saying, "Remember, Lord, David and all his gentleness." But even the Savior himself commanded us to be imitators of his gentleness, saying, "Learn from me, for gentle am I and humble in heart and you will find rest for your souls." For if someone abstains from food and drink but rouses the irascible to anger through evil thoughts, that one is like a ship sailing the high seas and having a demon for a pilot. So, insofar as we can, we ought to guard this dog of ours and train him to only destroy the wolves and not to devour the sheep, to show every gentleness to all men. (Thoughts 13)

M 12 says that an irascible man will be terrified. Of course! A demon piloting the ship of the mind is not a comforting thought. M 12 says that a gentle man will be without fear. Of course! For he has learned from the Savior himself who promises rest for the soul.

Commentary on M 13, 14, 15

13. A strong wind chases away clouds;
    memory of injury chases the mind from knowledge.

Ἄνεμος σφοδρὸς ἀποδιώκει νέφη,
μνησικακία δὲ τὸν νοῦν ἀπὸ γνώσεως.

14. He who prays for his enemies will be forgetful
    of injuries;
    he who spares his tongue will not sadden his neighbor.

Ὁ προσευχόμενος ὑπὲρ ἐχθρῶν ἀμνησίκακος ἔσται,
φειδόμενος δὲ γλώσσης οὐ λυπήσει τὸν πλησίον αὐτοῦ.

15. If your brother irritates you,
    lead him into your house,
    and do not hesitate to go into his,
    but eat your morsel with him.
    For doing this, you will defend your soul
    and there will be no stumbling block for you at
    the hour of prayer.

Ἐὰν παροξύνῃ σε ὁ ἀδελφός σου,
εἰσάγαγε αὐτὸν εἰς τὸν οἶκόν σου,
καὶ πρὸς αὐτὸν μὴ ὀκνήσῃς εἰσελθεῖν,
ἀλλὰ φάγε τὸν ψωμόν σου μετ' αὐτοῦ.
τοῦτο γὰρ ποιῶν ῥύσῃ σὴν ψυχὴν
καὶ οὐκ ἔσται σοι πρόσκομμα ἐν καιρῷ προσευχῆς.

If, as was suggested in the previous commentary on M 12, gentleness can be considered a concrete expression of what love means, then perhaps this series of proverbs could be considered a concrete and more specific expression of what gentleness means. The concern here is with memory of injury versus forgetfulness of injury.[25] Understanding Evagrius on this theme can

---

[25] The flow of the proverbs in this section justifies this interpretation of increasing concreteness in the understanding of love. M 8 and 9 are about love versus hate, and M 10 is the first mention of memory of injury, rendering love and

clarify further why throughout his writings he claims such a close connection between love and knowledge. His insistence on this point stands within the very nature of the dynamic of love. Or, put the other way around, there is something in the dynamic of hate that makes knowledge of God impossible. What is this?

"Memory of injury" is a useful way to formulate how hate actually manifests itself, for the expression draws attention to a faculty of the mind (i.e., memory) and what it can be used for. Basically Evagrius's teaching on the question is this: he would say that obviously human and monastic experience shows that it is possible to use the mind to harbor the memory of injury. But if the mind is used for that, then none of its energies can be used for knowing God. In teaching thus, Evagrius is relying on the tradition of the desert fathers who preceded him. He specifically cites Macarius the Great as his teacher on this point, and the story he tells is helpful for clarifying how this dynamic works.

> The vessel of election, the elder Macarius the Egyptian, asked me why it is that when we remember injuries done us by humans we make the memory faculty of our soul disappear, but when we remember injury done by demons we remain unharmed? And when I found myself at a loss for an answer, I begged him to teach me the reason. So he said, "Because the first one goes against the nature of the irascible [part of the soul], while the second one is to use it according to nature." (TP 93)

In his commentary on this chapter, Guillaumont points out that the teaching can confidently be considered to be genuinely Macarian and not for the simple reason that because here Evagrius says so. An almost identical text exists in the *Apophthegmata Patrum* on Macarius, and yet the two texts seem to be independent one from another. Thus, from two different sources, Evagrius and the *Apophthegmata Patrum*, we have a witness to Macarius's teaching.[26] As this teaching points out, memory of

---

hate more concrete. M 12 is about gentleness versus irascibility. Now M 13–15 renders this more concrete. The same could apply in the interpretation of M 41 and 42, the former referring to forgetting injury versus remembering it, the latter referring to love versus hate.

[26] Guillaumont, SC 171, 697–99. The text in the *Apophthegmata Patrum* is Macarius 36.

injury makes the memory faculty of the soul vanish, and it is precisely this faculty that the monk must use to contemplate God, to remember his mercies, to remember the original union with him which the mind was created to enjoy. Thus, no small thing is at issue here: without this memory faculty being healthy, God cannot be known.[27]

This rich teaching is nicely encapsulated in M 13. The image of a strong wind driving clouds away is the image for how memory of injury chases the mind from knowledge.[28] The proverb is explicit in making the connection to knowledge and in specifying that it is the *mind* that is used for knowledge. In the text from the *Praktikos*, Evagrius cites Macarius as his source for such teaching; but he has made this feature of the tradition a major stress in his own spiritual doctrine. From various angles—irascibility, anger, hatred, rashness, memory of injury—Evagrius never says much about knowledge without mentioning how these threaten it. Many citations from throughout the Evagrian corpus would be possible. Attention to a few of these will have to serve our present purposes.

[27] Guillaumont likewise points out in his comment that, compared to Evagrius's citation of Macarius, the text from the *Apophthegmata Patrum* puts in sharper relief the opposition between memory of injury and memory of God, by which is meant specifically prayer. He sees in the end of the text cited in TP 93 the hand and formulation of Evagrius, that is, the application of the idea of the irascible part of the soul and its use according to nature. This is a valid observation for comparing the two *texts,* but everywhere the *teaching* of Evagrius is directly in the line with the point that Macarius 36 stresses. Thus, the final point of TP 93 may be Evagrian in formulation, but there is nothing in what Evagrius offers here that goes beyond the desert teaching on this point. This is an important clarification to draw. It means that Evagrius's language may be Greek and reliant on the Clement-Origen tradition about knowledge, but that the intimate relation that he stresses between love and knowledge is a basic insight of the desert tradition as represented by Macarius. Bunge for his part would see no reason to deny that the whole of TP 93 faithfully reflects the teaching of Macarius. See Bunge, "Évagre le Pontique et les deux Macaire," 338 n. 139.

[28] The language of M 13 is very close to that of a saying given by another father and cited by Evagrius in TP 99. Thus, consciously or not, Evagrius is citing the advice of yet another father in M 13. For the image used in M 13, cf. Lt 58:5, where Evagrius, speaking of his own weaknesses, compares himself to a waterless cloud carried along by the wind. He is alluding to Jude 12.

The *Chapters on Prayer* formulate some of the deepest fruits of Evagrius's spiritual life and doctrine. In this work, prayer and knowledge are closely associated; they are considered two different aspects of a same reality.[29] Warnings against various manifestations of trouble in the irascible part of the soul are a major feature of this treatise. One of its chapters explains how irascibility (in the form of memory of injury) ruins the mind, which is made for prayer. Evagrius formulates his thought quoting the Lord's own teaching from the Gospels about anger: "Leave your gift before the altar, it is said, and go first be reconciled to your brother, and then come and you will pray undisturbed. For memory of injury dims the ruling faculty [ἡγεμονικόν] of the one praying and darkens his prayers" (Prayer 21 [PG 79:1172B]; cf. Matt 5:21–26). The following chapter stays with the same theme: "Those who store up pains and memories of injury and yet imagine that they pray are like people who draw up water and then pour it into a broken jar" (Prayer 22 [PG 79:1172C]).[30] Actually this whole section of the treatise is filled with chapters that treat this theme from various angles, and these have already been usefully studied.[31] Here I would like to draw attention to several less-well-known texts of Evagrius which express this same traditional

---

[29] In the prologue Evagrius distinguishes two types of prayer, the kind used in *praktikē* (πρακτικὸς τρόπος) and the contemplative kind (θεωρητικὸς τρόπος). It is this latter that is to be associated with knowledge. Knowledge of the Trinity is the highest form of knowledge in the Evagrian system, and in the *Chapters on Prayer* this *knowledge* is identified with *prayer* in spirit and in truth. These points are amply demonstrated by Bunge, "The 'Spiritual Prayer.'"

[30] Evagrius is fond of images of the ridiculous when it comes to showing how impossible it is to combine anger and knowledge. In fact M 10 already introduces the theme of memory of injury with an image. See also Prayer 65 and G 5.

[31] See especially Hausherr, *Leçons*, 27–44, commenting on Prayer 12–27 with many references to other Evagrian works. For briefer comments, but ones that note the Macarian connection, see Bunge, "Évagre le Pontique et les deux Macaire," 335–38. In the commentary on M 12 I have already drawn attention to the fact that the theme is also prominent in the *Gnostikos*. The same theme found stressed in the *Chapters on Prayer* strengthens my suggestion about the level of audience intended in *Ad Monachos*. Gentleness (and the many other words associated with it) is talk appropriate for knowers who find themselves between imperfect and perfect passionlessness.

teaching in a genre similar to the proverbs found in *Ad Monachos,* namely, texts from the *Eight Spirits of Evil.*

A number of the formulations of this treatise in the chapters on anger directly connect memory of evil to the mind. "A cloud blocks the sun and darkens it; the thought [λογισμός] of the memory of injury does the same to the mind" (8 Spirits 9 [PG 79:1153C]). Memory of injury is identified with the technical term λογισμός, which is to highlight two things: first, that it is a demon; second, that it is a demon that works by means of thoughts. The mind, which should be bright with the knowledge of God, is made dark by such demonic thoughts.

The mind is meant by nature to be the dwelling place of God.[32] But God cannot dwell there if the mind is filled with thoughts that have nothing in common with God's own nature. "A serious man flees disgraceful stopping places; God flees the heart that remembers injuries" (8 Spirits 10 [PG 79:1156A]). Another meditation shortly after shows how the mind is meant for prayer. "Just as the smoke from chaff agitates the eyes, so does memory of injury agitate the mind at the hour of prayer" (ibid.). Prayer, contemplation, knowledge—these are the mind's true activity. The mind can enter these when it is rid of evil thoughts, when the irascible is healthy, when it is filled with love. Then, "the long-suffering man sees in visions assemblies of the holy angels, and the one who forgets injuries will exercise himself on spiritual reasons, receiving solutions to mysteries by night (cf. Ps 76:6)" (8 Spirits 10 [PG 79:1156B]).

Images and formulations as rich as these embody a desert tradition sanctioned by the great Macarius himself. All of this tradition and the "logic" of the dynamic it represents is meant to come flooding into the meditating mind which ponders M 13's, "memory of injury chases the mind from knowledge."

M 14 works off of M 13 as its contrast, speaking of being for-

---

[32] This is explained below on pp. 256–59 in commenting on the significance of the word *throne* in M 31. For a systematic study of the theme, see Bunge, "Der 'Zustand des Intellektes,'" in *Geistgebet,* 62–73. Evagrius is sparing in his use of the word *mind* in *Ad Monachos.* It occurs only here and in M 107 and M 136, these latter two being among the most important proverbs of the whole text. Always at issue is the highest level of knowledge.

getful of injuries in place of memory of injury. The proverb offers a practical plan for how to achieve this, a plan that has two parts: prayer for the enemy and sparing one's tongue. Praying for an enemy is clearly based on the Lord's own admonition to do so (cf. Matt 5:44), but another portion of the scripture also suggests to Evagrius the same course of action. Commenting on the psalm verse, "Instead of loving me, they falsely accused me, but I kept on praying," he says, "Whence we know that when someone speaks against us, it is necessary to pray for our enemies, lest caught up by the memory of injury, we be driven away from knowledge" (In Ps 108:4).[33] In this text and in M 14, prayer for the enemy would be the kind of prayer associated with *praktikē* (πρακτικὸς τρόπος), which is a part of the struggle against demons or evil thoughts. Some dimension of an injury done keeps trying to work its way into the mind (more specifically, into the memory), yet the monk can be like the psalmist and say, "but I kept on praying." This prayer of *praktikē* fills the mind with other things and pushes out the memory of injury. Thus, as M 14 suggests, the one who so prays "will be forgetful of injuries."

In the proverb's second line, the advice of sparing the tongue has the scope of not saddening one's neighbor. This echoes a concise, straightforward saying from the *Chapters on Prayer:* "If you wish to pray as you ought, then sadden no soul. Otherwise, you run in vain" (Prayer 20 [PG 79:1172B]). Hausherr remarks that this chapter summarizes all of the doctrine of chapters 12 to 26.[34] The doctrine of those chapters means to undergird this brief line from *Ad Monachos* as well.[35]

Both M 13 and M 14 are short proverbs of two lines apiece; but as the foregoing has shown, each can provoke an extended meditation that is meant to flow out of the already pondered M 12 on gentle versus irascible. I have suggested that the movement is increasingly concrete in what is proposed. This concreteness is put forward with insistence in the next proverb, M 15, which is a specific plan of action for reconciliation. It roughly

---

[33] Pitra, *Analecta sacra spicilegio Solesmensi,* 3:222.
[34] Hausherr, *Leçons,* 35.
[35] Compare the advice of M 87, "If your brother is sad, console him." The reward is knowledge, expressed as "great treasure in heaven."

echoes Matthew 5:21–26.[36] If there is trouble with a brother, one must go to him and be reconciled before one can hope to go to prayer, "to go to the altar." Evagrius suggests an action that is always a strongly symbolic action for a Christian: sharing a meal, however simple a thing that might be for monks.[37]

The word *brother* in this proverb should not go unnoticed. It has a specific meaning for Evagrius, nicely defined in one of the scholia on Proverbs. "They are brothers who have the grace of adoptive sonship and who depend upon the same father; namely, Christ" (In Prov 6:19 [G 78]). The scriptural verse on which he is commenting is interpreted by Evagrius as an indication of the dangers that can divide brothers. He continues, "They [the brothers] are the ones whom 'the witness of injustice' tries to divide by throwing into their midst agitations and 'quarrels.' I think the word 'kindles' has been used [in the verse interpreted] because of the passionate thoughts which inflame the irascible [part of the soul] toward anger and hatred and because of those which inflame the concupiscible [part of the soul] to shameful actions" (ibid.).[38] The advice of M 15 is directed against the "the witness of injustice" who tries to divide brothers by agitations and quarrels.

In this proverb the expression "hour of prayer" should be seen as referring ultimately to contemplative prayer (θεωρητικὸς τρόπος), that is, to the kind of prayer directly associated with knowledge. M 15's relation to M 13, with that proverb's explicit reference to knowledge, requires this interpretation of "hour of prayer." So does the affinity of the teaching in M 13–15 with the teaching in the *Chapters on Prayer*.[39] It is this contemplative kind

[36] These verses are more closely cited at Prayer 21.

[37] The advice here can be compared with that given in TP 26, which, as the last in a series of chapters offering remedies against anger, recommends the giving of a gift to "extinguish memory of injury." See also V 41: "Love turns around anger and the irascible; gifts overthrow memory of injury."

[38] This text has already been cited above in the discussion of the proverbs that surround a chain on the spiritual father. There it was observed that the word *brother* was occurring frequently at that point in the text. This union among brothers and with their father was an essential prerequisite for the knowledge at which one hopes to arrive under a father's direction.

[39] Many of the chapters place prayer and knowledge in strict relation. See Prayer 10, 39, 45, 69, 76, 85, 86, 145. For the expression "hour of prayer," see Prayer 11, 13, 19, 44, 45, 114, 117, 120, 128, 148. Also in G 45 the expression

of prayer which memory of injury disturbs. "Whatever you do to get revenge on a brother who has wronged you, that becomes a stumbling block for you at the hour of prayer" (Prayer 13 [PG 79:1169D]; cf. Prayer 45). In fighting against this memory of injury, M 14 recommends the prayer of *praktikē*, a kind of prayer to use when the stumbling block is already there. The scope of the prayer in M 14 is always to serve the contemplative kind of which M 15 speaks.

I conclude these comments on M 13–15 with another of Evagrius's remarkably concise chapters, but I would like to point out that this little chapter can serve not only as a summary of the comments on M 13–15 but likewise as a summary of what was observed in the comments on M 12 concerning gentleness and what was observed in the comments on M 3 concerning love's relation to knowledge. Keeping in mind that prayer and knowledge are two dimensions of a same reality, volumes are expressed when Evagrius says, "Prayer is what sprouts forth from gentleness and absence of anger" (Prayer 14 [PG 79:1169D]).

Commentary on M 21

21. If you imitate Christ, you will become blessed.
     Your soul will die his death,
     and it will not derive evil from its flesh.
     Instead, your exodus will be like the exodus of a star,
     and your resurrection will glow like the sun.

Ἐὰν ζηλώσῃς Χριστόν, γενήσῃ μακαριστός,
τὸν δὲ θάνατον αὐτοῦ ἀποθανεῖται ἡ ψυχή σου,
καί οὐ μὴ ἐπισπάσηται ἀπὸ σαρκὸς αὐτῆς κακίαν,
ἀλλ' ἔσται ἡ ἔξοδός σου ὡς ἔξοδος ἀστέρος,
καὶ ἡ ἀνάστασίς σου ὥσπερ ὁ ἥλιος ἐκλάμψει.

This beautiful proverb with its suggestive images has much to offer. It is a proverb structured on the movement from *praktikē* to

---

"hour of prayer" clearly refers to contemplative prayer and follows upon mention of absence of anger.

knowledge, and it places Christ's death and resurrection at the center of this movement. The theological ideas in which the proverb is grounded are basically Pauline, involving as it does the notion of sharing in Christ's death so as to share his resurrection.[40] Evagrius uses these Pauline concepts and understands death to apply to *praktikē* and resurrection to knowledge. This is consistently his teaching, as the following will make clear.

How, more exactly, is Evagrius guided by St. Paul in the idea formulated in M 21? The proverb speaks of dying Christ's death. Philippians 3:10–11 expresses why a Christian would want to die Christ's death: "that I may *know him* [γνῶναι αὐτόν] [Christ] and the power of his resurrection, and may have communion in his sufferings, being conformed to him in his death, that I may attain the resurrection from the dead." With these biblical terms, within the framework of the movement from death to resurrection, Evagrius understands the movement from *praktikē* to knowledge. The proverb connects dying Christ's death to *praktikē* by means of its third line, saying that the soul "will not derive evil from its flesh." Elsewhere Evagrius uses both ideas (i.e., the soul dying Christ's death and its not deriving evil from its flesh) in ways that clearly designate the life of *praktikē*. These other texts enrich an understanding of M 21 and render its meaning more precise.

At the beginning of the *Praktikos,* explaining the significance of the monastic habit, Evagrius says, "The sheepskin is worn by those who 'always carry in the body the death of Jesus,' (2 Cor 4:10) and who muzzle all the irrational passions of the body, cutting off the evils of the soul by participation in good" (TP Prologue, 6). In this passage, carrying the death of Jesus in the body is put in conjunction with muzzling the irrational passions of the body, certainly one of the major goals of *praktikē*. Of further interest is the following phrase, which speaks of doing this by "participation in the good," an idea that, even if not as clearly christological in its focus, is similar to M 21's, "If you imitate Christ."

In another place, Evagrius speaks explicitly of the resurrec-

---

[40] Cf. Phil 3:10; Col 3:3; 2 Cor 4:10; 2 Tim 2:11; see also 1 Cor 11:1, "Imitate me as I imitate Christ," but where the Greek differs from M 21. The Pauline passage has μιμηταί instead of ζηλώσῃς.

tion which was left unspoken (but surely intended that the reader complete the passage in his own mind[41]) in the text from the *Praktikos*. Further, he specifically acknowledges that he is thinking with St. Paul. "The rational nature which had died through evil–Christ raises this through the contemplation of all the aeons. And his Father, through knowledge of himself, raises the soul which has died the death of Christ. This is the meaning of the Apostle's statement, 'If we have died with Christ, we believe that we shall also live with him' (cf. Rom 6:8)" (Thoughts 38). In this text Evagrius speaks with the precision typical of his anthropology and soteriology. It is the rational nature that has died, and it has died because of evil. Christ raises this nature by means of the contemplation of aeons, that is, a contemplation of the salvation arranged by providence. Further, the Father raises this nature by means of the highest knowledge, knowledge of himself. But the Father effects such a resurrection for this rational nature as it is found in a soul and when this soul dies the death of Christ. All this is said to be the meaning of the Pauline verse cited. This same anthropological and soteriological precision undergirds the reasoning of M 21, which likewise speaks of a soul dying the death of Christ and of a resurrection. These texts show clearly how Evagrius understands the biblical and christological terms: death–*praktikē;* resurrection–knowledge.

The description of the soul not deriving evil from its flesh is noteworthy for the formulation "*its* flesh." The idea, basic to *praktikē*, is that the flesh belongs to the soul as its instrument so that the soul can do what it ought. From one perspective, of course, a soul placed in a body is a troublesome thing; but ultimately for Evagrius it is a great act of mercy on the part of the Creator. Thus Evagrius speaks of, "those who *by means of this body* obtain passionlessness of the soul" (TP 53, emphasis added). But if instead, one simply nourishes the flesh, then one has lost sight of the saving purpose of the body. "Those who nourish the flesh wrongly and take thought for it, exciting its desires [εἰς ἐπιθυμίας] (cf. Rom 13:14) should blame themselves and not the flesh" (ibid.).

---

[41] 2 Cor 4:10: "always carrying in the body the death of Jesus, so that the life of Jesus may also be manifested in our bodies."

Christ is a model of the proper use of the flesh. M 118 places the flesh of Christ in direct relation to the virtues of *praktikē* and sees the culmination in passionlessness. Christ is similarly presented as a model in M 21. By imitating Christ the soul will not derive evil from its flesh.

The notion of *praktikē* as death can be likewise understood in terms of how Evagrius defines anachoresis, the technical term for monastic withdrawal. In the *Praktikos* he gives a definition that he notes as coming from the tradition. He says, "Our fathers called practicing death and flight from the body 'anachoresis'" (TP 52). M 21 shows that this death which monks practice is Christ's death. Their practice of death is done in imitation of him. This text from the *Praktikos* also defines anachoresis as flight from the body. In M 21 the reason the soul does not derive evil from its flesh is precisely because it is practicing such a flight, again in imitation of Christ. To die Christ's death, to not derive evil from one's flesh—this is the goal of *praktikē*, the goal of anachoresis.

Yet *praktikē* always opens up to knowledge; it prepares a way for true prayer. It does not open to knowledge as some next stage unrelated to itself. Rather, because *praktikē* is an imitation, a becoming like Christ, it gradually becomes a knowing of Christ and of what Christ knows. "Christ raises this [nature] through the contemplation of all the aeons" (Thoughts 38). Evagrius describes this movement suggestively in the following text, which echoes in part M 21: "When your mind in its great longing for God gradually withdraws [ὑπαναχωρῇ] from the flesh and turns away from all thoughts [νοήματα] which come out of the senses or from memory or from bodily temperament [compare: 'not derive evil from its flesh'] and when it becomes full of reverence and joy, then can you conclude that you are close to the frontiers of prayer" (Prayer 62 [PG 79:1180C]).[42]

In its last two lines M 21 also opens up to knowledge with striking images. A brief comment that Evagrius makes on a psalm verse can lead into an examination of these lines in such a way as to keep attention focused on the role of Christ. The psalm verse reads, "to deliver their souls from death and to nourish them in

---

[42] Here I follow a reading different from that given in Tugwell's text, reading αἰσθήσεως instead of ἐνθυμήσεως, as in three of the manuscripts.

famine." Evagrius comments, "First it is necessary to save from death, then to nourish. Through *praktikē* the Lord saves from death; through knowledge he nourishes" (In Ps 32:19 [PG 12:1305D]). In M 21 one is saved from death through *praktikē*, that is, through not deriving evil from the flesh. Then the soul is ready for knowledge, and four images or terms for the realm of knowledge are presented: exodus, star, resurrection, and sun. Each of these deserves examination.

EXODUS

It should first be noticed that a progression is marked in the last two lines of the proverb where these images are used. An exodus like a star's is less than a resurrection, which glows like the sun. Yet both refer to the realm of knowledge, to lesser and greater degrees. More specifically, *exodus* actually functions as a transitional term for the passage from *praktikē* and knowledge. Evagrius uses this biblical term for describing the death that the monk dies with Christ. In a scholion on a text from Proverbs it is clear how he understands it. "Here he calls 'exodus' the soul's exit from evil and ignorance" (In Prov 1:20–21 [G 12]).[43] An exit from evil is a description of reaching *praktikē*'s goal. An exit from ignorance is to enter into knowledge. Thus, the term is at once suited for describing what happens both in *praktikē* and in knowledge.[44]

STAR

These exits from evil and ignorance are likened to the exodus of a star. Evagrius is fond of images of stars for knowledge, an idea found in the theological tradition to which he is heir. To take an example close to Evagrius, Didymus the Blind, whom

---

[43] A similar understanding of the term is found in In Prov 8:3 (G 99). In the *Kephalaia Gnostica* Evagrius frequently uses images of the exodus, of the wandering in the desert, and of the entry into the promised land as images for describing the movement from *praktikē* to knowledge. See KG IV, 64; V, 6, 21, 30, 36, 68, 71, 88; VI, 47, 49, 64.

[44] *Exodus* is used also in M 54; see comments on that proverb below.

Evagrius much admired,[45] speaks of stars in a way that seems to be presumed by Evagrius's own theological use of this image. Commenting on Genesis 1:14–19, Didymus says, "These luminaries themselves [the sun, the moon, the stars] serve as signs. According to the letter they indicate a kingdom or a drought or rain or some other event with important repercussions. In the anagogical sense they indicate the progress of the soul and also often its desolation" (*Commentary on Genesis* 1:14–19).[46] In M 21 the star is an indication of the soul's progress. A soul that does not derive evil from its flesh is a soul making progress. A star's exodus is a sign of this.

The difference in brightness among the stars also serves as an indication of the progress of souls. In commenting on the psalm verse "He numbers the multitude of the stars and calls them all by name," Evagrius says, "The number by which God numbers the rational beings indicates the differences in the condition of the stars, and the names which he gave them means the differences in spiritual knowledge" (In Ps 146:4 [PG 12:1676C]).[47] If the difference among stars indicates different levels of progress, it does so within a particular level of knowledge; for in general stars refer to a lesser level than that indicated by the sun. The knowledge associated with stars refers to the second natural contemplation. "The whole of the second natural contemplation bears the sign of the stars, and the stars are those to whom it has been entrusted to enlighten those who are in the night" (KG III, 84). We will see that the sun refers to knowledge of the Father himself.

In combining the term *exodus* with *star* Evagrius composes a proverb rich in its power to evoke the progress from *praktikē* to

---

[45] Evagrius cites Didymus in TP 98 and in G 48. Lt 59 perhaps makes allusion to him. Thus, Bunge, *Briefe,* 378 n. 13. For the possibility of Didymus and Evagrius having met and the ideas they share in common, see Guillaumont, SC 171, 707–8.

[46] Text in SC 233, 107; translation mine. Cf. In Prov 9:13 (G 113): "David says, 'I will see the heavens, the work of your fingers, the moon and the stars which you established,' which is to say, 'I shall see the reasons concerning the heavens and the moon and the stars.'"

[47] For other instances of the stars as symbols of rational beings, see KG III, 37, 62, 84; IV, 29; VI, 88.

knowledge. Both images seem suited for the way in which he wishes to describe especially the bridge from one to the other. Thus, an exodus is an exodus from both evil and ignorance. A star in its degree of brightness indicates degrees of progress, more specifically, degrees of progress within the second natural contemplation. The mind itself is destined to shine like a star when all the work of *praktikē* has been completed, a condition in which the monk's "passionlessness has given birth to love."[48] Thus, "If you desire pure prayer, then guard your irascible part, love chastity . . . and put memory of injury far away from you. . . . Then passionlessness of the heart will arise in you, and you will see your mind shining like a star while you pray" (Thoughts 43).[49]

RESURRECTION

The images of resurrection and sun describe yet a higher level of progress. If the Pauline term *death* is understood as referring to *praktikē*, then, not surprisingly, we have seen that Evagrius interprets *resurrection* in reference to knowledge. Yet resurrection is not simply a biblical code word for knowledge, even if it is always closely associated with it. It is a term that focuses knowledge within its eschatological dimensions. And eschatology in Evagrius is set in the context of his cosmology and particularly in the context of his understanding of the body. This is to say that resurrection is a term that covers far more than the "exit from ignorance" which a monk may hope for in this present life. The details of Evagrius's teaching on this subject are complex, but

---

[48] See TP 81 and Prologue, 8 for this expression.

[49] Evagrius employs the striking expression "fasting mind" (νηστεύοντος νοῦς) in another sentence that uses the image of the star and shows (with a remarkable swiftness in the poetic movement!) the unity between *praktikē* and knowledge. "The fasting mind: a star shining in the open sky" (8 Spirits 1 [PG 79:1145B]). The expression "fasting mind" shows the mind as the ultimate subject of the monastic life, the ultimate subject of salvation. Normally it would be expected that the body fast, and it is in fact the body that does the fasting even for the fasting mind. But the formulation is Evagrius's way of indicating that the body is the mind's instrument. When the mind uses the body rightly within the effort of *praktikē*, then it shines like a star.

some of the basic lines of his thought can be attempted here for the interpretation of M 21.[50]

In a chain within the *Kephalaia Gnostica* Evagrius describes three resurrections: of the body, of the soul, and of the mind. "The resurrection of the body is the passage from a defective quality to a superior quality. . . . The resurrection of the soul is the return from the order of being subject to the passions to the state of passionlessness. . . . The resurrection of the mind is the passage from ignorance to true knowledge" (KG V, 19, 22, 25). In order to understand what Evagrius means by these three resurrections, it must be understood that in distinguishing these three he is highlighting dimensions or aspects of what needs likewise to be understood as a single resurrection of a single subject. The dimensions are body, soul, and mind. These chapters from the *Kephalaia Gnostica* explore the consequences of the one resurrection for the body, soul, and mind. The resurrection described for each is characteristic of how Evagrius conceives the role of these "instruments."[51]

The resurrection of the body is the passage to a superior quality of the body. A body appropriate to the condition of the fall was received at the judgment. It was received as an instrument, as the gift of providence, to enable the fallen mind to reascend to the "place" from which it fell. A passage to a superior quality of body is precisely what can be expected for a body that is used as it ought to be, when the soul does not "derive evil from its flesh." The resurrection of the soul is described as a "return" to a condition in which one is no longer bothered by the passions.

---

[50] For more extended examination of the theme, see A. Guillaumont, *Les "Képhalaia Gnostica,"* 113–17; Bunge, "Origenismus-Gnostizismus," 35ff.; O'Laughlin, *Origenism in the Desert*, 145–50.

[51] What Evagrius is describing here will be misunderstood if it is interpreted simply in terms of time and space, that is, something like an interpretation that would crudely explain Evagrius to mean that *first* there is a resurrection of the body somewhere, and *then* later somewhere a resurrection of the soul. And *then*, since the mind is more important for Evagrius than the body, the real resurrection is that later resurrection of the mind and not that of the body. This is not what Evagrius is saying. The nature of the subject does not permit the same application of language of time and space as in its everyday usage, even if that is the only language available to describe these mysteries. "The movement of bodies is in time, but the transformation of the incorporeals is outside of time" (KG II, 87).

The soul of the fallen mind is afflicted by passions in its various parts; but when health is reestablished in this soul, when it does not "derive evil from its flesh," then it reaches a condition of passionlessness. This is its resurrection. Evagrius's description of the resurrection of the mind focuses squarely on that for which the mind was originally created, on that condition from which it fell, namely, knowledge. The resurrection of the mind is the passage from ignorance to knowledge, which depends on the passage to a superior quality of the body and passionlessness of the soul.

In his thinking on resurrection Evagrius seems to be basing himself especially on the Pauline distinction between "a physical body and a spiritual body" (1 Cor 15:44).[52] This distinction, sanctioned by the authority of scripture, enables him to be loyal to what he would perceive as the tradition's insistence on the resurrection of the body while at the same time stressing a more subtle interpretation of the resurrection than simply a raising up of the body that is "sown, which is perishable" (1 Cor 15:42).[53]

The Pauline expression "spiritual body" is used in various ways by Evagrius to describe the passage to a better condition, be that of the body, the soul, or the mind.[54] "Spiritual body" or "resurrection" are terms that describe a return to original unity of those elements into which the mind "disintegrated" (i.e., into soul, into a body) in falling from essential knowledge. This can be expressed in other ways too, but the basic idea of return to original unity is the key to understanding the various ways in which

---

[52] A. Guillaumont points out that 1 Cor 15 is a text fundamental to the debate between the Origenists and anti-Origenists on the question of the identity of the risen body with the body that is buried. He rightly points out that it must be admitted that the Pauline passage can be interpreted equally well to support the two opposing positions (*Les 'Képhalaia Gnostica,'* 115 n. 153).

[53] Origen already faced this problem. See Chadwick, "Origen, Celsus, and the Resurrection of the Body"; and Dechow, *Dogma and Mysticism in Early Christianity,* 349–90, with much more bibliography; also Crouzel, *Origène,* 319–31. On this more subtle understanding of what resurrection of the body would mean in Evagrius, see KG III, 25. How the spiritual body actually comes about is regarded as a perplexing question for which he attempts no answer. See KG VI, 58.

[54] Bunge points out that the notion "spiritual body" plays a major role in the *Kephalaia Gnostica* (see the many references in "Origenismus-Gnostizismus," 51 n. 75).

Evagrius expresses himself. "Spiritual body" and "resurrection" are Pauline terms for the reality. But basing himself on other scriptural texts, Evagrius might express a similar idea, stressing, say, not so much the bodily aspect as that of the soul. For example, in commenting on the psalm verse, "Return, my soul, to your rest," he says, "As the sick person returns to health, so the soul returns to its rest [ἀνάπαυσιν]. Or: at one time the soul was at rest in the same way that at one time a sick person was healthy. The apostle puts it this way: 'I want to depart and be with Christ' (Phil 1:23). This is the departure of those who are returning upward to their first place" (In Ps 114:7).[55]

M 21 speaks of resurrection without specifying a resurrection of body, soul, or mind. This leaves the possible meditation more open-ended. All three dimensions of the resurrection (all three resurrections) are well suited to the terminology of the proverb. The resurrection described in the proverb is to be associated with knowledge in that resurrection describes a condition necessary for knowledge. Body, soul, and mind must rise if the monk is to know God. Knowledge is always the ultimate scope of the resurrection. Evagrius expresses himself clearly on this. In a long passage in which he distinguishes between what we know from Christ in his Incarnation and what we know from him as eternal Logos, he says,

> But our Lord is himself the end and the final blessedness according to his title as Logos.[56] What in fact does he say in the gospel? "And I will raise him up on the last day," calling "resurrection" the passage from material knowledge to immaterial contemplation, and saying "last day" for that knowledge after which there is no other. Then our mind cuts loose and rises toward a blessed height where it contemplates the oneness and the unity of the Logos. (Ep Fid 7, lines 25–31)

---

[55] Pitra, *Analecta sacra spicilegio Solesmensi,* 3:235. This interpretation relies directly on Origen's use of the same psalm verse as support for his developed discussion of the soul as a term that basically describes a fallen condition (see *De Prin.* 2.8.3).

[56] In what immediately precedes, the Father is described as "end and final blessedness," distinguished from Christ "according to his title in the Incarnation" (Ep Fid 7, lines 13–19).

SUN

In relating the resurrection which the soul that dies with Christ will undergo to the glowing of the sun, Evagrius compares this resurrection to Christ himself, "the firstborn from the dead" (Col 1:18; Rev 1:5).[57] We have seen that stars represent knowledge, but they signify a lesser knowledge than that of the sun. "The moon and the stars illumine this earth, which remains in ignorance and cannot yet be illumined by the Sun of Justice" (In Ps 135:6 [PG 12:1656D]). Christ himself is the Sun of Justice. "Our Lord is the Sun of Justice in whom the Father dwells, as he said, 'I am in the Father and the Father is in me' (John 14:10). And again, 'The Father who dwells in me does his works' (John 14:10). And the Apostle, 'God was in Christ reconciling the world to himself' (2 Cor 5:19)" (In Ps 18:6 [PG 12:1142D–1144A]). This same interpretation is given in another scholion: "Christ is a tabernacle in whom God dwells. For he said, 'In the sun he placed his tabernacle' (Ps 18:6). And the Sun of Justice is the Lord" (In Ps 26:5 [PG 12:1280D–1282A]). Thus, as the sun, Christ is the bright image of knowledge, indeed knowledge of the Father; for the Father "has placed his tabernacle in the sun." Fixing this quite specific meaning for sun helps us to notice that the first and last line of M 21 (in which "blessed" stands in conjunction with "shine like the sun") have a tight theological coherence, but this is recognized only when the reader understands all that Evagrius's language and images imply. The one who imitates Christ will be blessed (first line), that is, he himself will glow like Christ the Sun (last line), in whom the Father dwells.[58] He will be blessed because Christ himself, whom he imitates, is "final blessedness" according to his title as Logos.[59] His resurrection is likened to the glowing of the sun because "the intelligible sun is the rational nature which contains in itself the first and blessed light" (KG III, 44).

This examination of the rich possibilities for meditation in M 21 can perhaps be best concluded by observing how the

---

[57] See the use of this expression in KG IV, 24. Christ is the first to receive a spiritual body.

[58] Recall that the Father is called "final blessedness" in Ep Fid 7 in the text just cited.

[59] Also, according to Ep Fid 7.

thoughts about death and resurrection here can be extended to the issue of love, which I have suggested is a key to understanding the whole text. From the analysis of the overall structure of the text, we know that we are in a part of the meditation that intertwines temperance and love. This would suggest to the reader who has discovered this key that M 21's talk of not deriving evil from the flesh is not merely to find its application in the realm of temperance. A clue to the wider application is touched off by M 8, when its "Anachoresis in love purifies the heart" is put in conjunction with the fact that "our fathers called practicing death and flight from the body 'anachoresis'" (TP 52).

It is a good thing to die with Christ and to not derive evil from the flesh. But that is not the end of the story. The resurrection follows. Only for that reason does one willingly undergo such a death.[60] Or in other words, a monk is willing to enter into *praktikē* because knowledge follows it. Learning to love is a death. But by learning to love, one comes to *know* God, who is love. This is a resurrection. It will glow like the sun. This application of the contents of M 21 to love is made explicit later in the text in M 40 to M 43, where, among the other things which are happening in that chain, there is a movement from Pentecost as the resurrection of the soul (M 40), to Pentecost as the resurrection of love (M 42), to the feast of God as true knowledge (M 43).

The personal pronouns of M 21 are worth observing carefully. In line 2 there is *your* soul and *his* death. The monk's soul is dying a death, but it is Christ's death. Then there is *your* exodus and *your* resurrection. Each Christian has his or her own exodus to undergo (cf. Luke 9:31) and will have his or her own resurrection. Each one must personally exit from evil and ignorance, but this personal exodus is in fact accomplished by participation in Christ's death, by imitating it. Thus is the individual's resurrection likened to Christ's own, that is, to the glowing of the sun. Christ has been in the movement throughout. It is he who makes progress possible. As Evagrius said in commenting on the psalm verse, "He led them out of darkness and the shadow of death":

---

[60] Cf. Phil 3:10–11, "becoming like him in death, that if possible I may attain the resurrection from the dead."

"Insofar as he is Light, the Lord leads us out of darkness. Insofar as he is Life, he leads us out of death" (In Ps 106:14 [PG 12:1565D–1568A]). Christ leads out of death by his own death, for "the crucifixion of Christ is the mortification of our old man, the cancellation of the sentence against us, and the remission which makes us come to life again" (KG VI, 40). And, "The death of Christ is that mysterious operation which leads to eternal life those who have hoped in him in this life" (KG VI, 42). The "mysterious operation" is what is happening in a hidden way throughout the monk's *praktikē*. His *praktikē* actually is "dying Christ's death." And, "his Father, through knowledge of himself, raises the soul which has died the death of Christ. This is the meaning of Paul's statement, 'If we have died with Christ, we believe that we shall also live with him'" (Thoughts 38).

Commentary on M 31

31. In the gentle heart wisdom will rest;
     a throne of passionlessness: a soul accomplished
     in *praktikē*.

     Ἐν καρδίᾳ πραείᾳ ἀναπαύσεται σοφία,
     θρόνος δὲ ἀπαθείας ψυχὴ πρακτική.

We have seen that quieting the irascible and making proper use of it is one of the goals of *praktikē*. If in the main the concern of gentleness is with the irascible, it is useful nonetheless to see how gentleness is associated with other terms denoting the goal of *praktikē*, terms that lie right along the borders of knowledge. M 31 is a proverb especially pregnant in this regard. It is a proverb that virtually quivers with meaning. Every word in it describes a goal. *Gentle, wisdom, rest, throne, passionlessness, praktikē*—all of these are words with precise meaning for Evagrius; each refers to something for which the monk must long struggle. It will be useful to take them one by one and see what each implies.

WISDOM

In order to take account of the significance of gentleness in this proverb, we can begin by attempting to fix with accuracy Evagrius's understanding of wisdom, which is here closely related to gentleness. In the flow of the proverbs as a whole, the word *wisdom* has occurred for the first time just shortly before, in M 28, where it is placed in parallel with knowledge. Now it is found with gentleness. To understand well what Evagrius means by wisdom, it must be viewed with its companion virtue, prudence.

A text in the *Praktikos* locates wisdom as a virtue in the rational part of the soul. Its task is contemplation. "[The task] of wisdom is to contemplate the reasons for the corporeals and the incorporeals" (TP 89). This role for wisdom is consistently held throughout Evagrius's writings, and it occurs frequently.[61] Because of this role Evagrius considers wisdom the highest of the virtues. He says, "If the rational part is the most precious of all the powers of the soul, and if only it is moved by wisdom, then one can say that wisdom is the first of the virtues. It is what our wise teacher called the spirit of adoption (Rom 8:15)" (KG VI, 51).[62]

Yet to understand well how wisdom functions in the rational part of the soul, it must be viewed in connection with, and to some extent in contrast with, another virtue located in the rational part, namely, prudence. Prudence and wisdom are also consistently associated throughout Evagrius's writings. Actually in the passage from the *Praktikos* just cited, the fuller text describes three virtues in the rational part of the soul: prudence, intelligence, and wisdom. "The task of prudence is to command [the battle] against the opposing powers and to protect the virtues and to throw up a front against vices; also it regulates what is neutral according to the circumstances. [The task] of intelligence is to harmoniously arrange everything which contributes to our goal. [The task] of wisdom is to contemplate the reasons for the corporeals and the incorporeals" (TP 89). What is interesting in this

---

[61] Many texts could be cited. It will serve to cite those texts in *Ad Monachos* that are characteristic. M 28, 67, 71, and 126 associate wisdom with knowledge. M 108, 119, and 123 associate wisdom with contemplating the reasons for things.

[62] Greek text in Hausherr, "Nouveaux fragments," 232.

conception is how virtues in the rational part of the soul are looking in different directions, as it were. Wisdom contemplates and is directed toward knowledge, while prudence is directed toward *praktikē*, commanding the battle against the demons. Intelligence manages some harmony between the two.[63]

Another text in the *Praktikos* explains a little more about how prudence performs its task, and the text likewise serves to show prudence's relation to wisdom. "Rest is wisdom's, but work is yoked to prudence. For there is no procuring of wisdom without war, and there is no successful war without prudence. For prudence has been entrusted with opposing itself to the irascibility of the demons, forcing the powers of the soul to act according to nature and preparing the way for wisdom" (TP 73).

Two things in this text are especially interesting for our purposes. First, it should be noticed that prudence opposes itself to the *irascibility* of the demons. This is precisely what we have seen to be a major concern of gentleness! Second, it is to be noticed that prudence gets the powers of the soul to act according to nature. In the discussion above on trouble in the irascible part of the soul, it was observed that the goal is not actually to get rid of the irascible part but to establish health there (cf. Thoughts 17). This health is what prudence "forces" in the powers (or parts) of the soul. Health in the irascible, we have seen, is using it against the demons and showing gentleness toward all.[64]

---

[63] In the *Gnostikos,* citing his teacher Gregory, Evagrius assigns a different role to prudence: "to contemplate the intelligible and holy powers, independent of their reasons" (G 44). This is done independently of contemplating these reasons because, as in TP 89, these reasons "are revealed by wisdom alone." This difference in the role assigned to prudence is probably explained by the fact that in the text from the *Gnostikos* Evagrius explicitly states that he is speaking of prudence and other virtues particularly as they have to do "with contemplation itself." TP 89 speaks of prudence insofar as it concerns a monk involved in *praktikē*. Thus, in *praktikē* prudence "commands [the battle] against the opposing powers [τὸ στρατηγεῖν πρὸς τὰς ἀντικειμένας δυνάμεις]," while for the gnostic it "contemplates the intelligible and holy powers [τὸ θεωρεῖν τὰς νοερὰς καὶ ἁγίας δυνάμεις]." For the knower who has passed through the battles of *praktikē*, that virtue which once had to beware of demonic powers now can enjoy the contemplation of the holy powers, the angels, who will help him toward knowledge. But the deepest nature of these powers, their reasons, are known by the virtue of wisdom.

[64] This was expressed clearly in the passage from Thoughts 13 discussed in

Getting the powers of the soul to act according to nature is also what TP 89 assigned to prudence when it spoke of "regulating what is neutral." The irascible and concupiscible parts of the soul are neutral and become either good or bad according to the use to which they are put.[65] Making these parts work for the good is the war without which wisdom is not procured (TP 73). On the other hand, the war is undertaken not from love of war but precisely so that wisdom can be procured, that is to say, precisely so that one can enter contemplation or knowledge.[66]

---

the commentary on M 12, especially the conclusion, "So, insofar as we can, we ought to guard this dog of ours and train him only to destroy the wolves and not to devour the sheep, to show every gentleness to all men."

[65] For this interpretation, see the comment of Guillaumont in SC, 171, 684–85; see also TP 86, 88; KG III, 59.

[66] Wisdom and prudence together are the subject of four of the proverbs in *Ad Monachos:* M 68, 123, 126, and 131. In M 68 the companion virtues form part of the center (M 66–68) of the center (M 63–72). It is commented on below. In the analysis of the chains it was observed that M 123 introduces a chain whose principal structural component was the presence of wisdom and prudence. At first glance this proverb may appear to have wisdom pointed in the wrong direction, concerned as it is with the demons, which we have seen to be the concern of prudence. But TP 50 clears up the difficulty and shows that this sentence remains consistent with Evagrius's teaching on wisdom. The text is advice to the monk who would familiarize himself with the art of the demons. He is advised to observe his thoughts carefully, to see how they come and go and which demon comes following upon another. This is prudence at work. Then he is advised to ask from Christ "the reasons for these things" (καὶ ζητείτω παρὰ Χριστοῦ τούτων τοὺς λόγους). The reasons for the corporeals and incorporeals that TP 89 assigned to wisdom for contemplation would include the reasons why the demons conduct themselves in the way that they do. This would be knowing about the dogmas (δόγματα) of the demons. The first part of TP 50, observing carefully how the demons come and go is prudence's task, as described by the texts just examined (TP 89 and TP 73), or as M 123 says, "Prudence tracks down their crafty ways." The second part of TP 50, asking the reasons for these things, is wisdom at work. In essence TP 50 is simply a longer version of M 123. But demons not only trouble the monk involved in *praktikē*. They also make their trouble for knowledge. According to KG I, 10 the demons specialize in these various types of trouble. Thus, wisdom's work in knowing the dogmas of demons not only involves the reasons they act the way they do, but it also involves discerning the difference between true and false knowledge. Discerning this difference is actually the concern of the chain that M 123 begins. In this same chain it becomes clear that in M 126, in its exact center, the statement "There is no prudence and there is no wisdom in their [false teachers'] teachings" is an accusation that they are lacking in the two main virtues of the rational part

This somewhat lengthy explanation of the role of wisdom has been necessary in order to measure with accuracy the significance of the presence of *gentleness* in M 31's statement, "In the gentle heart wisdom will rest." In this proverb in the place where one might have expected the word *prudent,* instead *gentle* is found. This is not an inappropriate or inconsistent "surprise." Gentleness, like prudence, does war with the irascible. Gentleness is virtue established in the irascible part of the soul. This is something that can come about only with the help of prudence "commanding the battle" and "regulating what is neutral," that is, regulating the irascible and the concupiscible.[67] Only in such a heart, a gentle heart, a prudent heart, could wisdom rest. And when wisdom rests there, then the monk has passed from the life of *praktikē* into the life of contemplation, to the life of knowledge. Gentleness has been its door of passage. As M 133 says, "a gentle monk will know the reasons of the incorporeals."

REST

Another word deserves attention in M 31, in this sentence that I described as quivering with meaning. It is the word *rest* (ἀναπαύσεται), which also has its special overtones for Evagrius. The key is given in the opening sentence of TP 73, already cited: "Rest [ἀνάπαυσις] is wisdom's, but work is yoked to prudence." Wisdom, as has been noted, is something that comes after the battles, after the work of prudence. It is not something that comes and goes.[68] If one has achieved gentleness, it means that

---

of the soul. It is equivalent to saying that they have a proper teaching neither on *praktikē* nor on contemplation. M 131 closes this chain with the same virtues, wisdom being associated with the heart raised up (to knowledge), prudence with its being purified (in *praktikē*).

[67] The way in which some of the chains of *Ad Monachos* are intertwined presents an image of the regulating of both the irascible and the concupiscible. Thus, for example, the intertwining of temperance (concerned with the concupiscible) with love and gentleness (concerned with the irascible) as represented, among other places, in the movement from M 93 to M 106.

[68] This is not to say that it is impossible to fall from wisdom or knowledge. Evagrius everywhere warns of that possibility. Yet a monk would not fall in and out of wisdom from day to day in the same way that one involved in *praktikē* might one day defeat the demon of gluttony and the next day not.

there has been a tremendous battle in the irascible and that at last the victory went to gentleness. Then it is time for wisdom to rest there. The battle has, as TP 73 says, "prepared the way for wisdom"; or as M 31 says, "In the gentle heart wisdom will rest." Evagrius uses ἀνάπαυσις with several emphases. He may contrast it with the work of *praktikē*, showing it as what follows the struggle. Or, with a slightly different nuance, he simply emphasizes rest as a dimension of knowledge. Both emphases can be operative in a meditation on M 31. Several examples can serve to show all that the term connotes.

Concerning the contrast with *praktikē*, in the *Bases of the Monastic Life* he says, "And if the temptation toward bodily rest comes upon you, think of what is more important. I mean spiritual rest. For truly better is spiritual rest than bodily rest" (Bases 5 [PG 79:1256D]).[69] In commenting on Proverbs 21:20, "A desirable treasure will rest in the mouth of the wise," Evagrius writes, "The wisdom of the Lord will rest in the heart of the wise" (In Prov 21:20 [G 228]).[70] Evagrius's exegetical method here is a quick and simple movement to the spiritual level of the text, repeating the scriptural verse and substituting for the literal sense of *treasure* the spiritual sense *wisdom*, for the literal sense of *mouth* the spiritual sense *heart*.[71]

Yet "rest" for Evagrius means more than simply resting up after the long fight of *praktikē*. It has also the positive sense of knowledge. "The rest of the Lord [κατάπαυσις] is his knowledge. Those who enter into it will rest [ἀναπαύσεται] in it" (In Ps 94:11 [2] [PG 12:1556B]). In fact, *rest* is also a term, a description, of the progress that is made within the realm of knowledge itself, such that moving from one level of knowledge to another can be called "rest." This is beautifully expressed in a passage from *On Evil*

---

[69] Guillaumont in commenting on TP 73 in SC 171, 662, also cites In Ps 114:7 and KG IV, 44. For the text of In Ps 114:7, see above, p. 246 n. 55.

[70] This interpretation of treasure here can be compared with its use in M 122. It is an image for knowledge; cf Lt 47:1; 61:1; M 25, M 28, M 87.

[71] There could be added to these occurrences Evagrius's use of a cognate verb in TP 15: "Psalmody and long-suffering and mercy put to rest [καταπαύει] an agitated irascible."

Thoughts. "The soul which has rightly done *praktikē* with God and has loosed itself from the body reaches those places of knowledge where the wings of passionlessness bring it to rest and from where it receives those wings of the holy dove which it spreads out wide through the contemplation of all the aeons and then comes to rest in the knowledge of the adorable Trinity" (Thoughts 29).[72] In this passage rest describes two things: the place where passionlessness has brought the soul, and, more importantly, knowledge of the Trinity itself.

Finally, it should be noticed that there would be a specific christological reference to Evagrius's use of ἀνάπαυσις especially when it is found in conjunction with gentleness, as in M 31. The vocabulary as well as the general idea of M 31 is based on the Lord's words, "Come to me, all who labor and are heavy laden, and I will give you rest [κἀγὼ ἀναπαύσω ὑμᾶς]. Take my yoke upon you, and learn from me; for I am gentle and lowly in heart [πραΰς εἰμι καὶ ταπεινός], and you will find rest for your souls [καὶ εὑρήσετε ἀνάπαυσιν ταῖς ψυχαῖς ὑμῶν]" (Matt 11:28–29). It is not only the terms *gentle* and *rest* that Evagrius borrows from the Gospel passage, but also the way he uses the terms *heart* and *soul* reflects their use in the Gospel. The gentle heart of M 31 stands in relation the gentle heart of the Lord in the Gospel passage. The monk will learn to have a gentle heart by learning from the Lord.[73] The Lord promises rest for *souls,* and the proverb connects soul with passionlessness. We could say again, "The wings of passionlessness will bring it to rest."[74] That in the proverb *wisdom* is said to rest in the gentle heart is a formulation based on

---

[72] The Greek for rest in this passage is based on καταπαύω. The passage draws its use of the image of the dove from Ps 54:7 (see In Ps 54:7). A similar distinction in a rest associated with *praktikē* and another associated with knowledge is found in KG III, 68.

[73] Evagrius cites this Gospel text in a passage we have already seen which lists examples of gentleness. He mentions Moses, David, and "even the Savior himself [who] commanded us to be imitators of his gentleness, saying, 'Learn from me, for gentle am I and humble in heart and you will find rest for your souls'" (Thoughts 13; for the fuller passage, see above, p. 229).

[74] This is the formulation from Thoughts 29, cited immediately above; cf. In Ps 114:7.

another dimension of the Gospel passage, namely, "learn from me." Christ as wisdom is the teacher of gentleness.[75]

THRONE, PASSIONLESSNESS, *PRAKTIKĒ*

This strong sense of the word *rest* functions as a clue for opening up a fuller meaning to be found in the second line of the proverb; the words *throne, passionlessness,* and *praktikē* all suggest something firmly planted in the soul. A little time spent on each term as it is used here will greatly enrich an understanding of the proverb.

The word *throne* is a scriptural code word with a specific meaning. Its use here is designed to give the proverb an unspoken but definitely present christological sense, meant to be discovered by the careful meditator. The meaning of this biblical term is explained very briefly and straightforwardly when Evagrius is commenting on the scriptures. His interpretation consistently gives it a christological reference. Thus, in commenting on the psalm verse, "God is seated on his holy throne," Evagrius explains, "The throne of God is Christ. The throne of Christ, the rational nature" (In Ps 46:9 [PG 12:1437C]).[76]

A slightly longer comment on a text from the book of Proverbs directs us in a proper interpretation of the word as used in M 31. The Proverbs text is "Kill the impious in the presence of the king, and his throne shall be set up rightly in justice." Evagrius says, "He who with a spiritual word kills the old man which was corrupted through 'deceitful lusts' [κατὰ τὰς ἐπιθυμίας τῆς ἀπάτης] (Eph 4:22) would be setting up his own mind in justice, the mind, which is said to be the throne of God. For wisdom and

---

[75] The specific christological interpretation of wisdom in this proverb is demonstrated in what follows.

[76] In at least two other places Evagrius comments on the word in the same double sense of Christ as throne of God and rational nature as throne of Christ. Thus, "The temple of God is Christ. And the intellectual and holy powers [αἱ νοεραὶ καὶ ἅγιαι δυνάμεις] are the temple of Christ. Therefore, Christ is said to be seated on the throne of David his father" (In Ps 17:7 [PG 12:1225D–1227A]). And again, "The throne of God is Christ. The throne of Christ, the incorporeal nature [ἡ ἀσώματος φύσις]" (In Ps 9:5 [PG 12:1188C]). See also In Prov 28:22 (G 354): "The throne on which the mind is enthroned is spiritual knowledge."

knowledge and justice—and Christ is all of these!—are enthroned nowhere except in the rational nature" (In Prov 25:5 [G 300]). This text identifies wisdom, knowledge, and justice as the specific way in which Christ himself is seated on the throne of the mind. It suggests interpreting M 31 along the same lines and identifying Christ himself as passionlessness seated on the throne of the mind, here described in its present condition as a soul accomplished in *praktikē*. Such an interpretation is in line with M 118, which explicitly identifies the flesh of Christ as passionlessness for the monk who feeds on that flesh.[77]

This interpretive key provided from the *Scholia on Proverbs* suggests also moving backwards a moment in M 31 to reconsider the sense of *wisdom* there. It too is susceptible of a christological interpretation. Christ is wisdom.[78] Thus, in the gentle heart Christ will rest! If Christ is in the soul as passionlessness, it means that he has brought that soul to the term of *praktikē*. If he is in the soul as wisdom, it means that he is helping the soul with wisdom's task, "the contemplation of the reasons for the corporeals and incorporeals" (TP 89). This explicit identification of Christ with wisdom is made at M 119, the proverb that follows immediately upon the one that explicitly identifies Christ with passionlessness. "The blood of Christ: the contemplation of created things; / he who drinks it, by it becomes wise."[79] So, if the reader were to miss the hidden christological sense of M 31 in a first time through the text, M 118 and 119 are waiting later in the text to render the suggestion more explicit.[80]

---

[77] I think that interpreting "the throne of passionlessness" to mean throne of Christ is legitimate on the basis of the exegetical procedure employed by Evagrius in the text cited from *Scholia on Proverbs*, but the claim will be further justified in the discussion below on M 118. Basing himself on an idea dear to Origen, Evagrius names Christ as each virtue. Relying on Clement, Evagrius sees Christ as a model of passionlessness. See pp. 333–34 n. 228.

[78] "For wisdom and knowledge and justice—and Christ is all of these!" As in In Prov 25:5 (G 300) cited immediately above.

[79] In the chain M 118–20 passionlessness and wisdom are put in just as strict a relation as in M 31. The other place where this happens is in M 68, that is, in the chain on passionlessness found at the exact middle of the text.

[80] M 28, the first proverb in the text to mention wisdom, urges, "Procure knowledge and not silver, / and wisdom rather than much wealth." This proverb opposes spiritual riches to material riches. A proverb in a different text is formu-

Praktikē as it is used in this proverb also conveys a strong sense of something firmly established in the soul. Though Evagrius does not always do so, he usually uses the word πρακτική to describe someone who has achieved the goals of *praktikē* and reached the frontiers of passionlessness.[81] So, not only does wisdom resting suggest something firmly established, not only does throne of passionlessness, but so also does πρακτική as an adjective for soul. Thus, the throne of passionlessness is the soul that has come through *praktikē* and arrived at its immediate term, passionlessness.[82]

This discussion of M 31 can be concluded by drawing all these strands together around the theme of gentleness. Gentleness is here placed as the defining term of a monk who has reached the goal of *praktikē* (passionlessness) and entered into contemplation (wisdom). It turns out to be, more than might at first be suspected, a proverb that associates gentleness rather directly with knowledge; for in essence it is saying that in the gentle heart, Christ as wisdom will rest. And wisdom is contemplation of the reasons for the corporeals and incorporeals (TP 89).

---

lated in a manner very close to M 28, that is, with the same opposition between the spiritual and the material; yet in this proverb the spiritual riches are given an explicit christological reference. "Procure wisdom and not silver; put on the bright garment of Christ our Lord, better than any robe of linen, which does no good on the day of death" (Inst ad mon [PG 79:1237D]).

[81] Guillaumont demonstrates this in SC 170, 49–51.

[82] Evagrius's distinction between an imperfect and perfect passionlessness, discussed in the commentary on M 12, comes into play in the interpretation of M 31 as well. Perfect passionlessness describes a monk who has reached victory over all the demons that have opposed his *praktikē*. Imperfect passionlessness refers to the relative power one has achieved over a particular demon (cf. TP 60). In M 31 virtually every word argues for the sense of perfect passionlessness; but the real key is that gentleness is established there, so that there is control not only over the concupiscible but over the irascible as well. "Passionlessness is the calm state of the rational soul which comes from gentleness [in the irascible part] and chastity [in the concupiscible part]" (Skemmata 3) (Muyldermans, *Evagriana* [1931], 38). Another text speaks of perfect passionlessness in relation to wisdom and the state of prayer to be associated with knowledge. "The state of prayer is the condition of passionlessness, which by a supreme love [ἔρωτι ἀκροτάτῳ] snatches up on high the mind in love with wisdom, the spiritual mind [τὸν φιλόσοφον καὶ πνευματικὸν νοῦν]" (Prayer 53 [PG 79:1177C]). Bunge comments on this sentence showing that "wisdom" refers to Christ and "spiritual" to the Holy Spirit (see *Geistgebet,* 75–76).

The blood of Christ is this contemplation. He who drinks it becomes wise (M 119). The gentle monk will know reasons of the incorporeals (M 133).

The Greek construction is a tight chiasm, the beginning and end terms being gentle heart and soul accomplished in *praktikē*. In the middle of the chiasm, wisdom and passionlessness (two names for Christ!) are put immediately side by side. Thus, gentleness is what is meant by a soul accomplished in *praktikē*. Gentleness is knowing Christ as passionlessness and wisdom.

Commentary on M 53

53. Conversion and humility have set the soul up;
    compassion and gentleness have made it firm.

Μετάνοια καὶ ταπείνωσις ἀνώρθωσαν ψυχήν,
ἐλεημοσύνη δὲ καὶ πραΰτης ἐστήριξαν αὐτήν.

In the analysis of the text's structure, this proverb was identified as standing free in the collection, functioning as a hinge between two rather substantially developed portions of the text. Its terms look in many directions, both summing up what has come before and what will follow. It is striking that once again in a proverb of considerable weight in terms of its placement, gentleness is found. Three other virtues are mentioned along with it. We shall examine these here, focusing on what is of special interest, namely, seeing how humility and gentleness are associated.[83]

This proverb offers a good occasion for sharing a story from Evagrius's life which I think lends an insight fundamental to understanding the nature and tone of his spiritual teaching. The story goes some way toward explaining this theme found to be so

---

[83] There will be no need here to examine specifically the term "compassion." It is a companion virtue often associated with gentleness and other virtues that calm an agitated irascible. For this, see especially In Prov 3:24–25 (G 36), cited above, p. 227. Also TP 20: "Anger and hatred make the irascible grow; compassion and gentleness diminish that which is there." In some instances Evagrius's use of ἐλεημοσύνη has the concrete sense of almsgiving, as in In Prov 22:2 (G 234), cited here below. Cf. ἀνελεήμων in M 25 within a chain on poverty and wealth.

central to his thought, namely, the importance of love, be it called gentleness, mercy, compassion, or another of its many names. Evagrius was a much-sought-after teacher, according to accounts of him from other monastic sources. His correspondence also gives clear evidence of it; many of his writings are in answer to requests made of him. And we know that many monks used to come to him and especially on Saturday night would hear his spiritual conferences and receive his advice (*Coptic Life,* 114ff.). On one such occasion he shared with his brothers the experience of an extraordinary vision he had had. His own account of it is recorded by Palladius. Evagrius told his fellow monks,

> I was seated at night in my cell with the lamp burning, reciting one of the prophets. In the middle of the night I fell into an ecstasy and I found myself as if I were in a dream in sleep and I saw myself as suspended in the air up to the clouds and I gazed at the whole inhabited world. And the one who was holding me said to me, "Do you see all these things?" (For he had raised me up to the clouds that I might see the whole world at once.) I said to him, "Yes." He said to me, "I will give you a command. If you keep it, you will become ruler over all these things which you see." He also said to me, "Go, be merciful and humble and fix your thought correctly in God. You will be prince over all these things." (*Coptic Life,* 117)[84]

---

[84] I am indebted to Mark Sheridan for this translation from the Coptic. The relation of humility and mercy (the terms cited in this version of the command Evagrius received) to gentleness will grow more clear in what follows. However, the *Coptic Life* does at least allow us to wonder if the wording of the original command that Evagrius received may not have been to be gentle and humble. Immediately after the passage cited, Palladius continues with a remark on how much Evagrius had excelled in these virtues, and then quotes Evagrius as citing Ps 24:9, which reads, "He will teach the gentle his ways." Evagrius himself cites this verse in a way that shows how fundamental it is to his teaching. He comments on the psalm verse, "Your ways, O Lord, make known to me," in this way: "He who wants to know the ways of the Lord, let him become gentle. For it is said, 'He will teach the gentle his ways,' ways that put to rest [καταπαύσαντας] the never ending war in the soul of the irascible and the concupiscible and of the passions which are subjected to them" (In Ps 24:4 [2] [PG 12:1269C–D]). In any case, the ambiguity in vocabulary created by the *Coptic Life* can perhaps be considered useful for reflecting on M 53, which employs terms also used in the Coptic text as well as from this conjectured Greek text.

Evagrius took the advice of this vision to heart. The insistent recurrence of the themes we have been examining in *Ad Monachos* (love, gentleness, forgetting injury, and now compassion and humility) are but one instance of how. As with other proverbs, M 53 can be considered a "variant" expression of the command Evagrius received in his vision of the air.

The two lines of the proverb mark a certain progress in *praktikē*. The first line, mentioning conversion and humility, speaks of virtues that come at the beginning of *praktikē*, especially—and rather obviously—conversion. But the verbs note the progress as well. The first two virtues set the soul up. Once set up, other virtues make it firm. These are gentleness and compassion.

Conversion (μετάνοια) is, of course, a biblical term, characterizing the preaching of both John the Baptist and Jesus (Matt 3:2; 4:17). Evagrius and the circle of monks around him would have heard special overtones in the Greek word, overtones expressible in a phrase something like "return of the mind [νοῦς]." In the theological tradition of which Evagrius is both heir and practitioner, it is the νοῦς, constituting the core of each person, that is the definitive object of salvation. (The salvation of the soul and the body serve this end.)[85]

All that having been said, it is not a term that is used with special frequency in Evagrius. He seems to understand it in its obvious sense of conversion, making a change in one's life. A line dropped almost by chance in the *Scholia on Proverbs* indicates this understanding and locates it at the beginning of the monastic life, associating it with the fear of the Lord. In commenting on the word *shame* in the scriptural text, Evagrius says, "And perhaps also he calls shame the reasons concerning conversion and shame [τοὺς περὶ μετανοίας καὶ αἰσχύνης λόγους], which lead us to realize our own sins" (In Prov 9:12 [G 113]).[86] In a different context

---

[85] In at least one other instance Evagrius uses μετάνοια in a sense that is not the standard religious notion of conversion but instead refers to a change of mind. In In Prov 20:25 (G 219) he says, "Changing the mind regarding good things does not happen to the just but to the unjust" (Ἡ ἐπὶ τοῖς ἀγαθοῖς μετάνοια οὐ δικαίοις συμβαίνει, ἀλλὰ ἀδίκοις). In any case, this text shows how Evagrius would have heard νοῦς under the word μετάνοια.

[86] In the fuller context Evagrius associates it with fear of the Lord. On fear of the Lord at the beginning of the monastic life, see TP Prologue 8, 81; M 4.

Evagrius defines the term more closely in line with the principal coordinates of his understanding of the spiritual journey: "Conversion is the ascent from the movement and from evil and ignorance toward the knowledge of the Holy Trinity" (KG VI, 19).

Humility is a word with a far more developed Evagrian meaning. Two texts in the *Praktikos* show how humility is produced within the monk. Explaining the symbolism of the cowl, Evagrius says that those who wear it on their head can sing the psalm, "If the Lord does not build the house." He freely quotes the first verse from the psalm and then notes, "Words like this produce humility [ταπεινοφροσύνη]." It is opposed to pride, which he calls the original evil (TP Prologue 2).[87] Elsewhere in the *Praktikos* Evagrius, instead of quoting a psalm, unfolds the idea with his own words and creates a rather more striking text as a result. The suggestion is for the monk to remember his former life and all his ancient faults, to recall how Christ's mercy saved him, how many humiliations he [the monk] endured even while in the world. He is also urged to remember who it is that has protected him in the desert and chased the demons from him. After all this he says, "Thoughts [λογισμοί] like this produce humility" (TP 33).[88]

Another text is interesting for the way in which it lists humility along with some other virtues of *praktikē*, namely, "with compunction, tears, an infinite desire for the divine, and an unmeasurable zeal for work" (TP 57). What is interesting is that these virtues are said to accompany one of two "peaceful states of the soul," which is another way of speaking of passionlessness.[89] This is a peaceful state that results from virtues finding their natural place in the soul. The other peaceful state is more dangerous, though one might not think so at first. It is the peaceful state that results from the demons' withdrawal. The danger comes

---

[87] The psalm quoted is Ps 126:1. Pride as the original evil is a theme examined below in the commentary on M 62. Ταπεινοφροσύνη is Evagrius's most usual expression for humility. Ταπείνωσις in M 53 seems to carry the same meaning, unless it means to accent an action: *humiliation*, as it could also be translated.

[88] Apart from the difference between *words* and *thoughts*, the Greek is the same in TP 33 and Prologue 2. The text cited here shows, rather unusually, a positive use of λογισμοί.

[89] Guillaumont demonstrates this in his comment at SC 171, 634–35.

from the fact that after the demons withdraw, the monk is especially susceptible to the demons of pride and vainglory, proud that *he* is rid of demons and vain in thinking that it was *his* own efforts that produced their withdrawal. Thus, passionlessness as the goal of *praktikē* must be continually accompanied by humility and the other virtues mentioned in order to remain in that peaceful state and not be robbed of it by the sudden appearance of pride and vainglory. In fact the very next chapter in the *Praktikos* says, "Being able to drive away the thought of vainglory through humility . . . would be proof of a very profound passionlessness" (TP 58).[90]

So much for a general notion of humility. It is a virtue of *praktikē*. It is an antidote to pride and vainglory. It protects the condition of passionlessness. But another feature of humility makes it especially interesting for the present focus and serves to show more clearly its connection with gentleness. Humility is closely associated with the irascible. In one of the scholion on Proverbs Evagrius states this clearly and also associates it with compassion, another of the virtues mentioned in M 53. He says, "The rich man purifies his irascible part through almsgiving[91] and thus acquires love. The poor man through poverty learns to be humble" (In Prov 22:2 [G 234]). Géhin's commentary on the text seems just right. "La charité et l'humilité sont considérées comme les vertus du *thumos*. Par deux voies différentes, le pauvre et le riche sont parvenus au même résultat: la guérison de la partie irascible de leur âme."[92] Elsewhere in the same work Evagrius speaks of how someone who is passionless will linger in contemplation and no longer worry about his "house" because "the irascible is clothed in gentleness and humility, the concupiscible with chastity and temperance" (In Prov 31:21 [G 377]).

---

[90] See also In Prov 17:9 (G157), "And we hide pride through humility." See the fuller quotation of the text on p. 228 above, where gentleness is also mentioned.

[91] The Greek is ἐλεημοσύνη, which from the context can be specified as almsgiving; but it is the same word that is used in M 53, there translated more broadly as "compassion."

[92] Géhin in SC 340, 329. This same text with Géhin's comments helped us to see the logic of a proverb on humility (M 19) following a chain on poverty and love (M 16–18).

A text from *Ad Monachos* makes it equally clear that humility's work is in the irascible part: "As water makes a plant grow up, so humiliation of the irascible raises up the heart" (M 100).[93] One of the strongest texts that Evagrius has written on humility is also one of the briefest. He says, "The Lord opposes himself to the arrogant because he *is* humility" (In Prov 3:34 [G 39]).[94] This can suggest that at base the inspiration for Evagrius associating humility and gentleness is probably to be found in the Lord's own words, "I am gentle and humble in heart [πραῢς εἰμι καὶ ταπεινός τῇ καρδίᾳ]" (Matt 11:29).

There is in the first line of the proverb an implied upward movement that is expressed, as it were, almost "between the words." The verb "to set up" (ἀνορθόω) is explicit enough, but the root sense of ταπείνωσις, "being brought low," is meant to be heard ironically next to it; and the irony is that expressed in the Lord's words, "Whoever humbles himself will be exalted" (Matt 23:12).[95] The word *conversion* would also help build the implied upward movement for the monk who knows Evagrius's definition, already cited, from the *Kephalaia Gnostica:* "Conversion is the ascent . . ." (KG VI, 19).

I suggested that the story of Evagrius's vision, in which he received a divine command to be merciful and humble, can help to intuit the spirit that stands behind the formulation of a proverb like M 53, a proverb typically expressive of Evagrius's concern for love and gentleness. But M 53 is a proverb in which it may also be possible to hear a distant echo of more concrete dimensions of Evagrius's personal life. Such echoes are rare, and one must listen carefully for them. Yet those echoes that can be caught are helpful, for they can add an element of feeling to the sentence

---

[93] This is the third member of a little chain constructed around the theme of irascibility, long-suffering, gentleness, and knowledge. This chain shows where humility fits into this dynamic of virtues with their drive toward knowledge.

[94] Emphasis mine. The Lord as humility itself should be compared with the statement of Christ as wisdom, knowledge, and justice in In Prov 25:5 (G 300), cited above in the commentary on M 31. In the fuller text of In Prov 3:34 the Lord is also said to be justice and truth.

[95] M 96 and M 100 are structured on this same dominical saying, and M 130 states the same principle, only backwards.

involved and lend the authority of personal experience.[96] It is well known both from the *Lausiac History* (38:7–9) and the *Apophthegmata Patrum* (Evagrius 7) that Evagrius was established in the monastic life in Egypt only after a conversion that was very difficult for him, a conversion, in fact, that he had to attempt several times (*Coptic Life*, 107–11). Eventually, however, Evagrius became well known for his humility.[97] The stories from the various sources reveal some of the actual struggles that Evagrius himself would have had with conversion and humility and the path by which he came to them. His fellow monks knew the story of his life which one of their number, Palladius, tells in the *Lausiac History;* they knew the difficulty of his conversion; and many may have witnessed the scene of his humiliation by the priest of Cells (Evagrius 7).[98] These same monks, who now were able to profit from his own gentleness, of which the sources also speak, would have found much in which to put their confidence in hearing Evagrius say, "Conversion and humility have set the soul up; compassion and gentleness have made it firm."

Commentary on M 54, 55, 56

54. In all things remember your exodus,
       and do not forget the eternal judgment,
       and there will be no transgression in your soul.

Μέμνησο διὰ παντὸς σῆς ἐξόδου
καὶ μὴ ἐπιλάθῃ κρίσεως αἰωνίας,
καὶ οὐκ ἔσται πλημμέλεια ἐν ψυχῇ σου.

55. If the spirit of listlessness mounts you,
       do not leave your house;

---

[96] I examined above the personal experience of Evagrius which stands behind the construction of the whole of *Ad Monachos*. See pp. 181–94.

[97] The evidence is discussed below in the commentary on M 61 and M 62.

[98] The text is cited and discussed below in the commentary on M 61 and M 62.

and do not turn aside in that hour from
profitable wrestling.
For like someone making money shine,
so will your heart be made to glow.

Ἐὰν πνεῦμα ἀκηδίας ἀναβῇ ἐπί σε, οἶκόν σου μὴ ἀφῇς
καὶ μὴ ἐκκλίνῃς ἐν καιρῷ πάλην ἐπωφελῆ.
ὃν τρόπον γὰρ εἴ τις λευκάνοι ἄργυρον,
οὕτως λαμπρυνθήσεται ἡ καρδία σου.

56. The spirit of listlessness drives away tears
and the spirit of sadness shatters prayer.

Πνεῦμα ἀκηδίας ἀπελαύνει δάκρυα,
πνεῦμα δὲ λύπης συντρίβει προσευχήν.

It was observed in the analysis of the chains that even though
in M 54 the word *listlessness* does not appear, with its advice on
remembering death it begins a three-member chain on listlessness.[99] Evagrius is deservedly well known for his astute observations about the nature of this perennial monastic problem and
for the sage advice he proposes for its resolution. This chain is a
good example of my claim that the proverbs of *Ad Monachos* manage to express with a wonderful conciseness what is elaborated at
greater length in Evagrius's other works. I want to illustrate that
here by viewing various statements of the proverbs against Evagrius's other teaching on the subject.

In the *Praktikos* there is found a long description and analysis of how this demon (this thought, this spirit, this temptation)
operates (TP 12). It is Evagrius's best known and most lengthy
description. But for our purposes here a comparable but less-
well-known description from the *Eight Spirits of Evil* can serve as
a general description of what Evagrius means by the spirit of listlessness and how it attacks a monk.[100] The description is quoted

---

[99] The commentary on these proverbs contains the results of an earlier
study of mine: Driscoll, "Listlessness in *The Mirror for Monks* of Evagrius Ponticus."

[100] Furthermore, this particular text helps to see more clearly than does the
one from the *Praktikos* that the placement of a chain on listlessness after one on

here in its entirety, for it expresses some of the most characteristic themes.

The eye of the listless [monk] gazes out the windows again and again, and his mind imagines visitors. A sound at the door, and he jumps up. He has heard a voice, and from the window he reconnoiters the scene and won't leave it until he has to sit down from stiffness. When he reads, the listless [monk] yawns plenty and easily falls into sleep. He rubs his eyes and stretches his arms. His eyes wander from the book. He stares at the wall and then goes back to his reading for a little. He then wastes his time hanging on to the end of words, counts the pages, ascertains how the book is made, finds fault with the writing and the design. Finally he just shuts it and uses it as a pillow. Then he falls into a sleep not too deep, because hunger wakes his soul up and he begins to concern himself with that. The listless monk—he's lazy in prayer, and he never speaks about it. For like a sick person who won't carry a heavy load, so also is the listless [monk] who does not do the work of God carefully. He ruins the strength of his body, and he unstrings the chords of his soul. Endurance cures listlessness. And so does everything done with much care and fear of God. Set a measure for yourself in everything that you do, and don't turn from it until you've reached that goal. And pray intelligently and with straining, and the spirit of listlessness will flee from you. (8 Spirits 14 [PG 79:1160B–C])

This passage and the one from the *Praktikos* are both descriptions filled with humor and irony, and I think that it is already part of Evagrius's disarming of the demon to help the monk laugh a little at himself caught in the despondency that this demon provokes. Listlessness, which can make the monk look so silly, is the demon against whom this chain of proverbs in *Ad Monachos* is directed, and the proverbs offer some of the most characteristic advice that Evagrius suggests should be used against this demon. Let us look now at each of the three proverbs in turn.

Before even mentioning listlessness by name in M 54, Evagrius speaks of one of the most important remedies against it,

---

sleep (M 46–52) is no accident. Sleep is one of the ways in which the demon of listlessness causes his trouble.

remembering death, here expressed as "remember your exodus."[101] In the *Praktikos* he indicates that this is a method that existed in the tradition before him and that he learned from his "master."[102] He quotes this master as saying, "The monk should always, on the one hand, hold himself ready as if tomorrow he were going to die, and on the other hand, he should make use of his body as if he were going to live with it many years. For the one cuts off thoughts of listlessness and makes the monk more zealous, and the other keeps his body in good health and always maintains his temperance evenly" (TP 29).[103] Later in the *Praktikos*, again explicitly referring himself to the tradition, Evagrius identifies anachoresis itself with this practice. "Our fathers called practicing death and flight from the body 'anachoresis'" (TP 52).[104]

In his work *The Bases of the Monastic Life* Evagrius has a rather long piece of advice to deliver to his reader, of which M 54 could be considered a three-line version. The advice begins, "Sit in your cell. Recollect your mind. Remember the day of your death." There follows a vivid imagining of the decomposition of the body and the bitter sufferings of hell, of pain that never finishes. The length and vividness of the description are rare in Evagrius, but the image strikes its mark. It shows what "remember death"

---

[101] As the following texts will show, Evagrius regularly relates remembering death as a remedy to listlessness so that even without the mention of the term, we can be sure that M 54 forms part of the chain. This same proverb is found in the alphabetical collection of the *Apophthegmata Patrum*, Evagrius 4.

[102] Probably Macarius the Great, according to Guillaumont, SC 171, 566–67.

[103] As Guillaumont points out in his commentary on this chapter, if Evagrius is citing Macarius, Macarius himself, who was considered Anthony's disciple, is probably relying on Anthony for this teaching (see SC 171, 568–69 and the text cited there from the *Life of Anthony* n. 19, in which Anthony says, "And so that we not become negligent, it is good to meditate on the Apostle's word, 'I die every day' [1 Cor 15:31]. For if we live as if dying daily, we will not sin" [PG 26:872A]; cf. PG 26:969B on remembering death and paying attention to oneself). The theme is widely attested to in the *Apophthegmata Patrum*. See the examination by Burton-Christie, *Word in the Desert*, 181–85. The practice of remembering death has strong classical precedents, as is demonstrated by Hadot in *Exercices spirituels*, 64ff., 72.

[104] We have already looked at this text to understand the relation of death to *praktikē* in M 21.

meant to him. But the description is followed by its balance. One ought also to think of the rewards reserved for the just and rejoice in that thought (Bases 9 [PG 79:1161A–C]).

Actually, by his use of the term *exodus* instead of *death* in M 54 Evagrius has managed to deliver this two-pronged piece of advice, to remember the frightening side of death and the rewards of the just, in one simple proverb. The proverb advises that one not forget the eternal judgment, so vividly described in the passage from the *Bases of the Monastic Life*. But using the word *exodus* for death swings the meditating mind back to the striking appearance of that word in M 21, where its use certainly referred to death, but death positively conceived as sharing in the death of Christ in *praktikē*. This is the second part of the advice in the long passage from the *Bases of the Monastic Life*, the advice to remember the rewards of the just. The term for this in M 21 was *exodus,* and it was immediately related to resurrection. The term has these same favorable connotations elsewhere in Evagrius.[105] With the mind finding its way back to M 21, it might find M 22 as well, which describes the death of the lawless man. These are the two choices before a monk, two possible ways of finishing his life. Remembering these, as Macarius used to say, "cuts off thoughts of listlessness." It does this because this demon of listlessness "depicts [to the monk his] life lasting a long time and puts before his eyes the drudgery of the ascetical life." He inspires in the monk a hatred "for the life itself" (TP 12). But when the monk reflects on his death, even "as if tomorrow he were going to die," the value of the monastic life and its struggles falls back into place; and life stretching out for a long time does not seem so long upon reflecting that one might die tomorrow.[106]

M 55 offers what is Evagrius's most fundamental remedy for

---

[105] See above, pp. 241.

[106] In his work *Antirrhetikos*, in remedies against listlessness, Evagrius offers some scripture verses to help the monk remember death in his fight against this demon. In Ant VI, 25, he suggests using Ps 102:15: "As for man, his days are as grass; as a flower of the field, so shall he flourish." In Ant VI, 32, Job 8:8–9: "Ask the previous generation and investigate among the race of the fathers. For we are from yesterday and we do not know. Our life on the earth is a shadow." In Ant VI, 33, Job 10:20–22: "Is not the time of my life short? Suffer me to rest a little before

listlessness: stay in the cell and do battle with the demon. The monk must do this with each of the demons, yet winning the battle against this demon is especially crucial for the monk. Why? In the *Praktikos* the answer is given. "One must not quit the cell at the hour of temptations no matter how plausible seem the excuses. Rather one should stay seated inside and be patient and receive nobly the attackers, every one, but especially the demon of listlessness who, because he is the heaviest of all, brings the soul to its most proven point. For to flee such struggles and to avoid them teaches the mind to be unskilled and cowardly and a fugitive" (TP 28).[107]

This is a battle that must be faced because there is something about listlessness that involves the monk in war of proper versus improper desires, of love versus hate. In a letter Evagrius says,

> Which house is it necessary for you to leave, the spiritual one or the bodily one [i.e., the cell], which the one tempted by that temptation [listlessness] greatly hates. For this alone of all the thoughts is an entangled struggle of hate and desire. For the listless one hates whatever is in front of him and desires what is not there. And the more desire drags the monk down, the more hate chases him out of his cell. He looks like an irrational beast, dragged by desire and beat from behind by hate. To leave this visible house is disgraceful, for it is a sign of defeat. (Lt 27:6)[108]

Texts such as these could be multiplied, but the point is clear and the descriptions always vivid. The monk must stay and fight. M 55 calls the fight a profitable wrestling. The wrestling is profitable because though this demon "move all his legions to make the monk quit his cell and flee the stadium," when the struggle is over, "a peaceful state and an ineffable joy follow in the soul" (TP 12). This is because one of the most difficult of all the demons

---

I go whence I shall not return, to a land of darkness and gloominess; to a land of perpetual darkness, where there is no light, neither can any one see the life of mortals."

[107] Cf. G 46: "Let the knowers know who it is that blows against them [i.e., which of the demons] and let them stand their ground nobly against every temptation."

[108] Translated from a Greek fragment found in C. Guillaumont, "Fragments grecs," 220–21, lines 70–77.

has been defeated, and now the monk is on the verge of passion-lessness. This peace and joy are described in M 55 as "so will your heart be made to glow."[109] This is fundamental for Christian liv-ing. "As it is impossible for an athlete to be crowned unless he wrestles, so one does not become a Christian without contests" (Inst ad mon [PG 79:1236B]).[110]

Several further dimensions of Evagrius's teaching about list-lessness are found in the next proverb, M 56, where the demon is said to drive away tears (of repentance), where it is connected with sadness, another of the principal thoughts, and where together with sadness it is said to shatter prayer. Tears of repen-tance are a necessary preparation to arrive at true prayer, and a little series on this theme is presented early in the *Chapters on Prayer* (Prayer 5–8).[111] But M 56 says that listlessness prevents these kinds of tears from flowing. And Evagrius often associates listlessness with sadness. In the little work *Vices Opposed to Virtues,* he says, "Sadness is . . . a schoolmate of listlessness" (Vices 3 [PG 79:1141D]). And a little later in the same work he adds, "Listless-ness is . . . the partner of sadness" (Vices 4 [PG 79:1144C]).[112] Here in M 56 these two vices certainly appear to be working as partners. Listlessness prevents a proper kind of "sadness"—repen-tance—and since tears of repentance are a prelude to true prayer, prayer is shattered by its presence. The very reverse expression of the same thought is found in the *Chapters on Prayer.* "Prayer is the exclusion of sadness and despondency" (Prayer 16 [PG 79:1172A]).

Tears of repentance actually are a remedy against both sad-ness and its schoolmate, listlessness, as the following expresses: "Heavy is sadness; intolerable, listlessness; but tears before God are stronger than both" (V 39). This sentence helps us to notice

---

[109] This should also be understood as referring to the realms of knowledge which a monk can enter only after he has successfully done battle with the demons. The metaphor of shining things or glowing things in reference to knowledge is very common in Evagrius.

[110] The advice to stay in the cell is present in many other places in the monastic tradition. See in the *Apophthegmata Patrum* Anthony 1, Arsenios 11, Moses 6. In the anonymous series, see Nau 198, 202, 204, 205.

[111] See Hausherr, *Leçons,* 19–22, for commentary and other Evagrian texts on the role of tears. See also TP 27 for tears as a remedy for listlessness.

[112] Commenting on these and other passages relating the two demons,

an advantageous ambiguity in the Greek of M 56, which actually could also be understood to say, "Tears drive away the spirit of listlessness" (Πνεῦμα ἀκηδίας ἀπελαύνει δάκρυα). In this Greek the very meaning saws back and forth like the vice and its remedy in a struggle with each other.[113]

The foregoing has shown that the battle against listlessness is one of the most crucial for the monk. Ultimately the reason is that all the other temptations somehow "collapse" into this one, which means that if this one can be defeated, so can all the others. "The other demons are like the sun either rising or setting; they fasten on only one part of the soul. But the noonday demon[114] is in the habit of enveloping the whole soul and suffocating the mind" (TP 36). This demon will fight furiously and employ many ruses because he understands what is at stake. But the monk also must understand what is at stake, and Evagrius's teaching helps this to happen. Above all the monk must not flee his cell but must stay for what will be a profitable wrestling. A text from Evagrius's commentary on the Psalms expresses rather clearly how the other thoughts (temptations, demons) are contained within listlessness and thus why no other thought or demon follows on the heels of this one's defeat. The comment is on the psalm verse, "They have devised injustice in their hearts; all the day they prepared war" (Ps 139:3). Explaining it, Evagrius says, "Through the thoughts the demons are drawn up in battle order against us, sometimes moving the concupiscible part, sometimes [moving] anger, and other times [moving] the irascible part and the concupiscible part in the same moment, from which is born what is called a complex thought. But this only happens in the hour of listlessness. The others [demons, thoughts] arrive in intervals, following one another. On that day no other thought follows the thought of listlessness, first because it lingers

---

Bunge says, "Traurigkeit und Überdruß sind also zwar nicht identisch, aber doch so nahe verwandt miteinander, daß vom letzteren weitgehend gilt, was Evagrios über die erstere sagt" (*Akedia*, 42). This entire book is a fine study on Evagrius's teaching on listlessness as well as the relevance of his teaching for today.

[113] See also Inst ad mon: "Perseverance checks listlessness, and so do tears" (PG 79:1236A).

[114] In TP 12 the noonday demon of Ps 90:6 (LXX) is identified as the demon of listlessness.

and second because it contains almost all the other thoughts in itself" (In Ps 139:3 [PG 12:1664B]).

This present brief study of Evagrius's teaching on listlessness, drawn from many different parts of his writings, can have served to illustrate a point I consider one of the main values of *Ad Monachos* to which I wish to draw attention. Three brief proverbs contain a wealth and richness not to be imagined by only a cursory reading. The proverbs are designed for meditation and depend (or at least are greatly enhanced) by the reader's knowledge of the details of Evagrius's teachings.

Commentary on M 61 and M 62

61. Strip down pride from yourself
    and put vainglory far away from you.
    For the one who does not obtain glory will be sad,
    and the one who does obtain it will be proud.

    Περίελε σεαυτοῦ ὑπερηφανίαν
    καὶ κενοδοξίαν μακρὰν ποίησον ἀπό σου.
    ὁ γὰρ ἀποτυχὼν δόξης λυπηθήσεται,
    ὁ δὲ ἐπιτυχὼν ὑπερήφανος ἔσται.

62. Do not give your heart to pride
    and do not say before the face of God, "Powerful
        am I,"
    lest the Lord abandon your soul
    and evil demons bring it low.
    For then the enemies will flutter around you
        through the air
    and fearful nights will follow you, one upon another.

    Μὴ δῷς ὑπερηφανίᾳ σὴν καρδίαν
    καὶ μὴ εἴπῃς πρὸ προσώπου τοῦ θεοῦ· δυνατός εἰμι,
    ἵνα μὴ κύριος ἐγκαταλίπῃ σὴν ψυχήν,
    καὶ πονηροὶ δαίμονες ταπεινώσουσιν αὐτήν.
    τότε γάρ σε δι᾽ ἀέρος πτοήσουσιν οἱ ἐχθροί,
    νύκτες δὲ φοβεραὶ διαδέξονταί σε.

I have selected this little chain for commentary here for several reasons. First, like the previous chain on listlessness, it reveals a wealth of Evagrian teaching in but few lines. I wish to examine once again how much has been condensed here. Second, these proverbs precede the important central chain of the text, and it will be interesting to see how Evagrius moves his reader into that chain from these proverbs. Third, a careful examination of M 62 is especially required; for as we shall see, it has a special relation to M 107, the whole text's turning point.

This short chain is about vainglory and pride, the last two demons in the list of eight principal demons about which Evagrius teaches. We have seen that a deep peace and joy follow in the soul after the defeat of listlessness, yet it is a constant feature of Evagrius's teaching about vainglory and pride that they can slip in very unexpectedly after the defeat of listlessness, coming as a sort of self-satisfaction at the state of virtue that has been reached. "Alone of all the thoughts, the thoughts of vainglory and pride survive after the defeat of the rest of the thoughts" (Skemmata 57).[115] The two demons are found working closely together, much like sadness and listlessness; but before seeing how they work together, it will be useful to first focus more closely on what vainglory means for Evagrius.

VAINGLORY

Vainglory slips in on monks who are well advanced in *praktikē* and who have been graced with some measure of progress in it. It is an especially subtle temptation because it bases itself on what is of genuine good in the monk's life. "When the mind of the anchorites reaches some little bit of passionlessness [i.e., when it is advanced in *praktikē*], then mounting the horse of vainglory, it immediately rides off toward the cities to be filled with out of control praises for its glory" (Thoughts 15). The result of being tricked by this demon is that one can fall back into all the old vices. The monk is subject to them all over again because he has sought glory for his spiritual gains, and it is vainglory's

---

[115] Muyldermans, *Evagriana* (1931), 44.

specialty to let all the other demons come rushing back in. "Alone of all the thoughts, that of vainglory is the richest in resources. Embracing nearly the whole inhabited world, it opens the gates to all the demons, like some evil traitor of a good city" (Thoughts 14).[116]

This demon is insidious and persistent. Even when the monk guards against it, that very being on guard can be used against him. "Difficult to escape is the thought of vainglory, for what you do to pull it down becomes for you another starting point for vainglory" (TP 30). Then, once that demon lets in all the others and the monk decides he must work to rid himself anew of these, vainglory will threaten again using the very resolve of the monk against him. "I have seen the demon of vainglory chased down by almost all the other demons, and when those chasing him fall [i.e., when the other demons are conquered by the monk], then he shamelessly steps forward and reveals to the monk the greatness of his virtues" (TP 31).

These texts show that vainglory often bases itself on the virtues of *praktikē* that the monk has acquired, but it can also work on one who has already entered into the realms of knowledge and prayer. The difference is seen in contrasting two texts. Similar to texts already cited, another chapter in the *Praktikos* clearly associates vainglory with those involved in *praktikē*. "The thought of vainglory is one most subtle, and it easily sneaks in among those who are doing right [κατορθοῦσι],[117] making them want to publish their struggles and chase after the glories that come from men" (TP 13). In the *Chapters on Prayer* Evagrius associates vainglory with knowledge within a series warning against desiring to see visions of angels, of Christ, or of God. "The beginning of the wandering of the mind is vainglory, by which the mind is moved to try to circumscribe the divinity in figure and forms" (Prayer 116 [PG 79:1194A]). The desire for visions and even the experience of them (visions seeming especially to

---

[116] In this text "good city" is an image for a monk who had been established in the virtues for his having conquered the other demons.

[117] This term of Stoic origin was common in the ascetic language of the period, used here by Evagrius to designate *praktikē*'s striving after virtues. See Guillaumont, SC 171, 532.

involve light) are typical of the ruses employed by vainglory against "the mind which prays purely and passionlessly" (Prayer 73 [PG 79:1182D]).[118] Thus in either direction, toward *praktikē* or toward knowledge, vainglory afflicts the monk who is well on the way toward his goal.

M 61 does not say all this about vainglory, but it is useful to know how much the term connotes for Evagrius, for this highlights the significance of the placement of such a chain after the chain on listlessness and before the long development in the following chain on *praktikē* and knowledge intertwined (M 63–72). In M 61's "strip down" and "put far away" we hear the immediate verbal links with the preceding chain on not letting evil thoughts linger.[119] By means of these connecting words the advice (with its strong imagery) of M 58 to M 60 is able to swing specifically into advice about immediately killing pride and vainglory when they appear.

M 61 does express one particularly succinct thought about vainglory. It shows its connection with sadness and with pride; that is, it shows how it can toss the monk in one direction or the other within the order of the eight principal thoughts. It was already noted that sadness is the result of being deprived of something desired (cf. 8 Spirits 11). Vainglory is desiring glory. If that desire is frustrated, another demon, sadness, can enter in. If that desire is fulfilled, a still worse demon enters: pride. In the *Praktikos* there is a long description of the way vainglory makes the monk imagine many wonderful things about himself: people crowding around just to touch his garments, many visitors seeking his counsel, his being forcibly made to accept priesthood. Then suddenly this demon "vanishes, leaving him to be tempted by either the demon of pride or of sadness" (TP 13).[120] This vivid

---

[118] See the whole chapter and also Prayer 74, both of which speak in detail of vainglory's attacks against those who have already reached knowledge.

[119] Thoughts 11 speaks of a demon that gets into the soul and makes it obtuse: Περὶ δὲ τοῦ δαίμονος, τοῦ τὴν ψυχὴν ποιοῦντος ἀναισθητεῖν . . . . Later in this passage it is explained that this demon is vainglory, and it is able to work its ill effects because "thoughts [allowed] to linger lead in this demon of vainglory [τοῦτον δὲ τὸν δαίμονα κενοδοξίας χρονίσαντες ἐπάγουσι λογισμοί]." For the significance of χρονίζειν, see p. 97 n. 56 above.

[120] For another text associating vainglory and sadness, see Lt 8:1, especially, "Where there is vainglory and sadness, there also are all the other desires."

description fills out M 61 a little, and a monk who may have heard Evagrius's colorful descriptions could have it all come flooding back to mind in the several short lines of M 61.

One cannot help but admire the astuteness and accuracy with which Evagrius describes a very subtle set of tricks that the mind can work on itself, or to put it more as Evagrius would: a very subtle set of tricks that the demons using thoughts work on the mind. His descriptions, observations, and advice leave the impression of much personal experience standing behind them. He describes subtleties in thoughts working against thoughts that seem to have come from experiencing and observing the process within himself.

This impression receives some confirmation from outside the Evagrian corpus in the description of his life left us in the *Lausiac History*. Its author, Palladius, drops two little clues that indicate why Evagrius may well have had to struggle much with vainglory. Describing his early career as a promising young theologian in Constantinople, Palladius says that Evagrius was "most skillful in refuting all heresies [διαλεκτικώτατον ὄντα κατὰ πασῶν αἱρέσεων]" (LH 38:2, lines 17–18). His talents and personality won him the amorous attentions of a lady highly placed in the imperial courts, and feelings between the two were mutual. Fleeing to Jerusalem on a warning given in an "angelic vision," he experienced an initial conversion; but he fell back once more into the hands of the devil and "changing his clothes again, vainglory came back into his speech [πάλιν ἐξαλλάσσων τοῖς ἱματίοις καὶ ἐν τῇ διαλέκτῳ ἐκάρου αὐτόν ἡ κενοδοξία]" (LH 38:8, lines 67–68).

Even after he joined the monks in the deserts of Egypt, there is still evidence of his struggle. The story is told in the *Apophthegmata Patrum*:

> One day at the Cells, there was an assembly about some matter or other and Abba Evagrius held forth. Then the priest said to him, "Abba, we know that if you were living in your own country you would probably be a bishop and a great leader; but at present you sit here as a stranger." He was filled with compunction, but was not at all upset and bending his head he replied, "I have spoken once and will not answer, twice but I will proceed no further" (Job 40:5). (Evagrius 7 [PG 65:176A])[121]

---

[121] English translation from Ward, *Sayings of the Desert Fathers*, 54–55.

This story offers information about Evagrius across several different levels. First, one can hear in it a certain anti-intellectualism, a known fact of one particular school of Egyptian monasticism and something that would have been painful for Evagrius, intellectual that he was and intellectual that he remained.[122] But the second thing that can be noticed in the story is that Evagrius submitted to the rebuke he received. He came among monks who were far from being his equals in the intellectual sphere, and he submitted to learn from them.[123]

Another story gives a hint of how difficult this submission was for Evagrius, yet it likewise shows that he nonetheless embraced this difficulty. In a story found in the *Apophthegmata Patrum* under the name Arsenius, another of the intellectual monks, Evagrius is found coming to him and asking, "How is it that we, with all our education and our wide knowledge get nowhere, while these Egyptian peasants acquire so many virtues?" And Arsenius answers him, "We indeed get nothing from our secular education, but these Egyptian peasants acquire the virtues by hard work" (Arsenius 5 [PG 65:88D–89A]).[124]

These stories reveal some of the ways in which Evagrius would have struggled with vainglory and pride, but they also

---

[122] I do not use the term "intellectual" with any pejorative overtones. There were many well-educated monks in the Egyptian desert, and their learning worked to the advantage of their monastic life.

[123] In fact, the story likewise shows that before the actual outbreak of the Origenist crisis Evagrius (and one can presume other monks like him) was not only submitting to the less-well-educated masters but also that he himself felt able to "hold forth" from time to time. On this particular occasion, however, the priest of his community felt the need to rebuke him. Today we tend to presume that the division between educated and uneducated monks (the later so-called Origenist and anti-Origenist monks) was always sharply defined. The time would come when this would certainly be the case. But in this story and others like it we can detect monks with learning and monks without it living together and sharing their respective types of wisdom. Cf. Cassian, *Conferences* 10.3, which tells the story of Paphnutius bringing a man of learning into a gathering of monks in order to explain to the more simple brethren the subtleties of the much controverted interpretation of Gen 1:26.

[124] English translation from Ward, *Sayings of the Desert Fathers*, 8. On the identification of Evagrius as the questioner, see A. Guillaumont, *Les Képhalaia Gnostica*, 53 n. 20, 165–66. For a nuanced interpretation, see Bunge, "Évagre le Pontique et les deux Macaire," 354, especially n. 194.

show the path by which he actually came to humility.[125] His monastic confreres knew of these struggles in his life. This knowledge would have put considerable force behind advice like "strip down pride" and "put vainglory far away." These are evil thoughts that, as M 58 urges, must not be allowed to linger.

VAINGLORY AND PRIDE

M 61 speaks of the relation of vainglory to sadness and to pride. As such it looks backward to the chain on sadness (M 56–57) and forward to M 62, which is a proverb slightly longer than usual and concerned exclusively with pride. It was mentioned that Evagrius consistently associates vainglory and pride, and M 61 was identified as an example of how he sees the relation. "A flash of lightning precedes the noise of thunder, and the presence of vainglory announces pride" (8 Spirits 17 [PG 79:1161C]). After the chapter on vainglory in the *Praktikos*, Evagrius describes the demon of pride in a manner that is directly in line with M 62. He says, "The demon of pride . . . persuades the soul to declare that God is not its help and to think that it is the cause of its own good actions" (TP 14).[126]

This saying before God "Powerful am I" and its attendant results are presented in M 62 in a way that recalls the original fall. The scriptural allusion is to Isaiah 14:12–17, the fall of the Morning Star (ὁ Ἑωσφόρος) from heaven, who in his pride thought to mount up to heaven and "be like the Most High." Instead he was cast down to hell. Every monk who is proud follows Satan's same pattern of thinking to mount up to heaven and be like God (say-

---

[125] I agree with Bunge that the main purpose of the story of the rebuke of Evagrius by the priest of Cells (this likely was Macarius of Alexandria), perhaps before its present redaction, is actually to draw attention to the example of the humility with which Evagrius received the rebuke. See Bunge, *Briefe,* 82. And yet the story also indicates that in the desert Evagrius would have had to keep his talents in check and that he probably had some trouble doing so. For more on Evagrius's personal experience standing behind his teaching on vainglory, see Bunge, *Briefe,* 82-85.

[126] Guillaumont points out in his commentary on this chapter that this is a major idea of the section of the *Antirrhetikos* which deals with pride. See Guillaumont, SC 171, 532, for comment and texts.

ing, "Powerful am I "); and the pattern continues in his being cast down to hell, which is described in the second part of M 62.

This scriptural allusion would perhaps be difficult to catch for someone not familiar with Evagrius's teaching, but that it is definitely intended is made clear by other texts that connect pride to Satan's fall and to the original evil, all of them alluding to the Isaiah passage. In the treatise *On Evil Thoughts* he says, "Out of this thought [vainglory] birth is given to the thought of pride, which cast down to earth the seal of [God's] likeness and the crown of the beauty of heaven" (Thoughts 14). Another text proposes humility as an antidote to pride and suggests several scriptural verses that would function as a counterpull to a statement like, "Powerful am I." (This is the method of *antirrhētikos*.) Evagrius says, "An aversion against loving to rule and against preeminence gains hospitality; and an unmeasured humility, one which says, 'I am dust and ashes' (Gen 18:27) and again, 'If the Lord had not built the house, in vain would the builder have labored' (Ps 126:1)–this puts pride to rest, the original evil, blasphemy before the Lord, which even God resists" (Inst ad mon [PG 79:1236B]).[127] Here pride is clearly identified as the original evil. So the suggestion in the first part of M 62 is that a monk not repeat in his own life, by means of pride, the pattern of the original evil, the original fall, as described in the Isaiah passage. And the description of the second half of the proverb about the demons fluttering around in the air continues in the same vein as the scriptural passage.

It is worth following up a little on this striking description of the second part. Within *Ad Monachos* itself, the notion of being abandoned by God and demons bringing the soul low recalls at least two previous proverbs. There is M 23, "the souls of the wicked, demons will snatch up." There is also M 52, "a demonic dream agitates [the heart]."[128] M 62 expands these proverbs

---

[127] See likewise TP 33, which suggests a series of thoughts that will "produce humility and prevent the demon of pride from entering." These thoughts include the monk's remembering his old sins, how he was subject to passions, how Christ's mercy has brought him to passionlessness, how God has protected him from the demons. Likewise, M 19 has already contrasted humility and pride.

[128] See Refoulé, "Rêves et vie spirituelle d'après Évagre le Pontique," which supports this connection.

somewhat, and it is significant that the expansion is undertaken in a proverb on pride, the original evil. Two stages can be distinguished in M 62 which follow when the monk says, "Powerful am I." The first is that the Lord "abandons [ἐγκαταλίπῃ] the soul." The second is that it is left to the demons. One of the chapters in the *Chapters on Prayer*, when read carefully, offers an unexpected clue to noticing the precision with which Evagrius is speaking here and what he is suggesting. The chapter reads, "Pray first to be purified of passions and second to be delivered from ignorance and forgetfulness and third [to be delivered] from all temptation and abandonment [ἐγκαταλείψεως]" (Prayer 38 [PG 79:1176A]). As Hausherr points out in his commentary on this verse, the order of the three requests here follows three stages of the spiritual life. The first petition concerns *praktikē*, which is a fight against the passions. The second petition concerns the initial stages of knowledge, which are a fight against ignorance. Yet it is precisely because the monk has advanced this far that he is especially subject to temptations of a more subtle kind.[129] The chapter cited does not specify it, but the texts we have examined here show that these more subtle temptations would be vainglory and pride. So the third petition is to be delivered from those temptations and from the results if one were to fall to pride.

If the soul is abandoned by God, then it falls to the demons, who will bring it low; and it will be subjected to terrible visions and fantasies. "Do not give your soul to pride, and you will not see chilling fantasies. For the soul of the proud is abandoned [ἐγκαταλιμπάνεται] by God, and it becomes a source of glee for demons. By night it [the soul] will fantasize about hoards of invading beasts, and by day it will be agitated by thoughts of cowardice" (8 Spirits 17 [PG 79:1161C–D]).[130]

---

[129] Hausherr, *Leçons*, 55.

[130] The theme of abandonment by God is developed with considerable nuance in Evagrius and was destined to be influential in subsequent monastic literature. In G 28 Evagrius speaks of five causes of abandonment among which the knower must be able to distinguish in order to be a good interpreter of such experiences for others. One of the causes has to do with chastisement and bringing the soul back to humility. Many texts in which Evagrius speaks of these various types of abandonment are collected and commented on by Guillaumont, SC 356,

Actually it is not often that one can find Evagrius speaking of pride without mentioning such terrible visions. In the main chapter on pride in the *Praktikos*, after describing the kinds of thoughts a proud monk has, he says, "Then there follow anger and sadness and then the last evil: losing the wits, and frenzy, and a vision of a crowd of demons in the air" (TP 14). Such a "frenzy" and "chilling fantasies" are described: "[the proud monk] sees the air around his cell on fire, bolts of lightning flashing against the walls. Then voices of pursuers and pursued. And chariots with horses etched against the sky and the whole house filled with Ethiopians and commotion" (Thoughts 23). In short, for Evagrius pride is a form of madness because it carries one so far from the truth. What could be farther from truth, Evagrius would ask, what more insane, than saying before God, "Powerful am I"?

The opposite of all this is, of course, humility and being helped by the angels. It is M 23, "The souls of the just, angels guide," or it is M 52, "An angelic dream gladdens the heart." It is M 19, "In the tents of the humble, the Lord will make camp; but in the houses of the proud, curses will abound." In the *Chapters on Prayer* Evagrius establishes all this with a scriptural verse: "Strive for a profound humility and courage, and then the taunt of the demons will not touch your soul, and 'the scourge will not approach your tent, for God will give to his angels a command for you, that they guard you' (Ps 90:11 LXX) and invisibly chase away the whole operation brought against you" (Prayer 96 [PG 79:1188D]).[131]

The regularity and the vividness with which Evagrius discusses the attacks of the demons has, like his talk on vainglory, the flavor of personal experience standing behind it. Once again the *Lausiac History* confirms this impression: "He [Evagrius] was beaten by demons and had such experiences with them that it is impossible to count them all" (LH 38:12, lines 107–9). In his experience with demons and in his understanding of their attacks

---

135–43. See also Driscoll, "Evagrius and Paphnutius on the Causes for Abandonment by God," 259–86.

[131] Compare with the following chapter, Prayer 97, which speaks of a man of prayer being unafraid of "weird sounds and crashes and voices and beatings from the demons" (PG 79:1188D).

and how to deal with them Evagrius was heir of an already well developed tradition of the desert fathers. His living links were both Macarius the Great and Macarius of Alexandria. His written link would have been the *Life of Anthony*.[132]

The meditation that M 62 offers is in a sense a version of a method proposed in *On Evil Thoughts* as a means of combating unclean thoughts. There Evagrius suggests "slinging" questions at the evil thought that is troubling the monk.[133] Among the examples of possible questions, he suggests asking, "How was the Morning Star which rose at dawn cast down to the earth, making the deep boil like a cauldron (Job 41:22 LXX) . . . agitating all by his evil and wanting to rule over all?" After his several examples, he concludes, "Contemplation of these things [these questions] greatly wounds the demon and puts all his troops to flight" (Thoughts 19). M 62 is a proverb that proposes these kinds of images of the fall. Meditating on it is a contemplation designed to wound a demon. It can wound a demon because it is a meditation on the very origins of evil, namely, pride, which is saying "Powerful am I" in the presence of God.

Finally, it should be observed that M 62 is a proverb to which the meditating mind could come back from a proverb yet to appear in the collection, M 107, which reads, "Like a morning star in heaven and a palm tree in paradise, / so a pure mind in a gentle soul." A careless reader would see virtually no connection between these two sentences, but they stand as each other's polar opposite, for "pride [is] the original evil which caused to fall to the earth the Morning Star which rose at dawn" (TP Prologue 2). The morning star in heaven is an image of the mind before the fall. A pure mind in a gentle soul is like this morning star again. It is a soul that would never say before God, "Powerful am I."[134]

M 61 and M 62 are meditations on two of the most subtle, and thus most dangerous, of the demons: vainglory and pride. These are the last in the list of eight demons which the monk

---

[132] See the convincing demonstration by Bunge in "Évagre le Pontique et les deux Macaire," 330–32.

[133] The image comes from David slinging stones at Goliath; see 1 Sam 17.

[134] This interpretation of M 107 is developed in a particular commentary below.

must defeat in order to enter into knowledge and to remain there. With a vivid warning against these two demons, the text turns now to a splendidly intricate chain on the relation between *praktikē* and knowledge.

Commentary on M 63 to M 72

The placement of this chain in the center of the overall arrangement of *Ad Monachos* is certainly an indication of its importance, and for that reason it is the subject of comment here.[135] The themes presented in these proverbs are interpretive keys to the tone of the whole text. The chain treats the relation between *praktikē* and knowledge. Each proverb contributes a particular insight to this relation.

The importance of keeping both these dimensions of the spiritual life always in focus is a major tenet of Evagrius's teaching; and at this point in the meditative exercise he has designed, he wants the reader to reflect on this relationship at length so that as the monk makes ever greater progress toward knowledge of the Trinity, he may not find himself vulnerable to demonic attacks for not having kept watch over *praktikē*. "Praiseworthy is the man who binds the life of knowledge to *praktikē* so that from both springs he might irrigate the field of his soul to grow virtue. For the life of knowledge unfurls the intellectual essence [πτεροῖ τὴν νοερὰν οὐσίαν] by means of the contemplation of better things, while *praktikē* 'puts to death what is earthly: fornication, impurity, passion, evil, wicked concupiscence' (Col 3:5). Those who surround themselves with both of these as their armour will easily tread under the evil of the demons" (Eulog 15 [PG 79:1112D–1113A]).

---

[135] The proverbs will be dealt with one by one. The text is printed at the beginning of the commentary of each single proverb.

63. Knowledge keeps guard over a monk's way of life;
but he who descends from knowledge will fall
among thieves.

Πολιτείαν μοναχοῦ διαφυλάττει γνῶσις,
ὁ δὲ καταβαίνων ἀπὸ γνώσεως περιπεσεῖται λῃσταῖς.

M 63 begins the whole series with this statement about keeping demons away from the life of knowledge. It says that knowledge guards "a monk's way of life"; that is to say, that a monk who has entered into knowledge must continue to keep the virtues of *praktikē* intact. The word πολιτεία, which I have translated "way of life," is used elsewhere by Evagrius to describe the life of *praktikē*. He uses the term once in a positive sense, once in a negative sense in comments on the word παιδεία in the *Scholia on Proverbs*. On a biblical text that reads, "Listen, my son, to the instruction [παιδείαν][136] of your father, so that you may become wise at your end," Evagrius comments, "After a right way of life [ὀρθὴν πολιτείαν] comes knowledge. For here the words 'at your end' do not mean time but the purity that comes after the virtues of *praktikē*" (In Prov 19:20 [G 201]).[137] Another scholion shows that the term πολιτεία can also describe a negative reality. On a biblical text that reads, "Instruction [παιδεία] guards the roads of life; instruction without reprimand causes wandering," Evagrius comments, "He calls instruction without reprimand the evil way of life of the soul [τὴν κακὴν τῆς ψυχῆς πολιτείαν], which becomes a sort of ambassador for its wandering" (In Prov 10:17 [G 119]).[138] It is clear that in M 63 Evagrius uses πολιτεία with a similar force.

[136] On παιδεία as a word especially associated with *praktikē*, see In Prov 1:2 (G 3) with comments by Géhin, SC 340, 93–95.

[137] For this interpretation of "at your end," see the commentary by Géhin in SC 340, 297.

[138] In G 13 πολιτεία also clearly refers to *praktikē* and is contrasted with natural contemplation and theology: "It is proper to explain to monks and to people in the world about a right way of life [περὶ πολιτείας ὀρθῆς] and to clarify in part dogmas concerning natural contemplation and theology, 'without which no one will see the Lord' (Heb 12:14)." Here, as Guillaumont explains, Evagrius is using

It was mentioned in the analysis of the structure that the image of descending from knowledge and falling among thieves is a link with the previous proverb's (M 62) more extended and vivid statement of the same. The remarks that we have just made in the commentary on that proverb, especially on this fall repeating the original fall, would hold valid for M 63 as well. When knowledge keeps guard over a monk's way of life, it must especially beware of pride.

The language of M 63 contains a scriptural allusion, one that Evagrius would certainly expect his reader to catch in order to expand the possibilities of how the proverb could be meditated on. The allusion is to the parable of the so-called Good Samaritan, which speaks of "a certain man who went down [κατέβαινεν] from Jerusalem to Jericho and fell among thieves [λῃσταῖς περιέπεσεν]" (Luke 10:30). It is no accident that M 63 follows this biblical language exactly. Evagrius considers Jerusalem a scriptural code word for knowledge. One text can serve as an example, in which other code words are likewise interpreted. "Egypt signifies evil; the desert, *praktikē;* the land of Judah, the contemplation of the corporeals; Jerusalem, that of the incorporeals; and Zion is the symbol of the Trinity" (KG VI, 49).[139] So the parable's man going down from Jerusalem (κατέβαινεν) is M 63's man descending from knowledge (ὁ δὲ καταβαίνων ἀπὸ γνώσεως); and the thieves can well be taken as a symbol of demons, the demons who in M 62 "flutter around you in the air." In a different context Evagrius expresses clearly Christ's role in making it possible to ascend again from the place of the fall. In his long dogmatic letter he speaks of the Incarnation of Christ as a search after the one who went down from Jerusalem to Jericho and fell among thieves, a search conducted so that Christ can "lead him [the one who fell] up again, cured, to his proper homeland" (Ep Fid 5, lines 18–20).

---

the word *monk* in a restrictive sense to refer only to those involved in *praktikē*. See SC 356, 107. It is possible that this sense is intended in Evagrius's use of the word in M 63. The use of πολιτεία in a text of the *Praktikos* should probably also be understood as a reference to *praktikē*, though there the context would permit it being understood to refer to the life of knowledge as well. The text reads, "That their [monks'] hands are bare shows that there is no hypocrisy in their way of life [τὸ ἀνυπόκριτον τῆς πολιτείας]" (TP Prologue 3).

[139] See also KG V, 6, 21, 88, for Jerusalem also as a symbol of knowledge.

64. From the spiritual rock, a river flows;
the soul accomplished in *praktikē* drinks from it.

Ἐκ πέτρας πνευματικῆς ἀπορρεῖ ποταμός,
ψυχὴ δὲ πρακτικὴ πίεται ἀπ᾽ αὐτοῦ.

M 64 is based on a biblical image for knowledge. Once again, hearing the allusions can open up the proverb to a wider meaning. "Spiritual rock" is language taken from 1 Corinthians 10:4, where St. Paul utters his own authoritative interpretation for the word *rock:* "For they drank from the spiritual rock which followed them [ἐκ πνευματικῆς ἀκολουθούσης πέτρας], and the rock was Christ." Evidence of the influence of this Pauline text on Evagrius is found in the way in which it seems almost unconsciously to influence his interpretation of scriptural passages in which the word *rock* occurs. He automatically, as if it were obvious, interprets *rock* as a reference to Christ. For example, he begins a comment on the psalm verse, "He led me out of the trap of misery," in this way: "The trap of misery is evil and ignorance. 'And he set my feet on a rock.' The rock is faith in Christ. 'And he directed my steps' through *praktikē* and through true doctrine" (In Ps 39:3 [PG 12:1409C]). Another example of this sort of automatic interpretation is a scholion on the psalm verse "Blessed is he who takes their children and smashes them against the rock." He says, "Whoever kills the little thoughts [νοήματα and not λογισμούς] of his soul against the teaching of Christ, he is the one who smashes the children of Babylon against a rock" (In Ps 136:9 [PG 12:1660A]).[140]

So much for the rock. But what might the river that flows from it signify? First, it should be noticed that "river" stays within the image of the Corinthian passage. In that text it is not just any rock that is Christ; it is a rock from which water flows for drink-

[140] In another passage Evagrius contents himself with simply citing 1 Cor 10:4 as the interpretation of a psalm verse. "'From the ends of the earth I cried to you . . . and you raised me on a rock.' How, being in Judah, does David say, 'From the ends of the earth I have cried to you,' unless he said it perhaps, having gone out from evil, which now speaking typologically he calls earth. And the rock was Christ" (In Ps 60:3; Pitra, *Analecta sacra spicilegio Solesmensi,* 3:68–69).

ing. But rivers, water, drinking—these are all scriptural words in which Evagrius finds a wealth of meanings, which usually refer to the realm of knowledge or at least lean very far in that direction. To gauge how Evagrius might have intended the word *river* in M 64 there is a passage that offers a fairly clear picture. He is commenting on a text in the book of Proverbs that reads, "Abstain from strange water and do not drink from a strange fountain." He says, "Just as with God there is a fountain of life, so also with the devil there is a fountain of death. And if the fountain of God is the fountain of virtue and knowledge, then the fountain of the devil is obviously the fountain of evil and ignorance. And words like *rivers* and *wells* and *waters* should be understood in the same way" (In Prov 9:18c [G 116]).

With this sort of interpretive key, Evagrius finds some beautiful[141] meanings in various verses of the psalms which speak of rivers. His interpretation is often influenced by the words of Jesus in John 7:38: "He who believes in me, as the scripture has said, 'Out of his heart shall flow rivers of living water [ποταμοὶ ὕδατος ζῶντος].'" Commenting on the psalm verse, "The river of God is filled with water," he says, "'O the depths of the riches and the wisdom of God!' (Rom 11:33). And again, 'In every way,' says Paul, 'you have been made rich in all knowledge.' (1 Cor 1:5). The knowledge of God has been filled up with rational creatures since rivers of water flow out of the heart of the one who believes in Christ (John 7:38). The scriptures customarily call the rational natures waters, for thus even David said that the waters which are above the heavens praise the Lord" (Ps 148:4) (In Ps 64:10).[142] The suggestion of this interpretation is one of a most intimate union between God and the rational creatures. God is the river; the rational creatures are waters flowing into the river. This is what the psalmist means in saying, "The river of God is filled with water."

This sense of intimate participation in God is likewise found in other passages that comment on the word *river* in other verses

---

[141] The word is his. See In Ps 97:8 cited shortly below.

[142] Pitra, *Analecta sacra spicilegio Solesmensi,* 3:75. Evagrius's way of "reasoning" here is basically a pastiche of scriptural passages, interpreting scripture with scripture.

of the psalms. In these passages Evagrius is guided in his interpretation by the next verse in the Johannine text, which after
quoting Jesus as saying, "Out of his heart shall flow rivers of living water," adds, "Now he said this about the Spirit" (John 7:39).
On the verse, "The flowings of the river gladden the city of God,"
Evagrius comments, "The city of God (or the Church)—this is the
rational soul. The flowings of the river are the gifts of the Spirit.
For rivers, he says, flow out of his heart as living water. For he was
speaking about the Holy Spirit" (John 7:39) (In Ps 45:5 [PG
12:1433C]).[143] Those who participate in the Holy Spirit are likewise called rivers. "'The rivers shall clap their hands together,
etc.' If the gifts of the Holy Spirit are called rivers according to
the statement, 'Rivers of living water shall flow from his heart'
(John 7:38), then beautifully those who participate in these rivers
are themselves called rivers. And the word 'together' applies to
the rivers, so that all can say the same thing and so that there may
be no division among them" (In Ps 97:8 [PG 12:1557A]).[144]

The consistency with which the word *river* is interpreted by
Evagrius as referring to the realms of knowledge (based so frequently on the Johannine text which provides him with the interpretive key) indicates rather clearly the direction for interpreting
M 64. The proverb's content translated without the poetry and
biblical images would read something roughly like this: from
Christ come the gifts of the Holy Spirit, and these same gifts are
found in those rational natures who share in knowledge by participation in Christ and the Holy Spirit. Clearly, the poetic, biblical expression is to be preferred to something like this.

This interpretation is strengthened by noticing that the
adjective for rock, *spiritual*, is no casual flourish. For Evagrius this
word almost always has direct reference to the Holy Spirit, and

---

[143] Pitra, *Analecta sacra spicilegio Solesmensi*, 3:45.

[144] This passage shows that for Evagrius there can be no division in teaching
or in anything at all among those who share in knowledge. This is worth keeping
in mind for the development of the chain M 123–31 on true and false knowledge.
For still another example of rivers referring to the rational creatures united to
God, see "'The rivers have lifted up their voices, etc.' He calls the holy rational
natures rivers because rivers of living water flow out from their heart (John 7:38)"
(In Ps 92:3 [PG 12:1553A]).

this seems the case here.[145] A commentary on a psalm verse, working with different images, makes a connection similar to that of M 64 between *praktikē* and the gifts of the Holy Spirit. The comment is on the verse, "I opened my mouth and drew in spirit, for I longed for your commandments." Evagrius says, "The one who opens his heart through *praktikē* draws in the Holy Spirit, who reveals to him the mysteries of God" (In Ps 118:131 [PG 12:1616D]). This brief text expresses very concisely the relation between *praktikē* and the Holy Spirit, and at the same time it shows the Holy Spirit's role in the realm of knowledge, namely, revealing the mysteries of God. M 64 makes the same point. The soul accomplished in *praktikē* drinks in the Holy Spirit, drinks in Christ, that is, the spiritual (Holy Spirit) rock (Christ).

To say that the soul accomplished in *praktikē* drinks from such a river means that such participation is for those who have passed through the work of *praktikē*. Likewise it means that the monk still involved in *praktikē* looks toward knowledge as his goal, as a source that sustains him, waters toward which he travels in *praktikē*'s journey through the desert. And even after one has entered into knowledge, *praktikē* must continue; for it is a soul accomplished in *praktikē* that drinks from this river. This was the force of M 63 in saying, "Knowledge keeps guard over a monk's way of life." The same point is illustrated at length, again under the image of a river, in a fine passage from one of the letters.

> Oh, if only I were the "river of the Lord" (Ps 64:10) and could joyfully flow into the sea of the world in order to sweeten the bitterness of the evil of the reasonable souls of men. But instead I am a "waterless cloud" (Jude 12) which has been blown by the wind into the desert. Dangerous it is for the monk, still immature, to leave his cell before he has reached the perfection of *praktikē* and contemplation. It would be better for him had he not from the beginning sought the war and had he not enlisted himself in the battle with the beasts. (Lt 58:5)

---

[145] For this interpretation of *spiritual*, see Bunge, "'The Spiritual Prayer,'" 196–98, and *Geistliche Vaterschaft*, 37–39.

65. A vessel of election, the pure soul;
     but the impure soul will be filled with bitterness.

Σκεῦος ἐκλογῆς ψυχὴ καθαρά,
ἡ δὲ ἀκάθαρτος πλησθήσεται πικρίας.

This next proverb in the series also expresses the relation between *praktikē* and knowledge by means of several scriptural allusions either to Pauline texts or to Paul himself. The expression "vessel of election" is the Lord's own name for St. Paul as in the vision reported in Acts 9:15. Evagrius uses this same title for several of those whom he considered his greatest teachers. In the *Praktikos* he uses it to refer to Macarius the Great, whom he especially considered a model of the gnostic life (TP 93).[146] With the same title he refers to a different kind of teacher, namely, Gregory Nazianzus, the theologian (Ep Fid 1, line 15). Bunge points out that it is not without significance that Evagrius has used this same title (and reserved this same title) for these two teachers.[147] In this way Evagrius means to signal the two poles within which he attempts his own theological synthesis: Cappadocian orthodoxy as symbolized in Gregory and the ascetical and spiritual tradition of the desert as symbolized in Macarius.[148] So the term with which Evagrius refers to knowledge in M 65 is one that is meant to evoke for the reader familiar with his use of this expression these two great models of knowledge. Yet the proverb does not refer directly to them. Instead, it invites whoever reads the proverb to be a pure soul as these models were and thus to become oneself a vessel of election.

The word *vessel* can evoke yet another passage of the Pauline corpus which Evagrius cites at least twice in contexts that have directly to do with purifying oneself, as does M 65. It is useful to

---

[146] On Macarius the Great as a master especially of the gnostic life, see Bunge, "Évagre le Pontique et les deux Macaire," 223–25.

[147] That is to say that, including St. Paul, he reserves the title to them insofar as he uses it to refer to specific persons. Obviously in M 65 its application goes beyond Macarius and Gregory.

[148] Bunge, "Évagre le Pontique et les deux Macaire," 224.

cite the several verses surrounding the word *vessel* since it helps to see how the term is appropriately used in the present proverb. "If someone purifies himself from these things, he will become a vessel with a noble purpose, made holy and useful to his master, ready for any good work. So flee the desires of youth and strive after justice, faith, love and peace, together with those who call upon the Lord from pure hearts" (2 Tim 2:21–22).[149] This scriptural passage combines well with the allusion to Paul in Acts 9:15. The noble use to which the vessel of the pure soul can be put is precisely knowledge itself. And Evagrius uses the expression "vessel of election," which he otherwise reserves for Gregory and Macarius, to refer also to Paul himself in this very context, calling Paul "vessel of election" in citing him for his capacity to speak on the intricacies of the relation of Father, Son, and Spirit.[150]

This use to which the purified vessel can be put is another way of saying that purity is not an end in itself. This is, of course, a characteristic emphasis of Evagrius's teaching. The monastic life is not merely an ascetical workout. The goal of asceticism is always knowledge. In terms of M 65, the pure soul is not an end in itself. It becomes a vessel of election; that is, it becomes a Macarius, a Gregory, or a Paul. This pointing beyond purity can be found in many places throughout the Evagrian corpus, but a passage from one of the letters perhaps expresses it best for the understanding of the present proverb. In the letter Evagrius says,

> Therefore, just as there is no possibility that the incorporeal approach corporeal things, even so it is also impossible without an incorporeal mind to see the Incorporeal. To be sure, it is not the mind itself which sees God, but rather the pure mind. "Blessed are the pure of heart, for they shall see God" (Matt 5:8). Note that he does not praise purity as blessed but rather the one seeing [i.e., contemplating]. Purity is passionlessness of the reasonable soul, but seeing [contemplating] God is true knowledge of the one essence of the adorable Trinity, which those will see who have perfected their conduct here and through the commandments purified their souls. (Lt 56:2)

---

[149] Verse 21a is cited by Evagrius in In Prov 18:9 (G 179) and in In Eccl 1:15 (text in Géhin, SC 340, 274–75).

[150] See Ep Fid 3, line 35 for "vessel of election," but see lines 32–54 for the whole argument.

In the second line of M 65 Evagrius proposes the opposite image of a pure soul become a vessel for knowledge. It would be an impure soul filled with bitterness. The word *bitterness* is likewise a scriptural allusion to a Pauline letter, namely, Ephesians 4:31. It might be argued that a same Greek word found in a scriptural text and in a text of Evagrius can hardly constitute a biblical allusion; and, of course, it does not do so automatically. However, in the present case, reading the surrounding verses of the scriptural text offers convincing evidence that here Evagrius likely had this biblical passage in mind. The Ephesians text reads, "Do not sadden the Holy Spirit of God in whom you were sealed for the day of redemption. All bitterness [πικρία] and irascibility [θυμός] and anger [ὀργή] and clamor and blasphemy [κραυγὴ καὶ βλασφημία] should be taken away from you, together with every evil. Toward one another be kind, compassionate, forgiving one another just as God in Christ has forgiven you" (Eph 4:30–32).

Three observations about this text indicate that it probably influenced Evagrius in his choice of the word *bitterness* for M 65. First, bitterness is the first in a scriptural list of vices. That Evagrius was aware of such New Testament lists and influenced by them seems certain.[151] Second, within this same chain of *Ad Monachos,* at M 71, Evagrius likewise cites the last two vices of the list, clamor and blasphemy. Third, the surrounding verses fit the context well from several perspectives. The mention of not grieving the Holy Spirit flows nicely out of the way in which the previous proverb alluded to the Holy Spirit and can be a possible explanation for why at this point the words from this particular New Testament list find their way into the present chain. And, though irascibility and its opposite, gentleness, are not dealt with in the present chain, they would come to the mind of the monk who knew this scriptural passage well. The vices mentioned would be the vices that fill an impure soul.[152] The urging to be

---

[151] See Guillaumont, SC 170, 75–84. To the list of scriptural examples that Guillaumont offers (p. 76), this passage from Ephesians could be added.

[152] Indeed, in citing such lists Evagrius may cite only the first and last members of the list as he does in these several proverbs; but by implication the other vices or virtues are thus presumed "mentioned" as well, much like faith and love in M 3 imply all the virtues that stand between.

kind, tenderhearted, and forgiving, unmentioned in the proverb but all echoing behind the word *bitterness*, would be a description of a pure soul.

Thus, by means of biblical allusion the path of M 65's meditation could go something like this: a kind, tenderhearted, forgiving soul is a purified vessel elected for the noble use of knowledge like that of Paul, Gregory, and Macarius. On the other hand, bitterness, anger, and irascibility would grieve the Holy Spirit, "who reveals the mysteries of God" (cf. In Ps 118:131).[153]

66. Without milk, a child is not nourished,
    and apart from passionlessness, a heart will not
    be raised up.

Ἄνευ γάλακτος οὐ τραφήσεται παιδίον,
καὶ χωρὶς ἀπαθείας οὐχ ὑψωθήσεται καρδία.

This proverb opens a smaller unit within the chain, a unit structured around passionlessness. This first of three proverbs in the little chain speaks of passionlessness by means of an image. The image is clear enough in its own right. To say, "Without milk, a child is not nourished," is to speak of the absolute indispensability of passionlessness for reaching knowledge. But once again, the image is a scriptural one; and recognizing it greatly expands the directions in which the proverb can be pondered.[154]

---

[153] Cited in the commentary on M 64.

[154] This is the fourth proverb in a row in which the scriptural allusions have been strong, and it is worth pausing to make an observation about Evagrius's procedure. In general, one or two words or a simple phrase is meant to bring an entire passage to mind. Evagrius's words are often the Bible's words. Biblical language and biblical images flow naturally from his hand. This language, so well known and thus so easily alluded to, makes possible an economy of expression; and this is the economy with which a composer of proverbs (or any poet, really) must be able to speak. It is an economy based on a monastic culture, a culture that is itself profoundly shaped by the scriptures. And Evagrius (or any poet) will have to count on the reader's capacity to catch how much the single word is meant to convey. A reader who shares the same monastic, biblical culture will be prepared to do just that. For our part, we must attempt in our own right to ferret out what scriptural allusions are placed within the proverbs. We can know with relative certainty that Evagrius had a given passage in mind if we find him citing the passage

In M 66 three scriptural passages could have guided Evagrius in his choice of the image of milk as an image for *praktikē*, and all three are passages he cites elsewhere toward the same end. It will help to understand M 66 if all three of these passages are seen here together. The first is from the Letter to the Hebrews: "What you need is milk, not solid food. For whoever lives on milk is unpracticed in the word of justice, because he is still a child. But solid food is for the fully grown [τελείων], for those who have exercised their senses through the discernment of good and evil" (Heb 5:12–14). In this passage Evagrius reads the division between milk and solid food as the division between the life of *praktikē* and the life of knowledge, but in order to see just how he does so, several other passages that influenced him need first be noted. "I could not speak to you as I would speak to spiritual people, but as one speaks to the fleshy, as to children in Christ. I gave you milk to drink, not solid food, because you were not ready and are still not ready, because you are still fleshy. As long as there is jealousy and strife among you, are you not fleshy and conducting yourself in a merely human way?" (1 Cor 3:1–3) "So get rid of all evil and all guile and insincerity and envy and all evil talk. Like newborn babies, long for rational and unmixed milk [τὸ λογικὸν ἄδολον γάλα], so that by it you will grow up into salvation" (1 Pet 2:1–2).

All of these passages, each in its own way, not only associate milk with the beginning stages of the spiritual life; but each likewise speaks of a training in virtue and the need to be rid of vices in order to be given solid food. That Evagrius understands these texts to refer to the division between *praktikē* and knowledge is made clear in his reference to at least two of them in several of the scholia on Proverbs. Speaking of someone who is charged with dispensing the mysteries of God, he says, "He gives spiritual knowledge to each of the brothers in a way that accords with their state, making the Corinthian drink milk (1 Cor 3:2) and feeding the Ephesian with a more solid food (Heb 5:12)" (In Prov 17:2 [G 153]). The reason why Evagrius chooses the Ephesian as the

---

elsewhere in a way that accords well with the proverb in question. This has been our procedure throughout this study.

Corinthian's opposite here is that, as he goes on to explain, citing Ephesians 3:18, to the Ephesian is revealed the breadth and length and height and depth of the mysteries, which are understood to be references to various levels of knowledge (In Prov 17:2 [G 153]).

This same distinction between Corinthian and Ephesian is maintained in another of the scholia on Proverbs. Evagrius says, "The same Christ, according to the title in question,[155] can be both a father and a mother: father of those who have the spirit of filial adoption (Rom 8:15), mother of those needing milk and not solid food (Heb 5:12). For Christ, speaking in Paul (2 Cor 13:3), became a father of the Ephesians (cf. Eph 3:1–19), revealing to them the mysteries of wisdom, and a mother of the Corinthians, giving them milk to drink (1 Cor 3:2)" (In Prov 20:9 [G 210]).[156]

In its own way, the image of milk in M 66 makes a point similar to one made in the previous proverb, where part of its meaning was seen to be that purity is not an end in itself. On the other hand, purity is indispensable for knowledge. Something similar is said here, but the point is applied to passionlessness. Passionlessness is indispensable. Without it, a heart is not raised up; that is, there is no knowledge. But passionlessness is still only milk. It must be a preparation for the solid food of knowledge.

---

[155] The Greek is κατ᾽ ἐπίνοιαν. For Evagrius, following Origen, the scriptures express various dimensions of Christ's salvific action according to various titles (ἐπίνοιαι) used for him. For more on this, see Géhin, SC 340, 51–52.

[156] On "spirit of filial adoption" as referring to knowledge, see KG VI, 51. In In Prov 9:5 (G 107) Evagrius cites the passage from Hebrews directly. One might also compare Prayer 101: "As bread is nourishment for the body and virtue for the soul, so is spiritual prayer the nourishment of the mind" (PG 79:1189B). Hausherr comments on this, noting that to each stage of spiritual growth there corresponds a proper food (Leçons, 137–38). For a different use of milk, but still employed as an image of a lesser degree, see KG III, 67: "The whole of the second natural contemplation bears the sign of milk and the first [natural contemplation] that of honey; and this is 'the land flowing with milk and honey' (Exod 33:3)."

67. In front of love, passionlessness marches;
    in front of knowledge, love.

Πρὸ ἀγάπης ἡγεῖται ἀπάθεια
πρὸ δὲ γνώσεως ἀγάπη.

M 67 speaks directly of this solid food. It is the proverb that stands at the very middle of *Ad Monachos*. Along with M 3, the collection's specific beginning, it manages to sum up the themes of the entire meditation. Now the many insights from the sort of meditation which the commentary on M 3 brought to light are meant to be carried into this context. They are meant to be meditated on anew in the context of an extended chain that drives toward knowledge even while insisting on the permanent importance of *praktikē*. Within the dynamic of such a drive, love plays the role of hinge between the two realms. We have already examined this role of love in the commentary on M 3. Here I only wish to add a brief reflection on love's relation to knowledge, which seems to me to suit especially well the context of this chain.

In the theological tradition of which Evagrius was a part, there was a widely diffused tenet, stemming directly from Platonism, that only like could know like, that knowledge could be had on its deepest level only by a participation in the object to be known. Thus, to know God one must be like God; it must be a knowledge by participation. In at least one instance Evagrius specifically acknowledges[157] this Platonic principle of knowledge in his comments on a psalm. "Through like we know like. Thus, through love we know love, and through justice we know justice" (In Ps 17:2-3 [PG 12:1224D]).

---

[157] If I say "specifically acknowledges," it is to draw attention to Evagrius's definite knowledge of this Platonic commonplace about knowledge. The principle is everywhere presumed by Evagrius but by and large goes unexpressed. It is a major presupposition operative in the *Chapters on Prayer*, expressed succinctly in one of the chapters: "Do not somehow imagine the divinity within yourself when you pray nor allow some form to be imprinted on your mind. Rather, go immaterially to the Immaterial, and you will understand" (Prayer 67 [PG 79:1181A]). The theme is developed in the chapters immediately surrounding Prayer 67; cf. Prayer 114-17.

When Evagrius speaks of knowledge, when the emphasis of his spirituality falls on knowledge, this must not be allowed to distract from the fact that it is Love that is known. "Through love we know love." A letter explains why: "The first and greatest commandment is love (cf. Mark 12:28–31), with which the mind sees Original Love; namely, God (cf. 1 John 4:8). Through our love we see the love of God for us, as it stands written in the psalms, 'He will teach the gentle his ways'" (Lt 56:3). As the allusion here to the Gospel text shows, love is not only a question of love of neighbor but even more basically of love of God. For Evagrius the position he assigns to love could be said to be based on the ontology of things, for God is love (1 John 4:8). This is why *love* is the door to *knowledge*. Ultimately it is God whom one *knows*, and God is *love*.[158]

It can be recalled here that the difference between M 67 and M 3 is one suited to their respective positions in the text. M 3 speaks of love's connection to faith, the first of the virtues of *praktikē*, and then of its relation to knowledge. M 67 speaks of love's connection to passionlessness, the goal of *praktikē*, and then of its relation to knowledge. The middle of the text is the middle of the spiritual journey: the bridge from passionlessness to love.

---

[158] The same logic of seeing God, who is love, by means of the commandment of love stands behind the statement in TP 79, "The doing of the commandments does not suffice for completely healing the powers of the soul, unless the contemplations which correspond to them follow in the mind." The contemplations that correspond to the commandments would include discovering God's love in his created world and in the decisions of his providence and ultimately discovering love within the Trinity itself. Prayer 52 explains why: "We seek after virtues for the sake of the reasons [λόγοι] of created beings, and we seek these for the sake of the Logos who gives them their being. . . ." The movement here is from virtue to reasons [λόγοι] to the Logos himself. To render this idea more applicable to the present discussion, we might speak of a movement from the *virtue* of love to *knowing* and understanding what Love has created, so to *know* and understand Love Itself, that is, God.

COMMENTARY ON INDIVIDUAL PROVERBS: M 63 TO M 72   299

68. To knowledge, wisdom is added;
    prudence gives birth to passionlessness.

Γνώσει προστίθεται σοφία,
ἀπάθειαν δὲ τίκτει φρόνησις.

M 68 is the third proverb in a row to mention passionlessness, and it also introduces the important couplet virtues of wisdom and prudence. This couplet is developed in part in the proverbs that immediately follow, though its real development is in the chain on true and false knowledge in the second block of the text (M 123–31). In this proverb the two virtues of the rational part of the soul are found, each pointing in its own proper and different direction: wisdom toward knowledge and prudence toward passionlessness.

These couplet virtues were examined in the commentary on M 31. One observation on the present proverb is worth adding here. Evagrius is fond of the metaphor of giving birth when it comes to speaking of the relation of the virtues among themselves.[159] It is a firm metaphor and one especially suited for expressing his point, conveying a natural sense of one virtue leading to another, even containing the notion that it takes some time for the "child" to grow in the "womb" of the virtue that is giving it birth. The statement "prudence gives birth to passionlessness" has its precise sense for Evagrius. If the role of prudence is directing operations against demons in the war of *praktikē*, then in time it will result in (in time "it will give birth to") passionlessness, the goal of *praktikē*.[160] The work of prudence gives way to the rest of wisdom. It is quite appropriate to find such a meditation in the midst of a chain whose central theme is *praktikē's* relation to knowledge.

---

[159] This was seen in the passages of chains for virtues already cited; see TP Prologue 8, 81; M 5. The language is scriptural; cf. Prov 10:23.

[160] For another proverb that mentions prudence and passionlessness (but not wisdom), see M 105: "The prudent monk shall be passionless."

69. Fear of the Lord begets prudence;
faith in Christ bestows fear of God.

Φόβος κυρίου γεννᾷ φρόνησιν,
πίστις δὲ Χριστοῦ δωρεῖται φόβον θεοῦ.

This proverb builds on the mention of prudence in M 68. To say "fear of the Lord begets prudence" is similar to a statement such as M 3, "faith: the beginning of love," an expression containing the first and last of the virtues of *praktikē* and, by implication, all those between. But, as noted, for Evagrius fear and faith work very closely off each other such that it is possible to say that one or the other is actually the beginning of *praktikē*.[161] The reasoning which Evagrius has condensed into this first line of the proverb runs something like this: since prudence is the virtue in the rational part of the soul that directs the operations against the demons, and since fear of the Lord gives rise to faith, which gives rise to temperance and then the other virtues in their order, then "fear of the Lord begets prudence," since these virtues are developed under the directing influence of prudence.

The second line of M 69 is more difficult to interpret. It is not surprising to find the word *faith* alongside of fear; however, the proverb specifies a kind of faith that has a meaning clearly different from the faith that is spoken of in M 3 or in the other texts that speak of faith as the beginning of *praktikē*. M 68 says specifically "faith in Christ." This begets not fear of the Lord, which is the usual expression, but rather "fear of God." Evagrius speaks of faith in Christ in several other places in his writings, but these do not help to clear up the difficulty entirely.[162] We find a possible clue, however, in the *Kephalaia Gnostica*, where we read, "The contemplation of angels is named 'heavenly Jerusalem and mountain of Sion (Heb 12 ff).' Now if those who have believed in Christ 'have approached the mountain of Zion and the city of the living God (Heb 12 ff),' then those who have believed in Christ have been and will be in the contemplation of the angels, that

---

[161] See above, p. 75 and especially n. 10.

[162] See above, p. 75 n. 10 on the relations between fear and faith in the chain of virtues.

which their fathers left when they went down to the land of Egypt" (KG V, 6).[163] This text associates believing in Christ with contemplation. The placement of M 69 in a chain that holds in balance terms related to *praktikē* and terms related to knowledge lets the interpreter lean toward associating the term "faith of Christ" in it with contemplation. Contemplations associated with Christ involve the initial levels of knowledge,[164] which eventually give way to knowledge of the Trinity, which begins, according to this proverb, with fear of God. The proverb is stressing strongly the intermediary role of Christ in coming to the knowledge of God. (This may explain "fear of *God*" instead of the more usual "fear of the *Lord*.") This intermediary role is frequently stressed in Evagrius. All that is learned from Christ eventually gives way to a greater knowledge. In commenting on the psalm verse, "In your light we shall see light" (Ps 35:10), Evagrius says, "In the contemplation of created things we shall see Christ, or in the knowledge of Christ we shall see God" (In Ps 35:10 [PG 12:1316B]). M 69 can be interpreted along the same lines. Faith in Christ gives a knowledge of Christ, and "in the knowledge of Christ we shall see God." At least glimpsing that this first knowledge must give way to another is "fear of God."

> 70. A flaming arrow ignites the soul,
>   but the man of *praktikē* will extinguish it.
>
> Βέλος πεπυρωμένον ἀνάπτει ψυχήν,
> ἀνὴρ δὲ πρακτικὸς κατασβέσει αὐτό.

From its content this proverb can be considered a continuation of the development of prudence in that in its imagery it refers to an operation against the demons. The image and the language itself are once again based on a Pauline text. In a list of

---

[163] Lt 14 speaks of faith in Christ, saying that without it, it is impossible to be pleasing to God. The term faith in Christ occurs in TP Prologue, line 30, where it is said to sustain the monk in *praktikē*. The term faith in Christ occurs in In Ps 39:3, cited above on p. 287.

[164] In the text cited here, contemplations of angels.

virtues found in the Letter to the Ephesians we read toward the end of the list, ". . . and besides all these, take the shield of faith, with which you can quench [σβέσαι] all the flaming arrows [τὰ βέλη πεπυρωμένα] of the evil one" (Eph 6:16). The presence of the idea of faith with the image of the flaming arrow in this biblical text should not go unnoticed, for it is one of the links between M 69 and M 70. But the biblical text also confirms the identification of the image of the arrow as the work of the demons, here named "the evil one." Elsewhere, Evagrius offers confirmation of this identification. "The intelligible arrow is the evil thought which rises up from the passionate part of the soul" (KG VI, 53).

The idea expressed in M 70 with the image of a flaming arrow is expressed less poetically in a couplet of chapters found in the *Praktikos*, and that text's more straightforward way of speaking can secure a proper understanding of M 70. "The temptation of the monk is a thought which mounts through the passionate part of the soul and darkens the mind. The sin of the monk is consent to the forbidden pleasure which the thought suggests" (TP 74, 75). There is a distinction here between temptation and sin. It is not just the mere presence of an evil thought that is sinful for the monk. Rather, it is consent to the thought. In M 70 the flaming arrow is a thought, a temptation, launched by a demon. The man of *praktikē* will not consent to it. He will put the fire out.[165] If one does accept the thoughts, then the demon's arrow has done its damage. "As it is inexplicable that a man struck by an arrow not be weakened, so it is impossible for a monk who accepts evil thoughts not to be wounded" (Inst ad mon [PG 79:1237B]).[166]

In the analysis of the structure it was observed that this is the only proverb of the chain that does not have a clear reference to

---

[165] For fire clearly explained, see Evagrius's commentary on the numerical proverbs, Ad Prov 30:15–16, n. 13 (SC 340, 488): "Fire is the evil of the reasonable soul which destroys the virtues of God."

[166] Cf. Inst ad Mon. Muyldermans 5, 201: "A meeting with evil people is like a man struck by arrows, who if he lets them linger in him, will give up his own life." G 42 and 43 are another couplet based on the distinction between temptation and sin, but there the temptation and the sin are to false knowledge.

knowledge. However, in a letter in which Evagrius alludes to the same scripture passage, he shows that with such an image the idea of knowledge is not far away. He says,

> Nothing else "puts out the flaming arrows of evil" (Eph 6:16) like the knowledge of God. For a flaming arrow is the demonic thought which excites the concupiscible through unseemly things. And the mind, which through its vision (that is, the vision of itself) is enlightened and through the thought of God is recollected, either does not receive this arrow; or if it does receive it, it quickly throws it away, because knowledge carries it up as if on wings and separates it from the corporeal world. (Lt 27:4)

In this passage Evagrius says that *knowledge* puts the fire out. In M 70 *praktikē* does. Is there a contradiction here, or is it not rather that both are true—knowledge and *praktikē* are that intimately intertwined?

71. Clamor and blasphemy, knowledge turns aside;
     cunning words, wisdom flees.

Κραυγὴν καὶ βλασφημίαν ἀποστρέφεται γνῶσις,
λόγους δὲ δολίους φεύγει σοφία.

Again, in the analysis of the structure, it was noted that after mention of wisdom and prudence together in M 68, the following two proverbs are a development of prudence, while M 71 is a development on wisdom and wisdom's special relation to knowledge. M 71 also forms part of the scriptural allusion made in M 65, namely, to Ephesians 4:30–32, which reads in part, "Let all bitterness and irascibility and anger and clamor and blasphemy be put away from you." In this proverb knowledge itself is said to turn clamor and blasphemy aside.

For Evagrius, blasphemy, though not part of his list of eight principal demons, is nonetheless a demon that especially attacks the right doctrine which is necessary for true contemplation. What this demon's characteristics are and how he operates are described in the *Praktikos*. He is a demon who "seizes the mind [and moves it] toward blasphemy of God and toward forbidden

imaginings" (TP 46).[167] He is said to be particularly fast in seizing
the mind (TP 43, 51).

Several other texts make it clear that Evagrius envisions blasphemy as concerned with what we would call right doctrine.
Commenting on a text from the book of Proverbs, "Those who
accuse unjustly will not escape," he says, "Those who blaspheme
against the Creator, not knowing the reasons concerning judgment and providence—these are the ones who accuse unjustly" (In
Prov 19:5 [G 190]). Elsewhere in *Ad Monachos* the term *blasphemy*
is used in reference to a specific doctrinal error. "He who says
that the Holy Trinity is a creature blasphemes God, and he who
rejects his Christ does not know him" (M 134). M 71 claims that
knowledge knows how to turn aside such errors, to turn away
ignorance about the reasons of providence and judgment (as
specified by In Prov 19:5), to turn away a thought such as the
Trinity's being a creature (as specified by M 134). Wisdom, whose
task it is to "contemplate the reasons of the corporeals and incorporeals" (as specified by TP 89), knows how to flee the cunning
words that would be propounding such false doctrines. As mentioned, this idea, and especially the term "cunning words,"
sounds a theme that soon will be taken up and developed at
length, that of following the guidance of a spiritual father (M 88–
92) and then that of the difference between true and false knowledge (M 123–31).

72. Sweet is honey, its comb a delight;
    but sweeter than both is the knowledge of God.

> Ἡδὺ μέλι καὶ γλυκὺ κηρίον,
> γνῶσις δὲ θεοῦ γλυκυτέρα ἀμφοτέρων.

The final proverb in this long chain serves the function of a
conclusion to the whole, stressing the excellence of the knowledge of God in poetic terms that have clear biblical reference.

---

[167] In his commentary on this chapter, Guillaumont gives evidence that the
demon of blasphemy is to be closely associated with and even identified as the
demon of pride (see SC 171, 603–4).

Honey is the image Evagrius uses for knowledge, an image of which he is particularly fond. Two verses from the psalms seem to stand behind its being used for expressing the excellence of knowledge. First, I would like to cite these psalm verses and then see how they have influenced both Evagrius's choice of the image and his exegesis. This will make it possible to interpret his intention in M 72.

The two verses: "How sweet to my throat your oracles [τὰ λόγιά σου], more so than honey [ὑπέρ μέλι] to my mouth" (Ps 118:103). "Fear of the Lord and judgments of the Lord [τὰ κρίματα κυρίου]–sweeter than honey or the comb" (Ps 18:11). Evagrius uses the suggestion of these verses to construct one of the chapters of the *Kephalaia Gnostica*. In that chapter it is as if he were directly explaining M 72. "If among the things which one tastes there is nothing sweeter than 'honey and the honeycomb' (Ps 18:11), and if the knowledge of God is said to be superior to these things (Ps 118:103), it is clear that there is nothing among all the things on earth which give pleasure like the knowledge of God" (KG III, 64).[168]

The psalm verse "He fed them with the best of wheat and satiated them with honey from the rock," provides Evagrius with the occasion to draw a distinction between feeding and satiating, a distinction that corresponds to the two major divisions of the spiritual life. His interpretation presumes that honey refers to knowledge. Evagrius says, "God *feeds* [ψωμίζει] one whom he instructs [παιδεύει] through the commandments, but he *satiates* [χορτάζει] the one whom he delights through his contemplation" (In Ps 80:17).[169]

---

[168] In his scholion on Ps 118:103 Evagrius comments not on the word *honey* but on the word *mouth*. Nonetheless, the scholion associates honey and the mouth with knowledge. He says, "The mind which enjoys and feeds on the knowledge of God is called mouth" (In Ps 118:103 [PG 12:1608D). Evagrius has no scholion on Ps 18:11.

[169] Pitra, *Analecta sacra spicilegio Solesmensi*, 3:139. Emphasis mine. It is to be remembered that παιδεία is a term associated with *praktikē*. On eating in general as an image for knowledge: "'Man ate the bread of angels, etc.' The Savior said, 'I am the bread which came down from heaven.' Therefore, angels first ate this bread; now men do. But here 'to eat' means 'to know.' For the mind that knows eats this bread, and the mind that does not know does not eat it" (In Ps 77:25 [PG 12:1541C]).

In a passage from the book of Proverbs the biblical author suggests to the seeker of wisdom the example of the ant and the bee. These two little animals are an occasion for Evagrius once again to draw a distinction between the life of *praktikē* and the life of knowledge. The ant with its industrious work is the symbol of *praktikē*, while the bee in its work of producing honey is the image of knowledge (In Prov 6:6–8; 6:8a, b [G 71, 72]).[170] But in discussing the work of the bee as an image for knowledge Evagrius also draws a distinction between the wax that the bee produces and the honey itself, differences that enable him to see in the scriptural verse the various divisions of knowledge. He says, "And it seems to me that wax is a word which refers to realities themselves, while the honey it contains is a symbol of the contemplation of it [these realities]" (In Prov 6:8 [G 72]).

This same distinction can be understood to obtain in M 72. Thus, the first line "decoded" would mean that the created world itself and the contemplations that pertain to them are sweet and delightful. But the proverb goes on to say that the knowledge of God is sweeter than both these lower forms of knowledge. For Evagrius, knowledge begins with understanding the reasons of the created order and the reasons in God's salvific economy, but the ultimate goal is knowledge of the Trinity itself beyond the creation, beyond the economy. The Trinity's mark is found in created realities and by means of these the monk mounts up to knowledge of the eternal Trinity.

This interpretation is confirmed by another passage where Evagrius distinguishes between ants and bees following the same lines of his interpretation in the scholion on Proverbs. The context is the relation between created reality and knowledge of the Trinity, and with these words Evagrius concludes his *Epistula Fidei*: "He [Solomon] refers us to the wise bee's wax-moulding implement and through that suggests physical contemplation in which is blended the reason of the Holy Trinity, since from the beauty of created things the Creator is analogously contemplated" (Ep Fid 12, lines 37–40). Created realities are destined to pass away, whereas the knowledge contained in them will not.

---

[170] The same development is found in Ep Fid 12, examined immediately below.

"But the wax will pass away, for it is said, 'The heaven and the earth will pass away' (Matt 24:35). But the honey will not pass away, for the words [λόγοι] of Christ our Savior will not pass away (Matt 24:35), concerning which Solomon said, 'Good words [λόγοι καλοί] are honeycombs; their sweetness cures the soul' (Prov 16:24). And David says, 'How sweet to my throat your oracles [τὰ λόγιά σου], more so than honey to my mouth' (Ps 118:103)" (In Prov 6:8 [G 72]).[171]

M 72 can be read simply as a poetic statement that there is nothing on earth more excellent than the knowledge of God. In that case it is much in the same line as KG III, 64 cited above.[172] But the other texts cited here show that it would also be possible to find in the proverb a distinction between levels of knowledge. The knowledge of God (knowledge of the Trinity) is far more sweet than the already sweet contemplations of the creation and the economy.

It was observed in the analysis of the chains that with M 72 the first half of the text comes to a type of close.[173] The interpretation of M 72 offered here reveals a secret, then, contained in the way this first half of the text concludes and the way the whole text will do so. M 136, the final proverb (minus the formal conclusion) reads, "Knowledge of incorporeals raises the mind / and presents it before the Holy Trinity." This final proverb is

---

[171] In the biblical passages to which Evagrius refers, both those from the Old Testament and those from the New, λόγος in its most immediate sense means *word*. However, Evagrius plays also on its meaning as *reason*.

[172] Evagrius's use of honey is susceptible of other interpretations, as In Prov 24:13 (G 270) shows. There the distinction between honey and the comb is just the reverse of the texts examined here. In that scholion eating honey refers to the profit that a simple reading of scripture yields, whereas eating the comb refers to the doctrines that are derived from "the things themselves," that is, the literal level of the text. This distinction could perhaps inform the interpretation of the other proverb in *Ad Monachos* that mentions honey, namely, M 115: "He who loves honey eats its comb, / and he who gathers it will be filled by the Spirit." Interpreted in the light of In Prov 24:13, M 115 would describe a movement from literal level of the text, to the doctrines contained therein, to communion with the Spirit himself. Honey as an image for knowledge also occurs in G 25.

[173] This because it is the final proverb of the chain at the center of the text and also because M 73 is a fresh invitation to listen, in some senses constituting a new beginning.

expressing levels in knowledge, and it places knowledge of the Trinity in the highest position. This is precisely what we have seen as the point of M 72: the creation is good; the contemplation that corresponds to it is better; but better than these is knowledge of God. The way this central chain finishes is the way the whole text will finish, namely, with many stages of *praktikē* accomplished and many levels of knowledge climbed, the mind presented before the Holy Trinity. Nothing is sweeter than this.

Commentary on M 107

Like a morning star in heaven and a palm tree in
    paradise,
so a pure mind in a gentle soul.

Ὥσπερ ἑωσφόρος ἐν οὐρανῷ καὶ ὥσπερ φοίνιξ ἐν
    παραδείσῳ,
οὕτως ἐν ψυχῇ πραείᾳ νοῦς καθαρός.

I have called M 107 a turning point in the whole text and in the examination of the chains justified that claim on the basis of the proverb's placement in the overall arrangement of the whole. The claim is further justified by a remarkable range of meanings that emerge from the proverb when it is carefully meditated upon. In what follows I hope to indicate some of what that range might be.

M 107 is a proverb richer than most, and a meditation on it is inevitably complex. This complexity carries a richness of theological meaning intentionally desired by Evagrius and accomplished by the way in which he uses the scriptural images of morning star and palm tree. Therefore, the task of commentary will be to examine what Evagrius means by these terms and the significance of his using them as images to describe mind and soul.

MIND AND SOUL

Mind and soul have their exact Evagrian sense in this proverb. A mind that moves away from its original union with

God experiences a sort of disintegration wherein it can be said to "fall" into a soul that is joined to a body proper to its condition. Yet in this arrangement (this economy), by God's providence, there is hidden a plan of redemption in which the fallen mind can be purified by means of a purification of soul and body. All this is operative in M 107's "mind in soul." But the adjective for mind, *pure*, is critically important in the proverb. "To be sure, it is not the mind itself which sees God, but rather the pure mind" (Lt 56:2). The same text goes on to say, "'Blessed are the pure of heart, for they shall see God" (Matt 5:8). Note that he does not praise purity as blessed but rather the one seeing [i.e., contemplating]. Purity is passionlessness of the reasonable soul, but seeing [contemplating] God is true knowledge of the one essence of the adorable Trinity, which those will see who have perfected their conduct here and through the commandments purified their souls" (Lt 56:2). These words show with clarity the way in which Evagrius understands the relation of mind and soul. The soul is purified so that its effects can be felt in the mind, so that the mind can be pure again. Then the mind can fix itself once again on essential knowledge.

The mind's being fixed on essential knowledge is called pure prayer throughout the *Chapters on Prayer*. This pure prayer, or essential knowledge, is the condition for which the mind longs. "A *soul* purified through fulfilling the commandments renders the position of the *mind* immovable, making it capable of receiving the condition for which it longs" (Prayer 2 [PG 79:1168C]).[174] And there needs to be a firmness to this condition so that the mind will not easily move (again!) away from this knowledge. Commenting on the word "seat" in the biblical text, Evagrius says, "For the seat of the mind is the excellent state which maintains the one seated in a position difficult to move or immovable" (In Prov 18:16 [G 184]).[175] This relationship between soul and mind and the firmness in which the mind needs to be reestab-

---

[174] Emphasis mine. Note how the text distinguishes soul and mind. The soul is purified by the commandments so that the mind can receive the condition for which it longs.

[175] Cf. KG VI, 21, "Virtue is the most excellent state of the reasonable soul, according to which it becomes difficult to move toward evil." Greek text in Hausherr, "Nouveaux fragments," 231.

lished are both expressed very simply in M 107: mind *in* soul. Yet what is striking is the adjective for the soul in which the pure mind rests, namely, a gentle soul. Here *gentle* serves as an adjective summarizing the condition of a soul that has reached *praktikē*'s goal and in which the mind is "capable of seeing the condition for which it longs."

Turning now to the comparisons made of this pure mind and gentle soul to the images of morning star and palm tree, most could agree that they are beautiful and striking images. Their power and polyvalence gradually grow with some lingering on their meaning.[176] It is worth recalling that a monk who would linger on these meanings is someone who would naturally seek guidance in the scriptures for their explication. Following in those same tracks, a number of scriptural references can be collected that will help us to understand their sense.

MORNING STAR: CHRISTOLOGICAL REFERENCE

The image of the morning star, among other things, would be meant to evoke a christological reference. There are several New Testament texts that would be responsible for this kind of connection being made, the most clear one being the words of Jesus in Revelation, "I am the root and the descendant of David, the bright morning star" (Rev 22:16).[177] The Second Letter of Peter speaks of keeping attention fixed on the prophetic word "until the day dawns and the morning star rises in your hearts" (2 Pet 1:19).[178] Zachary's prayer speaks of salvation as a "day dawning upon us from on high [ἐπισκέψεται ἡμᾶς ἀνατολή ἐξ ὕψους]" (Luke 1:78). And elsewhere in Revelation, the Son of God, speaking to the church of Thyatira, says to the one who keeps his words

---

[176] This is true, of course, with any successful use of metaphor or simile in whatever genre. From time to time it is useful to draw attention to how this works in the proverbs of *Ad Monachos*.

[177] The Greek has ὁ ἀστὴρ ὁ λαμπρὸς ὁ πρωϊνός instead of M 107's ἑωσφόρος.

[178] Some Greek manuscripts have ἑωσφόρος and others have φωσφόρος. Evagrius and monks in his circle would likely read such a text making much of the fact that the star is said to rise is one's heart.

until the end, "I will give him the morning star [δώσω αὐτῷ τὸν ἀστέρα τὸν πρωϊνόν]" (Rev 2:28). Each of these scriptural texts either associates the morning star directly with Christ or closely to some dimension of the redemption he brings. In M 107, speaking simply from the point of view of technique in poetry, to say *like* (ὥσπερ) is to leave things a little more open and to allow a range of possible meanings of morning star to come to mind. One of those meanings, thanks to these scriptural texts, would likely be in reference to Christ himself: the pure mind in the gentle soul is likened to Christ the morning star. The scriptural texts indicate this interpretation, but there is also an Evagrian text that leads in the same direction.

Evagrius writes a letter in which the word ἑωσφόρος may refer directly to Christ and at least certainly refers to the redemption he brings. But not only that; the passage also connects not seeing the morning star with irascibility, the very thing for which gentleness is especially designed as remedy! Furthermore, the letter likewise employs the image of a tree, which can be compared to the palm tree of M 107. "An irascible temperate person is a dried-up tree, fruitless, twice dead, uprooted. An irascible person will not see the morning star rising, but will go to a place from which he will not return, into a land dark and gloomy, into a land of eternal darkness" (Lt 27:3).[179]

This passage can be read as the "expressed-in-prose" opposite of M 107's poetic expression. The concern of the letter is with irascibility, and it expresses a string of images to describe the irascible monk: dried tree, dark, gloom, eternal darkness, and no morning star. On the other hand, M 107's concern is with gentleness, and its images are the opposite of two of the letter's main images. Instead of a dried up tree, there is the palm tree in paradise. Instead of no morning star, there is the morning star.

So this much can at least be said so far: the pure mind in the gentle soul is like Christ himself.[180] And this is to say something

---

[179] Translated from a Greek fragment in C. Guillaumont, "Fragments grecs," 220, lines 66–69.

[180] Compare the strong christological explanation that was given in the commentary on M 31's statement, "In the gentle heart, wisdom will rest."

quite specific, for in Evagrian christology Christ is *the* mind par excellence.[181] What Christ is actually, other minds are potentially.[182] It is to a condition of union with essential knowledge like Christ's that each fallen mind is called to return. So to liken the pure mind to the morning star is not simply to choose a sweet and striking comparison. It is to choose a specific christological comparison with a clear awareness of the aptness of the comparison. The pure mind is likened to Christ for ontological reasons. Christ is pure mind which never fell. The pure mind of M 107 is the fallen mind become pure again, coheir with Christ in participation in essential knowledge.

MORNING STAR: REFERENCE TO RATIONAL CREATURES

All this having been said, there is a different direction in which the expression "morning star" could be reflected upon, a direction confirmed by other Evagrian texts. The mention of ἑωσφόρος would also easily call to mind the text of Isaiah 14:12, "How he has fallen from heaven, the morning star [ἑωσφόρος in LXX] which rose at dawn." This prophecy of Isaiah against the king of Babylon (Isa 14:12-24) has a history of being referred by Christian exegetes to Satan's falling from heaven.[183] Origen goes into it at some length in *De Principiis* in a section that treats of rational natures (*De prin.* 1.5.5). Didymus the Blind cites the Isaiah passage in a way that shows how readily it could come to mind in the context of a consideration of *praktikē* and its goal of return to an original condition. Commenting on a scriptural text in his *Commentary on Zechariah,* Didymus says, "This reading shows that the sinner is carried from higher to lower. Many passages of scripture show this, for example, 'How he has fallen from heaven, the morning star [ἑωσφόρος] which rose at dawn' . . . On the other

---

[181] Evagrius generally interprets "Christ" in the strict sense of meaning anointed; he is anointed "above his fellows" with essential knowledge. See In Ps 44:3.

[182] To make this potential actual is what it means to be a coheir with Christ, as mentioned in M 1.

[183] The notion of Satan falling from heaven like a star is already a theme in the New Testament; cf. Luke 10:18; Rev 8:10; 9:1.

hand, many other texts show that the one practicing virtue [ὁ σπουδαῖος] mounts upward. . . ."[184]

Evagrius fits into this same exegetical tradition concerning the Isaiah passage. On several occasions he refers to the text and uses other scriptural texts to shape his understanding of it. Basing himself on a very close reading of Ps 109:3, he understands ἑωσφόρος in that text to refer to a rational creature, distinguishing it from Christ in his generation. The comment reads, "'From the womb, before the morning star, I begot you.' Before every rational nature I begot you [i.e., Christ]. For a deep thing indeed it is to grasp the generation of Christ and the morning star; it is not within our power. For vast is the reason about that and hard for contemplation" (In Ps 109:3 [PG 12:1569B]).[185] If it is true that to speak of the generation even of this rational creature (to say nothing of the generation of Christ) is difficult, more is known and can be said of its fall. The creature falls because of pride, "pride, the original evil, which caused to fall to the earth the morning star which rose at dawn" (TP Prologue 2).

Evagrius develops this idea in several passages that are, compared to his usual style, relatively lengthy. This movement of pride caused the morning star to receive the name "devil." This is explained in a passage where Evagrius, arguing for the divinity of the Holy Spirit, distinguishes the divine essence from the nature of rational creatures. The argument goes like this: "But

---

[184] *Commentary on Zechariah*, book 1, 94, found in SC 83, 240. Translation mine. See also in the *Commentary on Job* the following text: "As an outcast he [the devil] thinks to himself, I need to be a hindrance to those who have citizenship in heaven so that they cannot mount up to the place from which I fell. For he sees the progress of men as a reproach to himself since he himself was the morning star of the heavens [ἑωσφόρος οὐράων] and the shining star rising at dawn." Text in *Didymos der Blinde, Kommentar zu Hiob (Tura-Papyrus)*, Teil I, *Kommentar zu Hiob Kap. 1-4* (Bonn, 1968), 28–30. Translation mine.

[185] Note how in his close reading of the text, Evagrius observes that there is a difference between the morning star and the generation of the one to whom the words of the psalm text are addressed, in this case understood by Evagrius as being addressed to the Divine Son. Thus, here Evagrius distinguishes the morning star from Christ, who (the psalm verse says) is generated before the morning star. This being so, Evagrius in his interpretation presumes then that morning star refers to rational nature since, we might say, "everyone knows" that the Divine Son was generated before these.

neither would you dare to call his [the Holy Spirit's] essence changeable if you consider the nature of the opposing power which fell like lightning from heaven (Luke 10:18) and fell out of true life. This was because his [the opposing power's] holiness was an acquired attribute and the change was a consequence of his evil decision. Thus, having fallen from the unity and thrown aside the angelic dignity, he is named devil on account of the change. His original and blessed state was extinguished; enkindled was the opposing power" (Ep Fid 10, lines 15–22).[186]

In another place Evagrius speaks of this same evil decision of the devil and shows that his fall is a movement away from knowledge. But of further interest in the passage is the fact that Evagrius moves rather naturally in his discussion toward the image of "the trees of paradise." We perhaps catch here some glimpse of the poetic structure of Evagrius's mind and how it is that he would combine the images morning star and palm tree in paradise as he does in M 107.[187] Commenting on several terms in a biblical proverb, Evagrius says, "The devil is called 'evil decision,' for he decided badly when he said, 'I will place my throne above the stars. I will become similar to the Most High' (Isa 14:13–14).[188] He had forgotten the divine knowledge, 'leaving aside the teaching of his youth.' 'Youth' here clearly means his original condition[189] which was his when he was envied by all the trees of paradise (Ezek 31:9)" (In Prov 2:17 [G 23]).[190]

---

[186] That Evagrius would have identified the image of Luke 10:18 with Isa 14:12 is likely. See the next passage examined here, In Prov 2:17 (G 23). Origen makes the connection explicit in the passage from *De Principiis* referred to above (1.5.5).

[187] It must be admitted that as such, without the particular understanding that Evagrius had of these biblical terms, the two images exhibit little connection with each other. Evagrius connects them on the basis of their both being found in biblical texts which refer to the original condition of rational creatures and of their both being susceptible of christological interpretation. For the christological reference to trees, see n. 190 below.

[188] This is pride, "the original evil." Cf. TP Prologue 2.

[189] Compare "original and blessed state" of Ep Fid 10, cited above, n. 186.

[190] Both stars and trees are symbols for Evagrius of the rational nature. This sense of star has already been seen in commenting on its use in M 21. See above, pp. 241–43. For trees as a symbol of rational nature Evagrius bases himself on an interpretation of Ezek 31:9, an explanation that he takes for granted in the con-

All this shows that Evagrius's choice of the comparison of the pure mind to the morning star is even more specific than its already specific christological reference had indicated. Something exciting is suggested in M 107. The pure mind in the gentle soul is compared to that most beautiful of rational creatures before the fall, namely, the devil before the fall. But there is something comparable to the devil's fall in the fall of every rational creature. What is described in the passages cited here of the devil's fall is applicable to the fall of every rational creature.[191] Every rational creature fell from a beautiful state "like the morning star's." This comes about for every rational creature as a result of an evil decision, a movement away from knowledge.[192] When this fallen creature becomes a pure mind in a gentle soul (into which soul it has fallen as part of a plan for its salvation), then it is "like a morning star" again.

HEAVEN AND PARADISE

A further nuance of interpretation is possible in M 107, perhaps so subtle as to elude many of the monks who would have meditated on it; but uncovering it can serve once again as an example of how much lies hidden in these texts and how the reader is rewarded for careful attention. In the same way that a

---

text of other rather more complex exegesis. Thus, in explaining the psalm verse, "I am a worm and not a man," he says, "The worm is not generated from copulation but from wood, and it devours wood, fodder, and stubble. And so perhaps our God is a fire that consumes wickedness and combustible material. If rational natures are called trees, as in, 'All the trees of paradise were envious of you' (Ezek 31:9), then in them [i.e., the trees = rational natures] Christ is born as wisdom and justice. Thus beautifully Christ is called a worm born in those trees" (In Ps 21:7 [PG 12:1253B–C]). The same interpretation of Ezek 31:9 is presumed in In Prov 2:17 (G 23), cited here; cf. also KG V, 67. The "tree of life" in paradise may also be meant as a christological reference. It is identified with "the Lord" in TP Prologue 7 and with Wisdom in In Prov 3:18 (G 32).

[191] All these remarks on the original evil can be brought to a meditation of that theme in M 62, as I already suggested in the commentary there.

[192] Evagrius makes this application explicit. The passage of Prov 2:17, which in the scholion on that verse is applied to the devil, is elsewhere applied to other rational creatures. See In Prov 5:18 (G 64). The movement described in these texts for the devil is applied to all the rational creatures in KG VI, 75.

hierarchy was observed between soul and mind (mind being the basic and original reality, soul being the arrangement of providence as a result of the mind's movement away from essential knowledge) it may be possible to observe a similar hierarchy between paradise and heaven and the image associated with each, namely, morning star in heaven and palm tree in paradise. The possibility of such an interpretation is suggested by a hint found in one of the scholia on the Psalms which describes paradise as a place of learning. "As paradise is the instruction place [παιδευτήριον] of the just, so Hades is the punishing place for sinners" (In Ps 9:18 [PG 12:1189D]).[193] This scholion suggests, among other things, why Evagrius would have specified the kind of tree (i.e., palm tree) in M 107. It is a symbol of the just, as in Ps 91:12, and the scholion on Ps 9:18 specifies paradise as a training place of the *just*.

Behind such a conception there likely lies a passage in Origen's *De Principiis* where he discusses a period of instruction after this present life in which we will come to understand clearly the reasons that lie behind the creation. Evagrius does not expose his own thinking in works the genre of *De Principiis*, but a passage like the following from Origen can help to fill out an understanding of such a brief text like Evagrius's on paradise as a place of instruction. Origen says,

> I think that the saints as they leave this life will remain in a place on the earth which the divine scripture calls *paradise*, remaining there as in a place of instruction, a lecture hall or a school of souls, so to speak, where they may be taught about all that they have seen on earth and receive also some outline of future things. . . . If someone will be *pure of heart* and even more so *pure in mind* and well-trained in intelligence, he will progress more rapidly, he will ascend quickly into the air and will reach the kingdom of the *heavens*, passing through those mansions of various stages which the Greeks call spheres (that is, globes) and the divine scripture calls heavens. (*De prin.* 2.11.6)[194]

---

[193] The reading παιδευτήριον is based not on the PG text but on a manuscript reading provided me privately by G. Bunge, who has it from M. J. Rondeau, who is preparing the critical edition. Cf. KG VI, 8.

[194] Translation mine. I have italicized *paradise* and *heaven* to draw attention

If Evagrius knew this passage or this line of thinking, then paradise as described here would be understood by him as a place of learning roughly equivalent to what are for him the initial levels of knowledge into which one enters after reaching *praktikē*'s goal. Evagrius would likewise have been struck by the way in which Origen connects purity of heart and mind with progress in this kind of knowledge. If this thinking is used to interpret M 107, then the palm tree in paradise is an image of the reasonable nature that has come through *praktikē*[195] and is now being instructed in what Origen calls "teachings about all that they have seen on earth" and what Evagrius would call "reasons of corporeals"; it is being instructed in what Origen calls "some outline of future things" and what Evagrius would call "reasons of providence and judgment." A reasonable nature that has reached *praktikē*'s goal and entered the initial stages of knowledge is "a palm tree (a reasonable nature in which justice is established) in paradise (a place of instruction)." Otherwise described, it is "a pure mind in a gentle soul."

In this interpretation, paradise is a "lesser" image than heaven, just as *praktikē* is subordinate to knowledge, just as knowledge of the reasons of corporeal things is subordinate to the essential knowledge for which the mind was originally created, just as soul is subordinate to mind. What Evagrius offers then in M 107 are two images for the mind *in* the soul, one image more particularly suited to the mind in its original condition (the morning star in heaven) and another image more particularly suited to the soul which, through *praktikē*, strives to return to the original condition (the palm tree in paradise). The two images reveal two different dimensions of the single reality of a mind in a soul. The morning star speaks of the original condition of the

---

to the way in which Origen distinguishes them. I have italicized *pure of heart* and *pure of mind* to draw attention to the similarity of concern between Origen and Evagrius.

[195] Thus, the palm tree is an image of the just man as in Ps 91:12; for the role of justice for Evagrius is to realize a harmony among the various parts of the soul (cf. TP 89). And, "the just, planted in the knowledge of the Lord, make many flourish in the world and in the churches, causing them to bear fruit through spiritual teaching" (In Ps 91:14 [PG 12:1553A]).

mind; the palm tree is a mind returning to this condition. What characterizes such a mind? A gentle soul! Once again, gentleness summarizes the whole life of *praktikē* and prepares the way for *praktikē*'s goal: the mind able to fix itself on that for which it longs. Such a mind is a pure mind. The Greek structure of the proverb is a chiasm difficult to repeat in less than clumsy English, but the structure lends weight to the interpretation I am offering here. In the center of the chiasm, the palm tree lies immediately next to the gentle soul, while the morning star and the pure mind are the two ends of the chiasm.[196]

The foregoing has, I believe, demonstrated the richness of M 107. With considerable care Evagrius has formulated the proverb which he places as the subtle turning point of the entire text's shift to a focus on knowledge that is sustained through to the end. I think it not out of line or too far-fetched to suggest that it may be possible to "sense" the influence of an important personal experience standing behind the formulation of this proverb. I refer to the experience to which I have already drawn attention in the commentary on M 53: Evagrius's own account of being caught up in a heavenly vision. He received instruction in the place into which he was caught up, an instruction that was summarized for him in the divine command which he received: Be gentle and humble.[197] It had been night when Evagrius had this vision. He had been sitting by the lamp reading. Immediately after he heard this command, he found himself again with book in hand and the lamp still burning. Intentionally using the words

---

[196] It is perhaps not possible to argue with certainty that such a hierarchy between heaven and paradise and the images associated with each was definitely the intention of Evagrius in composing this proverb, though I think it likely was. The scope of my remarks is, however, somewhat different. I wish to point out that whether Evagrius himself intended this particular meaning or not, the commentary offered here is the sort of insight this genre of poetic proverbs promotes. It is an insight consistent with all the tenets of Evagrius's cosmology and soteriology, an insight supported by other Evagrian texts. So the claim here is that whether Evagrius intended it or not, he could be pleased with such a meditation on his proverb, much like a poet is pleased with an interpretation of one of his poems which might include something he never was aware of saying but which strikes him nonetheless as a legitimate and valuable interpretation.

[197] On the exact wording of the command, see above, p. 260, n. 84.

of St. Paul to describe his experience at that moment, he says, "I do not know how I was taken up to the clouds; whether it was in the flesh, I do not know; God knows (2 Cor 12:3); or whether it was in spirit, I do not know" (*Coptic Life,* 117).

I suggested in my commentary on M 53 that this experience of this vision permeates Evagrius's teaching. It goes some fair way in explaining the insistent concern with gentleness and related virtues that is found throughout his writings and to which so many proverbs of *Ad Monachos* draw attention. The message of M 107 is about the critical importance of gentleness, and its images suggest something of the feel of the vision in which Evagrius received the command that was to so impregnate his teaching. One of the images is of a bright star in heaven, perhaps an image to which he was inclined from what he saw when suspended from the air and viewing the world in a single glance. The other image is an image of paradise, offered to him by seeing his own experience as comparable to that of St. Paul's. For St. Paul says, "I know that this man was caught up into *paradise*—whether in the body or out of the body I do not know, God knows" (2 Cor 12:2). For St. Paul also this "paradise" was a place of instruction: "He heard unspeakable words, which man may not utter" (2 Cor 12:4). For this same reason is Evagrius led to metaphor, which permits the mind a new grasp of mysteries, a deeper grasp, than what discursive reasoning could ever offer. The metaphor reaches for things "which cannot be told, which man may not utter."

This involved commentary on M 107 has not been meant to break down its meaning into some manageable and discursive form. It has not attempted to talk about what cannot be told. Rather, such commentary is a preparation necessary to allow the proverb itself in its two simple lines to find its mark. I have tried to indicate here directions for its meditation, but into what knowledge that meditation leads "only God knows." We, however, can say this much: no one goes into that knowledge without a gentle soul.

Commentary on M 118, 119, 120

118. Flesh of Christ: virtues of *praktikē;*
     he who eats it, passionless shall he be.

     Σάρκες Χριστοῦ πρακτικαὶ ἀρεταί,
     ὁ δὲ ἐσθίων αὐτὰς γενήσεται ἀπαθής.

119. Blood of Christ: contemplation of created things;
     he who drinks it, by it becomes wise.

     Αἷμα Χριστοῦ θεωρία τῶν γεγονότων
     καὶ ὁ πίνων αὐτὸ σοφισθήσεται ὑπ’ αὐτοῦ.

120. Breast of the Lord: knowledge of God;
     he who rests against it, a theologian shall he be.

     Στῆθος κυρίου γνῶσις θεοῦ,
     ὁ δ’ ἀναπεσὼν ἐπ’ αὐτὸ θεολόγος ἔσται.

In my remarks on these proverbs in the analysis of the chains, I suggested that no three proverbs are as tightly fitted together as these. Therefore, more so than in the previous commentaries on the individual proverbs, a commentary on these three must especially rely on attention to the structure of the proverbs and the way these are fitted together. Briefly summarizing the remarks made there, I remind the reader that these three proverbs trace a movement from *praktikē* through contemplation of creation and on to knowledge of God. This movement unfolds by means of images taken from the Last Supper, expressing a progress in intimacy with God by means of the movement from flesh to blood to the Lord's breast, which is a progress in what these symbolize, namely, passionlessness, contemplation, knowledge of God. Each proverb and all three together show a direct, a profound, and an indispensable involvement of Christ in this movement toward greater intimacy. I suggested that it was the eucharistic mystery itself that may account for the tight conjunction expressed between Christ and the various phases of the monastic life that these proverbs represent, such that Evagrius would be moved to say so strongly and so strikingly that Christ's flesh *is* virtue, his blood *is* contemplation, his breast *is* knowledge.

I would like to explore these ideas more deeply now. The discussion can be organized under several headings. First, I will look at other texts where Evagrius employs this same imagery and use these as a means of securing his intended meaning in M 118–20. Second, I will make some observations about the progress from *praktikē* to knowledge described in these proverbs. The movement is by now familiar enough and has been both presumed and often commented on throughout this study. However, these proverbs permit some comments on a detail of this movement that has heretofore gone unremarked, namely, the movement from contemplation of created things to knowledge of God. Third, I will make some comments on the images associated with each level of the movement and ask how apt they are. Thus, why is Christ's flesh associated with the virtues? Why is his blood associated with contemplation? Why is his breast associated with knowledge?

1. Evagrius's Use of These Same Images

These three proverbs would be badly misunderstood if the reader were to see in them merely a spiritualizing or allegorizing tendency such that the flesh of Christ is thought to be no more than a scriptural code word for virtue or his blood no more than something of the same for contemplation. The point is rather quite the opposite. The proverbs mean to express that the very possibility of progress within *praktikē* and from this to contemplation and from this to the knowledge of God is grounded in the mystery of the Incarnation. But here Evagrius says more. What the Incarnation makes possible is communicated through the action of eating Christ's flesh and drinking his blood and the intimacy that this implies. Further, it should be noted that the expressions "eat his flesh" and "drink his blood" are generally so closely associated with the Eucharist that it seems unlikely that Evagrius would not have wished the same connection to be made here.

One is invited toward such an interpretation by other places in which Evagrius uses the same imagery as that found in M 118-20. A text from *Epistula Fidei* is particularly worth examining in this regard. The context is a discussion of how the Father lives in his Only Begotten and how this relationship is transferred to us in the Incarnation. For Evagrius, basing himself on the Lord's own words, this transferal comes about through eating Christ's flesh and drinking his blood.

> Christ says, "He who eats me will live because of me" (John 6:57). For we eat his flesh and drink his blood thus becoming partakers [κοινωνοὶ γινόμενοι, cf. 1 Cor 10:16] in the Logos and in Wisdom through his Incarnation and his visible life. For flesh and blood is what he names his whole mysterious sojourn [among us], and he has revealed his teaching which consists in *praktikē* and natural contemplation and theology. Through this teaching the soul is nourished and prepared for the contemplation of the last things. (Ep Fid 4, lines 16-22)

Several things should be observed in this interesting text. First, from a methodological point of view, it is a text that can with confidence be used to interpret M 118-20, not only because of its reference to Christ's flesh and blood but also because the text sees in these a teaching associated with *praktikē* and natural contemplation and theology, just as in M 118-20. Second, Evagrius's expression "becoming partakers" alludes to Paul's words, "The cup of blessing that we bless, is it not a communion in the blood of Christ [οὐχὶ κοινωνία ἐστὶν τοῦ αἵματος τοῦ Χριστοῦ]? The bread that we break, is it not a communion in the body of Christ [οὐχι κοινωνία τοῦ σώματος τοῦ Χριστοῦ ἐστιν]?" (1 Cor 10:16). It would seem that with this language Evagrius means to associate himself with this strong Pauline understanding of union with Christ accomplished through the eucharistic sharing. In the text Evagrius is not speaking directly of the Eucharist but rather about how we become partakers of the Logos. Yet his way of arguing is possible only if there is a eucharistic understanding behind it. Evagrius's particular twist on the Pauline text is to specify that *by means of* the Incarnation (which in the text is put in strict relation with eating Christ's body and drinking his blood) we become partakers of the Logos and of Wisdom. For Evagrius, this is precisely how God is known and more specifically how he is known as Trinity, namely, from the position in which the Logos as God knows God. From participation in the Logos we know God as God knows God.[198]

A third observation worth making about this text concerns the expression "mysterious sojourn." With the term *sojourn* (ἐπιδημία) Evagrius refers specifically to the Incarnation.[199] But I wish to draw attention especially to the word *mysterious*. Evagrius is very likely using it here with the technical theological force common in patristic literature, which was already developed by St. Paul.[200] It refers to the secret plan of God hidden inside the events of sacred history. By extension, in the fathers, it refers to a deeper meaning hidden within some concrete reality, be that the text of scripture or saving events themselves. In the expression "mysterious sojourn" the concrete reality is the incarnate life of the Logos. According to Evagrius, Christ himself calls the whole sojourn "flesh and blood." Something is hidden within this concrete fact, within this flesh and blood; there is something *mysterious* in it. And this mystery has been revealed: "he has revealed his teaching which consists in *praktikē* and natural contemplation and theology."[201] M 118, 119, and 120 are proverbs that likewise reveal the mystery of what is hidden in Christ's flesh, his blood, his breast. Ultimately what is hidden there is participation in the Logos, through whom we know God. "The breast of the Lord: the knowledge of God."[202]

The eucharistic sense that I am suggesting underlies these texts (both the passage from *Epistula Fidei* and M 118–20) is

---

[198] This is developed below. See pp. 337–40 for the explanation of the fullest sense of "theologian" and the comments on Prayer 58–61. See also Prayer 52, cited below, p. 329 and Ep Fid 7, lines 25–26, 30–31: "But our Lord is himself the end and final blessedness according to his title as Logos . . . and our mind cuts loose and rises toward a blessed height where it contemplates the oneness and the unity of the Logos."

[199] Cf. In Prov 4:21 (G 51); 17:2 (G 153); 30:9 (G 287B); In Ps 44:3; 107:10; Ep Fid 4, line 12.

[200] See Rom 16:25–26; 1 Cor 2:7; Eph 1:9; 3:3, 9; Col 1:27.

[201] It is a dimension of the Pauline texts on mystery that a characteristic of the good news is that the mystery of God's plan has at last been revealed.

[202] For a similar use of *mystery* related to breast, see KG IV, 66. For other uses of *mystery* in this sense, see KG VI, 42, 65; In Prov 23:1 (G 250).

strengthened by two other places in which Evagrius uses the word *mystery* to refer to the Eucharist. In the *Praktikos* there is the expression "priests who purify us through the holy mysteries" (TP 100).[203] In the *Gnostikos* Evagrius speaks of "the mysteries celebrated by them [priests] and which purify the interior man" (G 14). In both texts the reference is to the eucharistic mysteries.[204] M 118–20 is a meditation that speaks of—to use an expression from the passage in the *Gnostikos*—"what these mysteries symbolize" (G 14). For the proverbs from *Ad Monachos* they symbolize *praktikē*, contemplation, and knowledge. The interpretation in the *Gnostikos* is slightly different. There the focus is on the vessels that contain bread and wine, which Evagrius says designate the passionate part of the soul and the rational part.

I think the texts from *Ad Monachos* and the *Gnostikos* can be used to interpret each other. M 118 would suggest that the vessel of bread mentioned in the *Gnostikos* refers to the passionate part of the soul. It is this which is purified in *praktikē*. "He who eats it, passionless shall he be." M 119 would suggest that the vessel of wine refers to the rational part of the soul. It is this part of the soul that is used for contemplation; wisdom is its principal virtue. "He who drinks it, by it becomes wise."

The text from the *Gnostikos* goes on to speak of a certain part of the eucharistic rite, "the inseparable mixture" of bread and wine when the priest places a piece of the consecrated bread into the chalice. This "inseparable mixture" reveals "the power of each separate part" of the soul and how they work together "toward one unique end," namely, knowledge. M 118–20 also speaks in this same tone. The parts of the soul are distinguished in the proverbs but inseparably joined in their scope. In the eucharistic rite itself there is a symbol of the inseparable joining of *praktikē* to knowledge. The flesh of the Lord is *praktikē*; his blood is contemplation. In the eucharistic rite these are inseparably joined and, we could add, inseparably received. This action of the rite works "toward one unique end." This end is, as M 120 says, "The breast of the Lord: the knowledge of God."[205]

---

[203] Part of what the mysteries do is "purify"; that is, they bring *praktikē* to its goal, passionlessness.

[204] See Guillaumont, SC 171, 711–12; SC 356, 109–11.

[205] It may be that Evagrius is inspired in these passages by 1 Cor 11:27-30,

The eating of Christ's flesh and the drinking of his blood are indispensable means for reaching the knowledge of God, which is to say that Christ himself, in the reality of his Incarnation, is indispensable. The scripture verse, "Who shall eat or who shall drink without him?" (Eccl 2:25) is occasion for Evagrius to remark, "For who, without Christ, will be able to eat his flesh and drink his blood, which are symbols of the virtues and of knowledge" (In Eccl 2:25 [G 13]).

We have seen in many places that in order to reach knowledge one must do war with demons. Christ is a power against the demons. He is power both in the monk's struggle against the passions and in his battle against ignorance. The texts we are examining here suggest that he is a power that is conveyed to the monk through the Eucharist. In at least two places Evagrius makes reference to the Eucharist in the context of the battle with demons. These texts implicitly confirm the eucharistic interpretation I am proposing for M 118–20. The idea is developed as the deeper sense of several scriptural passages. In the first instance, commenting on the verse, "When evildoers came against me to eat up my flesh, my persecutors and my enemies fainted and fell away" (Ps 26:2), Evagrius explains,

> If we eat the flesh of Christ (for he said, "He who eats my flesh and drinks my blood . . .") (John 6:54), the demons eat our flesh. But this does not in any way mean that the demons eat Christ's flesh as they try to destroy in us virtues and true doctrines. For in this verse "to eat" means "to destroy." . . . Or [a second interpretation], the demons are said to eat our flesh, that is, to eat that which comes out of our flesh. "Now the works of the flesh are plain," as the holy apostle says. "Adultery, fornication, licentiousness, idolatry," and the rest (Gal 5:19). (In Ps 26:2 [PG 12:1277A–B])

In this text "evildoers . . . eating up my flesh" is explained as the demons attempting to destroy virtue and knowledge. They do this by concentrating on our actual flesh, "and the works of the flesh are plain," that is, the list of vices mentioned in the Galatians

---

which speaks of "any one who eats and drinks judgment upon himself if he does not discern the body." Those who fail to discern the meaning "are weak and sick and some are dying." Cf. In Prov 5:11 (G 61) and two texts examined immediately below: In Ps 26:2; 67:24.

passage cited by Evagrius. But "if we eat the flesh of Christ," then Christ "abides in us" (John 6:56). He is in our flesh, according to M 118, as the virtues of *praktikē* instead of as the vices with which the demons attempt to destroy our flesh. Combining the viewpoint of this text with the ideas offered in M 118–20 and with the passage from *Epistula Fidei,* we could say that, for Evagrius, the battle with the demons is one that in a very real way takes place in the flesh and in the mind. The monk has hope for victory in the battle against the passions only because Christ himself is in his flesh. He sojourns there mysteriously as the virtues of *praktikē.* The monk has hope for victory in the battle against ignorance only because Christ sojourns in his mind as Logos, as Wisdom, or otherwise put, as contemplation (M 119), as knowledge (M 120). The whole reality of Christ's Incarnation and this reality conveyed in the eucharistic elements ("which are symbols of the virtues and of knowledge") are a counterforce to the demons present within, demons who "try to destroy in us virtues and true doctrines."

The second instance of reference to the Eucharist in the context of talk about demons is found in another scholion on Psalms which shows the blood of Christ directly related to his passion and at the same time rather automatically takes it to be an image of "knowledge of the truth." The psalm verse in question is, "That your foot may be dipped in blood, the tongue of your dogs with that of your enemies" (Ps 68:24 [Eng. 68:23]). Evagrius explains, "The foot of Christ, the man born from Mary, was dipped in blood through his passion, which blood the enemies hinder us from drinking, wanting us always to be dogs, so that we could never go into 'knowledge of the truth' (1 Tim 2:4). For they know that those who eat the flesh of Christ and drink his blood abide in him and he in them" (John 6:56) (In Ps 67:24 [Eng. 68:23]).[206] What the demons know is that Christ's flesh contains passionlessness for the monk (M 118), and Christ's blood, wisdom (M 119).[207]

Thus, all these texts combine to indicate that a real struggle is occurring, in which the concrete reality of Christ's flesh and

[206] Pitra, *Analecta sacra spicilegio Solesmensi,* 3:84.

[207] In the *Lausiac History,* a work written in the spirit of Evagrius (see Draguet, "L'Histoire Lausiaque, une œuvre écrite dans l'esprit d'Évagre"), there is

blood received in the Eucharist will prove decisive. If the demons are to keep the monk from knowledge, they must keep him from drinking the blood of Christ; for "he who drinks it, by it becomes wise." If the demons are to keep alive in the monk what comes from the flesh ("adultery, fornication, licentiousness, idolatry," and the rest), then they must keep him from the flesh of Christ; for, "he who eats it, passionless shall he be."[208]

2. The Movement from Praktikē to Contemplation to Knowledge

The movement described in these three proverbs, with its tri-partite division of the spiritual life, is a commonplace in Evagrian teaching. As such, there is no need for comment on it here. What is significant in the three proverbs is that this division is placed in tandem with eucharistic imagery; and, as we have seen, the proverbs from *Ad Monachos* are not the only instance of Evagrius's having done so. I wish to examine this imagery in the next section. However, before doing that, the arrangement of M 118–20 provides an occasion for looking at one of the details of progress within the spiritual life that has not yet received attention in this study, namely, the movement from contemplation of created things to knowledge of God. It is necessary to understand how

---

a series of three chapters that speak of fallen monks. It is interesting to note that in each case the monk is overcome by demons in connection with his refusal to partake of the eucharistic mysteries. Thus, Valens is overcome by pride and "thinks himself too good to participate in the Mysteries" (LH 25:2). He even went so far as to claim, "I have no need for Communion" (LH 25:5). Heron (whom we know was known to Evagrius since Palladius tells us that Heron once insulted him) "did not want to approach the Mysteries" (LH 26:2). Ptolemy "became estranged from . . . the continual communion of the Mysteries" (LH 27:2). On the other hand, Palladius makes it a point to note that before Evagrius's death, "he received Communion in the church on the day of Epiphany" (LH 38:13). This is contributing evidence to gain some sense that Evagrius is likely speaking in these texts of a concrete action, namely, celebrating the eucharistic mysteries. For the fuller context of the question of these fallen monks, see Driscoll, "Evagrius and Paphnutius on the Causes for Abandonment by God," 259–86.

[208] For other instances of this same understanding of the flesh and blood of Christ in battle with demons, see In Prov 5:11 (G 61) and 6:17 (G 77), both making reference to John 6:54.

Evagrius conceives of this movement in order to take account of the role assigned to Christ at this stage of the monk's progress and as this role is expressed in M 118–20.

Contemplation of created things is the level of the life of knowledge into which the monk can pass after having reached passionlessness. In what does such contemplation consist? The expression "contemplation of created things" (θεωρία τῶν γεγονότων) covers the knowledge of created things in all their conditions, thus contemplation of incorporeals and corporeals, of providence and judgment. Likewise included would be the worlds into which bodies are placed. It seems to be the all-embracing term of these otherwise more specified dimensions of contemplation. Evagrius mentions the name of this contemplation in many places, as he does in M 119; but as for actual descriptions of it, the best examples are probably to be found in the *Letter to Melania*. One example can suffice for our present purposes.

> And as the man who stands at the seashore is struck with amazement by its immensity, its taste, its color, by all that it possesses, by the fact that the rivers, torrents and streams which pour into it become themselves boundless and unlimited, possessing every quality which the sea has, thus also he who observes the making perfect of all intellects, is amazed greatly and marvels because he sees all these various distinct knowledges as they merge into one essential and unique knowledge, and that all those become this one, forever. (Ep Mel 12, lines 508–15)[209]

---

[209] Perhaps another descriptive example of what this contemplation actually consists in is to be found in a text from Cassian, upon whom the strong influence of Evagrius is not to be doubted (see Marsili, *Giovanni Cassiano ed Evagrio Pontico*). "But the contemplation of God is arrived at in numerous ways. . . . He is also clearly perceived in the grandeur of the things that he has created . . . when we consider with most pure minds [note the similarity to Evagrius's requirement of passionlessness] the things that he has accomplished with his holy ones over the course of generations; when with trembling heart we admire that power of his by which he governs, directs, and rules all things, as well as the vastness of his knowledge and the eye from which the secrets of hearts cannot be hidden; when we think that he knows the sands of the sea and that he has measured the number of the waves; when we contemplate with amazement the raindrops, the days and hours of the ages, how all things past and future are present to his knowledge" (*Conferences* I, 15; translation by Ramsey, *John Cassian: The Conferences*, 55).

This suggestive text is a fine example of how, for Evagrius, contemplation of creation is, yes, a marveling at its wonders. But more than that, it is seeing "mysteriously" hidden in the creation the very movement itself toward the eventual oneness of knowledge which is final blessedness. Indeed, details of the creation (the immensity, taste, and color of the sea) are amazing not only in themselves, but also for the way in which they are seen merging into one larger reality. To this merging of elements in the creation there corresponds a merging of minds into one essential knowledge. This is the mystery hidden in creation.

In every case the contemplation of creation is provisional. It serves a higher end, in the same way that the acquiring of virtues serves the higher goal of knowledge. "We seek after virtues for the sake of the reasons of created things [διὰ τοὺς λόγους τῶν γεγονότων], and from these we pass to contemplation of the Logos who gives them their being. And the Logos is accustomed to manifest himself in the state of prayer" (Prayer 52).[210] This explanation from the *Chapters on Prayer* describes the same movement that is found in M 118–20, and it adds to our understanding a focus on Christ in his dimension as Logos. As Logos, he has placed his reasons (λόγοι) in creation so that he can eventually be known in his eternal condition as Logos.[211]

M 119 says that this contemplation of created things makes one wise. This is not an arbitrary use of language for Evagrius. Wisdom, we have already seen, is associated with contemplation of corporeals and incorporeals, that is, with created things in their various conditions.[212] But why is *wise* the word that Evagrius associates with this particular kind of contemplation? For him the reason is clear. It is precisely because Christ "made all things with

---

[210] Similarly expressed in Prayer 132: "Let the virtues which have to do with the body accord to those of the soul and let those of the soul accord to those of the spirit. And let these accord to immaterial and substantial knowledge." See also KG III, 48, 61.

[211] See the longer development, very neatly explained, in Ep Fid 7, lines 31–39; see also In Eccl 1:2, examined below in the commentary on M 136.

[212] The classic expression of this is TP 89, a text we have encountered at many points throughout this study. To focus on the present point there could be added In Prov 1:2 (G 3), 6:20, 22 (G 79), 7:4 (G 88); KG III, 57.

wisdom."[213] By means of coming to know the "manifold wisdom" with which he created the world, the monk passes beyond to know Christ as Logos.[214] And through the Logos one knows God. All this is neatly and swiftly summarized as Evagrius offers two possible explanations of the psalm verse "In your light we shall see light" (Ps 35:10). He says, "In the contemplation of created things we shall see Christ, or in the knowledge of Christ we shall see God" (In Ps 35:10 [PG 12:1316B).

3. THE IMAGES

A question: In these proverbs how tightly are the incarnational and eucharistic images related to the conditions they describe? That is, is there some particular reason for associating Christ's flesh with the virtues of *praktikē*, or for associating his blood with the contemplation of created things, or for associating his breast with the knowledge of God? I think that in each of the correspondences of these proverbs there is an immediate coherence, a solid reason for the association that Evagrius establishes, and I shall try to indicate what I think it to be. But these are proverbs where it is also helpful to turn to some of Evagrius's possible sources, for the proverbs in themselves are so cryptic that their fullest sense seems to best unfold when placed in the con-

---

[213] Cf. Ps 103:24 as cited in KG I, 14; see also KG II, 1, 2. Origen has a longer explanation of the concept in *Commentary on John*, I, 39.

[214] The theme of "manifold wisdom," an expression taken from Eph 3:10, is very common when Evagrius speaks of this particular contemplation. See KG I, 43; II, 2, 21; III, 11; IV, 7; V, 84; Prayer 85; In Prov 27:9 (G 333). In the same way that Evagrius distinguishes between the Logos in his eternal condition and the reasons placed in creation, he also distinguishes between Christ as eternal Wisdom and the manifold wisdom with which the world was created. See In Prov 7:4 (G 88). In his comment on this text Géhin sees an allusion to the idea of Christ as a created intellect, but it seems to me that the text means to express something different, namely, that the wisdom involved in creation is not to be simply identified with the Son of God, who in other scriptural texts is called Wisdom but not in the text on which Evagrius is commenting. "Σοφίαν δὲ ἐνταῦθα λέγει οὐ τὸν υἱὸν τοῦ θεοῦ." See Géhin, SC 340, 188–89. The wisdom is manifold in that, according to the text from Ep Mel cited above, there are "immensity, taste, and color"; there are "rivers, torrents, and streams." More specifically, it is manifold because of the various worlds in which the fallen rational beings have been placed by providence.

text of the theological tradition that likely gave rise to them. Thus, for each of the correspondences of these proverbs I will indicate in what follows first what I think the immediate coherence to be and then what sources may have influenced Evagrius.

Flesh Associated with the Virtues of Praktikē

Behind this association stands the idea of why humans are found to be in the flesh in the first place and why Christ is in the flesh. The flesh is given to the fallen mind as its instrument. It is by establishing virtue in the flesh (or more accurately, by establishing virtue in the various parts of the soul which is in the flesh) that the mind is prepared again for the knowledge of God from which it fell. "Those who nourish the flesh wrongly and take thought for it, exciting its desires [εἰς ἐπιθυμίας] (Rom 13:14) should blame themselves and not the flesh. For the ones who know the grace of the creator are they who by means of this body obtain passionlessness of the soul and to some extent perceive the contemplation of beings [θεωρία τῶν ὄντων]" (TP 33).[215] It is by means of the body that passionlessness is reached. It is also by means of the body that "to some extent" contemplation of beings, or created things, is reached.[216] Eventually—and this is a sign of necessary progress—one reaches this contemplation even without the body.[217]

Christ is not in the flesh for the same reason that other humans are. He is not in it as a fallen mind but in order to help fallen minds (cf. Ep Mel 11–12). And among the helps he provides is a model for the proper use of the flesh.[218] The virtues themselves are this model. Because the mind is a soul in a body, it is subject to sensation (αἴσθησις) and, "It is by the sensations

[215] This text was already cited in part in the discussion on proper use of the flesh in imitating of Christ, as in M 21. See the discussion there.

[216] On the virtual equivalence of θεωρία τῶν γεγονότων and τῶν ὄντων, see Guillaumont, SC 171, 500–501, 623.

[217] See KG IV, 70: "Not to everyone is it given to say, 'Flee my soul from your prison' (cf. Ps 141:8), but to those who are able by means of purity of the soul and without this body to perceive the contemplation of created things." Greek text in Hausherr, "Nouveaux fragments," 231.

[218] This was the point of M 21.

that the passions are naturally set in motion. If love and temperance are present, the passions are not set in motion; but if they are absent, then the passions move" (TP 38). What M 118 is proposing is flesh (Christ's flesh!) in which love and temperance and perforce all the virtues are present.[219] The proverb is proposing flesh (Christ's flesh!) which is passionless and which, leaving behind what comes from the flesh ("adultery, fornication, licentiousness, idolatry," and the rest[220]), would know how to "perceive the contemplation of created things."[221] Thus, Christ's very flesh is virtue itself, each of the virtues of *praktikē*. The monk's flesh is involved in a struggle between either the passions being set in motion or love and temperance being present. Christ's flesh is the monk's victory in this struggle precisely because Christ's flesh is virtue itself. Thus, "he who eats it, passionless shall he be."

Origen—or at any rate, the theological tradition indebted to Origen—is likely Evagrius's source for such thinking. For Origen, the Logos forms himself in each person by means of the practice of the virtues. Among the functions or names of Christ (ἐπίνοια) are found the virtues. In his *Commentary on Matthew* is found the striking statement, "For Christ is each virtue" (XII, 14).[222] Or even stronger still is the remark in the *Commentary on John:* "The Logos, or more generally the Lord, is all virtue, entirely animated and alive" (XXXII, 11).[223] This statement, stressing as it does Christ's being alive in the virtues, very closely identifies the Logos with the virtues.[224] To practice the virtues, then, would be,

---

[219] Remember that love is the principal virtue for the irascible part of the soul, while temperance is the same for the concupiscible.

[220] Gal 5:19 as cited above in In Ps 26:2.

[221] As expressed in KG IV, 70 and TP 53.

[222] GCS Origenes X, p. 97, lines 2-22 for the whole development. The Greek reads, ὁ Χριστὸς γάρ, ἡ πᾶσα ἀρετή.

[223] GCS Origenes IV, p. 444, line 128. The Greek reads, ὁ λόγος δέ, καὶ ἁπαξαπλῶς ὁ κύριος, ἡ πᾶσα ἔμψυχος καὶ ζῶσα ἀρετή.

[224] For similar examples of Origen identifying Christ himself with his attributes, see also *Commentary on John*, I, 9 (GCS Origenes IV, p. 14, lines 52-53): "Let no one be surprised if we have understood Jesus to be announced in the Gospel under a plurality of names of good things." There follows a long list of examples; see also *Contra Celsum*, V, 39.

according to Origen, to participate in the very person of Christ. This is what Evagrius has managed to state so succinctly and provocatively in M 118.[225]

However, if Origen is the source for Evagrius's identification of Christ with each of the virtues, he cannot have been the source for the way in which M 118 reaches its climax, namely, in passionlessness. It is well known that Origen intentionally avoided this term, which he feared (rightly, it turns out) was subject to misunderstanding. Evagrius seems to have taken it into his vocabulary directly from Clement, even if his own understanding of the term is much more nuanced than Clement's.[226] Evagrius shares with Clement the idea of passionlessness as the summit of the ethical life.[227] But he also shares with him the notion of reaching passionlessness by means of imitation of Christ, who is the divine Logos concretely come to the aid of human moral striving.[228]

[225] For oneness among the virtues in Clement, see Méhat, *Étude sur les 'Stromates' de Clément d'Alexandrie*, 364ff. Compare Gregory of Nyssa, *Homily on Ecclesiasticus* V: "The one who has his eyes on the head (and by head we understand the beginning of all things) has his eyes on Christ, for Christ is virtue in its entirety [ἡ παντελὴς ἀρετή] in truth, in justice, in incorruptibility, in all good." Greek text in *Gregorii Nysseni Opera*, V, p. 358, lines 7–10. For oneness among the virtues in Evagrius, see Guillaumont, SC 170, 53–55.

[226] See Guillaumont, SC 170, 98–112, and "Le gnostique chez Clément d'Alexandrie et chez Évagre le Pontique," 198.

[227] This theme in Clement is usefully examined by Lilla, *Clement of Alexandria, A Study in Christian Platonism and Gnosticism*, 103–17. For Clement the ethical life is composed of two stages. First is μετριοπάθεια. But the perfect ethical life is expressed in the combination of two ideals, ἀπάθεια and ὁμοίωσις Θεῷ. The ideals are combined in this chain of reasoning: God is completely ἀπαθής. The way in which one becomes like God is by being passionless. Therefore, there is a tendency in Clement to identify ὁμοίωσις Θεῷ with ἀπάθεια.

[228] For Clement, not only God but also Christ is ἀπαθής. He is the teacher and model of perfect ἀπάθεια. It is Christ who must be imitated in order for one to become like God in passionlessness. Lilla gives a number of references to this theme in Clement (*Clement of Alexandria*, 111). Perhaps among the most relevant for the present study are the following: "[The Saviour] was completely passionless, inaccessible to any movement of the passions" (*Stromata* VI, 71, 2 in GCS, Clemens II, p. 467, lines 13–15). "[The perfect man] is compelled to become like his teacher in passionlessness" (*Stromata* VI, 72, 1 in GCS, Clemens II, p. 468, lines 3–4). "The image of God is the divine and royal Logos, the passionless man" (*Stromata* V, 94, 5 in GCS Clemens II, p. 388, lines 13–16). Lilla's study notes that though

Blood Associated with Contemplation of Created Things

It is not possible to establish quite so precisely with texts from his writings why Evagrius would make a connection between blood and contemplation of created things. He speaks far less frequently of blood than he does of flesh and body. Yet several dimensions of blood considered in itself and in its symbolic power indicate that the association is not inappropriate. In relation to flesh, blood represents a more interior dimension, more precious, as it were, more life-giving. Contemplation of creation is the same. It is the interior dimension of things, their λόγοι. The same can be said of the eucharistic form of Christ's blood, namely, wine. In relation to bread, it is the more precious, the more festive of the eucharistic elements.[229] Wine is a part of Wisdom's banquet as described in Proverbs 9, providing the scriptural base for M 119's "he who drinks it [blood = wine] by it becomes wise." Evagrius confirms this association in his scholion on "She [Wisdom] has mixed her wine in a bowl" (Prov 9:2). He says, "The bowl is spiritual knowledge which consists in the reasons concerning incorporeals and corporeals and judgment and providence" (In Prov 9:2 [G 104]).[230]

There is another dimension to blood and wine that, from a different perspective, likewise makes them suitable symbols for

---

Clement's ethical ideal of ἀπάθεια owes much to the ethics of Philo and Neoplatonism, it is distinguished from these in that for Clement human reason alone is not sufficient for achieving either moderation of the passions or complete passionlessness. The divinity itself in the person of Christ must come to the aid of human effort. Thus, the intervention of the Logos in human ethics is much more concrete, much more personal in Clement than in Philo or the Neoplatonists. It is in this tradition that M 118–20 stands, emphasizing Christ's role in each stage of spiritual progress. The intervention of the Logos in human ethics of which Clement speaks is "the grace from the Lord" which finds expression in M 122. On grace associated with progress in both *praktikē* and knowledge, see 8 Spirits 18; TP Prologue 2; G 4, 45; KG I, 37, 39; In Ps 106:3; Thoughts 39.

[229] Cf. G 22, where the knowledge of created beings is associated with joy and approachability, and TP 90, where knowledge and joy are associated.

[230] Compare the remark on bread in In Prov 9:5 (G 107) on "Come eat my bread." Evagrius explains, "She did not say 'my meat' because 'solid food is for the perfect' (Heb 5:14)." For wine as an image of *praktikē* come to fruition in knowledge, see TP Epilogue. In KG V, 32 wine is associated with knowledge of incorporeals and water with contemplation of corporeals. This is the cup "that Wisdom mixed" (cf. Prov 9:2). For drink referring to knowledge, see KG V, 13; G 47.

contemplation. This is the temporal dimension of the order in which bread and wine (flesh and blood) are handled by Christ in the Last Supper. *First* he took bread and *then* he took wine, in the same way that *praktikē* comes first and then contemplation. This might seem to be pushing the point were it not for the fact that these fathers did read the scriptural text that closely, and Origen himself says exactly this in a text that very likely could be Evagrius's inspiration not only for M 118–20 but for the other texts in which the typical divisions of the spiritual life are seen in the eucharistic symbols.[231]

Origen is discussing whether or not it seems appropriate to distinguish between the meaning of food and drink and in the course of the discussion offers his reader this challenge:

> You decide whether or not it is possible to apply such a distinction [i.e., such that food refers to action and drink to contemplation] to the text, "My flesh is truly food and my blood truly drink" (John 6:55). Someone might say that action is truly food and contemplation truly drink, and the one who so claims would say that that is why he *first* gave the bread to his disciples (Matt 26:26–27), blessing it and breaking it, because first there is action. And *after this* he took the cup, and giving thanks, gave it to them saying, "Drink of this all of you," since it is necessary that first the things that have to do with praxis must be set down and action done rightly, so that one can thus travel through things to the contemplation of them. (*Commentary on Matthew* XVI, 7)[232]

Thus, with some security it seems possible to suggest that there are at least two reasons for Evagrius's connecting blood with this contemplation: (1) the precious dimensions of blood and wine, and (2) the fact that in the eucharistic action wine comes after bread in the same way that contemplation comes after *praktikē*.

Breast Associated with the Knowledge of God

M 120 continues the forward movement toward greater intimacy with God. The term for this is knowledge of God. The

---

[231] Namely, the other texts examined here: Ep Fid 4; In Eccl 2:25; G 14.
[232] GCS Origenes X, pp. 487–88, lines 17ff. Translation and emphasis mine.

image is the breast of the Lord. The breast is an image that Evagrius uses infrequently.[233] In the present context he is remaining within the imagery of the Last Supper and is obviously inspired by the image of the beloved disciple in John's Gospel, who during the supper "was lying close to the breast of Jesus" (John 13:25).

The expression "knowledge of God" in its precise sense means knowledge of the Trinity for Evagrius.[234] What M 118–20 is saying is that this is a knowledge possible only through the incarnate Logos. Indeed, the image for such knowledge suggested in M 120, the breast, suggests that it is possible only through an intimate relationship with him.[235]

This image of the breast with the associated action of resting against it recalls a passage from Origen's *Commentary on John* that accords well with the way in which M 118, 119, and 120 climax in M 120. Origen says, referring to John the evangelist, "There is left to him who lay on Jesus' breast [τῷ ἐπὶ τὸ στῆθος ἀναπεσόντι τοῦ Ἰησου] the greatest and most complete discourses about Jesus. For none of these [other evangelists] so perfectly manifested his divinity as did John. . . . No one can seize the sense of [this gospel] unless he lay on Jesus' breast" (I, 4).[236] It could not be

---

[233] See Ep Mel 13, lines 519–22: "the great treasury which contains all the stocks of wisdom: this is the breast of Christ to which John lay close during the Supper. John was told who the traitor was; he understood it through the Supper. Thus without the Supper and without the Breast, the traitor was not known." For an image close to breast, see KG IV, 66.

[234] This is a logical deduction. Evagrius speaks of many kinds of knowledge, and for him knowledge of the Trinity is the highest form. Thus, this is what knowledge of God would mean for him. Sometimes he specifies "knowledge of the Trinity"; other times he contents himself with the expression "knowledge of God." Thus, "knowledge of God" in the opening proverb M 3 is made explicit by "the Holy Trinity" in the closing proverb, M 136. Likewise, see the commentary on M 72, where "knowledge of God" and the placement of the proverb were seen to stand in special relation to the Trinity as mentioned in M 136. See the commentary on M 136 below for the text of In Eccl 1:2, in which "knowledge of God" is put in apposition with "knowledge of the Trinity."

[235] The theme of intimacy or friendship with Christ is prominent in the *Scholia on Proverbs*. See the remarks with many references by Géhin in SC 340, 53–54. On this same theme as shown in the letters, see Bunge, *Briefe*, 74–75.

[236] GCS Origenes IV, p. 8, lines 8–17. Translation mine.

claimed with certainty that Evagrius knew this passage, though it is not unlikely. However, I wish to draw attention to the way in which Origen makes use of the suggestive incident from John's Gospel. John's Gospel speaks so loftily because the evangelist lay his head on Jesus' breast. To understand what this Gospel is saying, each reader must likewise lay his head on that breast. Evagrius works with the image in a similar way, trained as he is in the biblical tradition of Origen. For Origen also, resting the head on the breast of Jesus is a means of understanding the Godhead. Like Origen, Evagrius does not refer himself simply to John, but in his proverb invites the reader to do what John did. "He who rests against it, a theologian shall he be."

Theologian

The use of the word *theologian* here can move the meditating mind in any number of directions. Most immediately, the term is still within the Johannine imagery of the proverb; for it was the evangelist John who was known, well before Evagrius's time, by the title "the theologian."[237] Evagrius develops some of his most profound trinitarian theology on the basis of John's Gospel, particularly on the remarkable chapter 17.[238] His use of *theologian* in this proverb would be designed to suggest to the reader the line of thinking that emerges from a meditation on the Johannine pages.

Also to be associated with what Evagrius is suggesting here is the developed teaching on the theme of theologian by Gregory Nazianzus, who likewise was known to later generations by the title "the theologian."[239] Just one of Gregory's remarks on this theme can serve as an example of his influence on Evagrius's

---

[237] On this title for John, known since the time of Origen and developed in Eusebius, see Batiffol, "Theologia, Théologie," 215ff.

[238] See Bunge, "Mysterium Unitatis."

[239] For Gregory's understanding of this theme and for the title applied to him, see Szymusiak, *Elements de Théologie de l'homme selon Saint Grégoire de Nazianze,* 7–24. For the esteem with which Gregory and Evagrius regarded each other, see Gregory, *Letter* 228, and in Evagrius TP Epilogue; Ep Fid 1, line 16; Lt 12, 23, 46. On these letters as addressed to Gregory, see Bunge, *Briefe,* 177–78. On Gregory and the title "vessel of election," see the commentary on M 65.

conception of the theologian. "Do you want to become a theologian some day and be worthy of the divinity? Then keep the commandments; advance by means of observing commands. For praxis is a step toward contemplation. Out of the body, love the labor that concerns the soul" (*Oration* 20.12).[240] In this brief statement we see the same movement as described in M 118–20, beginning in *praktikē* and finishing in theology.

As in Gregory—perhaps more so than in Gregory—*theology* and *theologian* in Evagrius refer to a kind of knowledge far beyond what can be gained through discursive reasoning.[241] *Theology* is a term that Evagrius uses exclusively for what lies at the end of all lesser forms of knowledge and contemplation. Again, this is knowledge of the Trinity. "The end of *praktikē* is love; the end of knowledge is theology. Faith is the beginning of the one. Natural contemplation is the beginning of the other" (TP 84).[242] This text draws a fine distinction between knowledge and theology, the one a beginning, the other an end. The knowledge referred to is a knowledge that begins with natural contemplation but finishes with theology, or knowledge of God.[243] All this suggests that by "knowledge of God" in M 120 Evagrius means to refer to knowledge of the Trinity.

This suggestion can be made more firm by examining a series in the *Chapters on Prayer* in which the trinitarian dimension of knowledge of God climaxes with the term *theologian*. The chapters in question read as follows:

58. Even if the mind gets beyond the contemplation of corporeal nature, it has not yet seen the place of God in its perfection. For it can remain in the knowledge of intelligible beings and be caught up in their multiplicity. 59. If you want to pray, then you need God, who gives prayer to the one who prays (1 Sam 2:9). Therefore, call on him saying, hallowed be thy name; thy kingdom come (Matt

---

[240] SC 270, 82. Translation mine.

[241] The same could be said for the way in which the evangelist John speaks of knowledge.

[242] This text is directly in line with the use of *theology* in the similar texts already examined: TP Prologue 8; Ep Fid 4, lines 16–22; see also TP 1; G 13; In Prov 1:1 (G 2); 22:20 (G 247).

[243] The text from TP Prologue 8 makes this clear: "love is the gate to natural knowledge, and this knowledge gives way to theology."

6:9–10), that is, thy Holy Spirit and thy Only-begotten Son. For thus did he teach when he said that the Father is worshiped in Spirit and in Truth (John 4:23–24). 60. The one who prays in Spirit and in Truth no longer honors the creator on the basis of his creatures but praises him out of his own [God's] self. 61. If you are a theologian, you will pray truly. And if you pray truly, you will be a theologian. (Prayer 58–61 [PG 79:1180A–B])

A few remarks about each of these chapters can help us to see their relevance for interpreting M 120. Prayer 58 suggests that it is not enough simply to get beyond a contemplation of corporeal things. Prayer 59 goes on to say that if one wants to pray,[244] then God himself is needed. Then the chapter specifies that by this is meant God as Spirit and Son, who make possible the worship of the Father in Spirit and in Truth.[245] Prayer 60 is about intratrinitarian prayer. Spirit and Truth refer to the Holy Spirit and the Son. Their *eternal* relationship with the Father is participated in by the one who prays. This is praising God out of his own self (i.e., out of the Spirit and the Son), as opposed to praising him from the *temporal* creation. Prayer 61 climaxes the development by equating the theologian with one who truly prays and vice versa. The chapter means by its use of "truly" to refer to the Son.[246] Thus, we might paraphrase in a way that helps to see the close connection with M 120: if you are a theologian, you pray in the Son; if you pray in the Son, you are a theologian. Or we might paraphrase in a way that helps to see the trinitarian dimensions: if you know the Trinity (= theologian), you truly pray. And if you truly pray, you know the Trinity. Or, finally, to finish this discussion where it began: he who rests against the breast of the Lord, a theologian shall he be.

If *theology* is a term by which Evagrius means to connote a kind of knowledge far above what human reasoning can reach,

---

[244] Prayer is the *Chapters on Prayer's* way of expressing knowledge; see Prayer 10, 39, 45, 69, 70, 76, 85, 86, 145.

[245] Bunge calls this chapter "the key to Evagrius's trinitarian mysticism" and demonstrates that *spirit* and derivative words refer to the Holy Spirit, while *truth* and derivative words refer to the Logos ("The 'Spiritual Prayer,'" 196–98; "Mysterium Unitatis," 467).

[246] Demonstrated by Bunge in the articles cited in the previous note; see Prayer 10, 40, 54, 55, 80, 153.

this is already true for other dimensions of knowledge. "The knowledge of Christ requires not a dialectical soul but a seeing one. For dialectic is found among impure souls, but vision is only for pure souls" (KG IV, 90).[247] In the context of the present chain from *Ad Monachos*, such vision is possible for those who have become pure through the virtues of *praktikē* and become passionless.

Among the various statements in which Evagrius expresses himself in this regard—and there are many (Lt 62; G 4, 45; KG VI, 22)—perhaps none is quite so expressive and filled with feeling as is M 120. This results from the way in which Evagrius uses the image of resting against the Lord's breast. It is a proverb like this which gives the fullest and clearest sense of what Evagrius intends by placing knowledge as the highest goal of the spiritual life. He is not speaking of a dialectical knowledge. He is speaking of a knowledge that comes about through intimacy with the Incarnate Lord. The Incarnate Lord shares with the one who rests his head against his breast his own "knowledge" of God, which is a "knowledge" of himself being God, God the Logos, the eternally begotten Son. As John "the theologian" himself said, "No one has ever seen God; God the only Son, who is in the bosom of the Father, he has made him known" (John 1:18).

My stress on the trinitarian dimensions into which meditation on M 120 eventually leads may seem at first glance a case of reading too much into the text, but I am persuaded that it is not. The case rests first of all on what Evagrius means by the expression "knowledge of God." Second, it rests on how Evagrius understands the role of Christ in every stage of the spiritual journey. Christ helps the monk through *praktikē*. He shows him the manifold wisdom of the creation. He eventually reveals to him the Father. Finally, the case rests on the kind of knowledge that is implied by the term *theologian*.

---

[247] Greek text in Muyldermans, *Evagriana* (1931), 59. The Greek text has "knowledge of Christ," while the Syriac has "knowledge of God." On the reasons for choosing the Greek over the Syriac here, see Bunge, *Briefe*, 379 n. 1.

CONCLUSION

I hope that this study of M 118–20 can have served to show what a fine jewel Evagrius has carved in them. The beauty of a jewel–just a small stone–especially emerges when cut and polished. These three small proverbs, together one jewel, have been cut and polished with precision by Evagrius. The threefold movement from *praktikē* to contemplation to knowledge has been cut into the flesh, the blood, and the breast of the Lord. These have been polished by the mystery of the Eucharist itself, by the action of eating, drinking, and resting against the Lord's breast. As the jewel is turned, it shimmers ever more brightly. First, passionlessness shines. At the next angle it is wisdom that is seen, and something about it is as beautiful as the whole wonderful creation. Finally, the jewel is turned such that its whole splendor is seen in a glance. It is the mystery of the Trinity itself that shines there. And how wonderful that such a mystery could shine in so small a stone: someone resting his head on the breast of the incarnate Logos.

Commentary on M 136

> Knowledge of incorporeals raises the mind
> and presents it before the Holy Trinity.
>
> Γνῶσις ἀσωμάτων ἐπαίρει τὸν νοῦν
> καὶ τῇ ἁγίᾳ τριάδι παρίστησιν αὐτόν.

It seems appropriate to conclude these commentaries on selected proverbs of *Ad Monachos* by finishing where the whole text finishes, namely, with a proverb on the Holy Trinity. My scope here is not to present the details of Evagrius's trinitarian doctrine–the proverb does not do that–but rather to assess the significance and the mood created by finishing *Ad Monachos* with a proverb such as this.[248]

---

[248] For studies that summarize much of Evagrius's trinitarian teaching, see Bunge, "In Geist und Wahrheit," in *Geistgebet*, 88–109, and "'The Spiritual

Throughout the writings of Evagrius, knowledge of the Holy Trinity is mentioned very frequently as the goal of all knowledge. More precisely, we could say knowledge of the Father as he is known by the Son and the Spirit. The direction of movement toward this knowledge, "theology," has already been traced in the previous commentary. And yet, though Evagrius often mentions the Trinity and often alludes to it in the most subtle of ways,[249] it is really only in two works that he enters at any length into what could be called actual theological discussion on the Trinity. These are his *Epistula Fidei* and the *Letter to Melania*. What he says in these works functions as a guide for ferreting out what he says or only suggests more cryptically elsewhere.[250]

In *Ad Monachos* the Trinity is mentioned in three different proverbs. All three are appropriately found in the part of the text that follows the turning point of M 107, namely, that part devoted exclusively to knowledge. In M 110 the Trinity is placed in relation to the other contemplations: "Better is knowledge of the Trinity than knowledge of the incorporeals; / and the contemplation of it is beyond the reasons for all the aeons."[251] In M 134,

---

Prayer.'" This article and this chapter are basically the same study; but the German version, which is newer than the English, is fuller in its notes.

[249] As was seen for example in Prayer 58–61, examined in the previous commentary.

[250] Among a number of possible examples of Evagrius's refusal to enter into theological details about the Trinity, some few can suffice: "Let the ineffable [the reference is to the Trinity] be worshiped in silence" (G 41). Guillaumont comments on the influence of Greek philosophy, especially Neoplatonism, and of Gregory Nazianzus on Evagrius's thinking here (see SC 356, 169). "Do not overdo [thinking about] the Trinity, but simply believe and adore. For the one who overdoes it does not believe" (Inst ad mon [PG 79:1237D]). After some few remarks about the nature of the Trinity, Evagrius says, "You would not be able to comprehend the nature of God, even if you were to fly with wings. God is incomprehensible" (Inst ad mon [PG 79:1237C]). "Just as after perfect health is restored, medicine is vain, so also vain are the reasons of aeons and worlds after the knowledge of the Holy Trinity" (In Eccl 1:2 [G 2]). The fuller passage will be discussed below. "Remember Christ who guards you, / and do not forget the adorable Trinity" (V 56).

[251] The reader is reminded of what was observed about M 110 in the analysis of the chains. It is grouped with other proverbs (M 107–10) as a part of the first movement after the turning point, a movement that previews themes to be found in what follows. The mention of the Trinity in M 110 was seen to preview the end

as the text is wrapping up themes, there is a warning against a trinitarian heresy, namely, considering the Trinity as a creature: "He who says that the Holy Trinity is a creature blasphemes God."[252] M 136 speaks of the mind being presented before the Holy Trinity. In none of these three do we have any specific information or discussion of the Trinity per se. Evagrius's attitude toward the Trinity as expressed in *Ad Monachos* is an echo of what he once exclaimed elsewhere in its regard: "Let the ineffable be worshiped in silence" (G 41).

What I wish to draw attention to here is the way in which the whole text concludes with this open-ended mention of the Trinity. As I have argued in the analysis of the chains, with *Ad Monachos* Evagrius wants to create a text that in its very structure is an image of the various dimensions of the journey toward God. Given his notion that the Trinity is the goal of all monastic striving, he could not have finished this text, it would seem, in any other way than by mentioning it.

As a single proverb, M 110 is more complete in the types of contemplations it mentions; whereas M 136 only mentions knowledge of the incorporeals alongside the Trinity. (But, of course, M 136 is to be read in conjunction with the proverb immediately preceding, which mentions contemplations of worlds and reasons of judgment and providence.) Appropriately, the last knowledge that M 136 mentions before that of the Trinity is knowledge of the incorporeals. The worlds of M 135 and the providence and judgment mentioned there are the worlds to which the fallen minds, once incorporeal, were assigned at the judgment, an assignment designed by providence to lead the mind back to its incorporeal condition. Incorporeals are the subject of salvation. They are the mind contemplated in its original condition before its fall into the condition of a soul in a body. So, quite logically incorporeals are mentioned just before the mention of the Trinity; for the Trinity is that which the incorporeal mind was created to know.

---

of the whole text, ending the movement of the first chain of the second major block in the same way that the movement of the whole will end.

[252] This means considering the Son and the Holy Spirit as creatures. Much of *Epistula Fidei* is devoted to combatting these heresies.

Yet I think the real strength of the proverb, its suggestiveness and beauty, is the way in which it moves on from this knowledge of the incorporeals to speak of the mind being presented before the Holy Trinity. A mood is created by what the proverb leaves unsaid. The mind is presented before the Holy Trinity in a kind of silence that suggests that it must wait for the Trinity to reveal itself.[253] Absolutely every other thing drops away from the mind at this point, all the beauty contemplated in the creation, all the reasons discovered therein, the condition of the mind before the fall (incorporeal), after the fall (corporeal), and after its redemption (incorporeal)—all this becomes, to quote Ecclesiastes, "vanity of vanities, vanity of vanities; all things are vanity" (Eccl 1:2). With a suggestiveness echoing M 136, Evagrius comments on this verse. "To those who enter into the intelligible church and marvel at the contemplation of created things, the Logos says, 'Do not think that this is the final end [τὸ ἔσχατον τέλος][254] which is held in store for you by the gospel promises. All that is vanity of vanities before the knowledge of God himself. Just as after perfect health is restored, medicine is vain, so also vain are the reasons of aeons and worlds after the knowledge of the Holy Trinity'" (In Eccl 1:2 [G 2]).

At this point in our study it is perhaps no longer necessary to draw attention to the significance of the way in which M 136 specifies that it is the *mind* that is presented before the Trinity. The knowledge of the Trinity is precisely what the mind was created for. Many texts could be collected on this theme,[255] but here I would like to draw attention to several that seem especially characteristic and which fit the mood of M 136 particularly well.

The opening chapters of the *Praktikos* speak (with a precision

---

[253] "If you want to pray, then you need God" (Prayer 59, as found in the preceding commentary).

[254] Cf. τέλος in M 3 and Ep Fid 7, a detailed discussion of the significance of the term.

[255] Just to take examples from the *Kephalaia Gnostica* that specifically mention the mind and the Trinity: see KG I, 74; III, 6, 12, 13, 15, 30, 33, 69, 71; V, 52. KG I, 74 and V 52 express notions especially similar to M 136. For studies that examine this, citing many texts from other Evagrian writings, see Hausherr, *Leçons*, 16–18, 93–96, 117–19, 147–49; Bunge, "Der Zustand des Intellektes," in *Geistgebet*, 74–87; *Briefe*, 88ff., 137.

characteristic almost of a dictionary's definitions) of both a three-fold and a twofold division of the monk's spiritual journey. "1. Christianity is the dogma of Christ our Savior, which is composed of *praktikē,* natural contemplation, and theology. 2. The kingdom of heaven is passionlessness of the soul, along with true knowledge of beings. 3. The kingdom of God is knowledge of the Holy Trinity, coextensive with the substance of the mind and surpassing its incorruptibility" (TP 1–3). TP 1 speaks of the same three-fold division around which M 118–20 is structured. TP 2 and 3 distinguish within the realm of knowledge between various levels, and this is done by drawing a distinction between the kingdom of heaven and the kingdom of God.[256] The climax is, not unexpectedly, knowledge of the Trinity. What is noteworthy in the text is the way in which it speaks of this knowledge as being "coextensive with the substance of the mind." This knowledge is what the mind was made for. When the mind meets the knowledge it was made for, it has entered the kingdom of God. The reason this is said to surpass the mind's incorruptibility is that seeing this dimension of the mind is part of the "knowledge of beings" mentioned in TP 2.[257] These "definitions" help us to see why in M 136 Evagrius speaks of the *mind* being presented before the Holy Trinity. Trinity comes to meet mind, to become coextensive with its substance. Put in language more biblical: "The mind is a temple of the Holy Trinity" (Skemmata 34).[258]

In M 136 the mind is both "raised" and "presented." Raising is one of the most common expressions used by Evagrius to describe progress in knowledge.[259] A particularly striking image that he sometimes uses to speak of this upward movement is that

---

[256] TP 2 also nicely shows the border between *praktikē* and knowledge by mentioning passionlessness (*praktikē*'s goal) in conjunction with the first knowledge into which the monk enters after having reached it.

[257] For this interpretation, see Guillaumont, SC 171, 498–502, with texts that further the explanation.

[258] Muyldermans, *Evagriana* (1931), 41.

[259] It is influenced, of course, by how he understands the resurrection. See the commentary above on M 21 and especially Ep Fid 7, 25–31 discussed there. Worth remembering is the definition of the resurrection given in that text: "[He calls] 'resurrection' the passage from material knowledge to immaterial contemplation" (Ep Fid 7, lines 27–28).

of climbing a mountain, and several examples of this can fill out the sense of "raise" as used in M 136. In a letter Evagrius says, "The contemplation of created things has much into which to inquire [πολλὰς ἱστορίας] but knowledge of the Holy Trinity is one. For essential knowledge is revealed naked of passions and bodies. Impossible for the mind that does not climb this mountain to be saved. For an intelligible mountain [νοητὸν ὄρος] is what spiritual knowledge [γνῶσις πνευματική] of the Holy Trinity is, into which heights it is difficult to climb" (Lt 58:4).[260] Toward these difficult heights the text of *Ad Monachos*, with all of the themes "into which it inquires," has been climbing ever upward. In this, its final proverb, it reaches the peak of this "intelligible mountain."

The biblical Mount Sinai is an image of this mountain, and the theophany that occurs there is a manifestation of the condition of the mind, its substance coextensive with the knowledge of the Trinity. "When the mind has 'put off the old man' and 'clothed itself with grace' (Eph 4:22, 24), then it will see its own condition [τὴν αὐτοῦ κατάστασιν] at the time of prayer, looking like a sapphire or the color of heaven. Scripture calls this condition the place of God (cf. Exod 24:9–10 LXX), which was seen by the elders on Mount Sinai" (Thoughts 39). This color of the mind, which is the mind seeing its own condition, this blue of sapphire or of the sky, comes from the Holy Trinity itself. Indeed, it comes from the Trinity being coextensive with the mind, that is, from the Trinity being known by the mind, being known by the mind "at the time of prayer," prayer in Spirit and in Truth, that is, in the Son and in the Spirit. "The condition of the mind is the intelligible 'height' which resembles the color of heaven, over which the light of the Holy Trinity comes at the time of prayer" (Skemmata 4).[261] There is no other knowledge, no other light, for which the mind is ultimately made. "Prayer is a condition of the mind that comes into being alone through the light of the Holy Trinity" (Skemmata 27).[262] All this is echoing in M 136's "raised" mind.

---

[260] Translated from a Greek fragment found in C. Guillaumont, "Fragments grecs," 218, lines 5–9.

[261] Muyldermans, *Evagriana* (1931), 38.

[262] Muyldermans, *Evagriana* (1931), 41.

Evagrius has carried his characteristically careful choice of language through to the very end in speaking of the mind being "presented" before the Trinity. The term is Pauline, and certainly Evagrius meant this proverb to echo the scriptural texts that employ it. It is a term that the scriptures use in eschatological contexts, speaking of coming into the presence of God (or of Christ) after perseverance in a life of virtue. The choice of this word in M 136 would bring the Pauline texts to mind for the monk who knows the scriptures well, and the connection would add to the meditation of M 136 a strong sense of the fact that one arrives at the presence of the Holy Trinity by means of the salvation that Christ achieved. Thus, for example, "you, who once were estranged and hostile in your thinking, doing evil deeds [ἀπηλλοτριωμένους καὶ ἐχθροὺς τῇ διανοίᾳ ἐν τοῖς ἔργοις τοῖς πονηροῖς], he has now reconciled in his body of flesh [ἐν τῷ σώματι τῆς σαρκὸς] through his death, so as to present you [παραστῆσαι ὑμᾶς] holy and blameless and irreproachable before him" (Col 1:21–22).[263]

I have suggested throughout this study that the proverbs work off of each other inside the meditating mind. Perhaps then the remarks of this climax of the text can be appropriately concluded by suggesting a line of meditation provoked by bringing M 136 into contact with the text's turning point, M 107. In only three texts of *Ad Monachos* is the technical term *mind* used, and it is no accident that this sparing use of the term should occur in the text's turning point and in its climax.[264] The images of M 107

---

[263] It is useful to see the other texts where the word is used. Thus, "presenting yourselves to God as those who have been raised from death to life" (Rom 6:13); "knowing that he who raised the Lord Jesus from the dead will raise us also with Jesus and present us with you" (2 Cor 4:14); "For I betrothed you to Christ to present you as a pure virgin to her one man" (2 Cor 11:2); "that we may present every man perfect in Christ" (Col 1:28); "Strive to present yourself to God as one approved, a workman who has no need to be ashamed, correctly handling the word of truth [τὸν λόγον τῆς ἀληθείας]" (2 Tim 2:15); cf. Lt 52:6: "For the scope of the monk is not to loose the mind to these or those thoughts and then to join it again to some others, but rather wholly to present the mind, freed from all impure thought, before Christ." Translated from a Greek fragment found in C. Guillaumont, "Fragments grecs," 219, lines 27–29.

[264] The other instance is M 13, where the term was seen also to carry considerable weight.

were images of a pure mind in a gentle soul. They were seen to be images of Christ and of rational creatures restored by Christ to the mind's original condition. This pure mind is like the morning star in heaven. Or we could say with terminology similar to this, "like the color of heaven, over which [mind] the light of the Holy Trinity comes."[265] Christ has led this mind through the virtues, teaching the soul into which it fell to be a gentle soul. It is a soul that by its imitation of Christ "does not derive evil from its flesh" (M 21). Such a soul is ready for understanding the incorporeals. "Reasons of incorporeals, a gentle monk will know" (M 133). The meditation follows this line of progress through to M 136 again. "Knowledge of incorporeals raises the mind." Christ, the Logos, who taught gentleness (and perforce the other virtues) to the soul did this as a means to an end. "We seek after virtues for the sake of the reasons of created things, and from these we pass to the Logos who gives them their being. And the Logos is accustomed to manifest himself in the state of prayer" (Prayer 52 [PG 79:1177C]). It is from the place of the Logos within the Trinity that the Trinity is known. The pure mind in the gentle soul is the mind being presented before the Holy Trinity, a mind "once estranged and hostile but now reconciled in order to be presented holy and blameless and irreproachable before him."[266]

The interior journey which the monk has traveled in his meditation on *Ad Monachos* has been at once both challenging and consoling. The challenge to the life of virtue and true knowledge never let up in the text. Yet at the same time there grew stronger the promise of knowledge and its upward movement. There was a sweetness that drew the meditator along in hope. But the sweetnesses tasted were destined to be surpassed in knowledge of the Holy Trinity. The text has ended with a presentation before the Trinity which had been covertly promised much earlier. "Sweet is honey, its comb a delight; / but sweeter than both is the knowledge of God" (M 72).

---

[265] As above, in Skemmata 4 on p. 346.
[266] This language taken from Col 1:21–22, cited above.

CONCLUSION

Content and manner of expression, theology and literature—I suggest that in the intimate union between these two dimensions achieved in *Ad Monachos* there lies the text's power to attract. This study has tried both to examine this union and to gauge its effects. It seems possible to me to claim at this point that this text's theological content could not have been expressed without the careful choice of words, the poetic technique, and the literary structure that Evagrius employed. With these Evagrius created poetic proverbs that condense large stores of wisdom into several brief lines that require the reader's own participation to fill in the gaps between the condensation. And this filling in, promoted by the proverb's style, is part of the content supplied by the reader.

Recognizing the especially close connection between content and manner of expression in this text put us in a position to perceive accurately the message Evagrius wished to deliver, which can be considered a sort of mnemonic road map to guide the reader from the first of the virtues to the goal of knowledge of the Holy Trinity. This journey of spiritual progress is the text's content, a content that we saw stresses the intimate connection between *praktikē* and knowledge. This intimate connection is expressed first of all structurally, in the order of the proverbs, in the chain that forms the center of the text (M 63–72), in the movement that prepares for the text's turning point at M 107. This order of proverbs shows how much Evagrius's emphasis on knowledge as a goal is grounded in the very practical wisdom that claims that in order to know, one must transform one's life, or, to express it more theologically as does Evagrius, that one's soul must die Christ's death in order to rise with him.

The theme of the relation of *praktikē* to knowledge is not simply treated in general terms in *Ad Monachos* but is given a concrete and specific shape. Gentleness and love are seen to stand in very strict relationship to the knowledge of God, which is the goal of all monastic striving. Indeed, there is no knowledge unless love and gentleness are given a permanent place in the monk's life. Certainly, this content is one of the clearest messages that emerges both from the entire structure of the text and from some of its most important and most effectively expressed proverbs. Love is the goal of the transformation required for knowledge of God, for the God who is known is Love.

Content and manner of expression, theology and literature—this intimate connection was seen to exist not only in the structure of the whole text but also in the formulation of the individual proverbs. We examined a number of proverbs in detail and saw the range of theological and spiritual reflections that could emerge precisely because of the kind of language the proverb in question uses, be that language with strong scriptural allusions, be it effectively employed metaphors, be it language that vigorously condenses doctrinal positions, or the useful wisdom of *praktikē*. The study of these selected proverbs provided the occasion of detailed comments on some of the most effective formulations not only of *Ad Monachos* but of the whole Evagrian corpus.

Examining the content and manner of expression of *Ad Monachos* offered the opportunity in Part Three of the study to approach from some new angles the questions of Evagrius's relationship to the environments that formed him. *Ad Monachos* showed Evagrius to be very much a poet, a monk, and a philosopher (in the ancient sense of the term). He is a poet in his effective and suggestive use of language in the creation of literary proverbs in the biblical style. In his manner of teaching, which passes on wisdom from monastic fathers that he himself had gained through his own struggles, Evagrius shows himself to be a monk in the mainstream of a tradition. He is a philosopher in the love for wisdom that inspired him to create spiritual exercises that were the fruit of careful meditation on each subject penned and of actual living standing behind and in front of the exercise he creates.

When Evagrius shapes the exercise that *Ad Monachos* represents, he achieves a synthesis whose ingredients are the wisdoms contained in ancient Egyptian monasticism and in ancient philosophy. He is a desert father who delivers the words of scripture organized as a spiritual exercise for those who love wisdom. The monk who practices this exercise is made to live with spiritual questions and divine mysteries over a long slow period of time. He is made to face issues coming from unexpected directions and thereby to discover the overarching coherence which divine providence has hidden within the reasons for things. Yet as poet, monk, and philosopher Evagrius shows himself to be not only someone deeply immersed in biblical, monastic, and philosophical traditions, but also a capable innovator who was able to bring his own particular touch to each of these dimensions.

It may be hoped that the kind of richness discovered here in *Ad Monachos* might effect a new appreciation of this work within the Evagrian corpus. The way in which it holds in balanced arrangement the many various dimensions of the spiritual life can be used as a key for understanding the broader picture of Evagrius's thought when reading those works where he concentrates on one or another dimension only. The way in which the text summarizes in biblical language the whole spectrum of Evagrius's thought can be used to gauge the extent to which Evagrius's thinking is authentically biblical within the exegetical tradition to which he is heir. The way in which the proverbs teach can ask for a clearer recognition of how deeply involved Evagrius was in the monastic culture of fourth-century Egypt.

The attention I have tried to draw in this study to *Ad Monachos* is not meant, however, to suggest a new evaluation of the text only among Evagrian scholars. The text has an attraction, I think, that it can still exercise in contemporary spirituality. I have become convinced that many people can find spiritual guidance in the text, precisely because it is spiritual exercise. It is the biblical word extended to the concrete circumstances in which people who love wisdom today find themselves standing. It both acknowledges and elicits a desire for knowledge of God, which is a perennial longing of the human spirit. The tone with which this knowledge is treated is lofty and subtle in a way worthy of the subject matter. Yet the loftiness is clearly grounded on what has always been a bedrock of Christian common sense: love, very concretely expressed, as the door to knowledge.

Contemporary lovers of wisdom can find in *Ad Monachos* a program that promotes their spiritual progress. It is a program that requires patient transformation of self as the path of coming to know God. The God one comes to know is God who has revealed himself as Trinity. And a new dimension of self, freed from the blindness caused by untamed passions, is known in this process: self as made to know God. *Ad Monachos* is a program that can offer to the world some small part of the kind of theology for which it seems hungry: a theology that balances love and knowledge in the flesh and blood of Christ and where the heights of love and knowledge are found resting against his breast. "For he who rests against it, a theologian shall he be."

ABBREVIATIONS AND EDITIONS
OF PRIMARY SOURCES

Ant   *Antirrhetikos.* Edited by W. Frankenberg. In *Eva-*
              grius Ponticus. Abhandlungen der königlichen
              Gesellschaft der Wissenschaften zu Göttingen,
              Phil.-hist. Klasse Neue Folge 13/2. Berlin, 1912.

Bases   *Rerum monachalim rationes* or *The Bases of the*
              Monastic Life. PG 40:1252–64.

Coptic Life   The Coptic fragment of the life of Evagrius in E.
              Amélineau, *De Historia Lausiaca* (Paris, 1887),
              104–24. Cited according to page numbers.

CSEL   Corpus scriptorum ecclesiasticorum latinorum.

Ep Fid   *Epistula Fidei.* Edited by J. Gribomont. In *Basilio*
              di Cesarea: Le lettre, vol 1. Turin, 1983. Letter 8
              (pp. 84–113) = Evagrius's *Epistula Fidei.* Cited
              with the line numbers of this edition.

Ep Mel   *Epistula ad Melaniam* or *The Letter to Melania.*
              Edited by W. Frankenberg. In *Evagrius Ponticus.*
              Abhandlungen der königlichen Gesellschaft der
              Wissenschaften zu Göttingen, Phil.-hist. Klasse
              Neue Folge 13/2. Berlin, 1912. And G. Vitestam,
              "Seconde partie du Traité, qui passe sous le nom
              de 'La grande lettre d'Évagre le Pontique à
              Mélanie l'Ancienne,'" *Scripta Minora Regiae Soci-*
              etatis Humaniorum Litterarum Lundensis 1963–64,
              no. 3 (Lund, 1964), 3–29. English cited accord-
              ing to M. Parmentier, "Evagrius of Pontus and
              the 'Letter to Melania,'" *Bijdragen, tijdschrift voor*
              filosofie en theologie 46 (1985): 2–38, with his line
              numbers.

Eulog	*Tractatus ad Eulogium Monachum.* PG 79:1093–1140.
G	*The Gnostikos.* Edited by A. and C. Guillaumont. In *Évagre le Pontique: Le Gnostique ou a celui qui est devenu digne de la science.* SC 356. Paris, 1989.
GCS	Die griechische christliche Schriftsteller der ersten [drei] Jahrhunderte
In Eccl	*The Scholia on Ecclesiastes.* Edited by P. Géhin. In *Évagre le Pontique, Scholies a l'ecclésiaste.* SC 397. Paris, 1993. In the citations, G + number (G, standing for Géhin, with the number indicating the scholia in the Géhin edition).
In Prov	*The Scholia on Proverbs.* Edited by P. Géhin. In *Évagre le Pontique, Scholies aux proverbes.* SC 340. Paris, 1987. In the citations, G + number (G standing for Géhin, with the number indicating the scholia in the Géhin edition).
In Ps	*The Scholia on Psalms.* Cited according to the key of Rondeau in "Le commentaire sur les Psaumes d'Évagre le Pontique." PG 12; PG 27. J. B. Pitra, *Analecta sacra spicilegio Solesmensi, parata,* vol. 2, Frascati, 1884; vol. 3, Paris, 1883.
Inst ad mon	*Institutio ad monachos* or *The Instruction to Monks.* PG 79:1236–40, with supplement by Muyldermans, *Le Muséon* 51:198–204.
KG	*The Kephalaia Gnostica.* Edited by A. Guillaumont. In *Les six centuries des "Kephalaia Gnostica" d'Évagre le Pontique.* Patrologia Orientalis, no. 28, fasc. 1, no. 134. Paris, 1958.
LH	*The Lausiac History.* Edited by G. J. M. Bartelink. In *Palladio, La Storia Lausiaca.* Fondazione Lorenza Valla, 1974. Also C. Butler, ed., *The Lausiac History of Palladius.* 2 vols. Cambridge, 1898, 1904.
Lt	*Letters.* Edited by W. Frankenberg. In *Evagrius Ponticus.* Abhandlungen der königlichen Gesell-

schaft der Wissenschaften zu Göttingen, Phil.-hist. Klasse Neue Folge 13/2. Berlin, 1912. With Greek fragments in C. Guillaumont, "Fragments grecs inédits d'Évagre le Pontique," *Texte und Untersuchungen* 133 (1987): 209–21. Paragraph numbers according to Bunge, *Evagrios Pontikos, Briefe aus der Wüste, Eingeleitet, übersetzt und kommentiert von Gabriel Bunge.* Trier, 1986.

M *Ad Monachos.* Edited by H. Gressmann. In "Nonnenspiegel und Mönchsspiegel des Euagrios Pontikos." *Texte und Untersuchungen* 39, no. 4 (1913): 143–65.

Masters and Disciples *Masters and Disciples.* Edited by P. Van den Ven. In "Un opuscule inédit attribué à S. Nil," *Mélanges Godefroy Kurth,* 2:73–81. Liège, 1908.

PG *Patrologiae cursus completus.* Series graeca. Edited by J.-P. Migne. Paris, 1857ff.

PL *Patrologiae cursus completus.* Series latina. Edited by J.-P. Migne. Paris, 1857ff.

Prayer *De Oratione capitula* or *The Chapters on Prayer.* PG 79:1165–1200, with the edition of S. Tugwell, *Evagrius Ponticus: Practikos and On Prayer, translated by Simon Tugwell.* Published privately by the Faculty of Theology, Oxford, 1987.

SC Sources chrétiennes.

Skemmata *Skemmata.* Edited by J. Muyldermans, *Evagriana.* Extrait de la revue *Le Muséon,* vol. 42, augmenté de *Nouveaux fragments grecs inédits,* 38–44. Paris, 1931.

8 Spirits *Tractatus de octo spiritibus malitiae* or *The Eight Spirits of Evil.* PG 79:1145–64.

Thoughts *De Diversis Malignis Cogitationibus* or *The Treatise on Evil Thoughts.* Edited by P. Géhin. In *Évagre le Pontique, Sur les pensées.* SC 438. Paris, 1998.

TP   *The Praktikos.* Edited by A. and C. Guillaumont. In *Évagre le Pontique. Traité Pratique ou Le Moine.* SC 170, 171. Paris, 1971.

V   *Ad Virginem.* Edited by H. Gressmann. In "Nonnenspiegel und Mönchsspiegel des Euagrios Pontikos." *Texte und Untersuchungen* 39, 4 (1913): 143–65.

Vices *De vitiis que opposita sunt virtutibus* or *On Virtues Opposed to Vices.* PG 79:1140–44.

SELECTED BIBLIOGRAPHY

Amélineau, E. *De Historia Lausiaca.* Paris, 1887.

————. *Histoire des Monastères de la Basse-Égypte.* Annales du Musée Guimet, 25. Paris, 1894.

Balthasar, H. U. von. "Die Hiera des Evagrius." *Zeitschrift für katholische Theologie* 63 (1939): 86–106, 181–206.

————. "Metaphysik und Mystik des Evagrius Ponticus." *Zeitschrift für Aszese und Mystik* 14 (1939): 31–47.

Bamberger, J. E. "Desert Calm, Evagrius Ponticus: The Theologian as Spiritual Guide." *Cistercian Studies* 27 (1992): 185–98.

————. *Evagrius Ponticus. The Praktikos. Chapters on Prayer.* Cistercian Studies 4. Kalamazoo, 1981.

Bartelink, G. J. M. *Palladio. La Storia Lausiaca.* Fondazione Lorenza Valla, 1974.

————. "Les rapports entre le monachisme égyptien et l'épiscopat d'Alexandrie." In *ΑΛΕΞΑΝΔΡΙΝΑ: Mélanges offerts à Claude Mondésert S.J.* Paris, 1987.

Battifol, M. "Theologia, Théologie." *Ephemerides Theologicae Lovanienses* 5 (1928): 205–20.

Bernini, G. *Proverbi, versione, introduzione, note.* Rome, 1984.

Berthold, G. "History and Exegesis in Evagrius and Maximus." In *Origeniana Quarta: Die Referate des 4. Internationalen Origeneskongresses (Innsbruck, 2.–6. September 1985),* edited by Lothar Lies, 390–404. Innsbruck/Vienna, 1987.

Bertocchi, P. "Evagrio Pontico." In *Biblioteca Sanctorum,* 5:356–63. Rome, 1964.

Bettiolo, P. *Evagrio Pontico, Per conoscere lui, Exortazione a una vergine. Ai monaci. Ragioni delle osservanze monastiche. Lettera ad Anatolio. Practico. Gnostico. Introduzione, traduzione e note a cura di paolo Bettiolo.* Bose, 1996.

Bianchi, V. "L'anima in Origene e la questione della metensomatosi." *Augustinianum* 26 (1986): 33–50.

Bostock, G. "The Sources of Origen's Doctrine of Pre-Existence." In *Origeniana Quarta, Die Referate des 4. Internationalen Origeneskongresses (Innsbruck, 2.–6. September 1985)*, edited by Lothar Lies, 259–64. Innsbruck/Vienna, 1987.

Bouillet, M. E. "Le vrai 'Codex regularum' de saint Benoît d'Aniane." *Revue Bénédictine* 75 (1965): 345–49.

Bousset, W. *Apophthegmata: Studien zur Geschichte des ältesten Mönchtums.* Tübingen, 1923.

Bouyer, L. *La Spiritualité du Nouveau Testament et des Pères.* Paris, 1960.

Büchler, B. *Die Armut der Armen Ueber den unsprünglichen Sinn der mönchischen Armut.* Munich, 1980.

Bunge, G. *Akedia: Die geistliche Lehre des Evagrios Pontikos vom überdruß.* Cologne, 1989. (Traduzione italiana)

————. "<Créé pour être> une citation scripturaire inaperçue dan le <Peri Archon> d'Origène." *Bulletin de littérature ecclesiastique* 98 (1997): 21–29.

————. *Drachenwein und Engelsbrot, Die Lehre des Evagrios Pontikos von Zorn und Sanftmut.* Würzburg, 1999. (Traduzione italiana: *Vino dei draghi e pane degli angeli.* Magnano, 1999.)

————. "Erschaffen und erneuert nach dem Bilde Gottes: Zu den biblisch-theologischen und sakramentalen Grundlagen der evagrianishcen Mystik." In *Homo Medietas,* edited by Claudia Brinker-von-der Heyde and Niklaus Largier. Bern, 1999.

————. "Évagre le Pontique et les deux Macaire." *Irénikon* 56 (1983): 215–27, 323–60.

————. *Evagrio Pontico, Lettere dal deserto, introduzione e note a cura di Gabriel Bunge.* Bose, 1995.

————. *Evagrios Pontikos, Briefe aus der Wüste, Eingeleitet, übersetzt und kommentiert von Gabriel Bunge.* Trier, 1986.

————. *Evagrios Pontikos, Praktikos oder Der Mönch, Hundert Kapitel über das geistliche Leben.* Cologne, 1989.

————. "Evagrios Pontikos: Der Prolog Des Antirrhetikos." *Studia Monastica* 39 (1997): 77–105.

————. *Das Geistgebet: Studien zum Traktat "De Oratione" des Evagrios Pontikos.* Cologne, 1987.

————. *Geistliche Vaterschaft: Christliche Gnosis bei Evagrios Pon-*

tikos. Regensburg, 1988. (Traduzione italiana: *La paternità spirituale.* Comunità di Bose, 1991.)

————. "Hénade ou Monade? Au sujet de deux notions centrales de la terminologie évagrienne." *Le Muséon* 102 (1989): 69–91.

————. "Introduction aux fragments coptes de l'Histoire Lausiaque." *Studia Monastica* 32 (1990): 79–129.

————. "Mysterium Unitatis: Der Gedanke der Einheit von Schöpfer und Geschöpf in der evagrianischen Mystik." *Freiburger Zeitschrift für Philosophie und Theologie* 36 (1989): 449–69.

————. "Der Mystische Sinn Der Schrift: Anlasslich Der Veroffentlichung der Scholien zum Ecclesiasten des Evagrios Pontikos." *Studia Monastica* 36 (1994): 135–46.

————. "'Nach dem Intellekt Leben': Zum sog. 'Intellektualismus' der evagrianischen Spiritualität." In *Simandron: Festschrift K. Gamber,* edited by W. Nyssen. Cologne, 1989.

————. "Origenismus-Gnostizismus: Zum geistesgeschichtlichen Standort des Evagrios Pontikos." *Vigiliae Christianae* 40 (1986): 24–54.

————. "Praktike, Physike und Theologike als Stufen der Erkenntnis bei Evagrios Pontikos." In *Kirche aus Ost und West: Gedenschrift für Wilhelm Nyssen,* edited by M. Schneider, W. Berschin, 59–72. Cologne, 1995.

————. "The 'Spiritual Prayer': On the Trinitarian Mysticism of Evagrius of Pontus." *Monastic Studies* 17 (1987): 191–208.

————. *Vasi di argilla, la prassi della preghiera personale secondo la tradizione dei santi padri.* Magnano, 1996.

Bunge, G., and Adalbert de Vogüé. *Quatre ermites égyptiens, D'Après Les Fragments Coptes De L'Histoire Lausiaque / Présentés Par Gabriel Bunge; Traduits Par Adalbert De Vogüé.* Spiritualité Orientale, 60. Bégrolles-en-Mauges (Maine-&-Loire): Abbaye de Bellefontaine, 1994.

Burton-Christie, D. *The Word in the Desert, Scripture and the Quest for Holiness in Early Christian Monasticism.* Oxford, 1993.

Butler, C. *The Lausiac History of Palladius.* 2 vols. Cambridge, 1898, 1904.

Chadwick, H. "Origen, Celsus, and the Resurrection of the Body." *Harvard Theological Review* 49 (1948): 83–102.

————. *The Sentences of Sextus: A Contribution to the History of Early Christian Ethics.* Cambridge, 1959.

Chitty, D. J. *The Desert a City.* Oxford, 1966.

Clark, E. *The Origenist Controversy: The Cultural Construction of an Early Christian Debate.* Princeton, 1992.

Colombas, G. *El Monacato Primitivo.* 2 vols. Madrid, 1974.

————. *La Tradición Benedictina: Ensayo histórico.* Vol. 1. Zamora, 1989.

Comello, F. *Evagrio Pontico: Gli otto spiriti malvagi, a cura di Felice Comello.* Parma, 1990.

Congourdeau, M. H., et alia. *Évagre le Pontique, de la prière à la perfection. Au moine Euloge, Sur la Prière.* Paris, 1992.

Conio, C. "Theory and Practice in Evagrius Ponticus." In *Philosophy Theory and Practice: Proceedings of the International Seminar on World Philosophy,* edited by T. M. P. Mahadevan. Madras, 1974.

Contreras, E. "Evagrio Pontico: Su vida, su obra, su doctrina." *Cuadernos Monasticos* 11 (1976): 83–95.

————. "Evagrio Pontico en los catalogos de varones ilustres." *Salmanticensis* 33 (1986): 333–42.

Courtonne, Y. *Saint Basile. Lettres.* Vol. 1. Paris, 1957.

Crouzel, H. *Origène.* Paris, 1985.

————. "Origène, précurseur du monachisme." In *Théologie de la vie monastique,* 15–38. Théologie, 49. Paris, 1961.

————. "Origène a-t-il tenu que le Règne du Christ prendrait fin?" *Augustinianum* 26 (1986): 51–62.

————. "Recherches sur Origène et son influence." *Bulletin de Littérature Ecclésiastique* 62 (1961): 3–15, 105–13.

————. *Théologie de l'image de Dieu chez Origène.* Théologie, 34. Paris, 1956.

Dalmais, I. H. "L'héritage évagrien dans la synthèse de saint Maxime le Confesseur." *Texte und Untersuchungen* 93 (1966): 356–62.

Dattrino, L. *Trattato pratico sulla vita monastica, introduzione, traduzione e note.* Rome, 1992.

Davril, A. "La Psalmodie chez les pères du désert." *Collectanea Cisterciensia* 49 (1987): 132–39.

Dechow, J. F. *Dogma and Mysticism in Early Christianity: Epiphanius of Cyprus and the Legacy of Origen.* Macon, Ga., 1988.

———. "The Heresy Charges Against Origen." In *Origeniana Quarta: Die Referate des 4. Internationalen Origeneskongresses (Innsbruck, 2.–6. September 1985),* edited by Lothar Lies, 112–22. Innsbruck/Vienna, 1987.

———. "Origen's 'Heresy' from Eustathius to Epiphanius." In *Origeniana Quarta: Die Referate des 4. Internationalen Origeneskongresses (Innsbruck, 2.–6. September 1985),* edited by Lothar Lies, 405–9. Innsbruck/Vienna, 1987.

Dekkers, E. "MONACOS, solitaire, unanime, recueilli." In *Fructus Centesimus: Mélanges offerts à Gerard J.M. Bartelink à l'occasion de son soixante-cinquième anniversaire,* edited by A. A. R. Bastiaensen, A. Hilhorst, C. H. Kneepkens, 91-104. Steenbrugis, 1989.

Dempf, A. "Evagrios Pontikos als Metaphysiker und Mystiker." *Philosophisches Jahrbuch der Görresgesellschaft* 77 (1970): 297–319.

Desprez, V. "Des diverses mauvaises pensées (2 partie) traduction V. Desprez, " in *Lettre de Ligugé* 274 (1995): 24–36.

———. "Évagre le Pontique: Pratique, contemplation, prière." In *Lettre de Ligugé* 274 (1995): 8–23.

———. "Protreptique, Parénéntique, traduction V. Desprez," in *Lettre de Ligugé* 278 (1996): 8-17.

Dorival, G. "Origène et la résurrection de la chair." In *Origeniana Quarta: Die Referate des 4. Internationalen Origeneskongresses (Innsbruck, 2.–6. September 1985),* edited by Lothar Lies, 291–321. Innsbruck/Vienna, 1987.

Dornseiff, F. *Das Alphabet in Mystik und Magie.* Leipzig, 1922.

Draguet, R. "L'Histoire Lausiaque, une œuvre écrite dans l'esprit d'Évagre." *Revue d'Histoire Ecclésiastique* 41 (1946): 321–64; 42 (1947): 5–49.

Driscoll, J. *The 'Ad Monachos' of Evagrius Ponticus: Its Structure and a Select Commentary.* Roma, 1991.

———. "*Apatheia* and Purity of Heart in Evagrius Ponticus" in *Purity of Heart in Early Ascetic and Monastic Literature,* edited by H. A. Luckman, L. Kulzer, 141–59. Collegeville, 1999.

———. "Evagrius and Paphnutius on the Causes for Abandonment by God." *Studia Monastica* 39 (1997): 259–86.

―――. "Exegetical Procedures in the Desert Monk Poemen." In *Mysterium Christi: Symbolgegenwart und theologische Bedeutung, Festschrift für Basil Studer,* edited by M. Löhrer and E. Salmann, 155–78. Rome 1995.

―――. "The Fathers of Poemen and the Evagrian Connection." *Studia Monastica* 42 (2000): 27–51.

―――. "Gentleness in the *Ad Monachos* of Evagrius Ponticus." *Studia Monastica* 33 (1990): 295–321.

―――. "A Key for Reading the *Ad Monachos* of Evagrius Ponticus." *Augustinianum* 30 (1990): 361–92.

―――. "Listlessness in *The Mirror for Monks* of Evagrius Ponticus." *Cistercian Studies* 24 (1989): 206–14.

―――. "'Love of Money' in Evagrius Ponticus." *Studia Monastica* 43 (2001): 21–30.

―――. *The Mind's Long Journey to the Holy Trinity: The "Ad Monachos" of Evagrius Ponticus.* Collegeville, 1993.

―――. "Il pensiero malvagio dell'avarizia, o 'Amore del denaro' in Evagrio Pontico." *Parola, Spirito e Vita* 42 (2001): 219–32.

―――. "Penthos and Tears in Evagrius Ponticus." *Studia Monastica* 36 (1994): 147–63.

―――. "The Psalms and Psychic Conversion." *Cistercian Studies* 22 (1987): 99–110.

―――. "Spiritual Progress in the Works of Evagrius Ponticus." In *Spiritual Progress: Studies in the Spirituality of Late Antiquity and Early Monasticism,* edited by J. Driscoll and M. Sheridan, 47–84. Rome, 1994.

―――. "Spousal Images in Evagrius Ponticus." *Studia Monastica* 38 (1996): 243–56.

Duesberg, H. *Les scribes inspirés.* Paris, 1938.

Durand, M.-G. de. "Évagre le Pontique et le 'Dialogue sur la vie de saint Jean Chrysostome.'" *Bulletin de Littérature Eccléstique* 77 (1976): 191–206.

Dysinger, L. "The Significance of Psalmody in the Mystical Theology of Evagrius of Pontus." *Studia Patristica* 30 (1997): 176–82.

Elm, S. "Evagrius Ponticus' *Sententiae ad Virginem.*" *Dumbarton Oaks Papers* 45 (1991): 97–120.

―――. "The *Sententiae ad Virginem* by Evagrius Ponticus and the

Problem of Early Monastic Rules." *Augustinianum* 30 (1990): 393–404.

———. *Virgins of God the Making of Asceticism in Late Antiquity.* Oxford, 1994.

Evelyn White, H. G. *The Monasteries of the Wâdi 'N Natrûn.* Part II, *The History of the Monasteries of Nitria and of Scetis.* New York, 1932.

Festugière, A. J. *Hermes Trismégiste, III.* Paris, 1954.

———. *Historia Monachorum in Aegypto.* Subsidia Hagiographica, 53. Brussels, 1971.

Frank, S. ΑΓΓΕΛΙΚΟΣ ΒΙΟΣ. *Begriffsanalytische und begriffsgeschichtliche Untersuchung zum "Engelgleichen Leben" im frühen Mönchtum.* Münster, 1964.

Frankenberg, W. *Evagrius Ponticus.* Abhandlungen der königlichen Gesellschaft der Wissenschaften zu Göttingen, Phil.-hist. Klasse Neue Folge, 13/2. Berlin, 1912.

Géhin, P. "Un nouvel inédit d'Évagre le Pontique: Son commentaire de l'Ecclésiaste." *Byzantion* 49 (1979): 188–98.

Géhin, P., ed. *Évagre le Pontique, Scholies a l'Ecclésiaste.* Sources Chrétiennes, 397. Paris, 1993.

———. *Évagre le Pontique, Scholies aux proverbes.* Sources Chrétiennes, 340. Paris, 1987.

———. *Évagre le Pontique, Sur les pensées.* Sources Chrétiennes, 438. Paris, 1998.

Gould, G. *The Desert Fathers on Monastic Community.* Oxford, 1993.

———. "A Note on the *Apophthegmata Patrum.*" *Journal of Theological Studies,* n.s. 37 (1986): 133–38.

Grébaut, S. "Sentences d'Évagre." *Revue de l'Orient Chrétien* 20 (1915–17): 211–14, 435–39; 22 (1920–21): 206–11.

Gregg, R. C. *Athanasius, The Life of Antony and The Letter to Marcellinus: Translation and Introduction.* New York, 1980.

Gressmann, H. "Nonnenspiegel und Mönchsspiegel des Euagrios Pontikos." *Texte und Untersuchungen* 39, no. 4 (1913): 143–65.

Gribomont, J., ed. *Basilio di Cesarea. Le lettere,* vol 1. Turin, 1983. Letter 8 (pp. 84–113) = Evagrius's *Epistula Fidei.*

Guillaumont, A. *Aux origines du monachisme chrétien: pour une phénoménologie du monachisme.* Spiritualité Orientale, 30. Bellefontaine, 1979.

————. "La conception du désert chez les moines d'Égypte." *Revue de l'Histoire des Religions* 188 (1975): 3–21.

————. "Démon, 2. Évagre le Pontique." In *Dictionnaire de spiritualité, ascétique et mystique*, 3:196–205.

————. "Évagre et les anathématismes antiorigénistes de 553." *Texte und Untersuchungen* 78 (1961): 219–26.

————. "Evagrius Ponticus." *Theologische Realenzyklopädie*, 10:565–70.

————. "Gnose et Monachisme." In *Gnosticisme et monde hellénistique: Les objectifs du colloque de Louvain-la Neuve (11–14 mars 1980)*, 97-100. Louvain-la-Neuve, 1980.

————. "Le gnostique chez Clément d'Alexandrie et chez Évagre le Pontique." In *ΑΛΕΞΑΝΔΡΙΝΑ: Mélanges offerts à Claude Mondésert S.J.*, 195–201. Paris 1987.

————. "Histoire des moines aux Kellia." *Orientalia Lovaniensia Periodica* 8 (1977): 187–203.

————. "Une inscription copte sur la 'Prière de Jésus.'" *Orientalia Christiana Periodica* 34 (1968): 310–25.

————. "Un philosophe au désert: Évagre le Pontique." *Revue de l'Histoire des Religions* 181 (1972): 29–56.

————. "La 'preghiera pura' di Evagrio e l'influsso del Neoplatonismo." In *Dizionario degli Istituti di Perfezione*, 7:591–95. Rome, 1983.

————. "La prière de Jésus chez les moines d'Égypte." *Eastern Churches Review* 6 (1974): 66–71.

————. "Le problème des deux Macaire dans les Apophthegmata Patrum." *Irénikon* 48 (1975): 41–59.

————. *Les six centuries des "Kephalaia Gnostica" d'Évagre le Pontique*. Patrologia Orientalis, 28, fasc. 1, no. 134. Paris, 1958.

————. "Le travail manuel dans le monachisme ancien: Contestation et valorisation." In *Aux origines du monachisme chrétien: pour une phénoménologie du monachisme*. Spiritualité Orientale, 30, 118–26. Bellefontaine, 1979.

————. "La vision de l'intellect par lui-même dans la mystique évagrienne." *Mélanges de l'Université Saint Joseph* (1984): 255–62.

————. "Les visions mystiques dans le monachisme oriental chrétien." In *Colloque organisé par le Secrétariat d'Etat à la Culture*, 116–27. Paris, 1976.

Guillaumont, A., ed. *Les 'Képhalaia Gnostica' d'Évagre le Pontique et l'histoire de l'Origénisme chez les Syriens.* Patristica Sorbonensia, 5. Paris, 1962.

Guillaumont, A., and C. Guillaumont. "Évagre le Pontique." In *Dictionnaire de spiritualité, ascétique et mystique,* 4:1731–44.

———. "Evagrius Ponticus." *Reallexikon für Antike und Christentum,* 6:1088–1107.

———. "Le texte véritable des 'Gnostica' d'Évagre le Pontique." *Revue de l'Histoire des Religions* 142 (1952): 156–205.

Guillaumont, A., and C. Guillaumont, eds. *Évagre le Pontique: Traité Pratique ou Le Moine.* Sources Chrétiennes, 170, 171. Paris, 1971.

———. *Évagre le Pontique: Le Gnostique ou a celui qui est devenu digne de la science.* Sources Chrétiennes, 356. Paris, 1989.

Guillaumont, C. "Fragments grecs inédits d'Évagre le Pontique." *Texte und Untersuchungen* 133 (1987): 209–21.

Guy, J. C. "Les Apophthegmata Patrum." In *Théologie de la vie monastique,* 73-83. Paris, 1961.

———. "Un dialogue monastique inédit." *Revue d'ascétique et mystique* 33 (1957): 171–88.

———. "Écriture Sainte et vie spirituelle." In *Dictionnaire de spiritualité, ascétique et mystique,* 4:159–64.

———. "Educational Innovation in the Desert Fathers." *Eastern Churches Review* 6 (1974): 44–51.

———. "Note sur l'évolution du genre apophthegmatique." *Revue d'ascétique et mystique* 32 (1956): 63–68.

———. "Recherches sur la tradition grecque des Apophthegmata Patrum." Subsidia Hagiographica, 36. Brussels, 1962.

———. "Remarques sur le texte des *Apophthegmata Patrum.*" *Recherches de Science Religieuse* 43 (1955): 252–58.

Hadot, I. *Arts libéraux et philosophie dans la pensée antique.* Paris, 1984.

Hadot, P. *Exercices spirituels et philosophie antique.* 2d ed. Paris, 1987.

———. *Philosophy as a Way of Life, Edited and with an Introduction by Arnold I. Davidson.* Oxford, 1997.

———. "Théologie, exégèse, révélation, écriture, dans la philosophie grecque." In *Les règles de l'interprétation,* edited by M. Tardieu, 13–34. Paris, 1987.

Hammond, C. P. "The Last Ten Years of Rufinus' Life and the Date of His Move South From Aquileia." *Journal of Theological Studies* 28 (1977): 372–429.

Harl, M. "La préexistence des âmes dans l'oeuvre d'Origène." In *Origeniana Quarta: Die Referate des 4. Internationalen Origeneskongresses (Innsbruck, 2.–6. September 1985)*, edited by Lothar Lies, 238–58. Innsbruck/Vienna, 1987.

———. "Y a-t-il une influence du 'Grec Biblique' sur la Langue Spirituelle des Chrétiens? Exemples tirés du psaume 118 et de ses commentateurs d'Origène à Théodoret." In *La Bible et Les Pères*, 243–62. Paris.

Harmless, W. "Remembering Poemen Remembering: The Desert Fathers and the Spirituality of Memory." *Church History: Studies in Christianity and Culture* (2000): 483–518.

Harmless, W., and R. R. Fitzgerald. "The Sapphire Light of the Mind: The *Skemmata* of Evagrius Ponticus." *Theological Studies* 62 (2001): 498–529.

Hausherr, I. "Centuries." In *Dictionnaire de spiritualité, ascétique et mystique*, 2:416–18.

———. "Contemplation: Évagre le Pontique." In *Dictionnaire de spiritualité, ascétique et mystique*, 2:1775–85.

———. "Les grands courants de la spiritualité orientale." *Orientalia Christiana Periodica* 1 (1935): 114–38.

———. "Ignorance infinie." *Orientalia Christiana Periodica* 2 (1936): 351–62.

———. "Ignorance infinie ou science infinie?" *Orientalia Christiana Periodica* 25 (1959): 44–52.

———. *Les leçons d'un contemplatif: Le Traité de l'Oraison d'Évagre le Pontique*. Paris, 1960.

———. "Nouveaux fragments grecs d'Évagre le Pontique." *Orientalia Christiana Periodica* 5 (1939): 229–33.

———. "L'origine de la théorie orientale des huit péchés capitaux." *Orientalia Christiana* 30 (1933): 164–75.

———. "Par delà l'oraison pure grâce à une coquille: A propos d'un texte d'Évagre." *Revue d'ascétique et de mystique* 13 (1932): 184–88.

———. "Le Traité de l'Oraison d'Évagre le Pontique (Pseudo Nil)." *Revue d'ascétique et de mystique* 15 (1934): 34–93, 113–70.

Hombergen, D. *The Second Origenist Controversy: A New Perspective on Cyril of Scythopolis' Monastic Biographies as Historical Sources for Sixth-Century Origenism.* Rome, 2001.

Hunt, E. D. "Palladius of Helenopolis: A Party and its Supporters in the Church of the Late Fourth Century." *Journal of Theological Studies* 24 (1973): 456–80.

Ivánka, E. von. "ΚΕΦΑΛΑΙΑ: Eine byzantinische Literaturform und ihre antiken Wurzeln." *Byzantinische Zeitschrift* 47 (1954): 285–91.

Jaeger, W. *Early Christianity and Greek Paideia.* Cambridge, Ma., 1961.

Joest, C. "Die Bedeutung von Akedia und Apatheia bei Evagrios Pontikos." *Studia Monastica* 35, no. 1 (1993): 48–53.

Jones, C., G. Wainwright, and E. Yarnold, eds. *The Study of Spirituality.* New York, 1986.

Kelly, J. N. D. *Jerome: His Life, Writings and Controversies.* London, 1975.

Klauser, Th. "Apophthegma." In *Reallexikon für Antike und Christentum,* 1:545–50.

Kline, F. "The Christology of Evagrius and the Parent System of Origen." *Cistercian Studies* 20 (1985): 155–83.

———. "Regula Benedicti 73:8: A Rule for Beginners." In *Erudition at God's Service,* 97–108. Kalamazoo, 1987.

Labate, A. "L'esegese di Evagrio al libro dell'Ecclesiaste." In *Festschrift A. Ardizzoni,* 1:485–90. Rome, 1978.

Lackner, W. "Zur profanen Bildung des Euagrios Pontikos." In *Festschrift H. Gerstinger,* 17–29. Graz, 1966.

Langer, S. *Feeling and Form.* New York, 1953.

Le Boulluec, A. "Controverses au sujet de la doctrine d'Origène sur l'âme du Christ." In *Origeniana Quarta: Die Referate des 4. Internationalen Origeneskongresses (Innsbruck, 2.-6. September 1985),* edited by Lothar Lies, 223–38. Innsbruck/Vienna, 1987.

Leclercq, J. "L'ancienne version latine des Sentences d'Évagre pour les moines." *Scriptorium* 5 (1951): 195–213.

———. *The Love of Learning and the Desire for God.* Translated by C. Misrahi. New York, 1961.

Lefort, L. Th. "A propos d'un aphorisme d'Evagrius Ponticus." *Académie Royale de Belgique: Bulletin de la classe des lettres et des sciences morales et politiques,* 5 série, 36 (1950): 70–79.

Lemaire, J. P. *L'abbé poemen et la Sainte Écruture.* Licentiate thesis, University of Fribourg, 1971.

Levasti, A. "Il Più Grande Mistico Del Deserto: Evagrio Il Pontico (399)." *Rivista Di Ascetica e Mistica* 13 (1968): 242–64.

Lienhard, J. "On Discernment of Spirits in the Early Church." *Theological Studies* 41 (1980): 505–29.

Lilla, S. *Clement of Alexandria: A Study in Christian Platonism and Gnosticism.* Oxford, 1971.

Louf, A. "L'acédie chez Évagre le Pontique." *Concilium* 99 (1974): 113–17.

——. "Spiritual Fatherhood in the Literature of the Desert." In *Abba: Guides to Wholeness and Holiness East and West,* edited by J. R. Sommerfeldt, 37–63. Kalamazoo, 1982.

Louth, A. *Discerning the Mystery: An Essay on the Nature of Theology.* Oxford, 1983.

——. *The Origins of the Christian Mystical Tradition: From Plato to Denys.* Oxford, 1981.

Luibheid, C. *John Cassian, Conferences: Translation and Preface by Colm Luibheid.* New York, 1985.

Marsili, S. *Giovanni Cassiano ed Evagrio Pontico: Dottrina sulla carità e contemplazione.* Rome, 1936.

Méhat, A. *Étude sur les 'Stromates' de Clément d'Alexandrie.* Paris, 1966.

Melcher, R. *Der 8. Brief des hl. Basilius, ein Werk des Evagrius Pontikus.* Münster, 1923.

Messana, V. "La Chiesa orante nella catechesi spirituale di Evagrio Pontico." In *Biblioteca di science religiose* 46, 173–86. Rome, 1982.

——. *Evagrio Pontico. La Preghiera. Introduzione, traduzione e note a cura di Vencenzo Messana.* Roma, 1994.

Miquel, P. *Lexique du désert: étude de quelques mots-clés du vocabulaire monastique grec ancien.* Bellefontaine, 1986.

Moine, N. "Melaniana." *Recherches Augustiniennes* 15 (1980): 3–79.

Mondésert, C. *Clément d'Alexandrie: Introduction à l'étude de sa pensée à partir de l'Écriture.* Paris, 1944.

Mortari, L. *I padri del deserto: detti,* Rome, 1980.

——. *Vita e Detti dei Padri del Deserto.* Rome, 1975.

Moscatelli, F. *Gli otto spiriti della malvagità, sui diversi pensieri della malvagità, traduzione, introduzione e note di Francesca Moscatelli.* Milano, 1996.

Mühmelt, M. "Zu der neuen lateinischen Übersetzung des Mönchsspiegels des Euagrius" *Vigiliae Christianae* 7 (1953): 101–3.

Murphy, F. X. "Evagrius Ponticus and Origenism" In *Origeniana Tertia,* edited by R. P. C. Hanson and H. Crouzel, 253–69. Rome, 1985.

————. *Rufinus of Aquileia (345–411): His Life and Works.* Washington, D.C., 1945.

Muyldermans, J. *A travers la tradition manuscrite d'Évagre le Pontique.* Bibliothèque du Muséon, 3. Louvain, 1932.

————. *Evagriana.* Extrait de la revue *Le Muséon,* v. 44, augmenté de *Nouveaux fragments grecs inédits.* Paris, 1931.

————. *Evagriana.* Extrait de la revue *Le Muséon,* v. 51. Paris, 1938.

————. *Evagriana Syriaca.* Bibliothèque du Muséon, 31. Louvain, 1952.

Neumann, G., ed. *Der Aphorismus: zur Geschichte: Zu den Formen und Möglichkeiten einer literarischen Gattung.* Darmstadt, 1976.

Niescior, L. *Anachoreza W Pismach Ewagriusza Z Pontu.* Kraków, 1997.

Norris, F. "The Authenticity of Gregory Nazianzen's Five Theological Orations." *Vigiliae Christianae* 39 (1985): 331–39.

O'Cleirigh, P. "Knowledge of this World in Origen." In *Origeniana Quarta: Die Referate des 4. Internationalen Origeneskongresses (Innsbruck, 2.–6. September 1985),* edited by Lothar Lies, 349–51. Innsbruck/Vienna, 1987.

O'Laughlin, M. "The Bible, the Demons, and the Desert: Evaluating the *Antirrheticus* of Evagrius Ponticus." *Studia Monastica* 34 (1992): 201–15.

————. "Evagrius Ponticus in Spiritual Perspective." *Studia Patristica* 30 (1997): 224–30.

————. *Origenism in the Desert: Anthropology and Integration in Evagrius Ponticus.* Ann Arbor, 1987.

Parmentier, M. "Evagrius of Pontus and the 'Letter to Melania.'" *Bijdragen, tijdschrift voor filosofie en theologie* 46 (1985): 2–38.

Peterson, E. "Zu griechischen Asketikern, I. Zu Euagrius Ponticus." *Byzantinisch-Neugriechische Jahrbücher* 4 (1923): 5–8.

———. "Zu griechischen Asketikern, II. Noch einmal zu Euagrius Ponticus." *Byzantinisch-Neugriechische Jahrbücher* 5 (1926/27): 412–14.

———. "Zu griechischen Asketikern, III. Zu Euagrius, *Byzantinisch-Neugriechische Jahrbücher* 9 (1930–32): 51–54.

Pitra, J. B. *Analecta sacra spicilegio Solesmensi, parata,* vol. 2, Frascati, 1884; vol. 3, Paris, 1883.

Ramsey, B. *John Cassian: The Conferences, Translated and Annotated by Boniface Ramsey, O.P.* New York, 1997.

Refoulé, F. "La Christologie d'Évagre et l'Origénisme." *Orientalia Christiana Periodica* 27 (1961): 221–66.

———. "Évagre fut-il origéniste?" *Recherches de Science Philosophiques et Théologiques* 47 (1963): 398–402.

———. "La mystique d'Évagre et l'Origénisme." *Vie Spirituelle, Supplément* 64 (1963): 453–72.

———. "Rêves et vie spirituelle d'après Évagre le Pontique." *Vie Spirituelle, Supplement* 56 (1961): 470–516.

Regnault, L. "Les apophthegmes et l'idéal du désert." In *Commandements du seigneur et libération évangélique,* edited by J. Gribomont, 47–79. Studia Anselmiana, 70. Rome, 1977.

———. *Immerwährendes Gebet bein den Vätern.* Cologne, 1993.

———. "La priere continuelle 'monologistos' dan la littérature apophthegmatique." *Irénikon* 47 (1974): 467–93.

———. *Les sentences des pères du désert.* 4 vols. Solesmes, 1966–81.

———. *Les sentences des pères du désert: troisième recueil & tables.* Solesmes, 1987.

———. *La vie quotidienne des pères du désert en Égypte au IV siècle.* Hachette, 1990.

Rondeau, M. J. "Le commentaire sur les Psaumes d'Évagre le Pontique." *Orientalia Christiana Periodica* 26 (1960): 307–48.

———. *Les commentaires patristiques du Psautier (III–V siècles).* Vol. 1. Orientalia Christiana Analecta, 219. Rome, 1982.

Rousseau, P. *Ascetics, Authority, and the Church in the Age of Jerome and Cassian.* Oxford, 1978.

Rubenson, S. "Evagrios Pontikos und die Theologie der Wüste." In *Logos: Festschrift für Luise Abramowski sum 8. Juli 1993,* edited by H. C. Brennecke, E. L. Grasmück, and C. Markshies, 384–401. Berlin/New York, 1993.

————. *The Letters of St. Anthony: Origenist Theology, Monastic Tradition and the Making of a Saint.* Lund, 1990.

Rutherford, R. B. *The Meditations of Marcus Aurelius.* Oxford, 1989.

Sheridan, M. "The Controversy over ἀπάθεια: Cassian's Sources and His Use of Them." *Studia Monastica* 39 (1997): 287–310.

————. "Il mondo spirituale e intellettuale del primo monachesimo egiziano." In *L'Egitto Cristiano, aspetti e probelemi in età tardo-antico,* edited by A. Camplani, 177–216. Rome, 1997.

Skehan, P. "Wisdom's House." In *Studies in Israelite Poetry and Wisdom:* 27–45. Washington, D.C., 1971.

Spoerri, W. "Gnome." In *Der Kleine Pauly,* 2:822–29.

Stewart, C. *Cassian the Monk.* Oxford, 1998.

————. "From λογος to verbum: John Cassian's Use of Greek in the Development of a Latin Monastic Vocabulary." In *The Joy of Learning and the Love of God: Essays in Honor of Jean Leclercq,* 5–31. Kalamazoo, 1995.

————. "Imageless Prayer and the Theological Vision of Evagrius Ponticus." *Journal of Early Christian Studies* 9 (2001): 173–204.

————. "Radical Honesty about the Self: The Practice of the Desert Fathers." *Sobornost* 12 (1990): 25–39.

Stroumsa, G. G. "Ascèse et gnose: aux origines de la spiritualité monastique." *Revue Thomiste* 89 (1981): 557–73.

————. "The Manichaean Challenge to Egyptian Christianity." In *The Roots of Egyptian Christianity,* edited by B. A. Pearson and J. E. Goehring, 307–19. Philadelphia, 1986.

Szymusiak, I. *Elements de Théologie de l'homme selon Saint Grégoire de Nazianze.* Rome, 1963.

Taft, R. "The Egyptian Monastic Office in the Fourth Century." In *The Liturgy of the Hours in East and West,* part 1, chapter 4. Collegeville, 1986.

Tamburini, M. E. "Espejo de Monjes." In *Evagrio Pontico: Tratado de la Oracion, Tratado Practico, Espejo de Monjes, Espejo de Monjas,* 21–31. Publicación de Cuadernos Monásticos, 1976.

Thompson, J. *The Form and Function of Proverbs in Ancient Israel.* The Hague, 1974.

Torjesen, K. J. "Pedagogical Soteriology from Clement to Origen." In *Origeniana Quarta: Die Referate des 4. Internationalen Origeneskongresses (Innsbruck, 2.–6. September 1985)*, edited by Lothar Lies, 370–78. Innsbruck/Vienna, 1987.

Tugwell, S. *Evagrius Ponticus: Practikos and On Prayer, translated by Simon Tugwell.* Published privately by the Faculty of Theology, Oxford, 1987.

Van den Ven, P. "Un opuscule inédit attribué à S. Nil." In *Mélanges Godefroy Kurth,* 2:73–81. Liège, 1908.

Veilleux, A. "Monasticism and Gnosis in Egypt." In *The Roots of Egyptian Christianity,* edited by B. A. Pearson and J. E. Goehring, 271–306. Philadelphia, 1986.

Viller, M. "Aux sources de la spiritualité de S. Maxime le Confesseur. Les oeuvres d'Évagre le Pontique." *Revue d'ascétique et de mystique* 11 (1930): 156–84, 239–68, 331–36.

Vitestam, G. "Seconde partie du Traité, qui passe sous le nom de 'La grande lettre d'Évagre le Pontique à Mélanie l'Ancienne.'" *Scripta Minora Regiae Societatis Humaniorum Litterarum Lundensis* [Lund] 3 (1963–64): 3–29.

Vivian, T. "Coptic Palladiana II: The Life of Evagrius (Lausiac History 38)." *Coptic Church Review* 21 (2000): 8–23.

Vogüé, A. de. "La lecture du Matin dans les Sentences d'Évagre et le *De Virginitate* attribué à saint Athanase." *Studia Monastica* 26 (1984): 7–11.

———. "Un morceau célèbre de Cassien parmi des estraits d'Évagre."*Studia Monastica* 27 (1985): 7–12.

———. "Psalmodier n'est pas prier." *Ecclesia Orans* 6 (1989): 7–32.

———. *Les règles monastiques anciennes (400–700).* Turnhout, 1985.

von Rad, G. *Old Testament Theology.* Vol. 1. Translated by D. M. J. Stalker. New York, 1962.

———. *Weisheit in Israel.* Neukirchen-Vluyn, 1970.

Waddell, H. *The Desert Fathers.* London, 1936.

Ward, B. *The Sayings of the Desert Fathers, the Alphabetical Collection.* Kalamazoo, 1975.

Williams, J. G. *Those Who Ponder Proverbs: Aphoristic Thinking and Biblical Literature.* Sheffield, 1981.

Wilmart, A. "Les versions latines des sentences d'Évagre pour les vierges." *Revue Bénédictine* 28 (1911): 143–53.

Wipszycka, E., *Études sur le christianisme dans l'Égypte de l'antiquité tardive*. Rome 1996.

Wisse, F. "Die Sextus-Spruche und das Problem der gnostischen Ethik." In *Zum Hellenismus in den Schriften von Nag Hammadi*, edited by A. Böhlig and F. Wisse, 55–86. Wiesbaden, 1975.

Young, R. D. "Evagrius the Iconographer, Monastic Pedagogy in the *Gnostikos*." *Journal of Early Christian Studies* 9 (2001): 53–71.

Zandee, J. "Les enseignements de Silvanos et Philon d'Alexandrie." In *Mélanges d'histoire des religions offerts à H.-Ch. Puech*, 337–45. Paris, 1974.

————. "God and Man in 'The Teachings of Silvanus' (Nag Hammadi Codex VII, 4)." In *Proceedings of the XIIth International Congress of the International Association for the History of Religions*, edited by C. J. Bleeker, G. Widengren, and J. Sharpe, 209–20. Studies in the History of Religions (Supplements to Numen), 31. Leiden, 1975.

————. "Die Lehren des Silvanus: Stoischer Rationalismus und Christentum im Zeitalter der Frühkatholischen Kirche." In *Essays on the Nag Hammadi Texts in Honour of A. Böhlig*, edited by M. Krause, 144–55. Nag Hammadi Studies, 3. Leiden, 1972.

————. *"The Teachings of Silvanus" and Clement of Alexandria: A New Document of Alexandrian Theology*. Leiden 1977.

Zandee, J. and M. Peel. "The Teachings of Silvanus from the Library of Nag Hammadi." *Novum Testamentum* 14 (1972): 294–311.

————. "The Teachings of Silvanus (VII, 4), Introduced and translated by Malcolm L. Peel and Jan Zandee, edited by Frederik Wisse." In *The Nag Hammadi Library in English*, edited by J. M. Robinson. Leiden, 1977.

INDEX OF SCRIPTURAL CITATIONS
AND ALLUSIONS

The task of making a scriptural index to *Ad Monachos* presents some difficult decisions for the compiler. In some cases a proverb will clearly be seen to be citing directly or almost directly a particular passage in scripture. In many other instances the language of the Evagrian text is so saturated with the language of scripture that it is difficult to identify with certainty a particular scriptural text as the inspiration for the language in Evagrius's proverb. The following index seeks to distinguish between these various ways in which Evagrius lets himself be inspired by the scriptures. It offers first scriptural texts that are direct or near direct citations of scripture. These are designated by the signal (C) (meaning "close") after the scriptural reference. Other references are to scriptural verses that are in the same general direction of the proverb in question, either from the point of view of vocabulary or from a theological position expressed. The purpose here is not to claim that in every case Evagrius would have had these scriptural passages in mind, though I have tried not to stray far from collecting texts that seem to be his actual inspiration. The purpose, however, is to indicate, on the one hand, the extent to which Evagrius's thinking is shaped by the language of scripture and, on the other hand, to indicate the kinds of passages that are brought to the mind of a meditating monk who, knowing the scriptures well, receives Evagrius's proverb for his meditation. In some cases it is useful to take a single word from the Evagrian proverb and to indicate the extent of its use in scripture. Where a particular Greek term is important, it is indicated with the reference. Otherwise, the word on which the reference is based is given in English. Yet in every case, of course, it has been the Greek text that has been consulted. Some of the references are to the whole Evagrian proverb; others are to a particular line or even a phrase within the line. The latter are indicated by reference to the line by the letters **a, b, c,** (in bold), etc., referring respectively to the first, second, third line, etc., of a proverb. Finally, when a citation or allusion to a passage from the Psalms or the book of Proverbs is commented on by Evagrius in his scholia in a way that sheds light on the proverb from *Ad Monachos*, such references are followed by the designation (*). In short, the index that follows cannot be presented in a particularly "neat" fashion, yet I think it is the kind of index required by the nature of the text under examination. Pages of numbers are not especially inspiring for a reader, yet I would urge the one who wishes to understand the spirit of *Ad Monachos* well not to neglect to meditate on its proverbs inside the scriptural world in which it means to stand. This index is offered as a help toward that end.

M 1. Prov 1:1–2; 5–6 (C); Sir 18:29; Rom 8:16–17 (C). ἀκούειν: LXX makes very frequent use of the term, especially in wisdom literature, where it is a classical beginning to an exhortation. See below, references at M 73. Inheritance: Ps 15:5; 36:18; 60:6; 93:5; 134:12; Matt 25:34.

M 2. Luke 11:11–13; Heb 12:7 (C). ἀπόλλειν: frequent in Proverbs (LXX) for losing the fruits of good works.

M 3. For relation of faith to *praktikē*, see 2 Chr 34:12; Prov 15:27, 28. Faith and gentleness: Sir 1:26. Faith and knowledge: Sir 46:15; Eph 4:13. Love and knowledge: Col 2:2–3. Love and faith: 1 Tim 1:5. Add virtue to faith: 2 Pet 1:5. For knowledge as faith's goal based on biblical texts, see Evagrius In Ps 85:11; 94:11; 137:5; In Prov 4:10.

M 4. Prov 1:7 (*) and parallels. Ps 110:10. ἐγκράτεια ψυχῆς: Sir 18:15, 30.

M 5. Rom 5:3–5 (C); Jas 1:3–4; Ps 129:4–6. **b.** John 17:10; Rom 8:30; Ps 90:15.

M 6. a. 1 Cor 9:27 (C). **b.** Rom 13:14 as in TP 53; Eph 5:29.

M 7. Mark 7:21; Rom 1:29; 1 Cor 6:18; Gal 5:19; Col 3:5. Faith, love, holiness, chastity: 2 Tim 2:15.

M 8. Jesus and withdrawal: John 6:15. Purity of heart: Matt 5:8; Ps 23:4. Love from a pure heart, a good conscience, and sincere faith: 1 Tim 1:5. Love and purity: 1 Pet 1:22; 2 Tim 2:22.

ταράσσειν: very frequent in LXX. In NT see Mark 6:50; John 11:33; Acts 15:24.

M 9. "Better A than B" is a frequent structure in Proverbs. See 8:1; 15:16, 17, 29; 16:19, 32; 17:1; 19:22; 21:9, 19; 22:1; 24:5; 25:24; 27:5, 10; 28:6; 29:1.

M 10. Comparisons constructed with ὁμοιός, ὡς, ὥσπερ, ὅν τρόπον are frequent in Proverbs, as, for example, Prov 10:26; 11:22; 19:12; 21:1; 24:30–31; 25:11–26; 31:14. μνησικακεῖν: Ezek 25:12; Zech 7:10. **b.** chaff: Matt 3:12.

M 11. Prov 3:24 (*). **a.** Sir 37:30. **b.** Sir 31:20; Wis 18:17. **c.** Joel 1:19; same image, though use of image is different.

M 12. Prov 3:24–25 (*); Prov 13:3. Terrified in eschatological sense: Luke 21:9; 1 Pet 3:5. Terrified used with θύμος: Isa 31:4. Terrified is frequent in LXX in phrases like "Do not be afraid"; often used together with φοβεῖν. Without fear: Prov 1:33; 3:24–25 (*); 19:3; Luke 1:74. πραΰς: Num 12:3; Job 36:15; Ps 24:9; 33:2; 36:11 (with κληρονομήσουσιν); 75:9; 146:6; 149:4; Sir 3:18; 10:15; Isa 26:6; Zeph 3:12; Zech 9:9; Matt 5:5; 11:29 (with ταπεινός); 21:5 (citing Zech 9:9); 1 Pet 3:4. πραΰτης: Ps 44:4 (with truth and righteouness); 131:1; Sir 1:26; 3:17; 4:8; 10:28; 45:4 (with πίστις concerning Moses); Gal 5:23 (in a list of fruits of the Spirit); Eph 4:2 (with ταπεινοφροσύνη, μακροθυμία, ἀγάπη); Col 3:12–13 (with other virtues, including μακροθυμία), 1 Tim 6:11 (with other virtues); 2 Tim 2:25 (with other virtues and with the verb παιδειν); Titus 3:2; Jas 1:21; 3:13 (connected with wisdom); 1 Pet 3:16.

M 13. Prov 25:23 (*). ἄνεμος used in Synoptic accounts of storms at sea. μνησικακία: Prov 12:28; 21:24; Zech 7:10; Ezek 25:12. **a.** Jude 12.

M 14. Matt 5:44; Luke 6:28. "To spare the tongue": Job 7:11; 42:3 (same expression; different use); Prov 10:19; 17:27; Wis 1:11. "Sadden neighbor": Deut 15:10; Sir 3:12; 4:2; Tob 4:3; 10:13.

M 15. Prov 15:1; 21:14 (*); 25:21; Matt 5:24; Rom 12:17–21; Eph 4:25. **a.** 1 Cor 13:5. **b.** Gen 29:13; 43:17 (C). **d.** Judg 19:10; Prov 17:1; 23:7. **e.** ῥυεσθαι very frequent in LXX and also common in NT. For "deliver soul" see Job 33:30; Ps 6:4; 16:13; 21:20; 32:19; 55:13; 56:4; 85:13; 88:48; 114:4; 119:2;

Prov 14:25; 22:23; 23:14; Ezek 3:19, 21; 14:20; 33:9.
f. πρόσκομμα: Sir 17:25; 34:16; 39:24; Rom 14:13; 1 Cor 8:9.
M 16. Matt 5:3; Luke 6:20; Rom 12:9–16; Phil 4:4; 1 Thess 5:16; 1 Pet 4:13.
M 17. Matt 19:23–26 (C); Mark 10:23–27 (C); Luke 18:24–28 (C).
M 18. a. φιλάργυρος: 1 Tim 6:10; 2 Tim 3:2; Sir 31:5. **b.** Ps 38:6; Eccl 2:8; Zech 9:3. σκοτίζειν: Ps 68:23; Isa 13:10; Matt 24:29; Mark 13:24; Luke 23:45; Rom 1:21; 11:10; Eph 4:18; Rev 8:12; 9:2. συνάγειν with other negative things: Ps 40:6; Prov 10:10; Mic 1:7; Hag 1:6.
M 19. For the general tone see Num 24:5–6; Ps 14; 1 Pet 5:5. Contrast of humble and proud is frequent in LXX and NT. αὐλίζειν: frequent in LXX, as for example in Ps 24:13; 80:1; Sir 24:7; 51:23. ἀρά: frequent in LXX, but in NT only at Rom 3:14.
M 20. παραβαίνειν is frequent in LXX with "commands," "words," "ways," "law." Likewise for φυλάσσειν.
M 21. Rom 6:3–11; 2 Cor 4:10; Gal 2:19–20; Col 2:12–13; 2 Tim 2:11; 1 Pet 2:24. **a.** ζηλόω is not used with "Christ" in NT, but here the sense seems to be "imitate" as in 1 Cor 4:16; 11:1; 2 Cor 4:10; Phil 3:10; Col 3:3. μακάριος: frequent in LXX and very frequent in NT. **b.** Rom 6:3–11. **c.** Rom 6:12, 19; Gal 5:19–21. **d.** Comparisons constructed with ὅμοιός, ὡς, ὥσπερ, ὅν τρόπον are frequent in Proverbs, as, for example, Prov 10:26; 11:22; 19:12; 21:1; 24:30–31; 25:11–26; 31:14.
M 22. a. οὐαί: very frequent in Isa and Jer. ἄνομος: very frequent in LXX; also 2 Thess 2:8. "Day of death" and similar: Eccl 8:8; John 12:48. **b.** "Perish": used frequently in Prov as at Prov 11:7. Together with "woe": Jer 31:1. **c.** crow: Isa 34:11; Prov 30:17 (*). **c, d.** Prov 27:8 (*).
M 23. a. ὁδηγεῖν: for Exodus in Exod 15:13; Neh 9:12. See also Ps 22:3; 26:11; Wis 10:10. The verb is used frequently in the psalms, usually with God as subject. Here angels are intermediaries.
M 24. a. Prov 11:2 (C). **b.** Ps 15:10; 96:10 (with souls). Prov 22:11. "Holy ones": frequent in LXX.
M 25. The sense of this proverb is found frequently in Prov. See especially Prov 27:4 and also Wis 19:1; Eccl 5:9; Sir 22:23;

Matt 19:21 (C). **a.** ἀνελεήμων: Rom 1:31; Jas 1:6. **b.** Treasure: in NT frequently associated with kingdom of heaven, as for example, Matt 13:44; 25:34–35 (used together with "inherit"). See below references at M 87.

M 26. Sir 10:30; Heb 11:26.

M 27. Sir 6:30; 21:21; 22:17; 2 Tim 4:8.

M 28. The sense is expressed frequently in Prov. Matt 10:9.

M 29. a. Inherit: very frequent in LXX, as for example Ps 36:29; Isa 61:7–8. Also frequent in NT with some expression for salvation as object, as in 1 Cor 6:9, 10; 15:50. **b.** Matt 6:26; Luke 12:24; Rev 12:6, 14. "Holy ones": frequent in LXX.

M 30. a. Prov 14:21, 31; 19:22; 22:9; Ps 111:9; Sir 4:8; 2 Cor 9:9. **b.** Filled (πιμπλάναι) with good things: Ps 64:4, 11; 103:28; 125:2; Prov l5:4; Eccl 6:3; Sir 22:23; 37:24; 42:25; 48:12; Isa 27:6; Jer 27:19; 51:17. πιμπλάναι used in NT with Holy Spirit at Luke 1:15, 41, 67; Acts 2:4; 4:8, 31; 9:17; 13:9. Compare M 94, M 115.

M 31. a. ἀναπαύειν: Prov 21:20 (*); Ps 94:11 (*); Matt 11:28–29 (C). For gentle, see above at M 12. **b.** Ps 9:5 (*);17:7 (*); 46:9 (*); Prov 12:23; 25:5 (*); 28:22 (*).

M 32. Prov 14:22. μισθός: used in NT as reward for the Kingdom, as in Matt 5:12; 20:8; 1 Cor 3:8. See also Wis 10:17; Sir 51:30; Eccl 4:9.

M 33. Ps 9:15 (C); 30:4; 34:8; 56:6; 63:5; 118:110; 139:5; 141:3; Prov 6:2; 12:13; 18:7; Eccl 10:8.

M 34. "Better A than B" is a frequent structure in Proverbs. See 8:1; 15:16, 17, 29; 16:19, 32; 17:1; 19:22; 21:9, 19; 22:1; 24:5; 25:24; 27:5, 10; 28:6; 29:1.

M 35. Matt 12:30 (C); Luke 11:23 (C).

M 36. Comparisons constructed with ὁμοιός, ὡς, ὥσπερ, ὅν τρόπον are frequent in Proverbs, as, for example, Prov 10:26; 11:22; 19:12; 21:1; 24:30–31; 25:11–26; 31:14.

M 37. Matt 26:41; Luke 22:40, 46; Eph 6:18; 1 Thess 5:17. For διαλογισμοί and heart: Matt 15:19; Luke 2:35; 5:22; 6:8; 9:46–47; 24:38.

M 38. Prov 12:11; 20:1 (*); 23:20, 30 (*); Ps 104:33 (*). "Wine gladden" (in positive sense): Pss 103:15; Sir 40:20; Eccl 10:19.

M 39.

M 40. Pasch: very frequent in LXX. Pentecost: Acts 2:1.

M 41. b. μνησικακία: Prov 12:28; 21:24; Zech 7:10; Ezek 25:12.

M 42. b. Hate brother: 1 John 2:9, 11; 3:15; 4:20. Mighty fall: Job 18:12; 20:5; 37:16; Jdt 8:19.

M 43. 1 Tim 2:4; 6:20. **b.** προσέχειν: 1 Tim 1:4; 4:1; 6:3; Titus 1:4. "End shamefully": Prov 15:10 (C) (*).

M 44. "Better A than B" is a frequent structure in Proverbs. See 8:1; 15:16, 17, 29; 16:19, 32; 17:1; 19:22; 21:9, 19; 22:1; 24:5; 25:24; 27:5, 10; 28:6; 29:1. For content see Prov 15:17; 17:1. **b.** "Impurity of soul": Prov 6:16 (C).

M 45. Comparisons constructed with ὁμοιός, ὡς, ὥσπερ, ὅν τρόπον are frequent in Proverbs, as, for example, Prov 10:26; 11:22; 19:12; 21:1; 24:30–31; 25:11–26; 31:14. **a.** διαφθείρειν: frequently used in LXX for enemies. **b.** Ps 136:9 (C).

M 46. For the whole chain of M 46 to M 52 see Matt 26:36–46, especially v. 41. Comparisons constructed with ὁμοιός, ὡς, ὥσπερ, ὅν τρόπον are frequent in Proverbs, as, for example, Prov 10:26; 11:22; 19:12; 21:1; 24:30–31; 25:11–26; 31:14. **b.** Ps 101:8 (C) (*). Prov 31:15 (*).

M 47. b. "μὴ ἀπώσῃ": Prov 1:8; 6:20; 16:3. **c.** Prov 5:21; 15:3. **d.** Job 10:14; Sir 7:8; 11:10.

M 48. Prov 6:4 (*), 10; Sir 31:20.

M 49. Prov 6:4 (*), 10; Sir 31:20.

M 50. a. Ps 67:2; Isa 64:1.

M 51. "Better A than B" is a frequent structure in Proverbs. See 8:1; 15:16, 17, 29; 16:19, 32; 17:1; 19:22; 21:9, 19; 22:1; 24:5; 25:24; 27:5, 10; 28:6; 29:1. **b.** "Impurity of soul": Prov 6:16 (C).

M 52. a. Ps 126:2; Prov 12:25; Jer 31:26. **b.** Prov 4:16 (*); Sir 31:2; 40:5.

M 53. Matt 23:12; 1 Pet 5:6. **a.** μετάνοια: Matt 3:2; 4:17. ἀνορθοῦν: used for throne in 2 Kgs and 1 Chr; Ps 17:35 (with παιδεία); Ps 144:14; 145:8; Sir 11:12. **b.** στηρίζειν: frequently used in LXX with heart. For gentle, see above at M 12.

M 54. For M 54 to M 56 see Ps 142:3–6; Sir 38:20–21. **a.** μιμνήσκεσθαι: very frequent in LXX. ἔξοδος: very frequent in LXX. See also 2 Pet 1:15. **b.** κρίσις: frequent both in LXX and NT. **c.** πλημμέλεια: frequent in LXX, especially in Lev.

M 55. Comparisons constructed with ὁμοιός, ὡς, ὥσπερ, ὅν τρόπον are frequent in Proverbs, as, for example, Prov 10:26; 11:22; 19:12; 21:1; 24:30–31; 25:11–26; 31:14. **a.** Eccl 10:4 (C). Ps 118:28. "Spirit of listlessness": Isa 61:3. **c.** Eph 6:12. **d.** Prov 17:3.

M 56. Sir 30:21, 23; 38:19–21; Luke 22:45–46; 2 Cor 7:10.

M 57. Sir 5:1, 8; Matt 6:25; Mark 10:23; 1 Cor 7:32–34a. **a.** μεριμνᾶν: Matt 6:25–34; Luke 10:41; 12:22–34; 1 Cor 7:32–34a; Phil 4:6. **b.** πενθεῖν: Luke 6:25. πικρῶς: Matt 26:75.

M 58. Prov 6:27, 28 (*). σκορπίος: Deut 8:15; Luke 10:19.

M 59. **a.** ὄφις: Gen 3:1; Ps 57:4; 139:3; Wis 16:5; Sir 21:2; Luke 10:19; 1 Cor 10:9; 2 Cor 11:3; Rev 12:9; 20:2. **b.** ὠδίνειν: Ps 7:14; Sir 34:5. λογισμός is frequent in LXX. For λογισμός with heart, see Prov 19:21.

M 60. Ps 16:3; 25:2; 65:10; 67:30; 138:1, 23; Prov 17:3 (C); Sir 2:5; 31:6; Wis 3:6; Jer 9:7; 11:20; 12:3; 17:10; 20:2; Zech 13:9.

M 61. a. περίελε σεαυτοῦ: Prov 4:24. **c, d.** Jas 4:1–3.

M 62. Prov 3:24; Sir 10:7, 9, 12, 13, 18; Matt 23:12; Luke 14:11; 18:14. **b.** Isa 14:12–17; Ezek 28:6, 17. The opposite: Ps 88:8; Jas 4:10; 1 Pet 5:6. **c.** Ps 15:10; 21:1; 70:9–11; Jer 12:7. **d.** Prov 29:23 (*). **e.** πτοεῖν: frequent in LXX, as in Prov 3:25 (*). **f.** Wis 17:21.

M 63. a. φυλάσσειν: (here διαφυλάσσειν) very frequent in LXX. **b.** Luke 10:30 (C).

M 64. John 7:38; 1 Cor 10:4.

M 65. a. Acts 9:15 (C). 2 Tim 2:21–22. **b.** Eph 4:31. πίμπλημι: with something evil: Gen 6:11, 13; Jer 28:5; Ezek 8:17; 9:9; Ps 87:3; Prov 1:31; 12:21; Sir 23:11.

M 66. a. 1 Cor 3:1–3; Heb 5:12–14; 1 Pet 2:1–2. **b.** ὑψοῦν: very frequent in Psalms for salvation.

M 67.

M 68. Prov 2:6; 8:12; Eccl 1:16, 17, 18; 2:21, 26; 7:13; 9:10; Wis 6:22; Rom 11:33; Col 2:3. Wisdom and prudence: Eph 1:8. **b.** τίκτειν: Prov 10:23 with wisdom and prudence.

M 69.

M 70. Ps 10:3; 56:4; 63:7; 90:5; Eph 6:16.

M 71. a. Eph 4:30–32. **b.** χείλη δόλια, etc.: Ps 11:2, 3; 16:1; 30:18; 51:4; 108:2; 119:2, 3. δόλιος: Ps 5:6; 42:1; Prov 12:6; 13:9, 13.

M 72. Ps 18:11; 80:17; 118:103; Prov 16:24; 24:13 (*); 27:7 (*).

M 73. a. New beginnings with invitation to listen frequent in Proverbs, as in Prov 4:10; 5:7; 7:1, 24; 8:32–35; 22:17–18 (*); 23:19, 22–26. **b.** Prov 5:7 (C). **c.** Prov 6:22 (C).

M 74. a. ἐκθλίψει ψυχάς: Prov 12:13; Sir 40:14. **b.** μνησικακία: Prov 12:28; 21:24; Zech 7:10; Ezek 25:12.

M 75. a. Luke 16:1ff (C). **b.** Prov 11:21 (C) (*); 19:5 (C), 9 (C); 28:20 (C).

M 76. Ps 111:5; Luke 12:42; 16:8; Acts 2:45; 1 Cor 4:1–2; Titus 1:7; 1 Pet 4:10.

M 77. a. ἐξολεθρεύειν: very frequent in LXX. **b.** Prov 20:20; Matt 25:26.

M 78. Ps 36:21; 111:5; Prov 12:10; 13:9, 11; 21:26. "Better A than B" is a frequent structure in Proverbs. See 8:1; 15:16, 17, 29; 16:19, 32; 17:1; 19:22; 21:9, 19; 22:1; 24:5; 25:24; 27:5, 10; 28:6; 29:1.

M 79. ἄφρων contrasted with φρόνιμος: Prov 10:23–24; 17:10; 19:25.

M 80.

M 81. a. μελετᾶν: This is what the just man does with the Law, frequent in Proverbs and in Psalms. For negative: Prov 19:27 (C) (*); 24:2; Isa 59:3, 13. **b.** παραλογίζεσθαι: Col 2:4; Jas 1:22.

M 82. Matt 6:25. **a.** "Fills his stomach": Job 20:23. **b.** ποιμαίνειν: Prov 28:7 (*); 29:3 (*). **c.** Prov 3:32.

M 83. a. Prov 5:3 (*). **b.** Prov 9:18a (*). **c,d.** Comparisons constructed with ὅμοιός, ὡς, ὥσπερ, ὅν τρόπον are frequent in Proverbs, as, for example, Prov 10:26; 11:22; 19:12; 21:1; 24:30–31; 25:11–26; 31:14.

M 84. 1 Cor 13:5–6.

M 85. a. For gentle, see above at M 12. **b.** ἀπωθεῖν: frequent in LXX with Lord as subject.

M 86. Prov 22:13 (C) (*). Sir 10:5.

M 87. Prov 18:19; 2 Cor 1:4; 2:7. **c.** Ps 15:9; 72:21; 85:11; Prov l5:13; 17:22; 23:15; 27:11. **d.** "Treasure in heaven": Matt 6:20; 19:21; Mark 10:21; Luke 12:33; 18:22.

M 88. Prov 6:20; 19:13, 27 (*); 20:20, 29.

M 89. Prov 6:19 (*); 18:1 (C) (*).

M 90. d. "Book of the living": Ps 68:28; Phil 4:3; Rev 3:5; 13:8; 20:15; 22:19.

M 91. Prov 13:1; 15:5, 32; 19:8. **b.** ἐμπίπτειν εἰς κακά: Prov 13:7; 17:16 (*), 20 (*); 28:14.

M 92. a. μακάριος: frequent in LXX and very frequent in NT. φυλάσσειν: very frequent in LXX. **b.** διατηρεῖν: frequent in LXX.

M 93. a. ζημιοῦν: Prov 19:19 (C) (*); 21:11; 22:3; Matt 16:26.

M 94. a. Prov 3:6 (C); 4:24; 11:5 (C). Jas 3:5-12. **b.** Prov 4:23 (C). Filled (πιμπλάναι) with good things: Ps 64:4, 11; 103:28; 125:2; Prov 15:4; Eccl 6:3; Sir 22:23; 37:24; 42:25; 48:12; Isa 27:6; Jer 27:19; 51:17. πιμπλάναι used in NT with Holy Spirit at Luke 1:15, 41, 67; Acts 2:4; 4:8, 31; 9:17; 13:9. Compare M 30, M 115.

M 95. a. Prov 11:13 (C); Sir 5:9, 14; 6:1; 28:13. **b.** Prov 11:12 (C).

M 96. a. πείθειν: Prov 11:28 (C); 14:6; frequent in Psalms with Lord; frequent in LXX with idols; Luke 18:9 (C), thus connected with second line of M 96 and Luke 18:14. **b.** Matt 18:4; 23:12; Luke 14:11; 18:14.

M 97. a. "Trough of the stomach": Prov 25:15 (*). **b.** Prov 6:4 (*), 9 (*). **d.** Luke 1:35 (C).

M 98. Prov 15:18; 19:11 (*). ἡσυχάζειν: used frequently in LXX with "land" or "city" as subject.

M 99. For gentle, see above at M 12.

M 100. Prov 16:19; Sir 2:4; Matt 18:4; 23:12; Luke 1:48, 52; 14:11; 18:14; Jas 1:9. **b.** ὑψοῦν: frequent as word for salvation in LXX, especially in Psalms.

M 101. a. λαμπτήρ σβεσθήσεται: Prov 20:20 (C); 24:20 (C). "Track down banquets": Prov 23:30 (C). **b.** Prov 20:20.

M 102. Matt 12:43. **a.** Ezek 4:10-11 (C). **b.** 1 Cor 6:18.

M 103. a. Matt 25:31-46. **b.** Prov 5:11 (C) (*); 1 Cor 9:27.

M 104. Prov 17:5; 24:17-18 (C) (*). **c.** Ps 138:23; Prov 15:11; 24:12; Acts 1:24; 15:8. **d.** παραδιδόναι: very common in this sense in LXX, as in Prov 6:1 (*). See also Rom 1:24, 26, 28; 1 Cor 5:5.

M 105. ἄφρων contrasted with φρόνιμος: Prov 10:23-24; 17:10; 19:25. **b.** "Draw up evils": Prov 20:5.

M 106. Matt 6:22-23 (C).

M 107. Comparisons constructed with ὁμοιός, ὡς, ὥσπερ, ὅν τρόπον are frequent in Proverbs, as for example, Prov 10:26; 11:22; 19:12; 21:1; 24:30-31; 25:11-26; 31:14. **a.** Morning star: Job 3:9; 11:17 with verse 13; 41:9; Isa 14:12; Ps 109:3 (*);

Luke 1:78; 2 Pet 1:19; Rev 2:28; 22:16. Tree: Ps 91:12–15 (*);
Prov 3:18 (*); 11:30 (*); Ezek 17:24; 40:16–37; 41:18–25. **b.**
For gentle, see above at M 12.

M 108. a. John 5:39; 1 Cor 2:10; 1 Pet 1:11. **b.** "Mocks them": Prov
30:17 (*).

M 109. Comparisons constructed with ὁμοιός, ὡς, ὥσπερ, ὅν τρό-
'πον are frequent in Proverbs, as, for example, Prov 10:26;
11:22; 19:12; 21:1; 24:30–31; 25:11–26; 31:14. **a.** Hate: Prov
1:22, 29; 5:12. **b.** Ps 36:15.

M 110. "Better A than B" is a frequent structure in Proverbs. See
8:1; 15:16, 17, 29; 16:19, 32; 17:1; 19:22; 21:9, 19; 22:1; 24:5;
25:24; 27:5, 10; 28:6; 29:1. **b.** αἰών: very frequent in NT. See
also Ps 144:13 (*).

M 111. a. Gray: Prov 20:29; Sir 6:18; 25:4; Wis 4:9. For gentle, see
above at M 12. **b.** 1 Tim 2:4.

M 112. Isa 57:15; Ps 118:99–100 (*). **a.** "Bears many things": Prov
14:17 (C). For gentle, see above at M 12. **b.** Prov 18:14 (C) (*).
ὀλιγόψυχος: Prov 14:29 (contrasted with μακρόθυμος). **c, d.**
Prov 26:12 (C).

M 113. a. Scandal: Matt 18:6; Mark 9:42; Luke 17:2; Rom 14:21;
1 Cor 8:13. ἀτιμώρητος: Prov 11:21 (C) (*); 19:5 (C), 9 (C);
28:20 (C). **b.** 1 Cor 13:5.

M 114. Num 16:30–35; Ps 105:16–18. **a.** Agitating Church: Acts
15:24; Gal 1:7; 5:10.

M 115. a. Ps 18:11; 80:17; 118:103; Prov 16:24; 24:13 (*); 27:7 (*).
b. πιμπλάναι used in NT with Holy Spirit at Luke 1:15, 41, 67;
Acts 2:4; 4:8, 31; 9:17; 13:9. See also Prov 15:4 (C); Sir 48:12.
Compare with M 30, M 94.

M 116. a. τιμᾶν: Prov 3:9; 7:1 (C) (*); 14:31. **b.** δουλεύειν with
Lord as object: frequent in LXX. δεικνύειν with Lord/God
as subject: frequent in LXX. See also Rev 1:1.

M 117. a. ὑψοῦν: frequent as word for salvation in LXX, especially in Psalms. See also Prov 4:8 (*); 18:10 (*). **b.** Ps 1:3.

M 118. Matt 26:26–29; Mark 14:22–25; Luke 22:15–20; John
6:51–58; 1 Cor 10:16–21; 11:23–29.

M 119. Prov 9; Matt 26:26–29; Mark 14:22–25; Luke 22:15–20;
John 6:51–58; 1 Cor 10:16–21; 11:23–29.

M 120. John 13:25; 21:20.

M 121. a. Prov 22:2. **b.** Matt 18:20.

M 122. a. Treasure: See above references at M 25, M 87. See also Prov 2:4, 7; Wis 7:14. **b.** χάρις: Prov 12:2; 25:10 (*). χάρις καὶ ἔλεος: Wis 3:9; 4:15.

M 123. Prov 14:8 (C), 18 (*). Wisdom and prudence: Eph 1:8. **b.** ἐξιχνίαζειν: In LXX usually used for things concerning divine mysteries.

M 124. a. Prov 22:28 (C) (*). **b.** Prov 23:10 (C). **c.** ἐγκαταλείπειν: Jer 2:13; Ps 118:87; Prov 2:13; 4:2; 27:10 (*); 28:4. **d.** ἀπωθεῖν: Jer 6:19; Prov 1:8; 6:20; 16:3. **f.** σκεπάζειν: Ps 16:8; 26:5; 30:20; 60:4; 63:2; 90:14 (*). Evil day: Ps 90:14 (*); Prov 25:19 (*).

M 125. a. Job 20:15; 33:23; Prov 16:14. **b.** ἀπόλλειν: frequent in Proverbs (LXX) for losing the fruits of good works.

M 126. a. New beginnings with invitation to listen frequent in Proverbs, as in Prov 4:10; 5:7 (C); 7:1, 24; 8:32–35; 22:17–18 (*); 23:19, 22–26. **b.** Ps 118:85 (*). ἄνομος: very common in LXX. **c.** Ps 139:4; 141:3 (*). **d.** 1 Tim 6:20 (1 Tim 2:4). **g.** Ps 13:3; 139:3. **h.** Prov 21:30. Wisdom and prudence: Eph 1:8. **i.** ἀπολλύνα: very frequent in LXX, as in Ps 5:6; frequently constructed with πάντες. **j.** πιμπλάναι with something evil: Gen 6:11, 13; Jer 28:5; Ezek 8:17; 9:9; Ps 87:3; Prov 1:31; 12:21; Sir 23:11. Compare with πιμπλάναι in M 30, M 94, M 115 and references there. **l.** Acts 17:18. **m.** Jer 34:18. **n.** Col 1:28–29; Eph 6:12; 1 Tim 6:12; 2 Tim 4:7. **o.** Prov 13:9; John 3:19; 8:12; 2 Cor 6:14; 11:14; 1 John 1:5, 7.

M 127. a. ψευδής: very frequent in Proverbs and throughout LXX. **b.** ἀπωτᾶν: Gen 3:13; Eph 5:6.

M 128. Deut 11:10–11 (C); Jer 2:18. **a.** Paradise of God: Rev 2:7. **b.** Ps 64:9.

M 129. Deut 11:10–11 (C).

M 130. Matt 18:4; 23:12; Luke 1:48, 52; 14:11; 18:14.

M 131. Wisdom and prudence: Eph 1:8. **a.** ὑψοῦν: frequent as word for salvation in LXX, especially in Psalms. See also Prov 4:8 (*); 18:10 (*). **b.** Pure heart: Matt 5:8; 1 Tim 1:5; 2 Tim 2:22.

M 132. Prov 20:5; Rom 11:33. **a.** σκοτεινός: Ps 72:16 (*);118:7 (*); Matt 6:23; Luke 11:34–36.

M 133. a. Purity with seeing: Ps 23:3–4; Matt 5:8. **b.** For gentle, see above at M 12.

M 134. b. ἀθετεῖν: Luke 10:16; John 12:48.

M 135. a. πλατύνειν with heart: Ps 4:2 (*); 17:36 (*); 118:32 (*), 96 (*); Prov 1:20–21 (*); 18:16 (*); 22:20 (*); 2 Cor 6:11, 13. **b.** ὑψοῦν: frequent as word for salvation in LXX, especially in Psalms. See also Prov 4:8 (*); 18:10(*).

M 136. b. παριστάναι: Rom 6:13; 2 Cor 4:14; 11:2; Col 1:21–22, 28; 2 Tim 2:15.

INDEX OF EVAGRIAN WORKS CITED

INDEX OF PRINCIPAL GREEK WORDS
IN *AD MONACHOS*

The numbers following the Greek words are the numbers of the proverbs in which the Greek word occurs.